Martha Jefferson Randolph

Republican Daughter

&

Plantation Mistress

Billy L. Wayson

Palmyra, Virginia
Shortwood Press
2013

Shortwood Press
3 Shortwood Circle, Palmyra, VA 22963

Platinum Edition
ISBN-13: 978-0615800134
ISBN-10: 0615800130

ℰℐ

The cover and genealogical chart were created by Carole Ohl. The paintings used in composing the cover are "Martha Jefferson Randolph" (c.1836) by Thomas Sully, ©Thomas Jefferson Foundation at Monticello, photograph by Edward Owen, used with permission; and "Thomas Jefferson" (1788) painted for Maria Cosway by John Trumbull, courtesy of the White House Art Collection. The editor and project manager was Jean L. Cooper. This book uses the Garamond typeface in different sizes throughout. Headings are in 14 point, text in 12 point, and the endnotes and index are in 10 point.

DEDICATION

To the Willy Wonka adventurers:

Kaitlin Therese, Eamonn William Clarke,
Charles Ferguson, Sam Brody,
Owen Guthrie, and Felix Keppler

"[I]n order to understand him, you must understand those by whom he was surrounded."

—Ellen W. Randolph Coolidge
to Jefferson biographer Henry Randall, 1856

Genealogical Chart

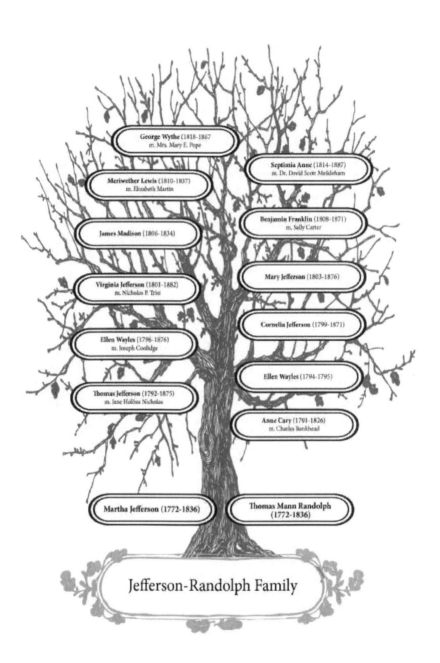

George Wythe (1818-1867)
m. Mrs. Mary E. Pope

Septimia Anne (1814-1887)
m. Dr. David Scott Meikleham

Meriwether Lewis (1810-1837)
m. Elizabeth Martin

Benjamin Franklin (1808-1871)
m. Sally Carter

James Madison (1806-1834)

Mary Jefferson (1803-1876)

Virginia Jefferson (1801-1882)
m. Nicholas P. Trist

Cornelia Jefferson (1799-1871)

Ellen Wayles (1796-1876)
m. Joseph Coolidge

Ellen Wayles (1794-1795)

Thomas Jefferson (1792-1875)
m. Jane Hollins Nicholas

Anne Cary (1791-1826)
m. Charles Bankhead

Martha Jefferson (1772-1836)

Thomas Mann Randolph
(1772-1836)

Jefferson-Randolph Family

Table of Contents

Acknowledgments

There were doctors in the house—two of them—who had, after all, been there, done that. Dr. Gail Funke—partner in life's enterprise, colleague, and spouse—weathered tempests and silent calms to signal messages of hope through even the darkest hours. Dr. Heather Wayson-Wilson, who had skillfully navigated the shifting sands of academe, shared her charts and was fearless in steering my fanciful and inflated ideas aground. It took both to provide the intellectual and emotional life support to complete the journey.

This book began as a much longer dissertation (500 pages), approved in 2008 under the title "Martha Jefferson Randolph: Educating a Republican Daughter and Plantation Mistress, 1782–1809" (UMI 3362906). It was a privilege to be guided along the way by two gentlemen of distinction. Despite his commanding knowledge of Thomas Jefferson's educational thought and a long career at Mr. Jefferson's University, Professor Emeritus Jennings L. Wagoner nonetheless patiently remained open to yet another overzealous research project on the Founder. His subject-matter expertise diverted the author from many conceptual cul-de-sacs and editorial pitfalls. Bridges across academic disciplines are sometimes fraught with rickety trusses; those transversing university colleges can be even more precarious. Peter S. Onuf, Thomas Jefferson Foundation Professor (Emeritus) virtually soars across these intellectual and institutional chasms to construct historical narratives that cause us to reexamine conventional assumptions, even about the iconical Thomas Jefferson. He inspired and persistently encouraged me to similar flights in this project, but saved a fledgling from Icarus's sad fate by demanding intellectual rigor grounded in solid historical context.

Two research fellowships at Monticello's Robert H. Smith International Center for Jefferson Studies were critical to shaping the final manuscript. These opportunities provided ready access to the precious research archives of the Thomas Jefferson Foundation but, more importantly, fostered a connection with historians and librarians dedicated to the scholarly study of Jefferson and his times. Early on, Center Director Andrew Jackson O'Shaughnessy was able to see behind the fog of "purple prose" to extend the benefit of this cherished association. The *Family Letters*, co-edited by James A. Bear, Jr., were, of course, essential to my research; but equally indispensable were his voluminous notations, jottings, and time-proven insights nestled in the files of the Foundation where he served so many years. His co-editor of *Jefferson's Memorandum Books*, Lucia A. Stanton, formerly Shannon Senior Historian, provided me the model for historical detail and thoroughness in that work which gives historians access to the grit of daily life, even that of a Founder. But the invaluable trove she left in careful transcriptions of letters between Jefferson and his son-in-law Thomas Mann Randolph, Jr. made it possible for me to discover the complexity and fine textures of a triangulated family array. I can only hope in my own way to make as significant a contribution to the field as these two dedicated historians.

Thomas Jefferson's granddaughter, Ellen Wayles Randolph Coolidge, advised his biographer: "[I]n order to understand him, you must understand those by whom he was surrounded." In the shadow of this icon were (and still are) not only notable colleagues and a plantation community but also beloved relatives and dear friends. Lisa Francavilla, Managing Editor of the *Papers of Thomas Jefferson: The Retirement Series*, enthusiastically pursues making accessible to the world attentively researched documents that provide an essential context for understanding a Thomas Jefferson heretofore available only to a handful of scholars. My research, drawing on the personal correspondence as it does, could not have been as thorough without the electronic archive Lisa has so carefully crafted for the Family Letters Project she directs. Moreover, her knowledge of Jefferson family affairs—arcane and notorious alike—and generosity in sharing insights made a distinct difference.

There is no "and finally" when acknowledging my indebtedness for a project of this scope and duration, but it cannot be left without expressing my gratitude to the guardians of history's treasures—archivists and librarians. Jack Robertson, Foundation Librarian, shared his enthusiasm for my computer-based analysis of historical documents and his vision for making the Jefferson archive electronically accessible to the world. Both his enthusiasm and his vision made me feel part of a larger, more significant scholarly enterprise of a different sort. Anna Berkes, Research Librarian, graciously accepted over nine months of my clumsy rattling on the Library's echoing surfaces and never openly took umbrage for my urgent interruptions of her work. Without the wry humor of Eric Johnson, who was Library Services Coordinator during my sojourn, the joy of research would have been unabated and unpunctuated with laughter!

Over a dozen readers, who undertook the labor of reading several hundred manuscript pages and proffered all matter of comment, will remain anonymous. However, they represented a cross-section of academic disciplines, a women's focus group, authors, editors, and even a few publishers, Baby boomers, and Gen-Xers. Editor Jean Cooper necessarily applied her sharp pencil and keen insights to a bulky manuscript as well as ably shepherding it through publication.

As much as I might like to lodge in those named and unnamed persons responsibility for errors in historiography, for poor interpretive judgment, and for other unflattering elements of this work, I am duty bound (and joyfully so) to be answerable for it all in exchange for the privilege of entering the realm of collective memory in search of meaning.

Billy Lee Wayson
Charlottesville, Virginia
billy@wayson.net

Introduction

"Nothing makes me feel your absence so sensibly as the beauty of the season," Martha Jefferson Randolph confided to her father. "Monticello shines with a transcendent luxury…Blest as I am in my family you are still wanting to compleat my happiness."[1] Thomas Jefferson's commitment to his daughter was no less ardent. "I with pleasure take up my pen to express all my love to you, and my wishes once more to find myself in the only scene where…the sweeter affections of life have any exercise."[2] This is the story of their relationship: its complexities, its ups and downs, its sustaining core. Martha and Thomas Jefferson shared words of elation and rejection, despair and hope, engagement and loneliness. The narrative emerges from a close textual reading and presentation of these words—words that bear on the relationship they created, nurtured, and defended against all interlopers. She lamented his departures, longed for their reunions, and fantasized a life together looking down from the summit on all other connections—spouse, children, cousins, congresses. As a relationship, it is not unlike countless others, whether of notables or nobodies, but Martha Jefferson's unqualified affection for and lifelong commitment to the happiness of her father was a display of what may seem old-fashioned values of fidelity and sacrifice. In that sense, she can claim the honor and esteem her father assured would come from persevering and actively engaging with life.

This fascinating relationship is explored along six principal themes. Affection, Plantation Household, and Public Sphere are familiar topics drawn from the extensive cultural, social, and political historiography of the late eighteenth and early nineteenth centuries. Their words to each other often reveal how a deeply felt daughter-father attachment was interpenetrated by the so-called public and private "spheres." Life in a Monticello household comprised of numerous farms spread across miles and overseen by an absent patriarch was further confounded with an affectionately bonded family embracing friends, in-laws, and blood relatives.

Three additional themes—Separation, Place, Debt—fill the pages of some 900 letters written by Martha, her father, husband Thomas Mann Randolph, and others. Jefferson's exercise of republican civic virtue from 1790 to 1809 required repeated, extended, and unpredictable periods of living apart, which was especially painful after daughter and father had been together almost uninterrupted from 1782 to 1789. To compensate, they constructed an imaginary family in their correspondence that was idealized as tightly bound by deep affection, isolated in a tranquil place atop Monticello Mountain, and sheltered from the rancor, tumult, and chicanery of politics. The family-of-letters became a mandated ritual with prescribed artifacts and liturgy intended to fill an emotional void and to penetrate the imaginary boundaries demarking intimate domestic space and the political public sphere. However, their emotional lives were tied to a place slowly collapsing under the burden of financial obligations as inexorably as wind, rain, and gravity were dragging its scant fertility into the Rivanna bottoms. Debt, which Jefferson thought made planters a "species of property," threatened to erode deeply cherished independence and along with it the Place where love resided. And ultimately, it was the burden of debt spawned by a complex plantation household and exacerbated by six decades in the public sphere that ultimately separated the Jefferson-Randolph family from its place.

The book describes milestones demarking many of the twists and turns encountered over the Jeffersons' life courses. Among the most prominent events were the loss of a young mother and dearest wife; extended engagement with the political public sphere; defending family esteem in the face of a relative's sexual shenanigans; and navigating domestic discord among imprudent in-laws. In rearing his daughters alone, Jefferson claimed he took into consideration that their husband might be lost, incapable, or inattentive. But, he did not quite figure the complications of hastily adding such a spouse as Thomas Mann Randolph, Jr. to their family constellation. Mann Randolph was the son of Jefferson's boyhood chum, and early on, as a student in Edinburgh and footloose in Virginia society, he was erratic, emotional, and inclined to deception. However, these were relatively minor faults compared to the imbroglios of later times. Farmer Randolph unexpectedly announced a plan to move his enslaved "family" to Mississippi; son-in-law Randolph (public servant) sought elected office against an ardent Jefferson supporter. A dejected and marginalized husband remained at the foot of the Mountain when his wife became undisputed mistress of the Monticello household in 1810. In death, he was "no longer an object of terror or apprehension," Martha conceded, but "one of deep sympathy."

A modern cliché posits "all politics are local," but observers seem surprised when they learn political life also is deeply personal, as ten-year-old Martha and her father soon discovered in 1783. The underside of republican civic virtue is nakedly exposed in the story of Martha and Thomas Jefferson's deep, abiding relationship amid the throes of a nation being invented. Martha unselfishly provided the emotional sustenance for Thomas Jefferson as he unmoored his skiff from the safe harbor of ideology, casting it adrift into the uncharted seas of a new republic. Martha and her children were the *Other* (to borrow from the anthropologists) against which Jefferson compared the self-interested, jiggery-pokery, and tempests of political life. He imagined sweeping theories of representative government freeing men from despotism and expansive designs for an "empire of liberty"; but together, the republican daughter and her father, also, imagined a family safely ensconced in a quiet, beauteous milieu, brimming with affection and comforted by its warmth. If family made a modern politics possible, to paraphrase a modern historian, then the couple's imagined family and its idealized life made politics emotionally bearable.[3]

Lastly, a finely textured and nuanced presentation of the words Thomas Jefferson chose to share with his most intimate companion reveals in a unique way the core of what he thought (and Martha came to believe) was the bedrock of a government "truly republican"—attachment to others or "moral sense" in the worlds of Scottish Enlightenment thinkers. The tension was never resolved between his need to be with those he loved and his desire to construct a massive edifice for guaranteeing the pursuit of happiness. Whether an educational institution seeking an "aristocracy of virtue and talent" for governing or declaring independence from subjugation, it was affection that impelled the enterprise. So too, conceiving himself as having suffered loss after personal loss, his solace was in clinging to Martha. It was the sort of emotional dependency some can interpret darkly; others construe it as a reminder of just how important abiding, emotional relationships are to existence itself. The pattern weaving through the weft and warp of individual, family, community, and country, as it did in Jefferson's philosophy, may have become frayed by modernity, but the binding threads of affection have not been rent if there is still pining in the twenty-first century for a classical civil society.

Chapters sequentially emphasize Affection/Family, Plantation Household, Public Sphere, Separation, Place, and Debt; however, each topic is present throughout. They are conjoined in the final two chapters, especially in "The Jefferson Family Story" that Martha and her family composed for the historical record.

The thread of Martha Jefferson's life is picked up at age ten, just after her mother's death and her father's return to public service in 1783, and traces influences on her development over the next six years. Grieving their loss in Philadelphia and Paris in starkly unfamiliar cultural surroundings and separated from the comfort of family and friends, the Jeffersons sculpted an emotionally dependent and impenetrable union (Chapters 2–3).

Living under matriarchal rule in a Paris convent, imbibing the delights of a *Madame*'s salon, or cheering the birth of another revolution had not prepared Martha and her father for their life together in a genteel plantation culture. The couple was confronted with the challenges of adding her new husband to a tightly knit nuclear family and inserting this social configuration into a complex plantation household extending for miles and encompassing all matter of acquaintances, kin, and enslaved relations. To cope with the loneliness of extended separations, Martha and her father constructed a letter writing ritual (a "family-of-letters") with prescribed content and scheduled regularity. A central trope of this literature detailed the unpleasant experiences of political life and emotional pain of living apart that, in turn, were juxtaposed to an imagined reunion at a place they called "Monticello"—a place of perfect harmony, tranquility, independence, and mutual affection. Thus, an internal, emotional sentiment was increasingly rooted to an external place whose material sustenance became irretrievably encumbered with debt during Jefferson's two decades answering the "call" of republican civic virtue (Chapter 4).

Faced with months apart for the first time in six years, Martha in 1790 confessed her "happiness could never be compleat" without Father's company; as a result, she supported his drawn-out efforts to incur more family debt so she and her husband could live at the foot of Monticello Mountain. The land purchase became a source of tension in the newly drawn emotional triangle, in the conflicts arising from an extended family circle, and revealed the social complexity of plantation life (Chapter 5).

Martha and her father were quickly and keenly made aware of the emotional and financial toll exacted by participation in a political public sphere (Chapter 6). After only two years as Secretary of State, Jefferson voiced his "weariness of public office."[4] Amid the "ruffled debates" of 1790–94, his solace was to imagine a future of "ease, domestic occupation, and domestic love and society," he wrote Martha, "where I may once more be happy."[5] Not only had his paltry salary fallen far short of expenses, but Jefferson returned home in 1794 to find his plantations in a "wretched condition" from the "unprincipled ravages of overseers."[6] He plunged into a quest for profitability by leasing his Shadwell holdings for sure money, manufacturing nails, and converting more cropland to wheat production. He soon learned that domestic society had its own perils. What the Hessian fly did not do to Jefferson's wheat crop, violent storms did to the corn, laying it "prostrate" with no recourse for paying long-overdue obligations. Mann Randolph was suddenly stricken with an unknown malady, frequently absent for extended periods seeking cures, and suffered a $42,000 court judgment against his father's estate.

Politics would not leave the family at ease: "Colo. Burr left [Monticello] two or three days ago," Jefferson informed a political ally in late 1795 before the Presidential election.[7] Emotional attachment was intensified even more during his Vice Presidential years and became more firmly planted on the Mountain. "I feel every day more strongly the impossibility of becoming habituated to your absence," Martha confessed in the spring of 1798.[8] The Mountain only aggravated her sense of loneliness. "Nothing makes me feel your absence so sensibly as the beauty of the season," she wrote. "Monticello shines with a transcendent luxury of vegetation above the rest of the neighbourhood."[9] Her father was sustained in political life with letters shining as "gleams of light, to chear a dreary scene, where envy, hatred, malice, revenge, & all the worst passions of men are marshaled to make one another as miserable as possible."[10]

Jefferson's political "revolution of 1800" was an irrevocable turning point in the family's life, its emotional dynamics, Martha's role within it, and the material well-being of the Monticello household (Chapters 7–9). Despite their pretensions to maintain an impregnable domestic sphere, the allure of the political public sphere for the next eight years permeated every aspect of Martha's being. It ordered her emotional, physical, conjugal, economic, and social life. More than a passive refuge for her father from the ravages of political life, this republican daughter became the emotional foundation stone of his career and their relationship a bane to her husband's very existence. "If my other duties could possibly interfere with my devotion to you," she assured her beleaguered father in 1804, "I should not feel a scruple in sacrificing them..."[11] When it came time for another retirement in 1810, she vowed to create for her father atop Monticello Mountain a "harbour from the cares and storms of life."

The interplay of deep affection, extended family, attachment to place, emotional separations, public sphere, and debt congealed between 1810 and 1836 to raze the household they had so artfully constructed (Chapter 10). When Father complained that "serious debts" would "materially affect the tranquility" of his retirement, Martha urged him to ignore her children's future, to sell portions of his holdings, and pledged her dowry lands "to provide them food and raiment."[12] Her part of the bargain, she pledged, was "to manage...[the] large establishment" and to "devote" herself to it. "With what tenderness of affection," she effused, "we will wait upon and cherish you My Dearest Father."[13] Mann Randolph ignited, fueled, and fanned emotional anguish with his erratic behaviors, until finally separating to a hermit-like existence at the foot of Monticello Mountain. Debt ultimately triumphed over all efforts to remove its "torment" and rang the final knell of family disharmony. A desperate financial scheme to save their place by selling land with a public lottery violated cherished family values of independence. Jefferson surrendered his claim of disinterested civic virtue by pleading lifelong public service as justification for gambling on the chance sale of property. Their jealously guarded and most private affairs were exposed to public scrutiny throughout the Republic.

After her father's death in 1826, Martha vowed to accept "honorable poverty" and devise a "genteel" home, despite being "prostrate in heart and spirits" and with "eight children unprovided for" (Chapter 11).[14] Martha's legacy was to be the principal co-author of "The Jefferson Family Story" that sought to make meaning out of private lives laid prostrate by debt incurred in pursuit of republican civic virtue. But as daughter Cornelia reminded the family, their true inheritance was neither a place called "Monticello" nor freedom from the thralldom of debt but being "his children." "The energy [Grand Papa] has shewn in public affairs, is in our blood & we will shew it in our private affairs."[15] The political public sphere had completely enveloped their self-consciousness and collective identity.

The lens we don colors the world we interpret. No claims are made here that the relationship between Martha and Thomas Jefferson is representative of some abstract, trans-historical force shaping the personal, familial, or political contours of what was called "The United States"—itself a mere abstract construction at the time. The couple's experiences, living conditions, and life course were specks in the vast stream of cultural, social, and political change that was occurring somewhere from the mid eighteenth to early nineteenth centuries. There is no doubt who was dominant in their relationship, but Martha knew well from an early age of her father's emotional dependency on her for his happiness; this is power of a quite different sort than conferred by "natural rights," statute, or political franchise. Thomas Jefferson was both a reluctant participant and an aggressive interloper into the maelstrom of practical politics; he chose the life, regretted the living, demanded deference, insisted on equality, nurtured the intellect, and tickled the fancy. But what follows does not attempt to resolve (or even admit to) any of the apparent "contradictions" in Thomas Jefferson's story that scholars, pundits, and schoolchildren have fretted and puzzled over since his arrival on the public stage. Few could meet a standard of consistency had they produced an archive so large that covered such a range of subjects for a period of over sixty years. (Both "head" and "heart" change over time—or so Jefferson believed.) This book is a story of a relationship—a social entity—not a full biography of Martha Jefferson. Much remains to be written about Martha's life in those years that she and her father had long-imagined as a "harbour from the cares and storms of life." The intimate details of this period emerge not from letters with her father but rather in the hundreds of written conversations his plantation mistress had with the once-spurned Anne Cary (Nancy) Randolph or with Martha's son-in-law Nicholas Trist; the prolix voices of granddaughters trapped in the mountaintop refuge Grand Papa had erected; gossipy observations of Eliza Trist and Catherine Bache; the inventive enterprises of sisters-in-law Virginia and Mary Randolph; or Martha's poignant efforts to preserve her father's memory and create a "genteel home" in "honorable poverty." These voices within Martha's hearing created an invaluable sub-text to historical events and social dynamics of the period that has not yet been given its due. A full treatment would necessarily concentrate on the women of the house—her daughters, sisters-in-law, and friends; only cameos of these other characters and their places in a network of intelligent, resourceful, and inspiring women are sketched in the final chapters.

This book does strive to slightly turn the kaleidoscope of Jefferson's multifaceted character as reflected through his most intimate relationship and presents a pattern of emotional expression different from that frequently presented in stories of the enslaved Sally Hemings or the European coquette Maria Cosway.[16] These pages chronicle the account of a tearful child emerging from the grief of a young mother's death to seed a relationship that became the emotional sustenance of her father's republican aspirations, and who grew to be an indispensible helpmeet and competent mistress of a plantation household in its waning days.

Chapter 1

"Time Wastes too fast":

Affairs of the Heart

"Time wastes too fast," the young mother wrote as she struggled to recover from the birth of their child. Her husband's favorite novelist, Laurence Sterne, provided the worlds to aptly describe ten years of marriage to Thomas Jefferson, already in 1782 an international figure.[1] Living with a meteoric political career, fleeing with a tiny baby from invading foreign forces, revolution, an unsettled household, and the death of three children had taken their toll on the thirty-four-year-old Martha Wayles Skelton Jefferson.[2]

Since their marriage on a bitterly cold New Year's Day in 1772, the devoted couple's family life had been as upsetting as the husband's political career had been flourishing. Martha, their eldest daughter, was just eighteen months old when sister Jane was born on 3 April 1774. She would have been unaware of Mother's postpartum difficulties with breast abscesses but certainly would have noticed the baby's absence eighteen months later. An only son passed unnamed after just two weeks in 1777.[3] Lucy Elizabeth, The First, had been born a romping 10½ pounds on 3 November 1780 at Virginia's newly established capital in Richmond. During her short life, Benedict Arnold's invasion forced the family's flight in the dead of winter, first, to the Randolphs of Tuckahoe, and then another eight miles westerly up the James. She died a few weeks later on 15 April 1781, "10. o'clock A.M," leaving young Martha, who was affectionately called "Patsy" by the family, and three-year-old Mary. Governor and Mrs. Jefferson had scant time to mourn in the face of another British incursion in May that drove them and the government to Monticello and beyond.[4]

All the while their father's political career was robust and rising. *A Summary View of the Rights of British Americans* (1774) and the *Declaration of Independence* (1776) had brought international prominence but also extended separations from family. Principal draftsman of 126 bills intended to create a Virginia code (1777–78) and a stint as wartime Governor (1779–81) had drawn him closer to home but consumed extraordinary amounts of time and exposed his family even more to political life.

During this unsettling and unsettled decade, little Patsy shuttled between the rudimentary quarters atop Monticello Mountain; a more established home with her Aunt and Uncle Eppes, while Father was off to Philadelphia; and a time in George Wythe's elegant, two-story, eight-room mansion on Williamsburg's Palace Green before moving into the cramped quarters of Ludwell Tenement. Shortly after arriving in the capital of a "new" government, Patsy's itinerate life was embellished with a new pair of shoes costing "3/9" and toys totaling "3/."[5] The Jefferson's eldest daughter, also, had experienced three births and two deaths in her short life.

When the Royal Governor dissolved the House of Burgesses in May, Jefferson's revolutionary stirrings became a boil, and he proposed with cohorts a Committee of Correspondence to communicate with other aggrieved Colonies. Father's step onto the national stage in Philadelphia separated the family for even longer periods, so Mother assumed not only her domestic chores but also some of her husband's, as well. She paid for stockings, chickens, making a gown, muslin, "John for dressing [her] hair," and whiskey. She also borrowed £10 from their Monticello steward, Tom Garth, and the same day "Lent Randolph Jefferson £10," her husband's brother; made payments for the "estate of Mrs. Jane Jefferson," her mother-in-law; and "Pd. for a book for Patsy 7½d."[6] All was not well, however.

As early as 30 July 1776, Jefferson had written John Page that "every letter brings me such an account of the state of her [Martha's] health, that it is with great pain I can stay" in Philadelphia.[7] Nearly five and having experienced her mother's previous illnesses, Patsy would have been anxious when they stopped at Doctor Brydon's en route to Williamsburg in the fall of 1776, or by "Dr. Mclurgh's" house call two months later.[8] Between these visits, Jefferson had declined to serve with Benjamin Franklin and Silas Deane in Paris as Commissioners to the Court of France. "[C]ircumstances very peculiar in the situation of my family," he wrote Congress President John Hancock, "compel me to ask leave to decline a service so honorable"[9]

The couple's first son was born the following spring on 28 May 1777, less than two months after Jefferson was elected to the newly-formed Virginia House of Delegates. "June 14. Our son died 10H-20' P.M."[10] Six children in ten years of marriage to a revolutionary had extracted a price. During her short life, Patsy had experienced a frequently absent father, a mother repeatedly ill from pre- and postnatal complications, and the joy of baby sister Mary born when she was almost six. She had lived in a rural home under construction, an elegant brick mansion in Virginia's Capital, and a two-room apartment. Thomas Jefferson at last had retired from public life in 1783. He felt thirteen years of public service had left his private affairs in "great disorder and ruin." His considerable skills and intense affections would now be focused on "a family advanced to years which require…attention and instruction."[11] French nobleman Chastellux visited in April, just before the second Lucy Elizabeth's birth, and found "a mild and amiable wife, charming children, of whose education [Jefferson] himself takes charge." His host at that time considered his "scheme of life…folded in the arms of retirement [and] rested all prospects of future happiness on domestic and literary objects."[12]

Time had wasted fast these ten years, but the times themselves, in the words from Sterne's *Tristram Shandy*, were "flying…like clouds on a windy day never to return."[13]

Social and Political Landscape

The world surrounding the Jefferson family was undergoing a watershed of political, social, economic, and cultural change.[14] They were in the very middle of a time when the future was rarely more contingent and the past so little guide. The new nation and everything within it was in a liminal state suspended between past and future, metropole and periphery, colony and state, confederation and union.

Even a return to plantation profitability might not have rescued the genteel way of life in post-revolutionary Virginia. An increase in free white labor seeking to become landowners, decline in Tidewater land productivity, and lowered land prices on the Virginia "frontier," combined with migration from the English borderlands into Virginia's Valley, had pushed settlement into the Piedmont and over the Blue Ridge. Slaveholding was dispersing socially and geographically, providing the necessary political support for its maintenance. But coupled with egalitarian political rhetoric and representative government following the Revolution, families of yeoman farmers and middling ranks with an individualistic bent were challenging the finely graduated hierarchies and political influence that elite Tidewater planters had constructed on foundations of wealth and social status.[15] Jefferson, who was raised on Virginia's colonial frontier, had been able through inheritance and a fortunate marriage to move beyond the yeoman origins of his father. But even vast landholding and civic engagement could not ensure elite status against a less tangible, effervescent menace of economic, social, and cultural discontinuities.

The very nature and constructs of family were also evolving. As early as mid-century, "the parent-child relationship had seemed to be so conditional, so much a matter of mutual consent, as to become something akin to a voluntary association."[16] The three "best sellers" in 1775, dealt with issues of parent-child relations: Daniel Defoe's *Robinson Crusoe*, Lord Chesterfield's *Letters to His Son*, and John Gregory's *A Father's Legacy to His Daughters*. The sentimental novel was a widely popular literary genre whose parental characters were critically appraised for demanding filial submission and asserting parental domination.[17] The content of magazines more frequently was referencing marriage in affective language connoting "love at first sight," "ideal loved one," and "love wins out," rather than emphasizing wealth or social status in marriage decisions. Women, as portrayed in publications in the period 1741–1794, increasingly used "subtle persuasion and indirect means…[to] exert considerable power in matters of morality, courtship, child-rearing, and other domestic situations."[18] This trend in the use of power in conjugal relations had its corollary in the political arena that increasingly questioned the hierarchical and monarchical origins of governance. Affectionate bonds were an important emotional dynamic in Southern plantation families as well, but commitment to collective needs muted individualism.[19] By century's end, constructs of both child and family would be in transition and fraught with ambivalence.[20]

The hierarchal ordering of family powers and unquestioned male dominance were confronted with an emerging view of the child as Rousseau-like, playful, and innocent; affectionate nurture would bring them to self-discipline and self-sufficiency.[21] In the new regime, fathers, mothers, and children were seeking to balance affection and authority, equality and hierarchy, nurture and nature. These social changes carried political implications in a Western culture that had tied government to a patriarchal family construct since Aristotle and had insisted on the divine origins of each. "[U]nder the combined impact of social evolution and political revolution, the explanatory power of the [traditional] familial paradigm was severely curtailed....[So] the commitment to republicanism entailed nothing less than a family of a new identity."[22]

The Revolutionary War and the political rhetoric surrounding it had irrevocably raised the question of women's domestic, social, and political roles. "Of how much consequence…it is in a republic," wrote Benjamin Rush, that women "be taught the principles of liberty and government; and the obligations of patriotism…Besides, the first impressions upon the minds of children are generally derived from the women."[23] The Revolution's iconography was gendered in the female form of Liberty, and her sister Columbia would sit atop the Republic's Capitol. Nevertheless, historians have described just how ambiguous and contentious women's roles were in republican ideology and practice.[24]

Three daughters in a family whose father was a Founder and ardent republican could not be isolated from the effects of the period's political ideology. What did the political rhetoric of individual rights portend for the daughters of America's preeminent republican? He looked unfavorably on women's involvement in the public sphere.[25] However, accommodating the needs of his political life was a significant dimension of Martha's social-emotional growth as she was learning to live apart from the person she loved the most. Neither "republican wife" nor "mother," the "dearest Daughter" had to invent with father's guidance her own devices to make meaning of these life experiences. Already by 1782, the lives of Patsy, Mary, their mother, and most assuredly the departed Lucy had been severely affected by Jefferson's engagement in practical politics to the point of "great disorder and ruin." Even in this first of several retirements in 1783, political maneuvering cast a pall over much-sought tranquility.

Paroxysms of Grief

The final weeks of wife Martha's pregnancy with their sixth child had been busy ones. Jefferson and Thomas Walker were re-elected to Virginia's House of Delegates in mid-April;[26] the anxious father was asked to inform Benjamin Harrison that the Continental Army stationed in Albemarle County was short of provisions;[27] the future Marquis de Chastellux was a guest from Jefferson's birthday on April 13th to the 17th. A few days before Lucy's birth, Jefferson sent his rye to Mrs. Meriwether's for distillation. Amid these affairs of business and daily plantation life, the note of a birth seems ominous: "Our daughter Lucy Elizabeth (second of that name) born at one o'clock A.M."[28] Recovering, Mrs. Jefferson from her sickbed continued copying the words Laurence Sterne had brooded during his tubercular decline: "[E]very letter I trace tells me with what rapidity life follows my pen." Her husband's nib on a *Summary View, Declaration*, and legislative drafts had hastened the pace of their times together in both material and intangible ways. There was no respite.

The Virginia legislature was demanding that Jefferson defend his performance as Governor during the British invasion, which had hastened the death of a daughter. Now, it seemed he had also lost the "only award ever sought" from public service—his countrymen's "affection." Surrounded by servitude and subservience on his mountaintop, Jefferson's intense emotions were conveyed in words starkly contrasting public duty and private domesticity:

> If we are made in some degree for others, yet in a greater are we made for ourselves. It were contrary to feeling and indeed ridiculous to suppose a man had less right in himself than one of his neighbors or all of them put together. This would be slavery and not that liberty which the bill of rights has made inviolable...I may think public service and private misery inseparably linked together...[29]

In the deepening crisis of Martha's illness, Jefferson was claiming a place separate from a meddling world, a place needing order, a place in need of succor from a long-absent patriarch. The "mental quiet" he sought in the family, the liberty he claimed as an individual right, were counterpoised to lost public affections, to enslavement, and perhaps most salient for Jefferson, an affront to his cherished republican civic virtue with alleged "treasons of the heart." But even a sympathetic Governor James Monroe would not let him separate from the world. For "as soon as circumstances will permit," Jefferson's advice would be sought "upon every subject of consequence."[30]

In the days following Lucy's birth and into the fall, her father saw to business—breeding mares for James Cocke and Colonel Harvie, giving a legal opinion for Doctor Reed, and paying taxes on his Natural Bridge property. He tended to the neighborly duties of loaning brown sugar to Mrs. Nicholas Lewis and Dr. Gilmer; and assumed the ailing Martha's domestic chores of buying "three turkies very young" from Mrs. Grey and giving Jupiter money to buy beer.[31]

On 6 September 1782, Jefferson noted, "My dear wife died this day at 11H–45' A.M."[32] His Memorandum Book went silent, but paper and ink bound the couple as both their hands had stroked Sterne's endearing words:

> Time wastes too fast: every letter
> I trace tells me with what rapidity
> life follows my pen. The days and hours
> of it are flying over our heads like
> clouds of a windy day never to return—
> more everything presses on—

A melancholy Jefferson finished their farewell duet:

> …and every
> time I kiss thy hand to bid adieu, every absence which
> follows it, are preludes to that eternal separation
> which we are shortly to make![33]

Death would prove the most significant watershed in the life courses of both her eldest daughter and husband.

What we know of the next few weeks comes from the adult recollections of a ten-year-old child's experience and the anguished ramblings of a grieving, single parent. Patsy recalled:

> [T]he violence of his emotion, when, almost by stealth, I entered his room by night, to this day I dare not describe to myself. He kept to his room three weeks, and I was never a moment from his side… [W]hen at last he left his room, he rode out, and from that time he was incessantly on horseback, rambling about the mountain, in the least frequented roads…In those melancholy rambles I was his constant companion—a solitary witness to many a violent burst of grief, the remembrance of which has consecrated particular scenes of that lost home beyond the power of time to obliterate.[34]

Physical place and emotional space would be inextricably bound for the remainder of Patsy's life. Monticello became hallowed ground, her heart engrossed by a single person. She would remain at her father's side over the next seven years as they extended their ramblings beyond the mountaintop, but a pattern that would recur for nearly three decades was set in these few months of grief: lonely separations, surrogate families, and longed for reunions.

As for Father, the family remnants became sacred, his parental duties blessed by an angel.

> This miserable kind of existence is really too burthensome to be borne, and were it not for the infidelity of deserting the sacred charge left me, I could not wish it's continuance for a moment....The care and instruction of our children indeed affords some temporary abstractions from wretchedness and nourishes a soothing reflection, that if there be beyond the grave any concern for the things of this world there is one angel at least who views these attentions with pleasure and wishes continuance of them while she must pity the miseries to which they confine me.[35]

Jefferson wrote sister-in-law Elizabeth Eppes, who had sat weeks with his dying wife, how he suffered a "stupor of mind," was "dead to the world," "blank" without "the spirits to fill up," except for the "care and instruction" of Patsy, Mary, and Lucy.[36] The "private miseries" associated in Jefferson's mind with ten years of public service paled in comparison with the dismal pain his heart felt from this "eternal separation." The palliative for grief, ironically, was to yoke his "sacred charge" to a life of republican civic virtue.

Following these days and weeks of shared grief, Patsy Jefferson and her father separated themselves from family, friends, and environs to live among strangers in locations considerably different from Piedmont Virginia's plantation culture. The isolation and circumstances of these experiences deepened an emotional bond of affection and commitment that could never be breached by husband or children, friends or kinfolk. To cope with extended periods of being apart, over the next twenty years Patsy and her father created in their letters an imaginary family that was situated at a place called "Monticello" and contrasted sharply with lives they were living separately. "Reunion"— symbol and enacted ritual—was an expression of their deepest affection for each other and attachment to the Mountain where it occurred. As husband Mann Randolph increasingly belied their family ideal of harmony, love, and tranquility, daughter-wife and Father intensified and deepened their commitment to each other and to the children. The material circumstances of inexorably growing debt finally and unavoidably intruded into their emotional refuge, but the couple was incapable of detaching either their imagined or their lived families from Monticello Mountain. Rather than part from the place where their love was rooted and where they had waited twenty years to achieve happiness, Martha and Father chose, instead, to suffer the ignominy of public scrutiny and enter their most feared condition—dependency.

Martha and her father recovered their imagined family, however, revised its narrative to accommodate life's contingencies, and created for posterity "The Jefferson Family Story." The plotline's protagonist was a benevolent republican and master who was absent for sixty years from his plantation in disinterested service to his fellow citizens; his opponents were greedy overseers, enslaved incompetents, and a national government favoring merchants and westward migration. The outcome was a family "destitute of a means of living," rending of the barrier guarding private family affairs from public scrutiny, and the sad realization that a republican ethos did not necessarily carry pecuniary expressions of public gratitude. Yet after her father's death in 1826, Martha would persist in maintaining that "honorable poverty" in the wake of civic virtue was preferable to genteel grandeur raised up by self-interested tides. Deprived of financial means, Martha Jefferson Randolph, former plantation mistress but still a republican daughter, inventively drew from the social and political capital Father had amassed over forty years to extract patronage for her children and to sustain a genteel, if modest, life for herself separated from both the person and place she loved the most.

This is the story of that relationship.

Chapter 2

"Educated as the heiress":

The Family of Memory, Imagination, and Life

"Unfortunately," Martha recalled in 1826, "I was educated as the heiress to a great estate, and was learning music, &c., &c., when I ought to have been acquiring dexterity with my needle; but I believe no good management of mine could have saved the estate." The patriarch had died. His material legacy to a grieving family was a mountaintop refuge burdened by debt; his emotional bequest, the embarrassment of exposing the most private affairs to public display. Yet, the mistress of Monticello hoped, "my education may still be the means of procuring us food and raiment."[1] In the silence of "&c., &c." was childhood reading in the "graver sciences," acquaintance with the "best poetry and prosewriters," translating ancient Italian, socializing with notable women in late eighteenth-century Paris, and supporting her father's political career.

From Private Misery to Public Service

Patsy had just passed her eleventh birthday when she began experiencing a world beyond Piedmont Virginia's insular plantation culture; it would ultimately serve to provide for the "food and raiment" her family so sorely needed. Leaving sister Mary and infant Lucy with Aunt Eppes on 19 December 1782, she departed the security of home with her father, who had accepted an appointment as a Peace Commissioner in Paris.[2] The grieving duo jostled along the Orange turnpike, following it northeastward and crossing the Potomac at Georgetown. They ferried Maryland's Patapsco, Pennsylvania's

Susquehanna and Schuylkill rivers, saw Bladensburg, Baltimore, and finally arrived at Philadelphia just after Christmas on the 28th.

An English visitor some years earlier described this city of substantial, three- and four-story homes standing neatly side-by-side and arrayed on ground rising gently from the broad Delaware River. Residences faced straight-running streets thirty feet wide that intersected to form an orderly checkerboard pattern. Government buildings, like the statehouse, hospital, a new gaol, almshouse, workhouse, barracks, and a "grand public" market house, had been deemed especially noteworthy by the visitor accustomed to ancient European cities. All in all "a very agreeable and elegant metropolis" that reflected the commercial, political, and intellectual dynamism of what would become a new nation's largest city.[3]

At 5th and Market right in the middle of this bustle was the home of widow Mary House; a block east was her upscale Indian Queen Tavern with sixteen rooms featuring liveried servants. Both establishments were favored by Virginia's representatives to political conclaves, and the Jeffersons followed suit until January 26th; then set off to Baltimore to await transportation to France.[4] When American negotiators in Paris reached agreement with Great Britain on a peace treaty, father and daughter returned to Philadelphia for a few weeks before leaving for home on April 12th.

Peace abroad, however, did not bring a cessation to internal political hostilities or tranquility to Monticello's heavily indebted patriarch. Madison's coded messages from Philadelphia were delivered to Jefferson outside Richmond at "Tuckahoe" plantation, one of Jefferson's boyhood homes owned by Col. Thomas Mann Randolph, Sr. They apprised him of disputes over such Treaty details as returning "Negroes [who] had eloped" to the enemy during the Revolution and opening trade through ports still held by the British. John Adams appeared to be petitioning for an appointment to negotiate a treaty of commerce with Great Britain. "The system for foreign affairs is not yet digested," his informant wrote.[5] Jefferson was "not a little concerned" over developments in Congress regarding federal assumption of states' war debts, so waited two weeks at Tuckahoe to confer with Virginia's representatives.

Some five months after leaving home Jefferson, with daughter Martha in tow, arrived back at Monticello in mid-May, but weighty public affairs were never far distant. Talk of a Virginia constitutional convention turned the draftsman's attention to a new charter during the summer months. Amid practical political maneuvering and lofty principles of governance to shape the future, Jefferson was reminded by creditor Wakelin Welch, Sr., that his London account of over £87 sterling was past due and had grown to £118.1.4 with interest during the late War.[6]

By late October 1783, Patsy and Congressman Jefferson were on the move again, trotting in a two-horse phaeton this time along a westerly route across the Blue Ridge Mountains, down the Shenandoah Valley, to view at Harpers Ferry, "perhaps the one of the most stupendous scenes in nature."[7] Leaving Twining's ordinary in Newport, Delaware, on October 29th, father and daughter again crossed to Philadelphia at the Schuylkill "ferrge."[8]

"Considerably Different" Experiences

Jefferson's first challenge in this "elegant metropolis" was to locate a place and persons which could serve as surrogates for the family and home Patsy had left behind. He drew into his lived family whomever could help with his "sacred duty."

> In either event of my being or not being in Philadelphia I propose to place Patsy there; and will ask the favor of Mrs. [Eliza House] Trist to think for me on that subject, and to advise me as to the person with whom she may be trusted. Some boarding school of course, tho' I am not without objections to her passing more than the day in such a one.[9]

James Madison reported that Mrs. Trist concurred in the idea of Patsy becoming a boarding school day student.[10] Over the next three weeks, Martha renewed her acquaintance with Mrs. House. Her father rejected a boarding school and chose an approach very similar to traditional female education in Virginia: a surrogate mother, tutors for the feminine ornaments, and a little reading.

Boarding with strangers, sleeping in taverns, ferry ride after ferry ride, two port cities, and unfamiliar households presented a bewildering array to a plantation girl from rural Virginia. The experiences were so impressive that memories of these early years were not dulled four decades later.

> The journeys that I had made with him in my childhood were still so fresh in my mind that in traveling the same road afterwards [1826] in my journey to Boston I was overwhelmed with melancholy recollections...Yet I

must do myself the justice to say that, great as that contrast was, it was not that, it was not the loss of fortune and of home, but of the being on earth I most idolized, and one of whom the thought had for years past become a habit of my mind.[11]

After several months as her father's principal companion and just a year from her mother's death, eleven-year-old Patsy was left at the Philadelphia home of Mary Johnson Hopkinson (1718–1804) in the center of a thriving American Enlightenment. Orphaned as a child, widowed in her early thirties with seven children under fourteen years, Mrs. Hopkinson was an able caretaker for little Patsy. (Her fervent religiosity may have given Jefferson pause, however.) The "good lady" was the mother of Jefferson's colleague and fellow-signer of *The Declaration*, Francis Hopkinson, and widow of Thomas, a founder of the Philadelphia Library Company in 1736.[12] While her father attended Congress in Annapolis, Patsy could associate with the children of clockmaker, astronomer, and mathematician David Rittenhouse as well as other notable and learned families.

Mrs. Hopkinson, her family, and their acquaintances in Philadelphia society were highly respectable company for Patsy's tutelage; however, the cultural environment was far different from her native "country"—Virginia. Typically, daughters of the plantation elite,

grew up in their mothers' shadows and under their tutelage. They learned the fundamentals of adult responsibilities from their mothers rather than from teachers, even when they had governesses or went away to school. Their mothers afforded the primary models of how to conduct oneself in a world that merged a woman's most important responsibilities of doing and being.[13]

Young girls helped with arranging chores for the enslaved servants, tending chickens, watching over the dairy, carrying keys to the larder, mending, receiving visitors, and a host of domestic duties that complemented farming operations and projected social hospitality.[14] However, Patsy's "shadow" would be letters from an exacting father; her conduct learned in the "world" of northern states and fashionable Paris; her "models" would be mother surrogates and nuns at a convent school. Jefferson's decision to assuage his grief by re-entering public service did not initially spawn "private misery," but it would engender a host of challenges to transmitting what he considered appropriate principles regarding gendered roles, plantation culture, and republican life.

Fearing public demonstrations by disgruntled Revolutionary War veterans demanding back pay, Congress adjourned first to Trenton and then Annapolis, where Jefferson stayed until May 1784.[15] This chance political event separated daughter and father by some 100 miles and three days travel. Circumstances, however, initiated a series of over 260 letters during the next three decades that reveal a deep-rooted affectionate bond, the emotional suffering from separation, a family ideal of being eternally together in solitude and serenity, and the harsh private miseries of public service. Father was forced to see to Patsy's education with a reading list, hired tutors, and regular instructions in letters.

Patsy was left behind with two popular Spanish-themed novels that Father considered "among the best books of their class," which he routinely recommended for both young girls and boys.[16] *Histoire de Gil Blas de Santillane* by Alain-René Le Sage recounts a youth who is placed by his impoverished parents in the home of a wealthy uncle for his education. He sets out from thence to learn about life, its temptations, and prospects from brigands, prostitutes, and persons of high degree. He successfully navigates these experiences in a corrupt society to become a landed nobleman. It concludes with a felicitous marriage whose sexual consummation on the wedding night is thwarted by groomsmen enticing the husband into a drunken stupor.[17] Cervantes' *Don Quixote* has a similar theme of roaming the world encountering brigands, errant women, unscrupulous traders, and other dubious characters but ends with a melancholy protagonist.[18] This reading, however, was only the preface, because "her time in Philadelphia [would] be chiefly occupied in acquiring a little taste and execution in such of the fine arts as she could not prosecute to equal advantage in a more retired situation."

> The plan of reading which I have formed for her is considerably different from what I think would be most proper for her sex in any other country than America. I am obliged in it to extend my views beyond herself, and consider her as possible at the head of a little family of her own. The chance that in marriage she will draw a blockhead I calculate at about fourteen to one, and of course that the education of her family will probably rest on her own ideas and direction without assistance. With the best poets and prosewriters I shall therefore

combine a certain extent of reading in the graver sciences. However, I scarcely expect to enter her on this till she returns to me.[19]

"America," "family," "considerably different," "proper for her sex," "blockhead," and "graver sciences" were among the words in this brief letter that carried significant implications revealed only in fragments over the ensuing years. By claiming Patsy's plan of reading was "considerably different...for her sex in any country other than America," her father was imagining a cultural context in which beliefs about family, parenting, human development, and children strongly influence the behavioral particulars of child-rearing practices.[20] These values can differ across communities, as Jefferson claimed they did from North to South along the Atlantic coast. Indeed, he contended with Adams that cultural differences between Virginia and Massachusetts explain variations in preferences for monarchal or republican forms of government.[21] He was aware of and acted on what he imagined would be a new republic's distinctive features and clearly situated his constructs of family, child, human development, republican government within a belief system that synthesized features from local, American, and Atlantic cultures, as he understood them.

Patsy would be reading *Gil Blas* and learning to draw in a city where her father believed regional differences arising from distinctive colonial histories were blended in a "people...free from the extremes of vice and virtue." Her Virginia "country" had characters that were an "aristocratical, pompous, clannish, indolent" sort; however, their "hospitable" and "disinterested" practices were essential to creating the social climate and personal generosity required by republican civic virtue. Navigating the shoals of political dissension in republican government would call for a "cool, sober, laborious, persevering, independent" temperament characteristic of Northerners.[22] Years later, Jefferson would advise a Paris convent student:

> It is part of the American character to consider nothing as desperate; to surmount every difficulty by resolution and contrivance....Remote from other aid, we are obliged to invent and to execute; to find means within ourselves, and not to lean on others.[23]

These values of persistence, industry, inventiveness, and more were drawn from what Jefferson considered the praiseworthy virtues of "North" and "South" that he imagined would be the emerging republic's distinguishing features.

"America"

The challenge for Jefferson was that the "America" for which Patsy presumably was being prepared had been undergoing a watershed, not only politically but also in matters of social and cultural imperatives. He had grown up on the Virginia frontier and spent a few years of his youth in the luxurious setting of Tuckahoe plantation just above the fall line of the James. He knew firsthand that the tobacco wealth of the eighteenth century's early decades had altered the plantation household. Abundant land, an enslaved workforce, and a world market had generated discretionary income that, in turn, fueled a consumer revolution and "dramatically transformed the domestic sphere and women's roles."[24] On the yeomen's farms, women were increasingly freed from the field and consigned to the house. For the better situated genteel women, wealth brought a "new set of burdens."

> She oversaw the house and its natural extensions, notably flower and vegetable gardens and perhaps the dairy. She had primary responsibility for clothing the white and black families. She oversaw all food for the white family and sometimes basic rations for the blacks...She presided over the infirmary if the household had one, and she helped in childbirth and illness if it did not.[25]

We might add to these, childbearing and rearing, proper external social relations, an elevated personal appearance and more—all of which had to integrate seamlessly with a production enterprise on the farms.

"Head of a Little Family"

Martha might be "head of a little family," but would it be dispersed like herself, Maria, and Lucy? Would she follow her mother's trajectory of a life slowly ebbing from the disabilities of multiple pregnancies? What kind of family was Father imagining—extended, multi-generational? Thirty-five years later, women's position in a plantation household in Jefferson's estimation had been elevated even higher and her role expanded to more than educating the children. He had added other possible spousal shortcomings to a "blockhead" husband:

> I thought it essential to give [my daughters] a solid education, which might enable them, when become

mothers to educate their own daughters, and even to direct the course for sons, should their fathers be lost, or incapable, or inattentive.[26]

Just four days after the birth of her twelfth and last child in 1818, Martha was "a better judge of the practical part" of educating children, her father admitted to this correspondent. Nonetheless, he offered explanations for various learning activities she had experienced. Novels—"this mass of trash"—should be avoided, because they inflated imagination, weakened judgment, and fostered "disgust towards all the real business of life." (Quixote's fantasies and Gil Blas' picaresque adventures were seemingly passé.) Some poetry was advised to form "style and taste;" dancing for exercise but only before marriage; drawing as preparation for teaching children; and music for recreation. French was requisite for both women and men, because it was used in the "general intercourse of nations" and was the language of "all science."

More critically, Martha and her father's shared experiences over three decades of struggling with an erratic husband, burdensome debt, a geographically dispersed household, and markets sensitive to foreign intrigues had obviously generated an expanded vision of the critical role women played in a plantation's viability.

> I need say nothing of household economy...We all know its value, and that diligence and dexterity in all its processes are inestimable treasures. The order and economy of a house are as honorable to the mistress as those of the farm to the master, and if either be neglected, ruin follows, and children destitute of the means of living.[27]

"Order and economy of a house" were insufficient surety against "ruin" or leaving future generations "destitute," because the farms never recovered to their pre-war levels of profitability. Provisions in the 1783 treaty ending military hostilities with Britain had further deepened planters' financial predicament and increased their dependency on faraway London and Glasgow merchant houses, until new financial institutions could be created in "America."[28] Some like Jefferson's neighbor John Cocke at Bremo on the James River's fertile bottoms, had successfully transitioned by the second decade of the nineteenth century to livestock and grain production for a domestic market. Others, like Christopher Smith in adjoining Louisa County from whom Jefferson leased laborers, had freed all his "slaves by name of Kinney" and given them 50 acres of land in 1804.[29] However, most planters tenaciously clung to a tradition of plantation agriculture whose product sailed into an Atlantic trade whipsawed by wars, capricious mercantilist policies, and nations' internal conflicts. In the turbulence of these economic conditions, Patsy's "music, &c., &c." probably served the house and farm as well as dexterity with the needle. Hospitality would prove to be a valuable skill for husbanding the household's social capital against eroding solvency as bankers' increasingly demanded tangible collateral to secure debts.[30]

"Considerably different"

However, it was not reading, dancing, drawing, French language, or even the picaresque novels that would be a "considerably different" upbringing; it was the location and circumstances in which Patsy lived during her formative years from age ten to seventeen. From late 1783 through the spring of 1784, Patsy was living in a more socially diverse environment, being encouraged to "accomplishments" in exchange for Father's affection, directed to treat Mrs. Hopkinson as a "mother," and urged to stay connected through letters with her kin in Virginia. Her father was beginning to create a family-of-surrogates and a family-of-letters, drawing Patsy even closer emotionally, and learning the challenges of being a widowed father.

Philadelphia was significantly "less retired" than an isolated rural mountaintop, where links to the outside world were tenuous and indistinct and where race clearly demarked social hierarchy. It was the new nation's largest city and eastern commercial center, where ships docked daily from France, Germany, and the West Indies. The population of the middle district of the city where she lived in 1784 had grown by 1790 to 13,674 (of those 71 were slaves), while the whole population of Albemarle County, Virginia that year was 12,585 (5579 were slaves). Mrs. House's residence accommodating eighteen persons would have approximated a hospitable Monticello, where Jefferson's sister, Martha Jefferson Carr, and her six children had lived for two years. By 1790, Patsy's Philadelphia neighborhood would have less distinct color lines than home, but its diversity of ranks would have been more marked. It was home to William Sheaff, wine merchant; William Jones, grazier; Benjamin Harbeson, coppersmith; Patrick McCormick, fish monger; and Robert Morris, Esq., merchant and prominent official at the U.S. counting house.[31]

The runaways in Philadelphia were somewhat different than Virginia, but in both locations the consequences of forced labor regimes were a ceaseless vexation to masters of all sorts. While Patsy was in Philadelphia, Captain Robert Shewell of the *Nancy* offered a sixty-dollar reward for ten seamen who had run away after receiving a month's advance pay. Among the absconders was Dutchman Clogner, who had a "smooth face" and spoke "broken English," and Andrew Barkus, "a Spanish Negroe, who neither speaks nor understands English."[32] Patsy would have been reminded of the other family relationships she had left behind by Morton Welsh's ad offering sixteen dollars reward for "a likely Negroe Man, named SAUL, of a yellowish complexion."[33]

"Good Lady" and "Valuable Friend"

Left behind in this unfamiliar environment, Patsy received letters from her father in Annapolis that reprised themes which would be echoed in correspondence until they were permanently reunited in 1809. His love made their separation a "difficult thing," but she would be "more improved in the situation" than in Annapolis. He demanded that she stay connected through letters to family and friends in faraway Virginia. Eliza Trist was installed as a "valuable friend." "Heaven has been pleased to afflict" Patsy with the loss of a parent, so "good lady" Mrs. Hopkinson was to be considered as her "mother" and the "only person to whom [she] can now look up." A month after installing this surrogate, Patsy was directed to be "obedient and respectful to her in every circumstance and that your manners will be such as to engage her affections."[34] Father would most likely have approved of "mother's" morality, if not its origins in fervent Christian spiritualism.[35]

In Jefferson's mind, ordering the flow of time and keeping incessantly busy was critical. So Mrs. Hopkinson would "see that you perform all your exercises, and admonish you in all those wanderings from what is right or what is clever."

> from 8 to 10 o'clock practise music
> from 10. to 1. dance one day and draw another
> from 1. to 2. draw on the day you dance,
>   and write a letter the next day
> from 3. to 4. read French
> from 4. to 5. exercise yourself in music
> from 5. till bedtime read English, write &c.[36]

Jefferson believed there was a quotidian pattern to mental vigor—strongest from 8:00–12:00 A.M. and best suited for reflective reading in the evening—and he routinely apportioned subject matter on this basis. There was a similar time-sensitive variation over a person's life span in the capacity of memory and reason. From ages eight to fifteen, the "memory is most susceptible and tenacious of impressions," and the "mind was not yet firm;" reason was best challenged from fifteen upward, when the mind was ready for "close examination;" and these two mental faculties were in decline at some indeterminate stage called "old age."[37]

The Family-of-Memory

Jefferson's busy schedule and incessant emphasis on affection as the tie that binds regardless of sanguinity were grounded in memories of his own childhood and youth.[38] His earliest memory was being separated from his Shadwell home and carried by a slave to a relative's Tuckahoe plantation where the family lived for the next several years.[39] Decades later, he recounted favorably his own father's achievements and contrasted them unfavorably with his mother's status attained through her Randolph genealogy. Peter Jefferson's education had been "quite neglected" in the opinion of his son, but personal qualities overcame this limitations: "strong mind, sound judgment, and eager after information." Persistent self-improvement enabled Peter Jefferson to gain entrée to genteel society and improve his economic status by marriage, of course, but also by associating with Joshua Fry of William and Mary College to complete the Virginia-North Carolina border survey that the prominent William Byrd II (1674–1744) had begun many years before. Individual effort, building upon innate faculties, was linked with being acknowledged by a learned person to continue work begun by a socially prestigious one. In the language of the times, Peter Jefferson had acquired "esteem." This memory also was manifested in the values of industry and persistence which were at the core of Jefferson's instructions to Patsy. As to his mother's Randolph "pedigree far back in England and Scotland…let every one ascribe the faith and merit he chooses." Achieved status clearly was more valued in Jefferson's remembrances than inherited aristocratic origins, just as Patsy's "accomplishments" would be the condition for his love.[40] These were his remembered "parents."

After childhood, his recollections were a youthful "Jefferson" outside a biological family, populated by paternal surrogates. "At 14 years of age," Grand Papa recalled for Martha's son Jeff in 1808, "the whole care and direction of myself was thrown on my self entirely, without a relation or friend qualified to advise or guide me."[41] This boy, like his father of memory, was "eager after information," was chosen by a professor and acknowledged by a notable person. Jefferson described for his grandson, who had just arrived in Philadelphia for his schooling, a frightful world in which a youth of his age (16) was threatened by a dangerous menagerie of "puppies in politics," "patients of Bedlam," "fiery zealots," and "angry bulls."[42] A youth's vulnerability to these unsavory characters was amplified at this age, Jefferson believed. "Man is an imitative animal. This quality is the germ of all education in him. From his cradle to his grave he is learning to do what he sees others do," even the "odious peculiarities" of tyranny experienced in a slave culture.[43]

On his own initiative, Thomas Jefferson at sixteen had recommended to his guardian that attendance at William and Mary College would provide him with "a more universal Acquaintance which may hereafter be serviceable."[44] Late in life, Jefferson recalled the surrogate fathers he had been fortunate enough to find in Williamsburg and consequently avoided the company of "horseracers, cardplayers, Foxhunters." Dr. William Small "became soon attached to me, and made me his daily companion," which "probably fixed the destinies of my life." He read law under George Wythe, who became a lifelong "faithful and beloved mentor." "I owed much instruction," he recalled, by joining these teachers at the table of Royal Governor Francis Fauquier, "the ablest man who had ever filled that office."

Jefferson remembered a family headed by an accomplished and ambitious patriarch who was married to a woman modestly distinguished by her genealogy with an eldest son independently finding his way in a potentially dangerous world. Just as Peter Jefferson inscribed the boundaries of a colony, his son constructed his family-of-memory from among faithful, beloved, affectionate, good-mannered, and liberal-minded parental surrogates. Recollection of these experiences contributed to his notion that "affectionate deportment...offers in truth the best example for the tutor and pupil" and was the principle guiding his "care and instruction" of Patsy. [45]

Clearly the feminine ornaments—dancing, drawing, music— were a priority for Patsy in the "less retired situation" of Philadelphia. He enthusiastically approved of her taking dance lessons at the home of David Rittenhouse, because in that family she would "see the best examples of rational life and learn to esteem and copy them."[46] Though Patsy routinely ignored his entreaties for reporting on what she read and drew, she did delight him with a letter in French indicative of her progress.[47] Foreign languages had been a traditional ornament considered desirable for refined, genteel women; but Patsy's father also considered such studies a practical matter for developing memory as well as to "impress their minds with useful facts and good principles" of history.[48]

Mary Hopkinson's son and Eliza Trist, also, were drawn into monitoring Patsy's progress. She "comes on finely in her Education," Francis informed Jefferson.[49] Eliza Trist affirmed that the young student now seemed happy but was more attentive to emotional, feminine, and spiritual concerns:

> [W]hen you write give her a charge about her dress which will be a hint to Mrs H. to be particular with her. De Simitière complains that his pupil is rather inatentive [sic]. you can be particular to these matters when you write but don't let her know you heard any complaints. I fance the old Lady [Mrs. Hopkinson] is preparing for the other world for she conceives, the Earthquake we had the other night is only a prelude to something dreadfull that will happen.[50]

The "charge about her dress" recommended by "valuable friend" Mrs. Trist was accorded only slightly less importance than doing a "bad" thing. Father sternly admonished Patsy that her clothes are to be "clean, whole, and properly put on" from the moment she rose until bedtime, as if "at the hours of dinner or tea." Aware of the fashion-conscious Philadelphia culture, he reminded her "a sloven or slut in the morning" cannot change this impression with fine dress and manners in the evening. Proper dress signified a gendered identity for "nothing is so disgusting to our sex as a want of cleanliness and delicacy in yours."[51] Jefferson had given a critical appraisal of Philadelphia fashion to Francis Eppes soon after their arrival in late 1783. "The high head is made as flat as a flounder....The shoulders are where the chin used to be, and the hips have succeeded to the place of the shoulders. The circumference of the waste [waist] is the span of the lady's own hands...[A] hoop...at each angle before projects like two bastions of a fort."[52] He obviously shared the opinions heaped on Philadelphia women by fellow Virginian Arthur Lee. "Extravagance, ostentation & dissipation distinguish what are calld [sic] Ladies of the first rank." Having spent so much time in this city, Jefferson would have been aware of the social, political, and cultural symbolism attached to fashion before and after the Revolution.[53]

Patsy was being assaulted by worldly fashion and spiritual fears. Word of the old Lady's prognostications and the dogma it embraced could not augur well for a father who abhorred religious sects and divine revelations. Mary Hopkinson's Commonplace Book noted Old Testament prophecies that had been fulfilled; described dreams of "universal salvation"; recorded what others had reported from the spiritual world; and, most portentously, contained excerpts from writings of a warrior in the late eighteenth-century's sectarian wars, Elhanan Winchester.[54] To counter the old Lady's influence, Patsy was instructed to "have good sense enough to disregard those foolish predictions that the world is to be at an end soon." He interpreted her experience in such a way as to emphasize the primacy of her "faithful internal Monitor" or moral sense. The "almighty" simply will not tell anyone "what time he created it...[or] when he means to put an end to it." The best preparation was to be guided by moral sense and "never do or say a bad thing."

> You will feel something within you...Our maker has given us all, this faithful internal Monitor, and if you always obey it, you will always be prepared for the end of the world: or for a much more certain event which is death. This must happen to all: it puts an end to the world as to us, and the way to be ready for it is never to do a wrong act.[55]

This "Monitor" was a naturally occurring faculty, just like hearing, seeing, and touch, and a necessary precursor to development of mental and physical capacities.[56] Moreover, Jefferson wrote years later, this "moral instinct...prompts us irresistibly to feel and succor [other's] distresses."[57] Sentiments of tenderness, attachment, and comity, along with physical health and learning, "will ensure your happiness...give you a quiet conscience, private esteem and public honour" Jefferson would later tell nephew Peter Carr. An "honest heart" (the location of moral sense) was the first blessing; allied with a "knowing head," it would "render you dear to your friends, and give you fame and promotion."[58] Perhaps Father's rationale for prescribing *Gil Blas* and *Don Quixote* for ten-year-old Patsy was to "exercise" and strengthen this moral faculty. Reading fiction, he advised cousin Skipwith, stimulates "the spacious field of imagination...to illustrate and carry home to the mind every moral rule of life."[59] On the other hand, history books were bound by facts and "cannot present virtue in the best & vice in the worst forms possible."[60]

"If you Love me"

With surrogates and tutors attending to the practical details of Patsy's reading, dancing, drawing, and French, her father was left to focus on their emotional relationship. "The acquirements which I hope you will make under the tutors...will render you more worthy of my love, and if they cannot increase it they will prevent it's diminution." Parental love was conditioned on the child's compliance with prescribed behaviors that, in turn, were expressions of filial affection: "If you love me then, strive to...acquire those accomplishments which I have put in your power." [61] If Father's conditional affection was insufficient reason for learning then a daughter's duty may be: "I have placed my happiness on seeing you good and accomplished, and no distress which this world can now bring on me could equal that of your disappointing my hopes." The theme of emotional interdependency and its contingent nature expanded over the years to become a dominant force in their relationship. Impending separation three years later would occasion Jefferson to write before leaving Paris for London: "The more you learn the more I love you, and I rest the happiness of my life on seeing you beloved by all the world."[62] Thus, her position in his heart, just like Grandfather Peter's status, had to be achieved and was not merely the result of being his daughter.

Jefferson encouraged Patsy to extend these emotional attachments by demanding a "habit" of letter writing to her Virginia family. In many ways, it would prove to be the most important preparation for her future as a republican daughter in a place called "America." "Write also one letter every week either to your aunt Eppes, your aunt Skipwith, your aunt Carr or sister Polly....I hope you will continue to [send] every week one for some of your friends in Virginia."[63] They reminded the reader of family members' well-being and illness: "Letters by yesterday's post inform me your sisters are well." And letters were written about not being written: "I have had no letters from Eppington...and have not received one from you...these two months."[64] The absence of letters excited Jefferson's emotions to such a degree he could lower his façade to confess "fear and trembling" from three months' silence on the condition of his "dear little ones."[65]

Jefferson was familiar with and accepted the special role letters played in establishing and maintaining relationships.[66] His surrogate parent, Professor Small, was "skilled at communication," had taught rhetoric and *belles lettres*, and most likely introduced his young student to the thought of a fellow Scotsman. "Epistolary Writing...is of the easy and familiar kind," Hugh Blair wrote in *Lectures on Rhetoric and Belles*

Lettres, "when it is conversation carried on upon paper, between two friends at a distance." While letters do not reveal the "whole heart of the Author…we may expect to see more of a character displayed in these than in other productions."[67]

Letters served, of course, practical purposes of arranging affairs, assigning tasks, and reporting events: "Inform me what books you read, what tunes you learn."[68] More importantly, however, their presence, absence, content, and regularity carried symbolic value. They were a material icon in a scheduled ritual to order personal relationships and reaffirm emotional attachment: "Your long silence had induced me almost to suspect you had forgotten me and the more so as I had desired you to write to me every week."[69] More important than travel plans, weather reports, and mundane daily affairs was his belief that letters, as Blair had claimed, were a public display of personal character: "It produces great praise to a lady to spell well," Patsy's father reminded her.

Experiences in Philadelphia, Boston, and Paris and the deluge of sensations they evoked had to be mentally collected, connected, and categorized in some way. Father's letters provided these interpretations for his daughter in such a way as to reinforce values of persistence, industry, invention, achievement, and others he deemed essential in "America."[70] Writing and reading letters were considered a means of personal development and satisfaction: "I wish [your letters] for my own gratification as well as for your improvement."[71] They were a vehicle for entreating behavior and extracting learning from a situation: "I do not wish you to be gayly clothed at this time." Cached letters were a repository of memories and a manual for directing behavior, learning etiquette, and creating proper social relations: "[K]eep my letters and read them at times that you may always have present in your mind those things which will endear you to me." Patsy's father reminded her, "I shall be very much mortified and disappointed if you become inattentive…to the directions of that letter which I meant for your principal guide." These were the details.

Creating a Family-of-Letters

Beyond particulars, the most prevalent theme in their correspondence was "Family." Father and daughter described their daily lives, reminisced about past times together, and enthusiastically discussed anticipated reunions. They created a verbal tableau in which they shared *in absentia* deeply felt emotional attachment, while at the same time coordinating their public and private lives and relieving the tensions of living apart. Letters ordering salt fish, linens, and garden plants; announcing arrivals and expected departures; and letters calling for even more letters were intended to shape family living to suit Jefferson's needs in public service.[72] Daughters, sisters, aunts, in-laws, uncles, and cousins were urged to write each other on an orderly schedule and instructed to pass letters around. The physical letters came to represent family members; their path on postal routes marked the relationships and distances between them; their content was the unhurried conversations of a family circle meandering from topic to topic and back again. Through their many periods of extended separations, the family-of-letters was a metaphor of family, a means of staying connected emotionally, a reaffirmation of affections, and a bridge between past and future.

Dealing with war debt, north-south enmity over the Jay Treaty, cession of western territory, and the practical details of Congressional proceedings, Father was "mortified and disappointed" when Patsy did not write weekly as demanded. The crush of work and Patsy's silence all contributed to an extended bout with his "periodical headache." A day after Congress approved the definitive Treaty of Peace with Britain, Father was "anxious to know what books" Patsy read and revealed that his ill-health made him "just able to attend to my duty in the statehouse, but not to go out on any other occasion."[73]

Launching a new nation in a time of peace was proving even more troublesome for Congressman Jefferson than organizing a state as Governor during a revolution. The political and financial detritus of internal conflict and colonial revolution floated on top of debates about where to seat government, how to gain status with foreign powers, who would pay for the War, what to do with the vast trans-Appalachian, and more. Amid this "agitation" in the public sphere, directing Patsy's "accomplishments" with letters from afar was made more difficult because of the tutored, in-home approach he had chosen instead of one of the many formal schools emerging in Philadelphia.

"Read by yourself"

Mrs. Trist could have recommended several educational opportunities that had arisen in the "elegant metropolis" since the Jeffersons had left the City in May 1783. The very next month in the *Pennsylvania Gazette*, Dancing Master Cenas, a former dancer in the Paris Opera, "BEGS leave to inform the Public, that being just arrived and earnestly recommended to several of the best citizens in this city, he intends without any delay to open a Dancing school for the young." He also purveyed "the renowned dictionary, called the Encyclopedia" and music.[74] This enterprising immigrant was retained by Jefferson at £3 for three months.

John Bentley, an English-born harpsichordist already appreciated for organizing the first regular musical entertainment in America, was paid the same as Cenas to teach Patsy. Her drawing tutor was Pierre Eugene du Simitière, whom Jefferson knew well for designing Virginia's Coat of Arms that included his defiant motto, *Rex est qui regem non habet* (Rebellion to Tyrants is Obedience to God).[75] A French instructor would round out the feminine ornaments in this "less retired" situation, provided they were attentive.[76]

Unlike her father, Patsy had a relative to "advise and guide" her, but his absence demanded independent action on the part of the eleven-year-old. "You must not let the sickness of your French master interrupt your reading." The French master's indifferent punctuality caused [Patsy] to lose time; but when he "can attend...receive his instructions, and read by yourself when he cannot." Her father was "sorry Mr. Cimitiere [*sic*] cannot attend [her], because it is probable [she] will never have another opportunity of learning to draw, and it is a pretty pleasing accomplishment."[77] However, their friend Francis Hopkinson discretely reported that Simitière felt "she has no Genius" for drawing.[78] Yet Father was persistent: "Have you been able to coax Cimitiere [*sic*] to continue?"[79] Two weeks later, he wondered whether Patsy has "been able to persuade Simetiere to continue."[80]

The diligence of Messrs. Cenas, Du Simitière, and maybe the French master as well, was probably hampered by their interests in the burgeoning opportunities in Philadelphia. Commerce with Europe, the islands, and South America required knowledge of Spanish, Portuguese, and French languages, and clerks who could write with a stylish hand. Patsy's tutors were examples of gifted artists seeking to create a cultural milieu the City's growing wealth demanded. A new nation's capital attracted the well-off along with the less fortunate to mine for prospects in the heap of government largess, land speculation, and outright chicanery.

Pierre Eugene du Simitière was already a notable figure in Philadelphia, having emigrated from Geneva via Barbados in 1773, and at the Revolution was co-curator with Rittenhouse of the American Philosophical Society's collection. Though his countryman Chastellux[81] critically judged Simitière's private cabinet "rather small and rather paltry," it did not deter the painter in 1784 from venturing to use his collection as "the foundation of the first American Museum."[82] No amount of coaxing and persuasion by Patsy Jefferson could probably have diverted this entrepreneur, but even more personal concerns complicated his business interests. In six months, the executors of his estate asked "all indebted to him to make immediate payment"; but neither these returns nor the auction of his papers, books, "collection of natural and artificial curiosities, paintings, &c." would likely have covered his debts.[83]

"The Principal Guide"

The "imperatives" of public duty did not allow for Patsy's continuing her education with tutors overseen by a surrogate mother in a home-like atmosphere among a "people free from the extremes both of vice and virtue."[84] While in Philadelphia, she began her "considerably different" education at a point in life when—according to her father's notions—the mind and body were "not yet firm," the memory was "susceptible and tenacious of impressions," and youth were vulnerable to imitating persons around them, whether good or bad. Patsy's still small voice was heard only faintly in her father's echoes. Her letters in French gave "great satisfaction," but those not sent on schedule garnered stern rebuke; she struggled with drawing and her dress was *en déshabillé*; she was an eleven-year-old child not always attentive to meeting parental demands, studying independently without a tutor, or forwarding news of the tunes she played. She had read in Father's letters, if not quite yet learned, that her "family" encompassed surrogates who were bound by affection not biology, that parental love was conditioned on her "acquirements" and reciprocal affection expressed similarly, and that Father expected she would follow his letters as her "principal guide." Patsy was urged to persist in getting Simitière to teach her; her schedule from 8:00 am to bedtime overseen by Mrs. Hopkinson was an industrious one; and with some inventiveness she could learn French without a tutor.

The Northern States

Patsy resumed her role as father's "constant companion" through the Northern states over the summer of 1784. As early as April, Jefferson had intimated to William Short that he was being considered as a minister to France for "negotiating foreign treaties of amity and commerce." Whether fatigue from political maneuverings or his periodical headache led him to demur, he was "in truth indifferent. If they desire it I shall go, for place is to me at present uninteresting."[85]

Written valedictories from Annapolis to friends and relatives preceded his departure on May 11th for a few bustling weeks in Philadelphia—settling accounts with Mrs. Hopkinson and others, preparing their luggage and securing locks, buying a panther skin for French naturalist Buffon, watching a balloon ascent, and getting Hugh Blair's *Lectures on Rhetoric* for James Madison.[86]

Accompanied by enslaved servants James and Robert Hemings, they travelled two days across the "Shamony" to Trenton, "Princetown," and Brunswick; across the Passaic River to "Hackinsack;" and over the Hudson for eight shillings on May 30 to lodge for the next six days with Mrs. Elsworth at 19 Maiden Lane. Jefferson bought chessmen, a bathing cap, and a Spanish dictionary for learning on the voyage, and saw to shoeing horses and mending harness.

The party was off again on June 6th for a two-week trip through Connecticut and a meeting with Yale President Ezra Stiles. The phaeton's axletree was mended in Rhode Island; then on to Boston by June 18th. A delay in gaining passage directly to France afforded Jefferson the opportunity for continuing his study of the northern states' commerce for a European correspondent. Patsy stayed behind at the home of Judge John Lowell in Boston, while her father made a flying trip (June 22–25) to Salem, Ipswich, and Newbury in Massachusetts with a stop in Portsmouth, New Hampshire.[87]

In just over two weeks, Patsy had seen four states whose people Father considered "sober," "laborious," "persevering," "cool," and "independent." She experienced at boardinghouses and taverns what Mesdames Elsworth in New York, Haviland in Rye, and Wells in Stamford, Connecticut did when their husbands were "lost."[88]

Boston, like Philadelphia, would have seemed starkly different from a rural mountaintop, but it too had its distinctiveness. A place "studded with pleasant islands," dotted by gray clapboard houses "rising amphitheatre-like, and forming along the hillsides a semicircle" was less orderly and planned than Philadelphia's "close built" red brick houses arrayed along parallel streets forming "exact squares."[89] Rochambeau's chaplain, l'Abbé Robin, just three years before (1781) Patsy's visit thought the "high regular buildings, intermingled with steeples, appeared...more like a long-established town of the continent [of Europe] than that of a recent colony." The "nineteen churches of all denominations" and "each member of the household engaged in reading the Bible" presented the Frenchman with a front of religiosity never witnessed in the scattered rural glebes of Virginia. The shallow

Rivanna wending the foot of Monticello Mountain—subject to the vagaries of freshets and droughts—was a slender thread to a broader Atlantic world. Philadelphia's harbor, "extending the length of the town…[with] spacious quays, and commodious wharfs," reminded the visitor of the City's connection "with almost all nations of the world." Similarly, the flourishing maritime commerce of Boston offered the promise of making it preeminent, "if one day this new continent spreads it formidable forces upon the sea." Shortly before Patsy was experiencing these "considerably different" environs, Comte Louis Philippe de Ségur had arrived in Boston, served with Rochambeau, and later left the new nation with a question that would shape her life as a republican daughter: "[T]his difference of manners and situation between the North and South; does it not lead us to apprehend in times to come a separation which would enfeeble and perhaps break this happy confederation…?"[90]

The dissensions Jefferson saw affecting foreign relations and the internal divisions over debt, Western territories, and residency he was trying to navigate would continue and widen while the family spent five years in Paris. Even more than her experiences in the northern states, the "music, &c., &c." Patsy learned in Enlightenment France would move her even further from the "manners and situation" Ségur noted in plantation Virginia, from family, and from being prepared to "head" a little one.

Chapter 3

"Judge of my situation:"

Matriarch, Mesdames, and Mistress

"A lovely passage…"

July 5. Sailed from Boston at 4. o'clock A.M. in the Ceres Capt. St. Barbe.[1]

"We had a lovely passage in a beautiful new ship," Patsy recounted to Eliza Trist a year after arriving in France. "I should have no objection at making an other voyage if I could be sure it would be as agreable as the first."[2] She may not yet have met father's letter-writing standards of spelling "agreeable," but she was soon to experience, according to daughter Ellen's account many years later, "a period of great happiness and great improvement."[3]

Accompanied by the *Ceres'* owner, Nathaniel Tracy, merchant Alexander Moore from England, and two unnamed passengers, the travelers saw sea birds, whales, and sharks; enjoyed balmy weather between 50 and 65 degrees; "a fine sun shine all the way, with the sea…as calm as a river."[4] Nineteen days later on July 26, they landed at West Cowes, England. Patsy's sea sickness delayed them two days before setting out by coach through Fareham, Titchfield, Gosport, a ferry to Portsmouth to await departure for Havré de Grace.

I cannot say that this voyage was as agreable as the first…It rained violently and the sea was exceedingly rough…and I was allmost as sick as the first time…The cabane was not more than three feet wide and about

four long. There was no other furniture than an old
bench which was fast to the wall. The door by which we
came in at was so little that one was obliged to enter on
all four. There were two little doors at the side of the
cabane was the way to our beds, which were composed
of two boxxes and a couplle of blankets with out eather
bed or matras, so that I was obliged to sleep in my
cloathes. There being no winder in the cabane, we were
obliged to stay in the dark for fear of the rains coming
in if we opended the door.

At home and Mrs. Hopkinson's, Patsy was safely insulated from
beggarly types and probably from the lower ranks, generally; however,
she soon came in contact with the social divisions of Europe.
Conveyance was a mark of Virginia gentility, but the "singularity" of
their carriage jostling through "the most beautiful country…a perfect
garden" in the Seine valley drew the unwanted attention of beggars,
sometimes as many as nine. The steeples of Boston and meeting houses
in Philadelphia paled in comparison to a twelfth-century church of
Notre-Dame at Mantes,

> …which had as many steps to go to the top as there are
> days in the year. There are many pretty statues in it. The
> architectures is beautiful. All the winders are died glass
> of the most beautiful colours that form all kinds of
> figures.

The beautiful country-side, "architectures," and "winders" were
surpassed on August 6, 1784, with the splendor and munificence of a
medieval city made modern in the last twenty years by private investors,
entrepreneurs, and nobles turned speculators. The tiny gardens
surrounding Philadelphia's homes would have been barely noticeable
spots on the Champs-Élysées; Boston's Faneuil Hall could not compare
with the Halle aux Blés grain market whose dome would inspire a new
nation's capitol; the gaol for Philadelphia's miscreants was a modest
affair compared to the presumably impenetrable Bastille.[5]

"When the mind is not yet firm"

The spectacles and sounds of a European countryside and city
with 500,000 to 700,000 denizens would have an impact on a twelve-
year-old considered in middle youth (ages 8–15), when the memory was
"most susceptible and tenacious of impressions," and the "mind [was]

not yet firm" enough for "close operations" (i.e., abstract reasoning). Dependency, vulnerability, and conflicting influences outside the family were some of the challenges for this age group in her father's opinion. Patsy would be well-situated to learn French without the trouble of an indifferent tutor; and she was an ideal age for learning "languages antient and modern" as well as reading books for "useful facts and good principles." It was a time for developing the essential habits of mental and physical "industry," otherwise, the "mind becomes lethargic and impotent, as would the body it inhabits if unexercised."[6] Patsy had been introduced to these principles through her father's letters while she was at Mrs. Hopkinson's. The situations she encountered in Paris over the next five years were used to reinforce the "virtues" of industry, inventiveness, and persistence.

While in temporary lodging at the Hôtel d'Orléans, Patsy and her father's first days were spent accommodating themselves to the fashions of Paris. On Friday, August 6th, Jefferson recorded in France's livre currency: "clothes for Patsy 167f," "cambrick and edging = 56f" and "lace ruffles 120f." On Saturday: "a hat 24f." On Tuesday, August 10, they moved to another Hôtel d'Orléans and bought "clothes for Patsy 27f8 , and through the balance of the summer a sword and belt, cane, knee buckles, shoe buckles, more lace ruffles and "6 shirts & making" for 18f8.[7] Perhaps suspecting "dear friend" Mrs. Trist had a part in her father's charge of being a "sloven and slut" when in Philadelphia, Patsy recounted these first few days and reaffirmed her casual attitude toward fashion:

> I wish you could have been with us when we arrived. I am sure you would have laughfed, for we were obliged to send imediately for the stay maker, the mantumaker, the milliner and even a shoe maker, before I could go out. I have never had the friseur but once, but I soon got rid of him and turned down my hair in spite of all they could say, and I differ it now as much as possible, for I think it allways too soon to suffer.[8]

"Judge My Situation"

"I was placed in a convent at my arrival," Patsy wrote Mrs. Trist, "and I leave you to judge my situation."

> The classe is four rooms excedingly large for the pensionars to sleep in, and there is a fith and sixth one for them to stay in in the day and the other in which

they take their lessens. We were the uniform which is crimson made like a frock laced behind with the tail like a robe de cour [dress for Court] hoocked on muslin cufs and tuckers. The masters are all very good except that for the drawing.[9]

America's *philosophe* and political draftsman was wise in the way of books and even the character of his countrymen, but he was an innocent among European aristocracy, a haughty abbess, and influential women. Whether from naïveté, self-deception, or simply to maintain appearances, Jefferson reassured his boyhood friend, James Maury, that,

> ...my daughter is indeed in a convent, but in one where there as many protestants as Catholics, where not a word is ever said to them on the subject of religion, and where they are as free in the profession and practice of their own religion as they would be in their own country. It is a house of education only...[10]

Despite her father's assurances to relatives and friends in America, Patsy was neither isolated from nor unaware of the religiosity of the sisterhood in which she lived. Just three months after these reassurances, while her father was away in the south of France, she received a book of instruction on Catholicism written expressly for Protestants.[11] After visiting Patsy at Panthemont on March 25th, William Short reported to her father: "She seems resigned to *faire ses paques*, and 'suivre les offices' de la semaine sainte *au convent*."[12] That is, she would participate in religious services throughout Holy Week from Palm Sunday on 1 April to Easter on the 8th. Dugnani, the papal nuncio in Paris, wrote on July 5th to Bishop John Carroll in Baltimore: "The eldest [Patsy] seems to have great tendencies toward the Catholic religion....Her father, without absolutely opposing her vocation, has tried to distract her."[13] Patsy's daughter, Ellen Randolph, remembered years later that her mother was "too young to remain an inmate of her father's family in a foreign country"; yet, "there was a spirit of proselytism which prevailed among the nuns."[14] Given father's critical opinions of French women, his aversion to papist theology, and his unfavorable opinion of aristocracy, Panthemont must have been a Faustian bargain.

The Abbaye Royale de Panthemont, which Patsy entered in late August 1784, had been for many years under the direction of a politically connected and willful Madame Béthisy de Mézières. Her aristocratic origins had enabled the abbess to launch an ambitious building program in mid-century that was continuing in the 1780s and supported by the future Louis XVI and other notable subscribers.[15]

Patsy's classmates were some fifty to sixty French, English, and American girls and young women, aged 6 to 30, from elite society;[16] her instructresses, *Soeurs* of the Order of St. Bernard; a tutor, Claude Balbastre from Cathedral Notre-Dame for music; and aristocratic widows and spinsters who regularly kept the young élèves apprised of Parisian society and political intrigue. Their daily schedule was probably similar to that practiced in other eighteenth-century convent schools.

7:00 AM Rising
8:00 AM Catechism Class
Breakfast
9:30 Mass
10:00 11:00 Reading
11:00 Music, Drawing, Geography, History
1:00 PM Dinner
Recreation
3:00 Arithmetic, Dancing, Harpsichord
7:00 Supper
7:30 Dormitory[17]

Decades later, Ellen Randolph related that her mother's recollections of Panthemont "were in the highest degree pleasant and favorable." The young American approved of the convent's attention to "morals and manners...habits of neatness, modesty and scrupulous regard to [purity?] and propriety." They were taught "arithmetic, geography, history, and modern languages...with the utmost care...[but] housewifery...and needle-work formed no part of the educational system of Panthemont."[18]

Protestant *pensionnaires* may or may not have attended catechism class and Mass, but it would have been impossible to isolate them from the "spirit of proselytizing" that permeated the situation. Father was an inadvertent contributor to familiarizing Patsy with one of the more profound, solemn rituals of the Catholic Church, when early in their stay they attended a taking the veil ritual as a social event with the Adams family. Patsy's account of the experience to Eliza Trist was brief: "I have seen two nuns take the veil. I'll tell you about that when I come to see you.[19] Seven years her senior, Miss Abigail ("Nabby")

Adams provided more elaborate details of unfamiliar rituals performed in a language unintelligible to the young girls. The abbess, sisters, novices, and "two English ladies" carried candles into the chapel. A French and an Irish girl wore "fine, white woollen dresses...loose and flowing" and white veils on their faces with "their hair all shaved off." Much "singing and chanting of prayers," "kneeling and rising," and the priest "made many signs that I did not understand," Nabby wrote. A sermon in French contrasted "a very good world" outside the convent to the "disagreeableness" of a life "confined" where every action "would be wrongly construed." Watching the "poor girls...lying on their faces" before the altar for half an hour, Nabby confided to her journal, was "an affecting sight; I could not refrain from tears." More prayers, a blessing of the veils with Holy Water and "frank incense," and another Mass in Latin concluded the spectacle for the American party.

There may not have been a "word on the subject of religion," as Father claimed, but it was hardly necessary in a place infused with religiosity and whose very existence was dependent on the Clerical Estate of monarchal France. The virtues of obedience and deference to which Patsy was being encouraged by Father could be experienced in a matriarchal French convent as easily as a patriarchal Virginia plantation. However, the widows, spinsters, and other ladies who sat at the Abbess's table were also a convenient source of gossip on marital infidelities, political intrigue, and dissension in the Royal family. The convent household, the community of sisters, and their connections with the public sphere were living testimony to a family "considerably different" than Patsy would have experienced in Virginia or even with her Philadelphia surrogates—Eliza Trist, Mrs. Hopkinson, and the Rittenhouse family.

"Much in debt...obliged to sell"

In the late summer and early fall of 1784, Patsy was adjusting to convent life. "I did not speak a word of french," she wrote Mrs. Trist, "and no one here knew english but a little girl of 2 years old that could hardly speak french." Father was seeking permanent quarters that reflected his diplomatic status but could also serve as a domicile for the legation's secretary, David Humphries, private secretary William Smith, and "servant" James Hemings. On October 16th, he signed a nine-year lease at an annual rent of 4,000 livres for the Hôtel Landrôn—located on the cul-de-sac Taitbout in a fashionable new residential district. Jefferson busily set about decorating, furnishing, and altering his "outfit": damask for curtains; books and bookshelves; teacups, silver forks, and sugar tongs; sofas and chairs; a pianoforte and music stand; a copy of Simon Vouet's "Herodiade with the head of John the Baptist," and other copies of artworks.[20] Civic virtue, personal debt, and grief once again were on converging paths for the Jefferson family in Paris and Virginia.

After his wife's death in 1782, Jefferson had told friend Monroe his retirement from public life was due to a "family in need of attention and instruction" as well as financial affairs in "disorder and ruin."[21] Ever since then, he had been fully engaged in public service. Again "his own affairs [were]...distressed," because Congress had "made no other provision for an "Outfit"—housing, furniture, carriage, horses, and clothes—beyond his annual salary of £2,100 sterling, roughly $9,000 or 48,600 *livres*.[22] Unless adjustments were made, Jefferson confided, "I shall return that much in debt, and be obliged to sell to pay it: a circumstance which I shall think hard....I think my expences should be paid in a stile equal to that of those with whom I am classed." A "hired carriage and two horses" were simply not in keeping with his position as Minister. Already in debt for 1,000 guineas (£1050 or about $4,500), he trusted to the "secrecy and delicacy" of friend James Monroe to discretely present his case to Congress.

This new debt for an outfit added to the pile he had already accumulated in Virginia. "The crops of 83. 84. 85.," he entered in the Summary Journal of Letters, "will I hope place me in peace @ home. A failure in this is [the] only thing which would dispose to stay longer here." Notes on a letter to Nicholas Lewis, who was managing his affairs, conveyed a similar optimism: "Crops of 83. 84. 85 I hope make my affairs easy."[23]

"Oh! could I do it myself!"

By late January 1785, Jefferson received news from home that would not only dash these hopes of clearing debt but also heighten tension between private and public responsibilities. A letter from Francis Eppes received on the 26th (but written in September the prior year), bore a foreboding message: "Your little Lucy, our youngest and Bolling are I think very ill" with "hooping cough." "Polly has it badly but she sleeps well and eats hartily." He continued that Nicholas Lewis, who was managing Jefferson's plantations, "gives a very bad account of crops at Monticello as well as Bedford" and Elk Hill may just cover taxes. Creditors were "very pressing"; one had already brought legal suit.

[W]e have every reason to expect that the other creditors will follow his example. Under these circumstances I fear it will be impossible to keep the Estate together. Mr. Lewis as well as myself…[await] instructions…what particular part of your property you wou'd wish us to dispose of. Have [you] heard from Jones of Bristol?[24]

The anxiety of separation could not have been more acute, as the messenger carrying this news—the Marquis de Lafayette—also brought a letter on 26 January 1785 from Doctor James Currie.

The good doctor bemoaned the "routine of drudgery" of his situation, thanked Jefferson for providing him a "Synoptical View" on the history of balloons, and congratulated him on his "quick passage" to Europe. As if he had been delaying the inevitable, unpleasant news, Currie then expressed sorrow to his "dear friend" for "the demise of poor Miss L. Jefferson, who fell a Martyr to the Complicated evils of teething, Worms and Hooping Cough which last was carried there by the Virus of their friends." The two-year-old, he wrote, was a "poor Innocent…a Child of the most Auspicious hopes and having among other early shining qualities an ear nicely and critically musical." Sensitive to his friend's sentiments and, perhaps, feeling the powerlessness of doing nothing, the good Doctor abruptly ended his report: "Enough of this too tender Theme."[25]

A day after the fateful news, Jefferson dined with John Adams's family, whose daughter Abigail (Nabby) witnessed "a man of great sensibility, and parental affection.…and this news has greatly affected him and his daughter."[26] Father's anguish was palpable in what for him was an unusual paucity of words but ones filled with emotion. "It is in vain to endeavor to describe the situation of my mind," he confessed to Eppes, who had also lost a child. "It would pour balm neither into your wounds nor mine; I will therefore pass on from the subject." And so he did, directing his brother-in-law how to disburse money voted by Virginia's Assembly to cover his expenses as governor from 1779–81.

The family living at Panthemont, Hôtel Landrôn, and Eppington—held tenuously together by letters, separated by the Seine and the Atlantic—was suddenly rent by death and harassed by persistent debt. When wife Martha had died, her husband withdrew to his private room or took solitary rides on his beloved Monticello Mountain. But in Paris his home was a public space, and he had only strangers to solace his grief and letters to send an embrace: "Kiss my dear, dear Polly for me." Jefferson urged his Virginia relative. "Oh! could I do it myself!"[27]

Ten days after learning of Lucy's death, a grieving Father optimistically hoped that "all very urging claims may be satisfied" with the '83 and '84 tobacco crops along with £500 voted by the Virginia Assembly.[28] He was cautioned in no uncertain terms by his brother-in-law not to "count too largely upon the crops of 1783 and 1784. They were not considerable." Moreover, Eppes wrote, "you must keep in mind our inormus [sic] taxes[,] the clothing of your people and the Education of Mrs. Carrs Sons...lessens your crop more than your aware of."[29] Despite his agents' efforts to secure Jefferson "peace @ home," to make his affairs "easy," and to satisfy "all very urging claims," his Virginia debt resisted diminution and current obligations were only increased by living in a "stile" appropriate for his public position.

Female Intrigue, Voluptuous Dress & Marital Infidelity

Patsy was almost twelve when the couple arrived in Paris in August 1784. She would learn that personal happiness required individual initiative to accomplish "good conscience, good health, [and] occupation." The imagined family and plantation household stood in sharp relief against a matriarchal convent whose daily life was regulated by the "brides" of an ancient moralist.[30] Rather than "gaining the affections" of a surrogate mother—Hopkinson or Eliza Trist—Patsy would be reminded that *she* was now a surrogate mother to her sister Polly and that father's happiness in his old age depended on her. She was entreated and cajoled to the virtues of industry, persistence, and inventiveness so essential to the "American character."

It is difficult to imagine a situation more antithetical to Jefferson's political and social views than a convent school for the children of Europe's aristocrats. Outside the home, it would prove insufficient insulation from the "degenerate" influence of Parisian *salons*, monarchal government, and fashionable culture. The deist's daughter not only was taught by and in daily contact with Catholic nuns but, also, was escorted to the opera and theater by *mesdames* who imbibed and influenced political affairs. She witnessed the tumultuous events leading to the Revolution and shared her lodgings with "aristocratic spinsters, widows, ladies separated from their husbands" such as Napoleon's future bride, Josephine de Beauharnais.[31]

For Patsy's father, cultural location was a vital contributor to personal development.

> Cast your eye over America: who are the men of most learning, of most eloquence, most beloved by their country and most trusted and promoted by them? They are those who have been educated among them, and whose manners, morals and habits are perfectly homogeneous with those of the country.[32]

Soon after his arrival in Paris, Jefferson's letters convey his strong criticisms of foreign education for American males. They may be more a reflection of his personal shock and dismay at experiencing a culture so different from Philadelphia, New York, or Boston than any reasonably objective comparison of cultural differences. In late 1784, he wrote to Charles Thomson: "I have always disapproved of a European education for our youth from theory: I now do it from inspection."[33] After a year in Paris, Jefferson elaborated to John Banister, Jr., his opposition. He had "entertained only doubts on this head before [coming] to Europe: What I see and hear since…proves more than I had even suspected….The consequences of foreign education are alarming to me as an American," Jefferson warned. "I sin therefore through zeal whenever I enter on the subject." A person under thirty studying in Europe would acquire a "fondness for European luxury…a contempt for the simplicity of his own country…[contract] a partiality for aristocracy or monarchy…[and] lose in science, in virtue, in health and in happiness."[34] Foreign cultures could infect body, mind, and spirit; suborn happiness, the ultimate purpose of life; and threaten republican government.[35] It is more likely that it was *his* education in Paris Jefferson found so alarming, amid what he described to his American correspondent as whores, female intrigue, voluptuary dress, and marital infidelity.[36] (This assessment may have received personal confirmation a year later when he met Maria Cosway.[37])

Amazons and Angels

If France was so treacherous for young males, what might it do to his twelve-year-old daughter? At this developmental stage, her father considered the mind not yet "firm" and "imitation" the germ of education. So would Patsy abandon the dress of a "sloven and slut," as her father had demanded in Philadelphia, to embrace "voluptuary dress" and attend the *coiffeur*? Would the "female intrigue" of a convent and the society around it influence the young Virginian's perception of the gendered role her father was constructing? Jefferson claimed distaste for women's position in Paris high society, compared them unfavorably with American counterparts, and deployed his binary rhetorical style customarily reserved for expressing deeply held convictions.[38] "You are…to tell me truly and honestly," he commanded Anne Willing Bingham, "whether you do not find the tranquil pleasures of America preferable to the empty bustle of Paris." At midday, a French madame is "propped on bolsters and pillows, and her head scratched into a little order"; in the afternoon, she will quickly "hobble around the cage of the Palais royal," have her hair arranged by the *Coeffeur*, and "flutter" through the streets paying visits. Evening is devoted to supper and cards; each day is "like a mill-horse, the same trodden circle over again." "Thus the days of life are consumed…without an object beyond the present moment…eternally in pursuit of happiness."

The foil to this bustling Parisian madame was an American woman situated in family and tending the household. She spends her time "in the society of [her] husband, the fond cares for the children, the arrangements of the house, the improvements of the grounds fill every moment with a healthy and an useful activity." Leisure is "filled by the society of real friends, whose affections are not thinned to cob-web by being spread over a thousand objects." [39]

This active, domestic life he imagined for the "head of a little family" and plantation mistress in America was at odds with the Parisian environs in which they lived. Wives shared their *salon* space with husbands and lovers; men openly fathered children with their mistresses and even occasionally their relatives. Moreover, the *salons* were a mediating space, intentionally blurring the public/private, domestic/political, female/male role distinctions that were essential to Jefferson's self-fashioning and to the task of defining the role for which his daughter was being prepared. *Salonnières*, whom he enjoyed so much, were a force shaping political affairs with carefully orchestrated discourses in their social spaces that reappeared in literary productions molding popular opinion.[40]

Anne Bingham was not flattered by her consignment to a subordinate domestic role and did not shy from sharply countering Jefferson's critical comparisons. She struck at the core of his argument by placing her skillful repartee in a cultural context and suggestively alluding to his recent liaison with their mutual friend, Maria Cosway:[41] Of course, women differ from society to society, Anne acknowledged. However more than in any other country, French women were better educated, socially more adept, and develop "a happy variety of genius, which forms their conversation to please either the fop or the philosopher." They do "interfere with politics" and, thereby, affect "the fate of empires." Not only was Jefferson using an incorrect standard but also the female qualities he admired in American women were not those necessary for the congenial, social intercourse he enjoyed with the *salonnières*.

Anne Bingham was not only an adept in the *salon*, but Jefferson knew well at least one "American" woman who could adapt to the politics of a "French" political culture. His coded letter to Madison shortly before receiving her repartee critically appraised Mr. Thomas Bingham as falsely claiming "intimate footing" with all European powers and having no "modesty" in the methods used. "If he obtained access afterwards, it was with such as who were susceptible of impression from the beauty of his wife."[42]

Anne Bingham's closing to her spirited response cut to the core of Jefferson's self-image and put her friend on notice of her capacity for self-defense.

> "We are therefore bound in gratitude to admire and revere [French women] for asserting our privileges, as much as the friends of the liberties of mankind reverence the successful struggles of the American patriots.[43]

Such a riposte might have silenced a patriot but not the felicitous, whimsical, and ever persistent Jefferson. Writing his feisty country-woman after her return to America, his opposing visions were both a social metaphor and a spiritual abstraction.

> You too have had your political fever [in America]. But our good ladies, I trust, have been too wise to wrinkle their foreheads with politics. They are contented to soothe and calm the minds of their husbands returning ruffled from political debate. They have the good sense to value domestic happiness above all other, and the art to cultivate it beyond all others....Recollect the women of this capital, some on foot, some on horses, and some in carriages hunting pleasure in the streets, in routs and assemblies, and forgetting they have left it behind them in their nurseries; compare them with our own countrywomen occupied in the tender and tranquil amusement of domestic life, and confess that it is a comparison of Amazons and Angels.[44]

Jefferson may have disparaged the political role of Parisian women, but he admitted to George Washington that they were the key to whether proposed governmental reforms would occur in France. "The manners of the nation allow them to visit, alone, all persons in office, to sollicit [*sic*] the affairs of the husband, family, or friends, and their sollicitations [*sic*] bid defiance to laws and regulations." The "omnipotence" of French women's influence had reduced political affairs to a "desperate state." He naively claimed to a President who knew better that even men of America were "in the habit of considering Right as a barrier against all solicitation," by anyone and that women did not venture beyond the "domestic line."[45]

Anne Bingham had proven her mettle in parrying Jefferson's unflattering caricature of French women. Perhaps more ominous were the examples presented to Patsy by her own countrywomen still in Paris. Mrs. Dorcas (Armitage) Montgomery was especially solicitous of Patsy and, therefore, a more immediate threat to Jefferson's image of American women. As a young widow, she had moved to Geneva in 1781 for her son Robert's education; had been a regular correspondent with Franklin; dined at Jefferson's Hôtel de Langeac; and invited father and daughter to tea.[46] Social occasions under careful chaperonage were acceptable but unescorted teas and a tour through Europe were not. A month after Maria Cosway left Paris, Jefferson declined Mrs. Montgomery's "friendly offer" of "shewing [Patsy] those countries...I have ever thought most worthy of being seen." He began the rejection with a skillful obliqueness: "I have unfortunately but a choice among difficulties and disagreeable things for her. Of the plans practicable in my situation I have been obliged to adopt that which presented the fewest objectionable circumstances." Were the "difficulties" travels in Europe with an American woman unaccompanied by a man? The other horn of the dilemma was Patsy's remaining at Panthemont. Was that "disagreeable" for her? His stated reasons for begging off were Patsy's insufficient "progress" in "French, drawing &c." and their not "very distant" return to America"—a leave not even requested for over a year.[47] But there may have been other, unspoken concerns of releasing his daughter into European society without his close supervision.

Patsy was invited to tea with Mesdames Montgomery and Barrett in November 1786, but the following spring, his private secretary, William Short, would not approve Mrs. Barrett's request to "have Miss Jefferson see her." "I never see Mr. or Mrs. Barrett," Short wrote, "without their bringing the affair on the *tapis*....I conjecture your failure to speak to the Abbess was intentional."[48] Father's opinion of

52

Mesdames Barrett and Montgomery are unknown, but he seemed reluctant to let Patsy venture far from the Abbess and her Sisters without his presence. Perhaps, he was becoming concerned with his daughter's emerging challenges to the imagined family and household he was constructing so assiduously. Sustaining this masque would become increasingly difficult after he withdrew Patsy from Panthemont in 1789, when "gay and thoughtless Paris [had] become a furnace of Politics."

du Beau Monde—Paris Society

Near the end of Patsy's stay in Paris, cousin Judith Randolph pleaded with her to "let me hear from you as soon as possible & tell me all the news in the Beau Monde."[49] The future sister-in-law from rural Virginia may not have been so generously "devoid of envy" had she known of the life her cousin was enjoying in Paris. Notwithstanding the alleged licentiousness of Paris and forwardness of its women, Jefferson enjoyed their company and introduced Patsy to a "considerably different" kind of womanhood than he claimed for America. He confided to Abigail Adams that he had "commenced an acquaintance with the old Countess d'Hocquetout [Houdetot]." He continued: "I received much pleasure from it and hope it has opened a door of admission for me to the circle of literati with which she is environed."[50] On a return trip in October 1785, Jefferson was sufficiently beguiled by her *salon's* amusements to overcome his aversion to gambling and lose "at lotto at Sannois 18s."[51] But even pleasure and the prospect of future companionship could not restrain the Minister from comparing the nightingale ("a bird of the third rank") at Sannois with the "unquestionably superior" mockingbird of America. After a visit to Monticello, Daniel Webster recounted that the former Minister had found "Madame Houdetot's society was one of the most agreeable." However, the *salonnière* Madame Suzanne Necker "was a very sincere and excellent woman, but she was not very pleasant in conversation," being "nervous and fidgety."[52] An earlier characterization of Madame Necker by Jefferson was decidedly more flattering and assigned her a large credit for the success of her husband, Jacques, who had "an ardent passion for glory without...those qualities required for its pursuit." Along with wealth and sociability, the Minister continued in writing to John Jay, "a virtuous, reasonable and well informed wife, procured for him [Necker] the acquaintance of many persons of distinction."[53] It was at d'Houdetot's that Jefferson became acquainted with the "fidgety" woman's daughter, Germaine de Staël, whom Patsy frequently encountered at the many balls she attended during their last months in Paris.[54]

After two years in Paris, Patsy was the guest of Mesdames La Borde de Mereville and Lafayette, enjoyed dinners with Mrs. [Nathaniel] Barrett and Mrs. [Robert] Montgomery, and was invited to accompany the latter on a grand European tour that father declined.[55] An even more dramatic spectacle of female agency was presented to Patsy in the summer of 1788, when she attended the opera *Médée a Colchis* with father and Madame de Corny. This example of a jealous, vindictive, and deceitful woman with magical powers was a stark contrast with the vision of Patsy as "head of a little family" responsible for her children's education rather than their death.[56] But the opera may have accurately recalled the views of a youthful Jefferson, who copied from Euripides' *Medea*: "'Yea, men should have begotten children from some other source, no female race existing; thus would no evil ever have fallen on mankind.'"[57] Once free of the convent in the spring of 1789, Patsy not only encountered the intellectual Germaine de Staël but also attended a dinner for the notorious Georgiana Cavendish, Duchess of Devonshire, who was pleased that the young Virginian's height was "equal to her own."[58] Jefferson considered the Duchess's garden at Chiswick as showing "too much of art [and its] obelisk of very ill effect." Most certainly, he would have objected to the "extravagant, reckless gambler" whose gaming debts have been estimated at £100,000.[59]

Patsy's father was sensitive to appropriate, if not fashionable, dress. He shared with Anne Willing Bingham his copies of *Cabinet des modes* that stimulated the "Ladies [of Philadelphia] with many Hints for the decoration of their Persons."[60] He regularly forwarded the magazine to Patsy after their return to America. This fashion publication must have held some interest for him displaying tight-corseted ladies with heads adorned by elaborate plumes, ribbons, and curls; their bodies clad in dresses with flounces and trains accented by brightly colored sashes. The *Cabinet's* men in tight-fitting pants topped by red waistcoats shrouded with striped coats were more flamboyant than the simple "republican" dress Jefferson would adopt as President.[61]

While in Philadelphia, Patsy's friend Eliza Trist had surreptitiously suggested that her father "give her a charge about her dress." He promptly complied by forcefully gendering and setting standards for clothes: "Nothing is so disgusting to our sex," he proclaimed, "as a want of cleanliness and delicacy in yours." Her dress should be "fine of its kind," "clean, whole, and properly put on." Upon

54

their arrival in Paris, they immediately attended "the stay maker, the mantumaker, the milliner and even a shoe maker."[62] Patsy was directed by her father to attend *soirées* outside the convent in other than her school "uniform" and to "hurry making the gown and also your reding-cote" for the dinner with "Marquis L'Fayette."[63] Nevertheless when she left the convent around 20 April 1789, Patsy was soon outfitted for the "gay whirl" of Paris that was ablaze in the "furnace of Politics." Some of the purchases were:

April [1789]
19   Pd. for linen for Patsy 274–16 [*livre*]
20   Pd. for lawn & cambrick for [Patsy] 332
      . . .
May
7   Pd. for a whip for Patsy 12
10   Pd. sewing acct. for Patsy 24
      . . .
17   Pd. shoes for Patsy 106
      Pd. for stays for do. 84
      . . .
June
15   Pd. for pocket book for Patsy 30
30   Pd for 2 lawn cloaks for Patsy 84
      . . .
July Pd. Mlle. Omont for Patsy's acct.
      in part[seamstress] 600
      . . .
Sep.
15   Pd. Mlle. Omont in full 296–17–6
26   Left Paris[64]

The total allowance for Patsy's outfit (1800 *livre* or very roughly, $333 US) was more generous than for other residents of her new home at Langeac. It could have paid for almost thirteen years of Sally Hemings's salary—she received 12 *livre* (about $2 ¼) monthly for her services—and just over six years of chef James Hemings's service. *Maître d'hôtel* Adrien Petit could be retained for two years at his rate of 72 *livre* monthly.

Patsy's father left no record urging her to consider a Madame or even a countrywoman like a "mother," "dear friend," or otherwise, as he had done with Mrs. Hopkinson and Eliza Trist in Philadelphia. She probably was not witness to lofty salon discussions or "lotto" games of these women active in the public sphere of the *ancien régime*. However, if imitation "is the germ of all education," as Jefferson claimed in *Notes on the State of Virginia,* then he would have been especially sensitive to Patsy's contact with American or French women whose lives were so at odds with the gendered role her father imagined for her.[65] The Abbess's table and the *dames en chambre* who lodged at Panthemont were a ready source of gossip on politics, marital dalliances, and international affairs. Even closely chaperoned visits outside the cloister to the home of Parisian notables could not have prevented the sixteen-year-old from observing how "considerably different" her environs were from what her father described she would experience in America.

Living as Family

Since Lucy's death in 1784, Jefferson had pressed his in-laws and sister to arrange Dear Polly's trip to France, but she had been delayed by a variety of factors. Father's heart and head were at odds—torn between his urgent desire to see her and his fear for her safety on the Atlantic passage. "Reason tells me the dangers are not great;" nonetheless he confided to Elizabeth Eppes:

> No event of your life has put it in your power to conceive how I feel when I reflect that such a child, and so dear to me, is to cross the ocean, is to be exposed to all the sufferings and risks, great and small, to which a situation on board a ship exposes every one.—I drop my pen at the thought.—But she must come. My affections would leave me balanced between the desire to have her with me and the fear of exposing her.[66]

His conditions for her travel were stringent: a ship no older than four or five years that had had at least one voyage and would be transiting in the months April through July. Moreover, her chaperone must be "a good lady" or a "careful gentleman" with a female attendant who has had a small pox vaccination. "My anxieties on this subject would induce me to endless details."[67] The "details," aided by the slow transit of letters, would work to the benefit of the Virginia family.

Affection stoked the urgency for reunion but also contributed to its delay. Father would painfully learn that affection conditioned on "accomplishments" was overshadowed by love based on care and comfort from two surrogate parents. Polly's family in France "cannot live without" her and what she learned in Paris would make her "more

56

worthy of the love of her friends." However, the central concern for
Father was more personal: "[B]y our care and love of you, we will teach
you to love us more than you will do if you stay so far from us."[68] Deep
affection and strong attachment required physical proximity. (This
theme will be a force shaping Jefferson family life for decades, as the
daughters married, set up housekeeping, and their father was away in
public service.) His uneasiness over Polly's affections was confirmed in
January 1785 by his brother-in-law: "I can't help feeling for her when I
recollect the length of time it will take her from this to Paris and that
altogether with strangers, her attachment to her Aunt is so great I am
certain it will be very difficult matter to persuaid her to leave this
place."[69]

The Virginians in 1785 and '86 missed the summer departure
prescribed by Jefferson, because his letters arrived so late and the
"necessary ceremony of enoculating Isabel" could not be
accomplished.[70] Moreover, Eppes thought it "impossible" because "the
situation it throws her into satisfies me that the scheme is
impracticable;...she is in tears when ever it is mentioned."[71]
Throughout 1786 and into 1787, sister Carr, Mrs. Eppes, and Polly
added their voices in protest. From Martha Jefferson Carr: "Polly's
aversion to going to France Increases dayly, and...she fears she must at
last be draged like a calf to the Slaughter...Your anxiety to have her
with you is quite natural, but how much do I dread her separation from
that family." With Mrs. Eppes, Polly "has Experienced the tenderness
and fondness of a parent." Aunt Eppes played to the other side of the
house by noting that Aunt Carr, Jefferson's sister, "has ingratiat'd her
self so much in dear Polly's good graces, that she concent'd to
accompany her home without me." And from Polly:

> I long to see you, and hope that you and sister Patsy are
> well; give my love to her and tell her that I long to see
> her, and hope that you and she will come very soon to
> see us...I don't want to go to France, I had rather stay
> with Aunt Eppes.

And nearly a year later: "I should be happy to see you, but I can not go
to France."[72]

Learning Virtues & Contesting Families

Through the Spring and Summer of 1787 just before Polly's
arrival and as Patsy was approaching her fifteenth year, the convent
student engaged her father in an epistolary dialogue in which contesting

notions of family, domesticity, and the public sphere were introduced but summarily avoided by her father with disquisitions on America and its women. Writing from the south of France, Jefferson used their extended separation as an opportunity to elaborate just how her situation at Panthemont was contributing to developing those virtues distinctive of the "American character" which would serve her as a plantation mistress. Moreover, the imagined family was subtly reframed and located for the first time within a multi-generational plantation household.

Patsy had learned well in Philadelphia most of her letter writing lessons and dutifully reported on learning a "beautiful tune with balbastre," drawing "a very pretty lanskip" with her tutor, Pariseau, and admitted going "very slowly" reading "*tite live*." Student qua teacher was emboldened enough to mention "being disappointed in my expectation of receiving a letter from my dear papa," but had "resolved to break so painful a silence by giving you an example that I hope you will follow."

A Bernardine convent or residence at Jefferson's Hôtel de Langeac was insufficient security against the dangers of voluptuous fashion, political intrigues, and marital infidelities in Paris. Reflecting the quality of independence and self-direction father urged, Patsy felt unconstrained in keeping him apprised of political events and their intrusion into the convent-family he had devised. "The kings speach and that of the eveque de Narbone has been copied all over the convent."[73] Such unwanted political intelligence would surely only increase if Patsy's status in her surrogate family was elevated by dining at the "abesse's table," as the matriarch had offered.

"Exercise" & "Industry"

Father's response to these challenges was to isolate his imaginary family in a tranquil setting insulated from political intrigues, to note the dangers of ennui, to stress the necessity of "industry and activity," and to assert the interdependence of mental, physical, and moral development. Patsy was concerned with "losing time" when her French instructor in Philadelphia was absent, but she was reminded in Paris of its dire, lifelong consequences:

> It is your future happiness which interests me, and nothing can contribute more to it (moral rectitude always excepted) than the contracting a habit of industry and activity. Of all the cankers of human happiness, none corrodes it with so silent, yet so baneful a tooth, as

indolence. Body and mind both unemployed, our being becomes a burthen, and every object about us loathsome, even the dearest. Idleness begets ennui, ennui the hypochrondria, and that a diseased body. No laborious person was ever yet hysterical. Exercise and application produce order in our affairs, health of body, chearfulness of mind, and these make us precious to our friends.[74]

Demarking potentialities and vulnerabilities by life stages, as Jefferson did, heightened the salience of time—a recurrent (if not incessant) theme in his parenting of younger family members. He prescribed strict schedules for both Patsy and nephew Peter Carr that began in the morning and extended to bedtime.[75] Time was to be filled up, used, and managed. "Lose no moment in improving your head, nor any opportunity of exercising your heart in benevolence."[76] Quotidian time must not only be used fully but also the times in life's course must be filled appropriately. Jefferson was "mortified" at Peter Carr's loss of time in his studies; at age fourteen his "time now begins to be precious." "It is while we are young," he instructed Patsy, "that the habit of industry is formed. If not then, it never is afterwards. The fortune of our lives therefore depends on employing well the short period of youth."[77]

This fixation with time was connected in Jefferson's mind with a more important issue central to developing independent adults—industry and activity." As he had informed Chastellux, indolence was one of the objectionable features of the "Virginia character." Presented in various guises, industry, doing, and busyness were critical to maintaining physical and mental health as well as to living happily in America; also, it was a feature that clearly demonstrates the interconnectedness of Jefferson's notions of human development and pedagogy. If the period of youth "be suffered to pass in idleness, the mind becomes lethargic and impotent, as would the body it inhabits if unexercised during the same time."[78]

Activity at the right time, structured in time, and filling time was a foundation stone, not only of life's ultimate purpose—happiness—but also of esteem, orderliness, and healthful living. Music, drawing, dancing, needlework, and exercise were a "resource…against ennui." Patsy asserted her self-confidence and reassured her anxious father: "As for the hysterics, you may be quiet on that head, as I am not lazy enough to fear them."[79]

"Means within ourselves"

Patsy's complaints about translating ancient Italian without her "master" were interpreted by her father as "an exercise in the habit of surmounting difficulties"; like all habits, it must be instilled in the youthful years when the mind is not yet "firm." Father's perceived cultural differences were used as a foil for describing the role Patsy would play later as mistress of a plantation household. Europeans have "shops for every want," he observed, but Americans were in isolated locations and required "to invent," "to execute," "to find means within ourselves," and learn "not to lean on others." In addition to "music, drawing, books, invention and exercise," the "needle and domestic oeconomy" prevent women's ennui in the "country life of America." If Patsy did not learn sewing, "how can the mistress of a family direct the works of her servants [slaves]?" Her fading memories of plantation life were reflected in her response a few weeks later: "I could not do much of [embroidery or netting] in America," because that country lacks "proper silks; however, they will not be totally useless."[80]

An Imagined Household

This tableau of busy feminine domesticity was immediately infused with an emotional charge that revealed dimly a more complex household whose details would emerge after their return to America. Lucy's death and Polly's increasing attachment to Aunts Eppes and Carr only stoked Father's dependency on his Dearest Patsy.

> No body in this world can make me so happy, or so miserable as you. Retirement from public life will ere long become necessary for me. To your sister and yourself I look to render the evening of my life serene and contented. It's morning has been clouded by loss after loss till I have nothing left but you. I do not doubt either your affection or dispositions. But great exertions are necessary, and you have little time left to make them. Be industrious then, my dear child.[81]

Patsy's father imagined a "serene and contented" future life that would serve as a palliative for the weight of "loss after loss" in the past as well as for his present life in the political public sphere. The tension was palpable; the anxiety, acute; time, as always, was critical. The "fortune of our lives" depended on the "dear child" developing the "habit of industry" in the "short period of youth." As an eleven-year-old in Philadelphia, Patsy's "accomplishments" were a condition for receiving father's affection as well as a means of expressing hers. The emotional dynamic had become somewhat more conflated since the death of Lucy. Happiness still remained life's terminal goal, but an imagined felicity had become enmeshed in a web of emotional interdependencies and sad memories of a lost family.

In a few strokes of his pen, Patsy's father was reinforcing what he considered essential features of the "American character" that had been described to Chastellux in 1782—industry, inventiveness, persistence, and independence.[82] By describing the remoteness of American plantation life and the mistress's role, he was isolating Patsy's future both in domesticity and in space. Though only intimated here, what would become the principal theme of their future was Father's public life juxtaposed to Patsy's filial duty of securing his happiness. Over the years, this interdependency would be strengthened (not weakened) by her marriage; it structured the Jefferson-Randolph household, and ultimately resulted in her installation as his plantation mistress in 1809.

Contesting the Imagined Family

Patsy's second introduction of the political world into their personal communications again was greeted by silence and a change of subject. "They make every day some new history on the Assemblee des Notables," Patsy reported. "I will not tell you any, for fear of taking a trip to the Bastille for my pains."[83] Father's riposte was to re-inscribe the domestic sphere by reminding her that sister Polly soon would be a "precious charge on [her] hands." As surrogate mother, she would need to teach Polly to be good, true, never angry, and to encourage her toward "industry and application to useful pursuits." By "teaching her these dispositions of mind," Patsy would become "more fixed in them" herself.[84]

She displayed the persistence her father encouraged so fervently by raising in her next letter even more sensitive topics, given father's estimation of Europe's dangers for young men:

> Mrs. Barett has wanted me out, but Mr. Short told her that you had forgotten to tell Madame L'Abbesse to let me go out with her. There was a gentleman, a few days ago, that killed himself because he thought his wife did not love him. They had been married ten years. I believe that if every husband in Paris was to do as much, there

would be nothing but widows left. I shall speak to Madame Thaubeneu about dining at the Abbess's table.[85]

Patsy had dined with Mrs. Nathaniel Barrett at Langeac the previous fall, but was not permitted to venture into Parisian society, even when accompanied by an American woman.[86] Next, the fourteen-year-old rhetorically sallied forth from the secure family rampart that her father had been imagining with an opposing family construction of conflict, betrayal, and death; and concluded with a reminder of her rising status in the matriarchal "family" of a Catholic convent. Father's response was again silence on matters of politics, French families, and going out into society. She was to "exercise your geography" by tracing his journey through the south of France on a map. He hoped the harpsichord would arrive soon, because it would give him "an opportunity of judging whether [she has] got better of that want of industry which [he] had began to fear would be the rock on which [she] would split."[87]

Neither entreaty nor silence, however, could stay the rush of political events and international affairs that flooded conversations at the Abbess's table. "The pays bas [Low Countries] have revolted against the emperor who is gone to Prussia to join with the empress and the venitians to war against the turcs. The plague is in spain." The political intrigue in the Royal family was thickening and becoming more serious. The King's minister, Baron de Breteuil, prepared an "apartment" at the Bastille for Queen Marie Antoinette's friend, Mde. De Polignac, because she had embezzled funds. Thieving governesses and conniving Royal families were far removed from the American situation but directing "servants" was not. More threatening to the imaged life for a plantation mistress was the report of a captured "virginia ship" with a cargo of "algerians" who would be sold as "slaves."

> Good god have we not enough? I wish with all my soul that the poor negroes were all freed. It greives my heart when I think that these our fellow creatures should be treated so teribly as they are by many of our countrymen.[88]

Father was silent on Patsy's challenge to his "family" ideal and directed her to "learn all your old tunes over again perfectly" on the new harpsichord.[89]

In the meantime, Father had turned her attention to the nightingale in the convent garden, so when she returned to her own "country," she could "estimate it's merit" compared to Virginia's mockingbird. His anticipation of Polly's long-delayed arrival summoned a near reverie on the family reunion and provided a coda to Patsy's challenges to the imagined family.

> It will be a circumstance of inexpressible comfort to me to have you both with me once more. The object most interesting to me for the residue of my life, will be to see you both developing daily those principles of virtue and goodness which will make you valuable to others and happy in yourselves, and acquiring those talents and that degree of science which will guard you at all times against ennui, the most dangerous poison of life. A mind always employed is always happy. This is the true secret, the grand recipe of felicity....Be good and be industrious, and you will be what I shall most love in this world. Adieu my dear child.[90]

In these exchanges, the child-becoming-youth expressed an independence from her father's imagined family, not only by introducing political events in family discussions but also by proposing three alternative constructs. One was the family of Paris where the attractions of love radiated beyond the marital circle. A second, the Royal family divided by political intrigue and financial misdeeds. Another family, similar to Monticello's, comprised of "our fellow creatures...treated so teribly...by many of our country men," that stood in complete dependence upon patriarchal benevolence. Jefferson for his part clung tenaciously to his family construct: first, by refusing even to acknowledge her rhetorical thrusts; and, second, by re-orienting the narrative to themes of motherhood, American character, Virginia culture, and Patsy's filial responsibility for his serenity and contentment. Father had assured the child four years earlier at age eleven that "you will feel something within...which will tell you it is wrong and ought not to be said or done." This was her "faithful internal Monitor."[91] He had not anticipated she would extend her benevolent sentiments to "wish with all my soul that the poor negroes were all freed." Even the security of the cloister could not shield Patsy from the culture of Paris. The "family" in Virginia that her Father had registered in his farm accounts, if not in his mind, was not beyond her moral sensibility.[92]

"United to what I hold dearest"

Just short of nine-years old, Polly finally reached London on 26 June 1787. The press of father's business, after being gone several months in the south of France, consigned her several days to the care of Abigail Adams. She found Polly was "indeed a fine child"; "of the quickest sensibility, and the maturest understanding," with an "intelligent countenance," "her temper, dispositions, her sensibility are all formed to delight."[93] Adams did not gloss over the emotional stress the nine-year-old was experiencing and did not allay Father's concern for the inconstancy of the child's affections:

> [A]t present everything is strange to her, and she was very loth to try New Friends for old. She was so much attached to the Captain [Ramsey] and he to her, that it was with no small regret that I separated her from him…I shew her your picture. She says she cannot know it, how should she when she should not know you.…If you could bring Miss Jefferson with you, it would reconcile her little Sister to the thoughts of taking a journey.[94]

But the candid New Englander gave no quarter in lecturing Jefferson and offering an opinion on his sending servant Petit as an escort from London to Paris. "[S]he last evening upon Petit's arrival, was thrown into all her former distresses, and bursting into Tears, told me it would as hard to leave me as it was her Aunt Epps." Polly, Mrs. Adams reported, thought her father "would have taken pains to have come here for her, and not have sent a man whom she cannot understand." Abigail warned Jefferson that he would lose "many pleasures…by committing her to a convent."[95] He was not unaware of the emotional stress of wresting Polly away from her newfound surrogate, and he feared she might even "think I am made only to tear her from all her affections." But "I cannot wait. Her distress will be in the moment of parting" from the Adamses.[96]

Despite objections from interlocutors and her own protestations, Polly was reunited on July 15th with the sister and father she "did not remember" after nearly four years separation. Patsy and Father had looked forward to her arrival and had even been pleased with Polly's claim to "rather stay with Aunt Eppes" than go to France. "I shall enjoy her presence very soon," Patsy wrote. "It will make up for a neglect that I own gives me the greatest pain." "United to what I hold the dearest in the world," their father confessed, "nothing more will be requisite to render my happiness complete." Having both daughters in Paris was "a circumstance of inexpressible comfort."[97]

Patsy dutifully assumed her role as surrogate mother by staying with Polly a week at Langeac and "leading her from time to time to the convent, till she became familiarized to it." Although the family had just been reunited, Patsy, according to her father, retained "all her anxiety to get back to her country and her friends. Her "dispositions" and "progress" gave him "perfect satisfaction; however, she [would] need the "finishing" of Aunt Eppes "to render her useful in her own country. Of domestic oeconomy she [could] learn nothing here; yet she must learn it somewhere, as being of more solid value than everything else."[98]

"The brightest part of a life"

In the "Siberian degree of cold" of a Paris winter in 1788, "Polly had a constant fever of 3. weeks from which she recovered for about a fortnight," but she had relapsed. Patsy, also, remained indisposed after "a cold and occasional fevers."[99] Perhaps, these illnesses, added to father's concern for Patsy's religious stirrings, were contributing reasons for a return to America.

Jefferson had revealed to Angelica Schuyler Church in August 1788 that he was planning a brief return home but had not yet requested leave. In November and December, he gave similar notice to John Jay, James Currie, John Adams, Nicholas Lewis, and the Eppes family. He planned to return for two months and depart via New York and Boston to resume his duties in Paris. Among his explanations were: "Patsy's age," "arrangement of my own affairs" regarding the legacy debt from John Wayles's estate, the children's "future welfare," and his claim that Patsy had "never lost her impatience to return to her own country."[100]

Jefferson candidly acknowledged the need to settle "matters of account" and urged the manager of his business affairs, Nicholas Lewis, to proceed with the sale of property and "renting the rest of [his] estate." For a European audience, the burden of debt had been cast by the American Minister in even more draconian language. Responding in 1786 to an author of the revised _Encyclopédie Méthodique_, Jefferson conceived planter indebtedness in conspiratorial terms. It was the result of chicaning British merchants, not the too "generous" character of Virginians he had suggested to Chastellux the year before. They offered planters "good prices and credit" until their debt was so large even selling land and slaves would not unburden them. The condition of indebted plantation owners was the very antithesis of the freedom and independence they esteemed. "These debts had become hereditary from father to son for many generations," Jefferson exclaimed, "so that the planters were a species of property annexed to certain mercantile houses of London."[101] Chronically indebted planters were like the men and women in the fields who made wealth accumulation and a genteel life possible. Jefferson certainly had inherited debt from John Wayles but, also, the property in land and slaves that enabled his exercise of republican civic virtue. Now, he was suggesting this legacy resulted in a kind of debt-slavery—"a species of property." Family necessities, financial affairs, and public service were and would continue to be inextricably conflated in Jefferson family life.

On April 20th of 1788, Father paid the Panthemont account in full (625 livres, 15 sous, 3 deniers).[102] There are several intriguing suggestions that he was concerned about sixteen-year-old Patsy's spiritual awakening. While her father was in the south of France, Martha signed the flyleaf of a book on Catholic religious instruction, dated 21 March 1787.[103] A letter from her friend Bettie Hawkins later that year in August asked whether Patsy's father had been informed about her plans for "abjuration." However, family lore later held that Martha informed her father of her interests in "abjuration" in early 1789, some two years after the Hawkins' query. More recent evidence draws on the correspondence of the Papal Nuncio in France, Antonio Dugnani, and suggests Martha was expressing interest in either converting to Catholicism, or perhaps, considering vows. The prelate's overtures were certainly concluded in 1818 when her father served notice that "my eldest daughter, who had the honor of being known to you in Paris," is married with grandchildren of her own. Regardless of degree, it seems reasonably obvious that Martha's religious sensibilities were being aroused precisely at the time when she was challenging Father on slavery, marriage, and sewing. In this context, it is just possible the nearly fifteen-year-old was testing the limits of her parent's tolerance and/or had devised a stratagem for release from the convent to enjoy Parisian society. Her religious sentiments, along with other material reasons, may have been one of several factors for Jefferson's long-delayed request for a "leave of absence."

Whatever the reasons for withdrawing from Panthemont, Patsy had completed what she recalled to her daughter was "a period of great happiness and great improvement." The last months in Paris would initiate a new phase of her development—immersed in Parisian society and witnessing the birth of a revolution that she had glimpsed only secondhand from the abbess's table. The time was "spent in the gay whirl of its fascinating society," though limited to "three balls a week."[104] Ellen Coolidge's diary recorded that her mother,

> remembered her residence in France as the brightest part of a life much shaded and saddened by care & sorrows....Her recollections of the Convent were in the highest degree pleasant and favorable. She always spoke with the greatest approbation of the system of education pursued there—of the attention paid to morals and manners...of the care which was taken to train them in the habits of neatness, modesty and scrupulous regard to purity and propriety...[105]

Besides alleviating "pain," providing "comfort," and engendering "happiness," the circumstance of a reunited family in Paris was an unsuspected metaphor of a "family" that would increasingly occupy the Jeffersons' imaginations and be frustrated by the lives they would lead. Patsy and Polly were safely ensconced in a convent-home just across the river Seine from the Hôtel de Langeac; Father would try a replication in the 1790s on the banks of the Rivanna. Over the years, the angst of separation and heightening anticipation of reunion would be interpreted as a fretful prelude to uncheckered happiness seeded atop Monticello—only to be delayed or followed by another lengthy absence. Affection was the dynamic that bound them together and attached them to others, but its intensity sometimes would threaten to break the circle asunder, as the family was extended by marriage and constricted by death. Being together was an "inexpressible comfort" that wedded physicality to emotionality and projected an internal impulse onto an external place, as it would be when Martha's dwelling at Edgehill was grafted to the Monticello household. Finally, it was during the Paris experience that Patsy and Father were learning to accommodate their situation by reconfiguring their lived family and what they expected from it, as they would with her marriage, his multiple "retirements," and unremitting financial crises.

Going Home

After two-and-one-half years together, the Jefferson family (including Sally and James Hemings) left Paris on 26 September 1789, accompanied by their French servant Adrien Petit. They traveled overland via Vernon and Bolbec and arrived at Le Havre on the 28th, where they joined with Nathaniel Cutting to await passage to Cowes,

England. "A terribly stormy night," Cutting recorded on Friday, 30 September; "Blustering, Rainy Tempestuous weather" the next day that continued to "squally, Dirty, tempestuous morning, and contrary Wind" on October 6th.[106] They finally departed Thursday the 8th on the packet *Anna* at "half before one in the morning" and arrived in Cowes "half after two." The water of the Channel had not calmed since their last passage five years prior, but a few hours rest followed by "a Comfortable Dish of Tea with butter'd roll" soon relieved the *nausea marina* of Patsy and Polly. Wasting no time, Polly's father was instructing her in Spanish the next morning, "instilling into her tender mind an accurate knowledge of Geography at the same time that he inculcated the purest principles of the language." Captain Cutting observed: "The lovely Girl was all attention, and discover'd a degree of sagacity and observation beyond her years…[W]hen her faculties attain their maturity, she will be the delight of her Friends, and a distinguish'd ornament to her sex."[107] He found seventeen-year-old Patsy "an amiable Girl…tall and genteel."

> Though she has been so long resident in a Country remarkable for its Levity and the forward indelicacy of its manners, yet she retains all the winning simplicity, and good humour'd reserve that are evident proofs of innate Virtue and an happy disposition.— Characteristicks which eminently distinguish the Women of America from those of any other Country.[108]

A north Atlantic ill wind held Captain Nathaniel Colley's *Clermont* in Cowes harbor for two weeks until noon on October 22nd, when it departed for a "quick and not unpleasant" voyage to Norfolk. However, the Jefferson entourage was again delayed in the Virginia capes by "thick mist," Martha recalled, and spent three days "beating about" off the coast. The "bold" captain finally decided to make what was an unsuccessful run for the harbor. Anchoring offshore after nightfall, a strong wind dragged the *Clermont* "one or two miles," but some other ships were "blown off the coast" and lost; others had to wait "three or four weeks longer" to safely dock at Norfolk. Still, the Jefferson's ship lost its topsail and was nearly rammed by a "brig coming out of port" that took part of its rigging. Their travails were not over: "[In] two hours after landing before an article of our baggage was brought a shore the vessel took fire and reduced to the mere hull…[but] everything in her was saved."[109] A dramatic ending to an eventful five years!

Nathaniel Cutting would write Martha several months later that America did not offer, as did Europe, "Persons of the same elevated Rank or the same degree of knowledge in the Etiquette of Courts." But in compensation, her country had "respectable examples of Polish'd Taste, genuine affability, and amiable sincerity."

> From your native good sense and from that just mode of thought which the conversation and instructions of your Father cannot fail to inspire, I dare venture to presage that you will soon be really happier in America than you ever thought yourself in Europe.[110]

Chapter 4

"Boys in tolerable order":

The Tangled Web of a Plantation Household

The family returned from France just as a new experiment in government was taking shape. Jefferson intended "to place [his] daughters in the society and care of their friends, and to return for a short time to [his] station at Paris." Aunt Eppes or some other of "their friends" was to become a stand-in parent to a girl of eleven and a marriageable seventeen-year-old.[1] Then having seen the end of the French Revolution, he recalled many years later, the plan had been to return home and "sink into the bosom of [his] family and friends" and to "devote [himself] to studies more congenial to [his] mind."[2] Six years prior, Jefferson had complained to a friend that "public service and private misery [were] inseparably linked together..."[3] Time, the "vaulted scene" of Paris, and having the girls live with him so long "to exercise [his] affections" seemingly had mitigated any compunction to serving in the New Republic. He deferred to the entreaties of President Washington to become Secretary of State and launched what was to become three decades of separations and reunions with the "bosom of family."

This decision cast Martha Randolph (née Jefferson) into a tangled emotional, social, and financial web of a far-flung plantation household comprised of unfinished houses, several farms, and scores of the "poor negroes" that had "grieved" her heart while in Paris. Adding husband Thomas Mann Randolph, Jr. had triangulated the family's emotional dynamics; the young couple's marriage portions of land and slaves located near Richmond and Lynchburg substantially expanded the Monticello household, increased its social complexity, and contributed to its ever-growing indebtedness. Martha was expected to manage the domestic side of this new enterprise, while simultaneously providing emotional and logistical support to a father actively exercising republican civic virtue.

How did the "family" Martha had been led in Paris to expect compare to the one she lived during the early years of marriage? What were the emotional dynamics and social demands in a family circle inscribed primarily by affectionate sentiments, rather than merely consanguinity? How did extending the family to in-laws and friends encroach upon it? How were the roles of daughter, son-in-law, father, wife, and husband in the Jefferson-Randolph family confounded by a household of extensive landholdings? The family construct Martha and her father had developed in France was first challenged by her hasty marriage to Mann Randolph, on 23 February 1790, followed by her father's immediate departure for New York. The abrupt change in circumstances and the distances separating them sharply reminded father and daughter just how much their mutual affection demanded physical proximity. An effort was launched to locate the newlyweds' plantation seat in Albemarle; meanwhile, letters were the balm to their empty, aching hearts.

From Imagination to Reality

Martha's first year back in America was a difficult one. Internal household affairs were "very troublesome," she confessed, but with the perseverance and industry her father admired so much, she could report by early 1791: "I have the boys in tolerable order....I have wrought an entire reformation on the rest of my household." She was not "relying much in the carefulness of the boys." The china had been preserved by locking it up; the spoons by a nightly inventory and stored safely with the silver under lock and key. Each day, Martha visited the kitchen, the smoke house, and tended the fowls (weather permitting). Receiving instructions, as usual, through Father's letters, she sent the "servants" their "meat cut out."[4] All this, because Jefferson had "silenced his reluctance, and...accepted yet another government appointment" as Secretary of State.[5]

Martha had entered into these domestic pursuits in 1790 without a scintilla of instruction in making a pudding, tending the garden, sewing clothes, caring for the sick, or overseeing the "servants." As a youngster in Philadelphia and Paris, letters from an absent father might have been an effective medium for conveying expectations;

interpreting life experiences; inculcating values of persistence, industry, and inventiveness; and constructing an imaginary family. But letters were an imperfect vehicle for developing practical skills in deciphering vague recipes, securing the silver from theft, coping with intrusive visitors, or integrating domestic and farming operations.[6] Nonetheless, father and daughter were dependent on regularly scheduled letters to mediate between the domestic family tranquility they longingly imagined and the unsettling household disorder they actually were experiencing. This "family-of-letters" alleviated somewhat the emotional pangs of separation by sharing the details of lives lived apart counterpoised to a conjured future of tranquility atop Monticello mountain.

Correspondence from New York following Patsy's marriage began to describe the revised family schema her father had in mind. At the same time, his language suggested the contradictions within their triangulated relationship that would eventually come to torment family life in the Jefferson-Randolph household. Drawing on his memory of five years with Patsy in Paris, her father now felt "heavily these separations:"

> It is a circumstance of consolation to know that you are happier; and to see a prospect of its continuance...Your new condition [marriage] will call for abundance of little sacrifices but they will be greatly overpaid by the measure of affection they will secure to you. The happiness of your life depends now on the continuing to please a single person. To this all other objects must be secondary; even your love to me, were it possible that could ever be an obstacle....Cherish then for me, my dear child, the affection of your husband, and continue to love me as you have done.[7]

Happiness—the ultimate purpose of life, according to Jefferson—depended upon resolving this tension between filial independence and conjugal submission. Father simultaneously noted feeling emotional separation, lamented that he "feels heavily," and demanded she "continue" to love him as in the past. His sense of loss was assuaged by "consolation" in her being "happier." For Father, she was a "dear child" who was to "cherish," as wife, the affection of her husband.

Martha did not miss the conundrum: "I assure you My dear papa my happiness can never be compleat without your company...I have made it my study to please [Mr. Randolph] in every<u>thing</u> and do consider all other objects as secondary to that <u>except</u> my love for you." Even at this early stage of marriage, and increasingly as she and her husband grew apart, Martha was beginning to feel the tangled web of living a Jefferson-Randolph family life—daughter, wife, and Father's plantation mistress—receiving from an absent parent through letters instructions on marriage, neighborly responsibilities, gardening, childrearing, and all manner of subjects. She assumed her domestic domain, though its burdens were nettlesome, and expectantly awaited father's return to the "bosom of family."

"Talents, dispositions, connections and fortune"

Martha and young Randolph's short courtship of a few weeks had been antedated by at least some contact while she was in Paris. The groom's relationship with Jefferson likewise had been intermittently maintained during the young man's studies at Edinburgh. Writing to Martha at Panthemont in 1785, a seventeen-year-old Randolph was delighted her "renewal of the correspondence...cannot fail of being very agreeable...the many obstacles which hitherto prevented it, being now entirely removed." He anticipated "great entertainment from [her] Epistles, knowing [her] to be highly capable of affording it."[8] Unfortunately, there are no other known letters between them, but Father had actively encouraged the Edinburgh student to study law in France.

Correspondence between Thomas Mann Randolph, Jr. and Thomas Jefferson during these years established a pattern of condescension and deference that would become the norm repeated after their return to America. Young Randolph at times accepted his subordination in the family circle, at others engaged in ambivalent participation, and finally by the early 1800s, sadly acknowledged he would never live among the "swans." Jefferson's approach was to proffer unequivocal, detailed, and sometimes conflicting advice; leave its implementation to Randolph's discretion; and convey veiled censure when it did not turn out to his liking. The subtext of letters during this early, 1790–93 period conveyed the emotional tensions of divided family loyalties Randolph was experiencing and would continue to do so when he attempted to breach the daughter-father relationship.

In 1785 and 1786, seventeen-year-old Randolph was urged by Jefferson to spend time on the European continent so "the talents with which nature has endowed you may be properly developed and cultivated so as to render you useful to your country and an ornament to your family."[9] Nine months later, a period in France was suggested to "acquire the habit of speaking French," become familiar with the "fine arts," and form "an acquaintance with the individuals and character of a nation."[10] In the spring of 1787, Randolph assured Jefferson he would show "gratitude" for his educational advice by "implicitly following it" while at Edinburgh. Spanish language studies would be undertaken, "provided my plan meets with your approbation." Trying to steer between his biological father and Jefferson, the young student wrote: "As my Father is very impatient for my return, I shall probably spend this winter in Paris, and set out the next summer."[11] This was unacceptable to Jefferson, so he "ventured to propose...another plan" to Randolph's father that involved a two-year stay reading law in some village near Paris and capped with a tour of France and Italy. The "plan," which included estimated costs and itinerary in Randolph, Sr.'s letter, was intended to further the youngster's decision to fix on "Politics as [his] principal pursuit."[12]

Despite acknowledging his "good fortune" and "honor" in having Mr. Jefferson "superintend" his education, young Randolph by early 1788 was marshalling reasons for his mother to acquiesce in "the request I have made my Father for permission to return home next spring." His "ardent desire for learning will prevent...ever relaxing in the pursuit of it," so he will not "abandon the prospect...of improvement from a residence of several years in France." However, separation at this time from his brother William is "extremely disagreeable" and likely to be construed as "partiality." Finally, the tutor who will accompany him to his home at Tuckahoe can instruct sisters Anne and Judy "in the sciences, which an accomplished woman cannot be entirely ignorant of." The attentive sibling would even "request Mr. Jefferson to give me his opinion concerning the method of conducting female education....[H]is honor, abilities [&] taste would have insured his adopting a proper system."[13] However, if mentor Jefferson "does not wholly approve" of his returning home, her son would "not think of it a moment longer."

At age twenty, Randolph left Scotland for Virginia in the summer of 1788 without completing his course of studies, visiting France, or seeking the approval of his adviser.[14] Anne Cary Randolph, mother of a "most affect. & dutiful Son," died in March 1789, and soon thereafter he left Tuckahoe for New York to further prepare for politics as his "principal pursuit." He lived with another of Jefferson's protégés, Peter Carr, who found young Randolph "extremely intelligent and cleaver [sic]."[15] Returning home in the fall, Junior's uneasy and tempestuous relation with his father resulted in a quarrel and another departure for a relative's plantation in Goochland County.

A seventeen-year-old Randolph had expected "great entertainment" from Martha's letters on her "studies, etc. in the convent," while lamenting his poor prospects for a "tolerable education."[16] However, he confided to his mother three years later in 1788 that it was "disagreeable" for an "accomplished women" to be too learned in the "tedious & abstruse enquiries into the causes of phaenomina [sic]." He wrote his mother that the "elegant and agreeable occupations of Poetry and the fine arts, surely become the delicate sex more…[It] will insure them pleasing far the greater part of the other sex…whose approbation only is to be sincerely wished for."[17] He may have overlooked Martha's "considerably different" education in the "graver sciences" and Parisian society. He most certainly was unaware that her "happiness" was "compleat" only with father's company and that "pleasing" Mr. Randolph would be secondary to love for her father.[18] But he may have expected from marriage the rapture promised in a poem from his journal, "To a Wife's Bosom."

> Open, open, lovely breast,
> Lull my weary head to rest;
> Soft & warm, & sweat and pain,
> Balmy antidote to care,
> Fragrant source of Sure delight,
> Downy couch of wellcome night,
> Ornament of rising day,
> allways constant, ever gay!
> …
> Open, open beauteous breast,
> angels here might seek their rest
> Caesar, fill thy Shining throne
> a nobler seat I call my own,
> Here I reign with boundless sway
> Here I triumph night and day[19]

Martha and Mr. Randolph may have renewed their acquaintance as the Jefferson family slowly wended its way from landfall in Norfolk on 23 November 1789, arriving at Monticello a full month later. Along the road, they visited relatives Eppes, Skipwith, Cary, Bolling, Burwell, and maybe the Randolph branch at Tuckahoe plantation.[20] They most certainly were together at Monticello in late December. Jefferson initiated on 6 January a complicated gambit to expand his holdings at nearby Edgehill which suggests the young couple found each other sufficiently "agreeable" to pledge their troth.[21] By 30 January, the groom's father noted his "real and extreme pleasure" from the "intended Union"; the bride's father considered the "talents, dispositions, connections and fortune" of young Randolph sufficient to make him the "first choice" for Martha's husband.[22]

There was a rush of events to re-order the past and structure the future in the three months since arriving home. The past weighed most heavily with the still outstanding debts inherited from his father-in-law, because the creditor's Richmond lawyer was demanding payment on money owed from the 1770s.[23] As family executor, Jefferson sent a flurry of letters settling accounts from the estates of his father Peter, wife Martha, and his sisters Jane and Elizabeth.[24]

A "Call" to Public Office

Late in the summer of 1789 before arriving home, Jefferson had unequivocally declined to "accept any appointment" in the New Republic. "You know," he wrote James Madison," the circumstances which led me from retirement, step by step and from one nomination to another up to the present." He would not "engage in any other office, and most especially any one which would require a constant residence from home."[25]

Jefferson learned of President Washington's request that he serve as the first Secretary of State on December 11th after docking in Norfolk and on the return to Monticello. He demurred:

> I cannot be insensible of my inequality to it: and I should enter on it with gloomy forebodings from the criticisms and censures of a public just indeed in their intentions, but sometimes misinformed and misled, and always too respectable to be neglected. I cannot but foresee the possibility that this may end disagreeably for one, who has no motive to public service but the public satisfaction…[26]

Fears, hopes, and inclinations do not "lead me to prefer a change," he replied to President Washington. "But it is not for an individual to chuse his post. You are to marshal us as may best be for the public good;…Whatever you may be pleased to decide, I do not see that the matters which have called me hither will permit me to shorten the stay I originally asked…"[27]

Two Virginia gentlemen were equally masterful in the dance of dissimulation. Washington felt "such delicacy and embarrassment," because Jefferson had placed the burden of decision on him; he did not wish to oppose "inclinations." "It must be at your option to determine relative to your acceptance of it, or continuance in your Office abroad." But the crafty President knew what would stir Jefferson's civic virtue and his appetite for the "affection" of his countrymen. News of the appointment, Washington assured Jefferson, "has given very extensive and very great satisfaction to the Public."[28]

With the "disorder and ruin" of his private financial affairs seemingly in hand by February 7th and the marriage settlement nearly complete, Jefferson finally acquiesced to George Washington's "call" to public service. "I no longer hesitate to undertake the office to which you are pleased to call me....I shall have to go by way of Richmond, [but] the circumstances which prevent my immediate departure, are not under my controul."[29] This completed a *pas de deux* of several weeks in which Jefferson, first declined, then demurred, delayed, and finally deferred to the President's "call."

The matter of the marriage settlement between the Randolphs and Jeffersons was unresolved, so James Madison was enlisted as interlocutor to advise Washington "the happiness of a child, for life, would be hazarded were I to go away" too soon.[30] (Unspoken, however, was the need to sign seven bonds totaling £4,444 sterling for the Wayles debt and settle other accounts with Richmond merchants.) Legacy debt in Jefferson's mind prevented him from following the "dictates of my heart" in providing for the newlyweds, so the "provision" for Thomas Mann Randolph, Jr. would be left to his father. Perhaps suspecting his old friend was in financial straits, Jefferson insisted they not rely on letters alone but prepare formal legal documents describing the terms of the marriage settlement and conveying deeds. "Come then, my dear Sir, and let us place them in security before their marriage." (Such arrangements were legally legitimated only before nuptials.) His concerns were verified by Randolph's response on February 15th which informed him that, indeed, the land at Varina contributed on behalf of the husband was mortgaged for "£1200 sterlg."[31]

The Household

The plantation household described in letters to Martha, while she was residing in a Paris convent, was "remote from all other aid" and required that the mistress be "inventive" or else loose "esteem" by being considered a "helpless creature." Since the "morning" of their father's life had been "clouded by loss after loss," the sisters were the only prospects to "render the evening of his life serene and contented." The household described to Martha while in Paris was tranquil, multi-generational, physically secluded, and insulated from public life.[32] Her father may have conveyed in more subtle ways a life similar to what he described to Anne Willing Bingham: husband, children, house, and "improvements of the grounds fill her every moment." The plantation mistress was "contented to soothe and calm the minds of their husbands returning ruffled from political debate." And, the "good ladies" of America valued "domestic happiness above all other, and the art to cultivate it beyond all others."[33]

Without the benefit of a mother's tutelage and with only the childhood memory of a two-parent family, In 1790, Martha was thrust simultaneously into learning the adult responsibilities of a plantation mistress, newlywed, surrogate mother, and republican daughter. Marriage had triangulated intimate family relations, and the affectionate impulse embedded daughter, husband, and father in a web of social connections that routinely intruded on tranquil domesticity. Dissension and imprudence in the extended family disrupted the order they were trying to achieve. Martha was sent forth as envoy of the Monticello household to "sooth" the contentious Tuckahoe Randolphs but, more importantly, to protect her "interests" in gaining title to Edgehill land near Father's Monticello that would assure her future "happiness."[34] She was asked to visit an imperious neighbor and suffer her foibles, because neighborly "ill-will…is an immense drawback on the happiness of life."[35] Shuffling people and things between multiple residences in New York, Henrico, and Albemarle along with balancing the demands of farming at three widely dispersed locations were imperfectly conducted by Jefferson *in absentia* with written instructions and contributed decidedly to muddled affairs. Wife-Martha would intermediate between husband and Father; Daughter-Martha would provide logistical and emotional support to a father actively exercising republican civic virtue; and simultaneously Mistress-Martha would be expected to manage the domestic side of an expanded Monticello household.

The notion of "household," as it took form in the family's minds over the years, was a constellation of physical, imaginary, and relational dimensions. Most obvious were houses, farms, quarters, gardens, and workshops dotting the mountain, scattered along the Rivanna River, and extending to far-off Varina near Richmond and

Poplar Forest outside Lynchburg. Ornamenting both physical structures and helpful associations were more subtle but intensely desired qualitative features of independence, tranquility, order, ease, harmony, and self-direction that was expressed repeatedly in their correspondence. Finally, letters between the three principals—Martha, her husband, and father—taken as a whole, also reveal that "Monticello" was a complex of mediating structures connecting the intimate family sphere with the "world" of merchants, governments, interests, and other external entities considered necessary for creating and sustaining a plantation household.[36]

A New Family-of-Letters

The imagined family Martha's father had created in letters during their years in Philadelphia and Paris was bound by deep affection; its members were dependent on each other for mutual happiness; they were accomplished, capable of overcoming difficulties, persistent, and most importantly, engaged in incessant activity to avoid ennui, that "canker of human happiness." With regard to the household in which the family would be situated, however, there had been only vague and indirect references. Sewing was a pastime with "dull company" and a skill requisite to "direct the works of…servants." Patsy had been directed to be a surrogate mother to sister Polly, whom she would teach to be "good," "true," "never angry," and industrious. Instantiating this ideal in a southern plantation of an absent republican patriarch would prove more challenging than anyone imagined.

Writing, reading, and receiving letters, as well as silence was infused with emotional overtones and symbolism early in the new family's life together and continued unabated until Jefferson's retirement in 1809. The most prominent aspect of both the family they were living and the one they were imagining was the warm, deep expressions of affection between father and daughters. Their letters' style, language, explicit content, and themes conveyed this emotional dynamic. Most obvious were stylized openings and closings in which "My dear Daughter" or "Dear Papa" bracketed explicit words of longing, requests to be "remembered affectionately," messages of "tender affections" and assurances of "sincere love." Emotional intimacy and interdependency were accentuated and deepened by writing letters about letter-writing, by physical distance, and by the sharp contrasts they draw between the lives they were living apart. Away at Lake George, New York in 1791, twelve-year-old Polly received a letter that read: "I write you merely to tell you that…I love you dearly, am always thinking of you."[37] Next year, months of experiencing detached and distinctly different experiences wore heavily on Martha and her father. Memories of a shared past "alleviate the toils and inquietudes" of her father's present situation:"

> Having no particular subject for a letter, I find none more soothing to my mind than to indulge itself in expressions of love I bear you, and the delight with which I recall the various scenes thro which we have passed together, in our wanderings over the world.

The past conjured a future image of,

> being at home once more, and of exchanging labour, envy, and malice for ease, domestic occupations, and domestic love and society, where I may once more be happy with you, with Mr. Randolph, and dear little Anne, with whom even Socrates might ride on a stick without being ridiculous.[38]

The act of writing in which a remembered past and an imagined future were foils for an unhappy present served as an emotional substitute for the warmth and affection that could only be truly affirmed with physical togetherness.

Mann Randolph was instructed by Jefferson to provide in "all [his letters] a particular account of the reasonableness of the weather and the state and prospect of crops of wheat, corn and tobacco as these things are very interesting to me."[39] Martha, her husband, and sister Polly were directed to write alternately each week. In turn, the absent patriarch would favor them with weekly accounts of his life in the political public sphere.[40] Letters became the artifacts representing an activity and physical token in a household ritual that mediated between the intimate family sphere, farming operations, and an external world of politics, commerce, and society. As the participants interpreted it, the ceremony included a strictly scheduled activity of writing and reading; required specific content describing personal feelings and conditions in the writers' situations; and carried the expectation that letters would evoke particular emotional responses such as "pleasure," relief from "anxiety," or reaffirmation of "affection." The rite served to bridge an existential space between imagined and lived experiences, past and present, separation and reunion.

Enduring Separations—Ritual & Artifact

While in Paris, Jefferson had written a letter to Maria Cosway he titled "dialogue between my head and my heart." His rational self had admonished his sentimental "Heart" that it disturbs their "whole system when you are parted from those you love…[T]heir return too depends on so many circumstances that if you had a grain of prudence you would not count upon it."[41] Similar intense feelings of separation were revealed by the emotive language of letters the family wrote to each other. The prescribed (but routinely violated) schedule for corresponding was intended to order potentially inconstant emotions. Not receiving a scheduled letter was objectified in a person's character as "indolence" or "weak affection." Jefferson's demand for regular letters continued as the lived family was transformed by Martha's marriage and became more insistent and clamorous as father's disaffection with the "hateful labours" of public life increased. His strident insistence on a strict, rotational letter writing schedule conveys a sense of isolation and the need for reassurances of emotional fidelity.

> I mentioned that I should write every Wednesday to him [Mr. Randolph] , yourself and Polly alternately, and that my letters arriving at Monticello the Saturday and the answer being sent off on Sunday I should receive it the day before I should have to write again to the same person, so as that the correspondence with each would be exactly kept up. I hope you [Martha] will do it on your part.[42]

After eleven weeks away in 1790 without "a scrip of a pen from home," he wrote a "scolding letter" to Martha, who was seven months pregnant: "I think it so easy for you to write me one letter every week, which will be but once in three weeks for each of you [Martha, Polly, and Randolph]."[43] If rebuke was ineffectual, perhaps piqued withdrawal would work: "I write to you out of turn, and believe I must adopt the rule of only writing when I am written to, in hopes that may provoke more frequent letters."[44] Father was "really angry at receiving no letter" from his youngest daughter; so much so, he subordinated personal character to emotional deficiency by ascribing her tardiness "first to indolence, but the affection must be weak which is so long overruled by that." If they wrote regularly, it would be "as exactly as if I were in Charlottesville."[45]

A common refrain during all their separations was just how emotional states were dependent on an orderly writing, receipt, and response to letters that, in turn, were contingent on factors beyond the control of even a Secretary of State. Letters and their absence evoked emotional responses. Family members awaited "impatiently" for news from home and abroad and were "uneasy" and "anxious" with long intervals between letters. Recipients were assured that failure to write did not signal waning "affection," and they, in turn, expressed "pleasure" at finally hearing from a loved one. Martha received her father's letter "with more pleasure than is possible for me to express." He conveyed that he was "anxious to hear from you of your health, your occupations, where you are &c." "In matters of correspondence as well as of money you must never be in debt," Father advised "dearest Maria," and presented her with an accounting of debits and credits neatly arrayed in columnar form.[46] Thirteen-year-old Polly dutifully reassured her father: "I am very sorry that my not having wrote to you before made you doubt of my affection towards you and hope that after having read my last letter you were not so displeased." When they failed to write, Jefferson engaged his new son-in-law as interlocutor: "Present my warm affections to the girls. I am afraid they do not follow my injunctions of answering by the first post the weekly letter I address to them."[47]

The salience everyone attached to the ritual of letters generated all manner of excuses for not corresponding. Silences were attributed to the press of visitors, illness, children, farming operations, public affairs, and undependable postal riders. A visit "up country" to aunt Carr prevented Martha from writing her father. He thought her "ambulatory life" a reason for not hearing from her for a month. While Martha was with her Aunt Eppes, Mr. Randolph was busily preparing "2 small houses with 2 rooms in each" in anticipation of "her coming to Varina" to settle. Even temporarily settled at Monticello, however, the Virginia correspondents had ready excuses for their tardiness. Martha was "prevented" from writing, because she mistakenly thought the Charlottesville post had been "discontinued." The rider between Richmond and Charlottesville, Randolph reported, was "extremely irregular." He leaves home "as it suits him on Wednesday, Thursday or Friday, and keeps the letters in his hand frequently 3 days…When the weather is bad he sometimes misses a week and even 2 or 3…I am afraid it will be difficult to establish it on a better footing." The family was "unhappy at not being able to transmit…regular accounts from Monticello as [Jefferson] was desirous of having."[48]

If delay and misdirection of letters by the postal riders were obstacles to performing the family's ritual, then the Secretary of State would invoke his political influence to remedy the matter. In mid-1791, Jefferson pressed Congress to authorize "a regular post" from Richmond through Columbia on the James and north to Charlottesville and west over the Blue Ridge to Staunton, "so as to cost nothing to the public." Certainly, the proposal was in his "interest," but "neighbors and friends…benefited" as well.[49] Government intervention, however, was only one factor in sustaining an orderly family-of-letters. "I am afraid," Father chided his daughter who would soon be a mother, "there is one kind of precariousness [a regular post] will not remove; that in writing of them."[50]

Imagining Places

This family-of-letters assuaged the emotional pangs of separation by sharing the details of lives lived apart counterpoised to an imagined future together at a place called "Monticello." Until physical, experiential, and emotional distances could be bridged, their pangs were alloyed with words calling up images that simulated proximity. Noting spring's blossoms called to mind a vision of Monticello's orchard; reporting an upset stomach evoked sympathy for a loved one's discomfort; and mention of falling tobacco prices reminded a reader how vulnerable it all was to the vagaries of commerce and international affairs.

When absent from America, Jefferson had urged Dr. Currie: "give me facts, little facts." While away from Virginia, he hoped John Page would report "occurrences passing daily" and "whatever is interesting to yourself." Separated from "Dear Daughter" and without a letter in almost three months, Father "scolds" her:

> Perhaps you think you have nothing to say to me. It is a great deal to say you are all well, or that one has a cold, another a fever &c., besides that there is not a sprig of grass that shoots uninteresting to me, nor anything that moves, from yourself down to [the dogs] Bergere or Grizzle.[51]

"Facts, little facts" of inclement weather, children's antics, Presidential travels, garden vegetables, Congressional votes and the arrival of bluebirds served to stimulate an image of the other's world in which to locate their reports of a "periodical headache," visiting aunts, political duplicity, unpacking furniture, and other details of daily living. These specifics recounting their separate lives were interleaved with an evocative language of affection and caring to ameliorate loneliness;

without gestures, movements, and facial expressions to embellish written words, they implored the other to kiss and remember them to loved ones. For Patsy and her father, happiness was constructed at a place called "home" on a foundation of love ornamented with leisure, mental engagement, and quiet domesticity.

Their correspondence during the 1790–1809 period exemplify style, language, and content that revealed deeply felt needs to be physically together, symbolize emotional intimacy, and detail the social and economic complexities of a plantation household. As Jefferson configured rented quarters in New York and Philadelphia to meet his needs and the young couple wandered among temporary residences in Virginia, the family was trying to solve the practical difficulties of living lives apart in anticipation of being reunited. Polly's trip to Aunt and Uncle Eppes was delayed for lack of horses. Did his youngest daughter know, Father asked, "How to make a pudding yet, to cut out a beef stake, to sow spinach or to set a hen?" Randolph's hogsheads of tobacco were commingled with Jefferson's and must be distinguished before sale. Martha complained "old George is so slow" in the garden she will never "shine" without father's assistance. When her father was detained in Philadelphia by personal attacks in the newspapers, Martha was alerted that Mr. Randolph would be called on to tell the canal workers "what is to be done and how, and to attend to levelling the bottom." She reported that the "divisions within the [Randolph] family encrease daily," because of an alleged sexual imbroglio by a sister-in-law.[52] After just a year in the Jefferson household, young Randolph had learned that a family-of-letters symbolized not only emotional attachment but also personal character traits. "You shall no longer have reason to complain of our irregularity in the correspondence," he assured Jefferson. "We are ashamed to have made you repeatedly desire what was before strongly sollicited by Affection and commanded by Gratitude, respect and Duty."[53]

Living the family they had imagined in a plantation household would prove more troublesome than either daughter or father could have anticipated. In early 1790, they were re-constructing their relationship to accommodate a new husband. Young Patsy while in Paris had obliquely challenged Father's imagined family by recounting the story of a French husband whose wife's infidelity had resulted in suicide. Faced suddenly with the practical challenges of actually living in a family, an unusual candor entered her letters. Affection for her father would never be subordinated to that for Mann Randolph. In addition to adapting to changing family composition and roles, the trio now had to deal with practical concerns of adding a home to the Monticello household; managing the "servants"; planting a garden; directing four farming operations; engaging in the lives of relatives, friends, and neighbors; and enduring extended separations. While the husband initially was not "unavailable," the head of the household was, which fueled feelings of loneliness and complicated their lives with the logistics of coming and going.

Chapter 5

"Much adverse to it":

Constructing a Household

Martha confessed her "happiness could never be compleat without [his] company." Father remembered their times together, felt "heavily the separation" but rationalized (as he had when leaving her in Philadelphia) that she would be "happier" in Albemarle. Their first separation in six years fueled a desire for physical proximity and revealed the emotional complexity of a triangulated family. Mann Randolph, inexperienced both in farming and marriage, was stretched between his new family's drive to relocate him near Monticello and managing his heavily mortgaged marriage settlement some sixty miles distant. Extending family membership and expanding the Monticello household became a source of tension in the family's newly drawn triangle and in the conflicts arising from competing family interests. Their plans to live near each other became ensnared in the vagaries of eighteenth-century property law, the petulance of Randolph in-laws, long-past political machinations, and the craftiness of a "dangerous neighbor."

"Beauteous Breast"

Martha's husband had copied a vision of marital bliss in his Notebook. However, locating a home for the "beauteous breast" and gaining even a modicum of "boundless sway" in a Jefferson-Randolph household were being obstructed by his wife's need for Father's company and his birth family's dysfunction. Young Randolph was tossed between an emotional Charybdis and Scylla. On one side was a father-in-law determined to establish the "bosom of family" at

Monticello—fraught with all matter of difficulty; on the other shore, an emotionally distant biological father was intent on saving his Edgehill property for a recent wife thirty-three years his junior and their new son, "Thomas Mann Randolph, III." This liminal state between two families made the newlywed susceptible to Jefferson's expressions of affection, confidence in his intelligence, and presumptive reliance on his farming skills.

Mann Randolph and his father-in-law continued to build on the pattern of deference and condescension initiated in their early letters while in Europe, but now such behavior significantly confounded relations in the several families. The young man acknowledged Jefferson's superior knowledge and experience in all matters. Monticello's patriarch did not hesitate to voice expectations and encouragement to study law in preparation for public office but "mix it with a good degree of attention to the farm."[1] His research on the opossum might expose him to a wider sphere with a paper for the "philosophical society" headquartered in Philadelphia.[2] At the expense of his personal responsibilities at Varina, twenty-two-year-old Randolph was enlisted for Jefferson's many "little commissions": plant trees according to detailed instructions, keep daily weather records in prescribed format, and discipline "servants" but not too harshly. Randolph was "unhappy at not being able to transmit regular accounts from Monticello," because the postal service had been discontinued and freight wagons were undependable. He was "sorry" that want of a thermometer made the desired weather diary impossible. It was not in his "power" to estimate the harvest of wheat and tobacco.[3] By degrees, young Randolph would be initiated into the role of executive overseer or proto-patriarch whose every action was overseen, judged, and not infrequently countermanded by an absent head of household. Randolph would defer, delay, and denigrate his own performances in farming, politics, and family responsibilities, while furtively seeking avenues for independent action.

Entangled in the Past

During the spring of 1790, letters between Martha and Father passed unread on the post road, but their thoughts on mutual happiness were in concert. By April, "Mr. Randolph has some thought of settling at Varina for a little while till he can buy a part of Edgehill," Martha told her father. She was "much adverse to it...but shall certainly comply if Mr. Randolph thinks it necessary."[4] Her father's reply reframed the discussion from their emotional need to live near each other to argue with a tortured logic that Edgehill was the wellspring for sustaining marital bonds. He was anxious the newlyweds would "suffer ennui" in Richmond, developing "a weariness of one another." "Interesting occupations," he advised, "are essential to happiness," and no "emploiment" was so engaging as "commencing housekeepers on [their] own farm." He hoped "Mr. Randolph's idea of settling near Monticello will gain strength; and that...some expedient may be devised for settling...at Edgehill."[5]

As early as 1773, and again before leaving for Paris in 1784, Jefferson had requested that Albemarle County surveyor Anderson Bryan lay off 1000 acres of the Edgehill parcel adjoining Monticello Mountain that had been authorized by the colonial Governor's Council. There was a difficulty, however, in locating the bounds of other properties (among them Thomas Mann Randolph, Sr.'s family tract), so the work remained undone when the nuclear family returned from France.[6] In January 1790, the long-absent claimant renewed his efforts to untangle the Gordian knot in his financial affairs but, also, most likely was anticipating his scheme to locate Martha nearby to "exercise [his] affections in the intervals of business."

Their long absence had opened the opportunity for neighbor James Marks to discover a Land Office warrant for the same general area and to have it surveyed by Bryan, and patented, thereby perfecting his claim. Unfortunately, the piece overlapped with about one-half the area described in Jefferson's unclaimed 1000-acre warrant. Marks later sold the parcel to his brother-in-law, John Harvie, Jr., and divided with Randolph, Sr. portions now being disputed.[7] Begging a chronic "bad state of health" for the uncompleted survey, Bryan claimed that Marks had assured him Colo. Randolph "would give up all title," if Jefferson could show his claim to the land was prior.[8] These issues of proving ownership were not unusual in the transition from colonial to independent status and resulted in several, sometimes conflicting, laws by the new state government that further clouded titles. This particular case, however, was complicated by the fact that the Jefferson, Randolph, and Harvie held different interpretations of law as well as incompatible recollections of informal conversations. These twists and turns served to mask the underlying family dynamics being played out during 1790–92.

Jefferson proposed to Randolph Senior that the bride's portion of a marriage settlement would include 1000 acres in Bedford County ("Poplar Forest") and 27 "slaves;" however, he kept the contribution separate from her new husband by granting it to "Martha and her heirs."[9] As Jefferson was tied up by creditors' demands for payment of his legacy debt, Randolph, Sr. was urged to make "the provision for your son." Jefferson's boyhood friend responded by conveying "40 negroes" and 950 acres in Henrico County ("Varina") , but also included a caveat that the land was heavily mortgaged for £1,200 sterling.[10] Even though the young couple had been given a total of almost 2000 acres and 67 "negroes," the parcels and people were far removed from Monticello; so, Jefferson would persist through all of 1790 and beyond to 1810 to clear his land claims against John Harvie, Jr., and Thomas Mann Randolph, Sr., to provide enough additional acreage at the foot of the Mountain for a viable plantation.[11] The tangled knot restraining his plans was only drawn tighter by events in the Tuckahoe household and neighboring families.

The legal land claims over Edgehill parcels, like many of this period, were complicated enough, but their resolution in this instance was layered with past political enmities and personal obligations. Family matters likely were instrumental both in Jefferson's sense of Bryan's ungratefulness and in Marks's design to preempt Jefferson's right to survey and patent Edgehill property. The surveyor's dalliance piqued Jefferson even more by a debt of gratitude he considered justly due. Bryan had boarded with Jefferson several years, served as clerk for his father-in-law, John Wayles, and had been amanuensis in 1774 for his patron's *A Summary View of the Rights of British Americans*. Most importantly, Jefferson had been instrumental in securing for Bryan the position of Albemarle County surveyor once held by Peter Jefferson.

Because of Jefferson's political machinations a decade before, Marks had family as well as pecuniary interests in thwarting Jefferson's claims by his land deals with Harvie and Randolph. In 1781 Marks had defeated Charles Lilburne Lewis, the husband of Jefferson's sister Lucy, to represent Albemarle in the Virginia Assembly.[12] Simultaneously, his political influence in the Country had been sufficient for the local court to nominate his brother as colonel in the local militia over Lewis, whose seniority by precedent should have prevailed. However in an action that further violated tradition, Governor Jefferson persuaded the Virginia Council of State to override the local court's recommendation of John Marks in favor of his twice-thwarted family member.[13] The hand of the past—reaching from politics to plantation and spanning in-laws and friends—was alive and well enough to throw obstacles on the path to making Martha's happiness complete.

"So many allurements...as Albemarle"

Jefferson began the Edgehill gambit by approaching John Harvie, Jr., in early January 1790 with a lawyer-like account of the situation and a declaration that there could be no "difficultly" between them as they both desire "nothing which is not just."[14] Harvie was having only a part of it when he proffered two weeks later on February 2nd an alternative legal opinion along with a very different recollection of his informal conversations with Randolph, Senior. He accepted, however, appointing arbitrators from Albemarle's "General Court Barr" with "some knowledge in Land Law" to decide the question.

Given the recent betrothal of Martha and Randolph, Jr., there was a complication. Harvie suggested that if the three disputants would meet "nothing can prevent the full Adjustment of our Rights, as each will endeavour to do the Strickest justice to the other."[15] More hitches arrived two days later from Randolph, Sr. , who expressed his "real and singular pleasure" at the "intended Union" of their children and proposed a gift of Varina to the couple. "[T]here is, or may be at a small expence made a very convenient dwelling."[16] But such a bargain did not indulge the need of Martha and her father to be physically near. Jefferson now had to devise a stratagem that was appreciative of a future in-law's apparently generous offer but at the same time reciprocated with one of comparable value. Without some of the Harvie and/or Randolph parcels at Edgehill, he would be left with what for him was an unpleasant choice of sub-dividing Monticello. Marital unions were creating as much difficulty as physical divisions.

The husband seemingly deferred to the importance of "emploiments" encouraged by his father-in-law but outmaneuvered his mentor by undertaking them at Varina. "Martha and myself," young Randolph wrote in late May, "have concluded that the advantage of constant employment in interesting tho' trivial affairs will more than balance the many inconveniences...[She] is so certain that [those inconveniences] cannot affect her happiness as to be impatient to encounter them." Perhaps to assuage his father-in-law, he proclaimed that "no situation in America has so many allurements for us as Albemarle." He would "immediately" buy a small farm of 100 acres "in the neighbourhood of Monticello, to build on, as soon as there is a prospect of [Mr. Jefferson's] retirement." Such a diminutive size would prevent the danger of "being wholly involved in the care of it," because "exercise in excessive heat" for even an hour had caused him "two Military eruptions."[17] This dalliance and restrained industry must have struck a discordant note in the ears of someone who considered activity, especially physical exercise, an essential antidote to ennui and an ingredient of good health. A month later Jefferson urged young Randolph to defer purchase of 100 acres in hopes the two fathers "will be able to accommodate [him] with as much at least of Edgehill," as the Colonel had proposed in the interim to sell to Mr. Harvie to raise money for his daughters' marriage "portions." Domestic affairs and land deals had become even more entangled, however. Randolph Senior had married Harvie's teenage daughter, Gabriella, and was confronted with overseeing a household in which his own two daughters were just two and four years younger than the new bride.[18]

"Link of love...for the whole family"

Mrs. Hopkinson, Eliza Trist, and the Rittenhouse children, along with Aunt Eppes, Cousin Judy Randolph, and sister Polly were all part of the "family" Patsy and her father had constructed during their years away. Jefferson, also, had begun to describe the image of what he envisioned the Jefferson family would be upon their return to America. Patsy would be engaged in quiet domestic chores tending the children, soothing a "ruffled" husband, seeing to the "servants," superintending gardens and grounds. Along with her sister, they would warranty Father's happiness in his old age. Not even their most fanciful conjuring, however, could have anticipated the complications of joining with the Tuckahoe Randolphs!

By summer, Jefferson seemingly accepted the couple's decision to set up housekeeping at Varina but nonetheless pressured them to postpone settling there, because Martha was "not yet seasoned to the climate" of Tidewater region where the plantation was located. He was determined "to come to Virginia in September or October and arrange their being fixed in Albemarle." But Gabriella's presence at Tuckahoe was complicating the Edgehill strategy, so Martha was sent forth as Monticello envoy in a flanking maneuver to soothe ragged emotions and cultivate social relations. The choice of such a young bride as Gabriella "may be liable to objections in point of prudence and justice," according to Jefferson; it should "not be the cause of any diminution of affection between him" and his son's family. He urged his "dear child" to "redouble [her] assiduities to keep the affections of Colo. Randolph and his lady." Martha should ingratiate herself to Randolph Senior and his new bride: "Avail yourself of this softness in him then to obtain his attachment. If the lady has anything difficult in her dispositions, avoid what is rough, and attach her good qualities to you."[19] A person's "rough" qualities should be ignored like a "bad stop in your harpsichord," and one should avoid rejecting friends just as you would "throwing away a piece of music for a flat passage or two."

"Domestic economy" was entailing more than simply keeping the "boys" in order, "sending out the meat cut up," and locking up the silver. Constructing a genteel plantation household, also, involved much more than just accumulating tangible capital in Edgehill land, dowry slaves, and appurtenances. Intangible social capital—family connections, esteem, honor, political alliances, affection, and more— were as critical as bricks, mortar, and lumber that physically distinguished the genteel planter household.[20] These were just that kind of features that had been forcefully urged on Martha and cousin Peter Carr.[21] Private esteem, public honor, and being loved by others, as her father had instructed, were markers of sentiments necessary for achieving life's happiness.[22] To further these ends, seventeen-year-old Martha, former convent student and denizen of Paris, was instructed to be "the link of love, union, and peace for the whole family" of Randolphs. But then again, there was more than magnanimous friendship at stake. The bride's father (John Harvie) owned "a good tract of land on the other side of Edgehill" near Monticello which Jefferson had been laboring several months to recover. It "may not be inadvisable to begin by buying out a dangerous neighbor," Martha's father warned her. "Besides your interests which might be injured by a misunderstanding be assured that your happiness would be infinitely affected." Her dual roles as daughter and daughter-in-law "will require peculiar attentions," so James Monroe was suggested as a "good and unsuspected hand" for inquiring about price and availability of the Harvie land.[23] Apparently the neighbor was so "dangerous" and Jefferson's need for situating his daughter nearby so urgent that eight days were all he could wait before taking independent action.

A Two-Pronged Strategy

The complex strategy he undertook in the summer is a measure of just how important it was for Martha and her father to live near each other. On July 25th, Jefferson penned five letters that reveal how family relations, business, and the dead hand of the past ensnared his plans for a physical reunion with his daughter. To his deceased wife's half-sister, Elizabeth Wayles Eppes, he made clear an intent "to bring about arrangements which may fix [Patsy] in Albemarle."[24] His "arrangements" were a two-part strategy: pursue the claim against Harvie for the parcel incorrectly surveyed and approach Randolph, Sr., as an interlocutor for the newlyweds to purchase part of his Edgehill holding inherited from Senior's mother.

There was but slight subterfuge in approaching the Randolphs. In a letter to Junior, he enclosed an unsealed one to Senior, noting he had "taken great liberties in hazarding ideas on which [his son-in-law] ought to have been previously consulted."[25] Projecting his desires and a concern for the newlyweds temporarily locating at Varina, Jefferson wrote Randolph, Sr. , to "see whether we could arrange together a matter which our children have at heart. I find it is the strong wish of both to settle in Albemarle. They both consider Varina as too unhealthy."[26]

The six hundred acres at Edgehill that Senior was considering selling to *his* father-in-law (Harvie) in order to raise *his* daughters' "portions" would suffice; moreover, the parcel would provide the bystanding son with "occupation and amusement," while the couple could use Monticello to relieve themselves of the "necessity of building and furnishing a house for some years." In addition to interposing young Randolph between his biological father and stepmother, Gabriella, in the proposed sale of 600 acres to Harvie, Jefferson opened an intricate ploy in the case of his "dangerous neighbor."

Candor had not served Jefferson well in dealing with John Harvie over the prior six months, so he undertook a more oblique approach. One subterfuge was to delay and obstruct his opponent's suit for debt against the estate of Jefferson's deceased brother-in-law, Dabney Carr. The estate's only asset available for debt recovery was a piece of land in the area of Edgehill. Still another tack was to bestow a political favor and personal encomiums on Harvie. Regarding the Carr suit, he advised attorney Nathaniel Anderson on the same day he wrote to Harvie that "every possible delay be used, because it will give more time to be receiving profits and paying off" the debt until his nephew, Samuel Carr, can come of age and "save the lands." Then, in an act of intentional deception, Jefferson claimed to be unsure who had been appointed guardian of Dabney Carr's children: he alone or jointly with another uncle, Overton Carr. If he alone (which he assuredly knew), "let them run out their tether against Mr. O. Carr," then Harvie "will have to amend [his] bill, and make me defendant." He even offered to further complicate the situation by suing his own sister Martha (Sam's mother) for committing "waste on the lands by working more hands than she ought to have done," thereby forfeiting her use of the land under the law and making her liable for treble damages.[27] So, even if Harvie was successful in his amended suit naming Jefferson as guardian, the land awarded would be encumbered by prior claims of debt subject to recovery by a nephew more amenable, perhaps, to Jefferson's scheme for locating his dear daughter near Monticello.

"Wars"—Foreign and Domestic

The fifth letter on July 25th was to Harvie himself in response to a favor he had asked of the Secretary of State regarding a contract with the national government. Jefferson denied the request but inverted the "favor." He effused his appreciation "for the occasion it's acknolegement furnishes…of resuming a correspondence which distance and business have long interrupted, but which has never wanted the urgency of motives of sincere friendship." The "dangerous neighbor" had become the object of "sincere friendship." Jefferson undertook a performance in genteel dissimulation by describing three conflicts arising from wars, their financial consequences, and his preference for peaceable outcomes.[28] There was a possible war between England and Spain that France might enter, but it might be averted through diplomacy. If not, "there will be war enough to give us high prices for wheat for years to come." The second and most fully elaborated clash referenced a consequence of war *not* diverted— national assumption of the states' Revolutionary War debts. A brief rhetorical sortie concluded his "wars" letter on a positive note regarding battles on the Georgia-Alabama frontier between white settlers and Creek tribes over land won in the Revolutionary War.[29] "McGillivray and his [Creek] chiefs are here. We hope good from this visit." In each "war" case, Jefferson averred preference for half-a-loaf over leaving conflict on the table. This tone was markedly different from his January letter to Harvie that read more like a legal brief.

The contrast of conciliatory tone and ominous topics in Jefferson's message appeared to have not been lost on Harvie; his response could apply equally to either the apparent or the deep meaning of the "wars" letter. Mimicking Jefferson's dissembling style, Harvie avoided any direct mention of their differences, but warned that assumption of war debt by the national government was a "Bitter pill" in Virginia. It "forebodes jealousy which some other Untoward proposition may kindle into a dissension dangerous to the Union."[30] But what "Union"? The States? The Jefferson family's Edgehill and Monticello tracts? The Randolph Senior and Junior families? Or the two marriages themselves?

An Unconsummated Family "Agreement"

On October 5th, Jefferson visited Colonel Randolph at his Tuckahoe plantation and believed agreement was reached for young Randolph to purchase 1600 acres of the Edgehill tract, some grain and "negroes" for £2000.[31] A wavering son-in-law had decided to "relinquish the purchase" because his father objected "to letting him take such of the slaves as he may chuse." Jefferson cautioned him that Edgehill was "really so convenient a one…ready stock and in order for furnishing…everything….nor indeed [does he] know any other purchase that can be made." It is probable the seller "means nothing more than that he will not abide by the agreement if all the articles are insisted on."[32] On the same day in a letter to the Colonel, an anxious Jefferson contradicted his July 25th proposal about the 600-acre Harvie contract and abandoned any semblance of negotiation. "I understand with much pain that you are dissatisfied with the articles of agreement…[but I do not] insist on those articles being enforced." The son and Jefferson felt "the contract should be moulded to [Randolph's] will"; he can "model the whole to [his] own mind." The Harvie issue was represented in the most ambiguous terms:

> With respect to the lands adjacent to the 1600. acres, certainly there was never a thought or word between us to the contrary of their being included. I do not mean any which your contract with Mr. Harvie extended to. I knew that that contract being prior must prevail, and meant to bargain for the residue only.[33]

Jefferson had essentially withdrawn from the field, conceding the petulant father any terms he chose, but departed with a final appeal to family heritage and owning up to his emotional investment.

> The sale being meant for a family purpose, you are a proper umpire between your son and your other children. If a contract can be adapted to your mind, I confess I have it much, very much at heart. It is impossible to find so convenient a settlement for them. They are ancient lands of your family, had got out of it, but were purchased in again by you.

The Tuckahoe patriarch could fulfill three family obligations by one sale: raise money for his daughters' portions, provide a seat for his son, and preserve the Randolph heritage in "ancient lands." His Piedmont counterpart, cousin, and in-law could sate his family's emotional needs: Martha, whose "happiness can never be compleat without [his] company"; Junior, for whom a "small farm" would provide "occupation and amusement"; and a lonely father, who felt "heavily the separation" and needed Patsy and dear Poll "to exercise…affections and chear…in the intervals of business."

The Randolph prong of his land acquisition strategy seemed uncertain, so Jefferson redirected attention to the Harvie flank eleven days later on November 2nd. Gone were vague discussions of "wars." He reiterated his legalistic argument and only slightly veiled a threat to pursue recourse in the courts. After all, both parties were "capable of understanding the law, and neither would wish to oppose it." The basis for a suit was an alleged collusion between surveyor Bryan, Jefferson's political opponent James Marks, and by implication the latter's brother-in-law, Harvie. They had "intended to effect by a juggle what could not be effected by law." He received no response from Harvie for almost three months.[34]

The orderly quadrille Jefferson had undertaken early in 1790 with his lawyer-like letter to Harvie was devolving into a ragged Virginia reel. Marriages, crafty gentlemen, political enmities long past, and to no small degree, Jefferson's urgency had muddled partners, tempos, and steps until it appeared Martha's "ambulatory life" would continue without end. In a few short months, the "dangerous neighbor" and benefactor of "sincerest friendship" had met each legal and dissembling parry with a deft sidestep. The "knot of friendship" Jefferson that anticipated would be "drawn closer and closer" by marriage had become entangled with Randolph Sr.'s inconstancy and the younger Randolph's impetuosity. Seventeen ninety ended with Monticello not hearing "how the Edgehill negotiation had terminated" with Tuckahoe.

"Domestic oeconomy"

While Jefferson was pursuing a "good tract of land" at Edgehill, and Randolph was preparing a temporary residence at Varina, Martha was struggling to get Monticello in "tolerable order," developing proper social relations in the neighborhood, and experiencing her first pregnancy. The emotional intensity of the daughter-father relationship was increased and complicated by the events of 1790. The salubrious effects of domestic "emploiments" on conjugal happiness had proven instead the bane of Martha's existence. Routine household responsibilities her contemporaries learned at their mother's apron hem were a struggle for someone whose formative years were spent in a Philadelphia boardinghouse and Paris convent.

Her father had interpreted these formal and situated learning experiences as opportunities to develop the habits of industry, persistence, and inventiveness. He had emphasized the web of relationships in which she was embedded by threads of affection that could be sustained with a family-of-letters filled with the details of daily living. Martha's father acknowledged, however, she was not prepared to assume her domain in the plantation household of a frequently absent patriarch.

On the other hand, Polly would "have opportunities of learning from [her aunt Eppes] many things of the most useful in life, which her sister also would have been the better for, had not circumstances necessarily removed her out of the way."[35] What the self-professed "vagrant" considered "more useful in life" was suggested by questions Father asked in his letters to the youngest daughter: "How many hours a day you sew? Whether you have an opportunity of continuing your music? Whether you know how to make a pudding yet, to cut out a beef stake, to sow spinach or to set a hen?"[36] Martha's maternal role model at a similar age was a forceful abbess; her household, a Bernardine convent; and the "fundamentals" of adulthood were learned from worldly European women and through a parent's letters that interpreted situations she encountered far removed from the plantation South. Years later, she would remember being educated to become "heiress of a great estate" and "learning music, &c., &c." but thought she would have been better prepared by "dexterity" with a "needle." The southern culture of hospitality demanded that the mistress "graciously, cheerfully, and efficiently" attend to maintaining proper relations with the world outside.[37] Her "plan of reading," experiences in Parisian society, and "music, &c., &c." had provided a solid ground, one visitor commented, for spending an "evening with the gentlemen" visiting Monticello and being accustomed "to join in the conversation, however high the topic may be."[38] However, running a genteel plantation household comprised of scattered locations, extended family, and several farms required much more than sociability, hospitality, and enlightened conversation. Hastily thrust into household duties, she would have to learn quickly from experience under the close attention of an absent father who was always discerning of the smallest detail.

The Monticello household was not limited to Virginia locations but had been extended to New York and Philadelphia by Jefferson's choice to continue his political life. Along with the newlyweds' unsettled life, this dispersal added significant difficulties to "domestic oeconomy." Provisioning the Virginia section with seeds, clothes, foodstuffs, furniture, and other necessities depended on its northern "agent"—the Secretary of State. He, in turn, relied on persons of "stupidity" and unpredictable coastal shipping for his supply chain. Sugar maple seeds sent from Philadelphia "failed entirely" as did all but one of *acacia farnesiana,* "the most delicious flowering shrub in the world."[39] Fifty-two yards of linen, nine yards of muslin, nine pair of cotton stockings, and other cloth for Martha's "housemaids" were shipped to Richmond in December but had not yet arrived by July the following year. "The miscarriage of the servants clothes has happened," Jefferson presumed, "from the stupidity of the person who carried them to the vessel," and he was beginning to suspect "roguery."[40] Martha asked her "Dearest Papa for a green silk calash lined with green also, as a hat is by no means proper for such a climate" as Virginia. Her "trusted" friend Eliza Trist was "so kind as to have the calash made," Jefferson reported, "but either by mistake of the maker, or of myself, it is not lined with green."[41]

Flowering shrubs and a green calash may have been optional, but the interdependency between Virginia and the northern cities extended to the necessities as well. "I am afraid you suffer inconvenience from the detention of your harness," Jefferson wrote. "[B]ut without it I could not have used my carriage till I receive my own harness from France." By December 1790, the shipping crates had arrived from Paris. Until his rented house was remodeled, however, Martha's father was "without a place to open" them, so was prevented from sending the mattresses for Monticello. "It is unlucky that the matrasses cannot be sent now," she replied, "as we shall soon be in great distress…[with] Aunt Fleming and probably one of her sons being expected here shortly."[42] The much needed mattresses were borrowed from Mrs. Nicholas Lewis and, by early 1791, Martha considered herself "far advanced" in the lady's "good graces." Good relations with neighbors are "almost the most important circumstance in life," her father wrote approvingly. "The ill-will of a single neighbor is an immense drawback on the happiness of life, and therefore their good will cannot be bought too dear."[43]

Martha's role as surrogate mother, however, was another matter. Although Sister Polly had improved her Spanish and been twice through her grammar, she proved "remarkably docile when she can surmount her Laziness of which she has an astonishing degree." Martha thought such "trifling" details would be of interest to her "Dear Papa."[44] And they were, he assured her. Such trifles would "contribute to [her] happiness," as "nothing is so engaging as the little domestic cares."[45] Just seven days after concluding her household was in "tolerable order," Martha's "little domestic cares" had multiplied with the January 23rd birth of her first child, Anne Cary. Father hoped less than three weeks later that she would soon be out to begin her garden because "nothing will tend more to give...health and strength."[46] Her efforts outside the house were understandably modest: "Polly and My self have planted the cypress vine in boxes in the window as also date seed and some other flowers."[47]

Father's letters while they were in France described how a plantation mistress would be burdened with "dull company" and far removed from outside assistance; however, he had failed to mention how her life would be affected by the household's connections with the social and commercial world outside it. Not only was Martha confronted with accommodating visiting family members, such as Aunt Fleming, but she was also sent forth to soothe dissensions at Tuckahoe between Randolph kin. In addition, she had responsibility for maintaining good relations outside the extended family with Monticello's neighbors. Instructing a teenage sister, caring for a newborn, and continuing to oversee her Father's household during 1791 left Martha little time for writing. Though infrequent, her letters were filled with details describing Polly's "habit of idleness," friends' ill-health, relatives' marriages, and when the strawberries were ripe. Each closed with the reminder to "Dearest Papa" that she was his "affectionate child."[48]

"Leisurely preparations for a settlement"

Three months after Jefferson's last letter on the subject, Harvie in January 1791 cleverly reframed their differences as "want of Recollection, or some Misunderstanding in Circumstances either in [Jefferson] or Colo. Randolph."[49] His proposed solution could not have been more unfavorable to Jefferson's two-pronged strategy for acquiring land near Monticello: "the Matter should be reffer'd to Mutual friends," rather than disinterested gentlemen of the "General Barr." Harvie's persistence was forcefully noted by recalling that the disputed tract adjoined his larger one which had been purchased from his mother, and by claiming it had "little Value" for the farming purpose Jefferson intended. He had skillfully deflected the legal rationale and confounded the process by introducing conflicted family relations into the game.

By the spring, Mann Randolph had reversed roles with his father, who "continues to press the purchase of Edgehill...and shews

so much eagerness that I have not as yet given him a decisive answer."
With the newlyweds now ensconced even more closely with him at
Monticello, Father encouraged them to "[t]ake all the time you please to
accommodate yourself with lands."[50] And fortunately so, because John
Harvie would re-enter the tangle by August. My father "appears not so
much disposed to part with Edgehill," Junior wrote, because Colonel
Harvey claims "the value of it has risen considerably."[51] The parcel had
been represented to Jefferson in January as of "very little Value," "not
more than 150 Acres can be cultivated," and the "rest is so pav'd with
Rock and Stone...as to be Altogether a Barren." The "dangerous
neighbor" seemed intent on blocking acquisition of any part of
Edgehill. Nevertheless, a day after reinforcing with Randolph, Jr., the
advantages of consummating an agreement with his father, Jefferson
countered Harvie's "family" tactic with an offer to relinquish his claim
to the portion sold by Randolph, Sr., to Harvie; he would, however,
continue his claim to acres that Marks took by "fraud and surprise"
with Bryan's "collusion." This converted the issue in Jefferson's
opinion to a legal matter that could be resolved with
"arbitrators...taken from among the judges, federal, or of the state."

Whatever transpired with Randolph, Sr. , over the remainder of
1791 is lost to history, but in January the following year Jefferson
informed his friend Philip Mazzei "my son in law...has bought
Edgehill."[52] But even that might be too far from Martha. His "ardor" to
retire would cool if he was "left alone," upon "coming home," so he
hoped they would make "only leisurely preparations for a settlement."
He would see to making them "both happier than [they] have been at
Monticello."[53] To his son-in-law, he related that Edgehill
"secures...what is essential to my happiness, our living near together."
Mann Randolph, in addition to ultimately taking his father's terms, had
apparently accepted those of his wife and father-in-law, as well:
"[T]here is nothing in the power of fortune which can add so much to
the happiness of your daughter and myself as your residence at
Monticello."[54]

"My domain"

Just a year after having the boys in "tolerable order," Martha
was frustrated with the difficulties of ruling her "domain" and
sheltering the household from intrusive neighbors. Mrs. Lewis had
provided the mattresses for Aunt Fleming's visit, but her family was
interfering in the "tolerable order" of Monticello. Martha intended to
visit young Nicholas Lewis and his new bride, but:

I have some reason to complain of the airs that family has given them selves of late with me. They find it so difficult to divest themselves of the authority they once enjoyed here that they continue to this day to exert it over every part of the enclosure to my great vexation as I look upon that to be my domain and of course enfringing upon my rights to take anything out of it with out my leave. I have how ever overlooked their impertinence with regard to that as I am determined not to fall out with them if I can possibly avoid it tho I acknowledge it hurts my pride not a little to be treated with so much contempt by those of whom I am conscious of not diserving it having allways been particularly attentive to the whole family as far as I had it in my power. I rejoice to think that this is the last year I have to put up with it.[55]

Not unexpectedly, Martha's father hoped she had visited young Mrs. Lewis and "borne with the old one so as to keep on visiting terms. Sacrifices and suppressions of feeling in this way cost much less pain than open separation." Indeed, she had attended both ladies but with faint praise considered the young one "a good little woman tho' most intolerable weak." As a near neighbor, however, she would be "worth cultivating."[56]

Martha could "rejoice" only briefly in imagining a reunion with her father. The long-promised retirement from public office—even then it would prove only a temporary one—was delayed by political events. She would have to "put up" with sustaining the household's neighborly relations and would be called into the public sphere of court proceedings to defend Monticello's much valued esteem in Virginia society.

Over the next several years until the "Revolution of 1800," the Jefferson-Randolph family would struggle to create a rudimentary plantation household that combined public service, domestic economy, and farming operations, but which was balanced dangerously on the brink of insolvency. The family within it would grow by birth, marriage, and purchase; contract by death and by sales to pay expenses and retire old debts. Martha and Father in the intervening years came to realize, but still not accept, that deep affection attached to a place could engender discord and tumult as readily as it could harmony and tranquility. Martha experienced the social complexities of a plantation household extended to aunts, uncles, cousins, and in-laws; learned to cope with the sometimes conflicting roles of devoted daughter, mother, and soother of her husband's mercurial "spirits"; endure, if not accept, separation; and to openly acknowledge how necessary Father's company was to her happiness. She learned from these experiences to deal with the emotional toll of indebtedness on her husband's adult identity, her father's diminishing patrimony, and her children's future prospects. Martha's development into a surrogate mother, wife, adult daughter, and plantation mistress had been left to her own devices and what little her father's letters could extract from situations she encountered.[57]

Chapter 6

"Blush for so near a connection":

Private Esteem and Public Honor

After two years, Martha had the domestic chores in "tolerable order," inscribed the boundaries of her "domain," and had tended to neighborly duties with the intrusive Mesdames Nicholas. She had been the "link of love" between feuding family members, when old Mr. Randolph imprudently married a teenage Gabriella Harvie—a fracas that had been discretely contained within the extended family. In the spring of 1793, the quiescence of a mountain-top refuge, victory in her garden, and cuddling two lovely children could be a welcome respite for the plantation mistress who had just endured the humiliation of another Randolph family escapade. Martha learned, however, that "so near a connection" in a family extended by affection could bring dishonor on the household and challenge its esteem in the public eye.

Martha's "considerably different" upbringing had not included a round of visitations to relatives that was typical of the late eighteenth century. Among the plantation elite, "parents allowed daughters in their late teens a time of considerable freedom before they assumed the adult responsibilities of marriage."[1] A convent school of the *ancien regime* did not afford the experiences of her near contemporary, Lucinda Lee: "[T]wo horred Mortals…seized me and kissed me a dozen times in spite of all the resistance….They really think, now they are married, they are prevaliged to do anything."[2] The Monticello Randolphs became ardent participants in the southern tradition of visitation, though perhaps not in the "dull company" Martha's father had cautioned her against while they were in Paris. Unhindered by negotiations for the Edgehill property, Martha, Mann Randolph, and ten-month-old baby Anne left Monticello in late November 1791 for a "few days"; but "the kindness of [their] friends" extended their absence to "a journey of 3 months."[3] They visited Mann's cousin: the David Randolph family at "Presque-isle." Sometime later, they moved on to the home of his sister Judith and her husband, Richard Randolph, at their plantation called "Bizarre," near Farmville, Virginia.[4] Sister Anne (Nancy) also lived with Judith after Randolph Senior married Gabriella Harvey. During these rambles among Virginia relatives, the family-of-letters was nearly silent from mid-October 1791 to late January 1792.[5]

While at Bizarre, Martha and her husband finally received on the last day of January 1792 a "packet" containing all Jefferson's letters from late November. They learned Polly (who increasingly was called "Maria") was at Mrs. Pine's Philadelphia boarding school wondering when she would be favored with a "few lines" from home and "whether dear Anne is christened yet."[6] The thirteen-year-old was being "honored with visits" from Martha Washington, Abigail Adams, Mesdames Edmund Randolph and David Rittenhouse, but was "particularly happy with Nelly Custis," granddaughter of Mrs. Washington.[7] Martha and Mann Randolph had been enjoying a genteel life in Virginia, but Father felt the despair of being separated from the people and the place he cared for the most. The Secretary of State brooded to Randolph:

> When I indulge myself in these speculations [of planting peach trees], I feel with redoubled ardor my desire to return home to the pursuit of them, and to the bosom of my family, in whose love alone I live or wish to live, and in that of my neighbors.—But I must yet a little while bear up against my weariness of public office.[8]

Just two weeks later, Martha's father would "delight" in a memory of "the various Scenes thro which [they] had passed together, in [their] wanderings over the world." The "reveries" served to "alleviate the toils and inquietudes" of his present political life, and he imagined a future at "home," where he could "once more be happy" with them.[9]

The couple planned to leave Bizarre plantation "certainly" on 5 February. Shortly thereafter, Richard Randolph's brother, Theodorick, died of consumption, though no mention of his lingering illness and bedridden condition was made in letters to Jefferson.[10] The couple and thirteen-month old daughter, Anne, returned to Monticello eleven days later, after a "tedious and disagreeable journey thro' the deepest snow within memory."[11] Because of the "dismal weather," Martha "never saw the end of anything with more pleasure in [her] life." But even freedom from unpleasantness and three months distraction from the "daily ailment" of being a "notable housewife" did not attenuate her "continual and ardent desire" of seeing her "Dearest Father." "The anxiety you express to be at home," Martha wrote, "makes me infinitely happy....I feel more and more every day how necessary your company is to my happiness." Her ambulatory life might end soon, also, for Mr. Randolph was "in possession of Edgehill. "[12]

Anne Cary (Nancy) Randolph returned her sister-in-law's visit at Monticello sometime in May 1792, perhaps to get away from the scene at Bizarre and ease the grief of having lost her "betrothed," Theodorick. She stayed until or returned with her sister Judith by 12 September, when Martha gave birth to her second child, Thomas Jefferson Randolph.[13] Late in the fall, Martha, daughter Anne—almost two and recovering from a long illness—baby Jeff, and their cousin Jane Barbara Carr were "determined to pay a visit to their friends at Bizarre...before the cold weather sets in."[14] It would prove a fateful decision, for a scandal was already afoot.

On the first day of October 1792, a party of young revelers left their ancestral home at Bizarre on the Appomattox River near the southernmost border of Cumberland County. Richard, Judith, her sister Nancy, and Richard's brother, John, were accompanied by Nancy's spurned suitor, cousin Archibald ("Archie") Randolph. They traveled north through tobacco country, arriving late in the day at Glentivar on the James River for a short visit with their cousin Mary Cary and her husband Randolph Harrison. Events over the next six days are clouded by participants' confounded motivations, internecine conflict, and the demands of defending family honor, esteem, and reputation in a genteel planter culture.[15]

Feeling indisposed, Nancy almost immediately after arriving went to bed and "appeared very unwell" when her hostess looked in after supper, but she had taken her "Gum guiacum."[16] The household was suddenly awakened during the night by agonizing screams from Nancy's room. The Harrisons rushed to her room to find Richard, "a negroe girl of about fifteen," and Nancy's six-year-old sister Virginia. They supplied "the ailing visitor with laudanum" to ease her discomfort and returned to bed. Later, the host and hostess, "while not completely awake," heard "heavy footsteps on the stairs" that they "imagined" were Richard's. From this point, the record is obscured by reconstructed memories, innuendo, and conflicting inferences.

A "Report among the negroes" on Tuesday alleged there had been a furtive miscarriage and the corpse "deposited on a pile of shingles." Mary Harrison saw blood on "the pillow case and some on the stairs." Her husband investigated the shingle pile "six or seven weeks afterwards" and found one that "appeared to have been stained." Several of the family in their court testimony seven months later recalled a "disagreeable flavor" or a "disagreeable smell" in Nancy's room but claimed at the time of the event they considered her malady "an hysteric fit, to which she was subject."[17] Attempts to contain the affair within the Glentivar, Tuckahoe, and Bizarre households were unsuccessful. Consequently, family members' memories of events and interpretations of appearances many months later were shaded by an aroused public interest.

Rumors of a scandal had been fanned in no small part by Richard's announcement in newspapers on 29 March 1793 that he would appear before the Cumberland Court to answer "any charge or crime" alleged by "any person or persons."[18] The course of events illustrates the complexities of plantation households, their dependence on social esteem, and the power that esteem confers on even the seemingly powerless servants. The scandalous story had arisen from the quarter; was embellished by relatives' observations of "heavy footsteps," "flavor," "smell," and "blood"; and associated in memory with the miscreants' expressions of fondness until the story incriminated Richard and Nancy Randolph with infanticide, incest, and a gross violation of southern honor.

As rumors escaped from the privacy of Bizarre and Glentivar into the neighborhood and beyond during the weeks and months following October 1st to 6th, Martha and her family's appearance at Bizarre in the autumn could not avoid associating the Monticello household with the alleged dishonor. Sitting at the bedside of her "little angel" at Bizarre, she despaired to her father on 18 November that little Anne's relapse placed her in "a continual state of anxiety," and her "distress" was compounded by "Mr. Randolph's absence."[19] Her unease would be only heightened by learning details of an emerging scandal but, more portentously, she might be perceived as a contributor to Nancy's misfortune.

The next spring on 29 April, Martha Jefferson Randolph was summoned into the public sphere at a packed Cumberland County courthouse to tell sixteen magistrates what she knew about the alleged infanticide and incest. Joined by a gaggle of Randolph cousins, aunts, uncles, and acquaintances, and with the skilled guidance of Patrick Henry and John Marshall, Martha was to answer the "slanderous" gossip initiated by a "negro-woman," passed around the quarter, and inflamed by Richard's own impetuous demand for a public hearing to clear his vaunted name.

John Marshall's notes on his "examination" of Martha in *Commonwealth vs. Randolph* recounted:

> In a conversation with Mrs. Richard Randolph [Judith], in presence of Miss Nancy; she [Martha] spoke of Gum Guiacum [*sic*] as an excellent medicine for the cholic, but observed at the same time that it was a dangerous medicine, as it would produce an abortion. This conversation happened about 12th September [1792]. Miss Nancy was silent but...[later] an application was made to her [Martha] by Mrs. [Carter] Page for some gum guiacum for Miss Nancy....[A] few days afterwards it was sent to her, but not in a considerable quantity. She [Martha] has known more to be given to a pregnant woman without producing mischief. She did suspect that Miss Nancy was pregnant.[20]

But how pregnant? If Theodorick was the father, as Nancy would claim in 1815, she was at least seven months into her term when Martha recommended a potentially abortive medicine. (He had died on 14 February 1792.) While this would have compromised her chaste condition—deemed so critical for a favorable marriage—it was moderately less dishonorable than incest with her sister's husband. Richard's tack was to deny there even was a pregnancy, since it would reflect negatively on him regardless of paternity. As master of the household, he was dishonored either for failing to protect Nancy, who was under his care, or for committing incest, thereby violating his marriage with Judith. By the time 29 April arrived, he had been found "guilty" at the bar of public opinion. "Impressions of wrong doing," James Monroe informed Jefferson, "were before deeply fixed."[21] John Wayles Eppes reported: "The people of Cumberland carried their prejudices so far that a strong guard was necessary to protect Mr. Randolph on his way from the prison to the court house." However, both correspondents were too optimistic in hastily concluding that the court's decision made the "accounts...universally in his favor" and he had been "acquitted with great honour."[22] Within the extensive

Randolph family linked across households in Cumberland, Albemarle, Henrico, and beyond, residue of the "Bizarre Affair" would linger for decades. After all, as Eppes observed:

> His own relations were his prosecutors and particularly active….It is a striking instance of the length to which the inveteracy and malice of relations may be carried when they once depart from that line of conduct which should be observed among near connections.[23]

Martha admitted to her father that "it is painful in an excess to be obliged to blush for so near a connection." She realized immediately that her drama-filled entry onto the stage of public scrutiny would affect the Monticello household and her family for years to come. The "poor deluded victim" has had her mind corrupted and her reputation destroyed by a "villain" and "vile seducer." Nancy would not suffer "disgrace…in the eyes of people of sense, yet the generality of mankind are weak enough to think otherwise." They gained little "honour" because "a small part of the world and those the most inconsiderable people in it were influenced…by the dicision [*sic*] of the court."[24] Martha's father had heard in Philadelphia the "rumor" about Nancy, which gave him "great uneasiness" for its effects on Martha and Mr. Randolph. For the "pitiable victim," it was a time of "trying the affection of her friends, when their commiseration and comfort become balm to her wounds." Just as he had done in the case of Gabriella, he urged the Randolphs to become "instruments not only of supporting the spirits of your afflicted friend…but of preserving her in the peace and love of her friends."[25] Martha dolefully wrote her father:

> The divisions of the family encrease daily. There is no knowing where they will end. The old gentleman [Randolph, Senior] has plunged into the thickest of them governed by the most childish passions. He lends the little weight his imprudence [in marrying Gabriella] has left him to widen the breaches it should be his duty to close. Mr. R's [Junior's] conduct has been such as to conciliate the affections of the whole family. He is the Link by which so many discordant parts join.[26]

Martha herself had "continued to behave with affection" to Nancy. "[C]ould I suppose her penitent," she wrote, "I would redouble my affection to her."

A family circle distended by affection was divided from within by an imprudent patriarch, humiliated before the public by an improvident "villain," and at least one family member "obliged to blush for so near a connection." Yet, the "pitiable" and "deluded victim" refused a "separation from her vile seducer" and remained at Bizarre amid ever increasing tensions with Judith until the "villain" died in 1806.

Martha had correctly assessed that the court decision brought more "honour" to lawyers Henry and Marshall than the parties to the sexual imbroglio, for it was in the end a matter of honor. St. George Tucker, wise in the way of Virginia gentry, thought so as well. As Richard's stepfather, he published a letter "to the public" following the court examination that read in part:

> The public mind is not always convinced by the decision of a *court of law*. In cases where the characters of individuals are drawn in question, there lies an appeal to a *higher tribunal*: A COURT OF HONOUR![27]

Personal embarrassment and family disharmony were secondary concerns to gaining, maintaining, and defending honor before "people of sense," as Martha noted. But she had learned that in the world beyond the Monticello, Bizarre, and Tuckahoe households, it was the "generality" of mankind—public opinion—who was the arbiter of personal "disgrace" and "reputation." Unlike what her father had imagined, Martha now realized private esteem and public honor were sometimes at odds with living among those whom you loved. After such an unsettling experience, she probably shared her husband's sentiments upon returning from Cumberland Courthouse to the isolation of Monticello: "Our journey has only increased our relish for retirement and our fondness for this charming spot which we quit allways with the greatest reluctance."[28]

"Cruel disappointment"

After just two years in the office to which President Washington had been "pleased to call" him, Martha's father was remembering with "delight" their experiences together in "wanderings over the world." His only reason for writing was to "indulge…in expressions of the love I bear for you." Living and remembering family experiences "alleviate the toils and inquietudes" of public service that is filled with "labour, envy, and malice." He imagined a future of "ease, domestic occupation, and domestic love and society, where [he] may once more be happy with [Martha], with Mr. Randolph, and dear little Anne." The family had returned from Paris and expanded its members but had not yet arrived home at a place envisioned as "Monticello." "The ardor of these [wishes] however would be abated," the lonely father wrote, "if I thought that on coming home I should be left alone. On the contrary I hope that Mr. Randolph will find a convenience in making only leisurely preparations for a settlement [at Edgehill] ."[29]

Financial settlement in 1792 continued to be as much of a struggle for the family as reuniting at Monticello. Randolph was "sorry" to inform Jefferson that the weevil had devastated his wheat crops in Albemarle and Bedford. It was "unfit for flour" and sold for "1/2 Dollar per Bushel." His own Varina wheat was "so injured" that purchasers refused to take it at any price.[30] By the fall, Jefferson had decided to "to sell a dozen negroes" from the Poplar Forest farm as well as "Dinah & her younger children" from Albemarle "so as to unite her to her husband." As for Caesar, who was "notorious for his rogueries" and whom Randolph had recommended for sale, the absent patriarch asked: "Would it not be practicable for you to sell their families at private sale in the neighborhood?"[31] But it was unlikely even this would settle affairs in 1792. In addition to a short wheat crop, Randolph reported by the next post that there would be "less Tobacco for market by one half" than in the previous year.[32]

As "retirement" drew near in 1793 and he expectantly looked forward to being with an even larger family, Father promised: "[W]hen I see you, it will be never to part again. In the mean time my affairs must be a burthen to Mr. Randolph."[33] Superintending from afar the farm and house construction with its mixture of enslaved and free workmen was a constant distraction to Jefferson and a bane to his son-in-law. George, the blacksmith, needed a larger bellows for work on the mill; snow delayed the carpenters in building the stable; the "slabs" for construction were bought by a "neighbouring blacksmith"; sawing the "scantling will be exactly attended" but probably not ready for house construction when Jefferson returned.[34] Matters were no less troublesome on the domestic side of the Monticello household.

When Martha's first child was born in 1791, her father had assured her that motherhood was the "the keystone of the arch of matrimonial happiness"; whereas, being a "notable housewife" was "it's daily ailment."[35] It was proving to be true for her in 1793. Only twelve of 140 bottles of cyder escaped forcing their corks—"the havoc is incredible"—and the "servants cloaths" had not yet arrived. However, Martha was "going on with great spirit in the garden," optimistic about conquering her "opponent the insect," and had added to the "accasia" and "lemmon" trees. "You will easily concieve," she wrote, "how great the satisfaction is I derive from the company of my sweet Little babies tho none but those who have experienced it can."[36]

In the fall of 1782, Jefferson had been wrenched from grieving a departed wife and from retirement to answer charges of maladministration during the British invasion of Virginia, lamenting that "public service and private misery are inseparably linked."[37] While in Paris, Patsy's father had hopefully sketched a family image in which he enjoyed "retirement from public life" and looked to her and Polly "to render the evening of life…serene and contented."[38] In 1790, Jefferson's impulse for civic virtue in answering Washington's "call" had thrust him once again into the throes of practical politics to the disappointment of loved ones and to the detriment of personal affairs. In both "retirements," all he ever claimed to have wanted was the "affection of his countrymen" and "nothing like a disapprobation of the public." The conflicting demands of public life and private affairs were heightened by expectations of impending retirement, family reunion, and disappointments at their delay.

Martha and her father also wanted more than family letters to "indulge…in expressions of love"; they wanted "never to separate again farther than Edgehill." Early in 1793, Father was "under an agitation of mind which [he] scarcely ever experienced before." A raging political mêlée would prevent returning to Monticello at the close of Congress. His "mind was fixed on it with a fondness which was extreme," but impartial friends had,

> urged that my retiring just when I had been attacked in the public papers, would injure me in the eyes of the public,…The only reward I ever wished on my retirement was to carry with me nothing like a disapprobation of the public…A circumstance which weighs on me next to the weightiest is the trouble I foresee I shall be constrained to ask Mr. Randolph to undertake.…I must therefore…get him to tell them always what is to be done and how, and to attend to the levelling the bottom [of the canal].[39]

Martha suffered no less "anxiety" for delaying the reunion they had imagined.

> It was a cruel disapointment to me who had set my heart upon the pleasure of seeing you in March never to

separate again farther than Edgehill. Having never in my life been more intent upon anything I never bore a disappointment with so little patience. ...Be assured dear and much loved Father than no one breathing possesses [my tenderest affections] more entirely than yourself.[40]

Dashed expectations "throws a gloom over our prospects of happiness this summer," Randolph wrote, and "gives no joy" at Monticello. It did, however, give him an opportunity to show his mettle to a father-in-law who considered his planned work on farm and house "too complicated to be pursued by any one less interested in it than my self."[41]

The different works over which you request my superintendance shall be forwarded with all my power and directed with all the little ability I have. My Gratitude and affection are so strong that they will come near to Self love alltho it is impossible for any motive to equal it in force.[42]

Contesting with Hamilton and staying clear of foreign war "produce daily incidents which add much to my occupations," Jefferson informed Randolph in the spring of 1793. "I am now quite unable to pay attention to my own affairs, which to be of any use should be followed up."[43] Public life had distracted him from farming and domestic responsibilities, just as his absence had diverted Randolph's attention from his own Varina plantation and delayed establishing a separate residence at Edgehill.

"Domestic occupation, domestic love and society"

Jefferson arrived home at last on 16 January 1794 to enter into yet another retirement. There was little time for the "ease" he had imagined on his return as he coped with nagging creditors, a son-in-law even more uncertain of his place in the Monticello household, and the necessity of reconfiguring farming operations. The early months would establish a pattern in which the husband was absent at Varina outside Richmond, or seeking relief from an unknown malady while Martha, her father, and the children enjoyed "domestic occupation, and domestic love and society."

Jefferson found his lands in "a degree of degradation far beyond what [he] had expected." He confided to President Washington that "10. years abandonment of them to the unprincipled ravages of overseers" would require 3. to 6. years" to rescue the "plantations from their wretched condition. Time, patience and perseverance must be the remedy."[44] Jefferson had returned to the "domestic occupation" he had longed for, thereby relieving Randolph of his many "commissions," but the wheat crop "must still be a miserable one."[45]

Matters were no better at the house. Detailed instructions the prior year for sawing lumber and construction were performed with much "dullness" while Randolph was absent from Monticello. The enslaved carpenters were "more awkward and clumsy than [Jefferson] could conceive and…really incapable of raising the coarsest building." Overseer Menoah Clarkson was "so totally ignorant of everything" but farming that "it would be better to employ some industrious white-person" to supervise the carpenters. Randolph himself had done little to allay his father-in-law's anxiety over the deranged affairs of the Monticello household:

> I shall not hezitate [*sic*] to take any step in this matter [of house construction] which it is manifest will advance your interests but shall be extremely cautious not to enter into any engagements which may not be dissolved, without giving umbrage, immediately upon you intimating your dislike.[46]

Jefferson never lacked for a plan—just frequently the wherewithal to implement it—and this "retirement" was no exception. He had advised Randolph that the 1793 season should be devoted to the canal as it "enters materially into my plan for renting my estate." The toll mill would provide a source of revenue, and when completed, attention could be turned to his "potash plan" to provide a "resource of money subsidiary to the farm." He intended to look for farm and mill tenants in Maryland. However, there were other demands on his resources. A "mason and house joiner from Scotland" would arrive soon and must have "something which may employ them" until he arrived home. Canal construction was to be interrupted so workmen could assist the mason in "cutting columns for the porticoes" of the house. Making "10. window frames" and sharpening the "old set of tools" would occupy the joiner. People as well as things would have to be rearranged on the mountaintop: "As I destine the stone house for [white] workmen, the present inhabitants must remove into…the new log houses." Implementing the plan, however, was left to the twenty-five-year-old Randolph: "[B]e so good as to marshal the troops & their employment as you please. If they are always employed, the order in which things are done will be less material."[47]

The spring and summer of 1794 found Jefferson busy hiring a Scottish gardener, Robert Bailey; commencing a nail operation to escape his financial straits; installing Eli Alexander of Elkton, MD, as Shadwell tenant; traveling to Richmond for two weeks to meet with creditors and confer with Francis Eppes on the Wayles debt payments. From early May to mid-September, Patsy, as he noted her in his memorandum books, was regularly receiving money for "small exp."[48] Meanwhile, her husband had left Monticello sometime in mid-July to seek the palliative of a sea voyage for some indeterminate illness that was to persist for the two years of Jefferson's temporary retirement at Monticello.[49]

Randolph wrote from "Hughes," (somewhere between Monticello and Richmond) on 15 July and the next day from Richmond. By the 28th, he was in Norfolk, in New York a week later on 5 August, then on to Boston. Randolph's health and Jefferson's public service were making it difficult to live the family they imagined or even to sustain a family-of-letters. "It has been impossible to write to you in return," Jefferson explained, "on account of the rapidity & incertainty of your movements." Nevertheless, the family ideal had not been abandoned:

> Be assured we are all tenderly anxious for your recovery
> and return. We are fully satisfied that the most solid of
> all earthly happiness is of the domestic kind, in a well
> assorted family, all the members of which set a just
> value on each other, and are disposed to make the
> happiness of each other their first object. The void
> occasioned by your departure is sensible to us all; we are
> impatient to see it filled again…[50]

The "void" was filled (temporarily at least) in late summer with the birth of the couple's third child, Ellen Wayles Randolph, on 30 August 1794. By late October, however, only Grand Papa, two-year-old Jeff, and his sister Anne Cary, almost four, remained at Monticello, and the children had "leant to say 'Mama is gone'."[51]

On each return from his health expeditions, Randolph was re-engaged by his father-in-law in a host of commissions on top of his own continuing and unsuccessful efforts to clear the Varina debt by selling land. While in Richmond in late October 1794, he was to "ascertain the price of wheat"; determine the monetary "exchange between Richmond & Liverpool"; see to the "hire of four negromen...on advantageous terms"; "pay £141–16 currency...to Mr. Lyle"; and forward clover seed "by the first safe waggon."[52]

"A ruinous condition"

Recovering his health and attending to the details of the household's seat at Monticello left Randolph little time for overseeing the outlying Varina farm. The couple arrived there in January 1795 to find "everything...in such a ruinous condition," Martha told her father, "that it is impossible to say what stay we shall be forced to make."

> The monstrous crop of wheat which was represented to be 3000. bushels has dwindled away to 800[.] most of the corn out still at the mercy of thieves hogs birds &c. and in short everything in such disorder that Mr. Randolph has been obliged to discharge the overseer and take the management of the plantation in to his own hands.[53]

A "doleful" report from Poplar Forest overseer Bowling Clarke did not brighten the prospects for improving the household's financial affairs: "a much shorter crop of tobacco" and "loss of horses."[54] Martha and her husband sometime in late-spring returned to Monticello from their unsuccessful attempt to satisfy their creditors, only to depart soon in search of a remedy for Randolph's persistent ailment.[55] Jefferson remained home with his sisters Bolling, Carr, and Marks who were suffering variously from rheumatism, ague, and dysentery.[56] The Randolphs' eleven-month-old Ellen was reunited with her Monticello family in its graveyard. "We all join in love to you both," Jefferson consoled the father, "and trust you are looking forward with hope to the restoration of your own health and as early a return to us as is consistent with that. God bless you both."[57] Grand Papa's letter five days later to daughter Martha made no mention of their loss, but did express his willingness to have a "homeless" Nancy Randolph get away from Bizarre and take up residence at Monticello—"a mere hospital of sick friends"—provided it was not "disagreeable" to her and Mr. Randolph. There was no word from the travelers. "We have had no letter from you since your arrival at the Warm-springs," Father reminded Martha, "but are Told you are gone on to the sweet springs." And to Randolph eleven days later: "We have no letter from you since that from Staunton [on 6 August]...We are very anxious to hear from you both."[58]

From August 16ᵗʰ to September 14ᵗʰ, Randolph dutifully maintained a meteorological record at Sweet Springs, where temperatures ranged from 63 to 86 degrees accompanied by rain, "slight showers," and about as many cloudy days as fair ones. The therapeutic benefits of their long absence from home are lost with Randolph's letters from this period.[59]

Illness and even death did not detract from the vital position farming and political affairs held in the family's life. Rainy weather, the pervasive Hessian weevil, and a "terrible storm" had conspired to lay the corn "prostrate" and reduce the wheat yield to "but 32 bushels to the acre." Scilla, a slave at Edgehill, was sick with dysentery. The flurry of opposition to the proposed Jay Treaty was in full boil in central Virginia. Albemarle County citizens met to express their opposition to "the monument of folly or venality," and surrounding counties would soon follow that lead.

There was neither a family-of-letters, a life of "ease," or "domestic society," but Jefferson maintained appearances before the world outside the Monticello household. He told friend Madison in the spring of 1795 that considering public office—including the presidency—was "for ever closed." His health was "broken down," age required that he put his private "affairs in a clear state," and the "delights" of family and farming were not to be abandoned. With "patience and perseverance," his "agricultural plan" would be accomplished.[60] He had "returned home" from Philadelphia, he resolutely told Mazzei, "with an inflexible determination to leave it no more." With Martha, her family, and Polly living with him, they comprised a "considerable domestic society," and he had "become the most ardent and active farmer in the state."[61] While his beloved Martha was away with her ailing husband, Jefferson blissfully drew an image for their friend Eliza Trist that belied his lonely situation.

> I am become the most industrious farmer in the world: and never had reformer greater obstacles to surmount from the barbarous mode of culture and management which had been carried on. I read but little. Take no newspapers, that I may not have the tranquility of my mind disturbed by their falsehoods and follies, and I have it in contemplation next to banish pen, ink, and paper from my farm....The society of my family and friends is becoming more and more the sole object of my delight...[62]

The firm disavowal to Madison and the contented quiescence Jefferson expressed to Trist and Mazzei were brief and would be violently disturbed by the approaching presidential election that thrust his private affairs and past politics before a critical public eye. Not even the autumnal beauty of Virginia could hide the ominous visit Jefferson reported to Wilson Cary Nicholas: "Colo. Burr left this two or three days ago, after a stay of one day." The campaign for presidential electors had begun; political parties would soon follow.[63]

Indeed, the prospect of settling his youngest daughter intensified Jefferson's fear of disturbing his "tranquility of mind" with political affairs. In the fall of 1796, Maria's cousin, John (Jack) Wayles Eppes in whose family she had lived until Paris "ventured to indulge and express sentiments, for a part of [Jefferson's] family."[64] Young Eppes trumpeted his success two months later by proclaiming that "all obstacles to [his] happiness" were removed. Probably the most striking chord to the father's sentiments was the suitor's pledge that "in every arrangement as to future residence, I shall be guided by yourself and Maria."[65] When the couple married a year later, Jefferson's drawn-out experience in trying to purchase Edgehill for Martha dissuaded him from a similar tactic for Maria. The couple was given 819 acres at "Pantops," just across the Rivanna from Monticello, the "Lego" farm of unspecified size, and thirty-one slaves listed by name.[66] He was certainly discouraged by impecunious conditions from adding to the household's Albemarle holdings.

Jefferson had been cautious in drawing the marriage settlement for his eldest daughter in 1790. He even delayed assuming the post of Secretary of State. Carefully drawn legal documents executed at the proper time and correctly recorded by Albemarle's clerk of court were insufficient warranty against volatile commodity markets, inexperienced farm management, a son-in-law distracted by Jefferson's many "commissions" and suffering from an unknown malady that affected his "spirits." Martha's father had concluded Randolph's chronic malady was "gout, because no other disease is so long in declaring itself, and because [he had] a hereditary expectation of that." The cure would not be found at the springs or in restorative sea air but, rather, through *vis medicatrix naturae* accompanied by moderate exercise and "soberly" eating. The more troublesome effect of the disease on Randolph's "spirits…[was] merely mechanical" and could be remedied by "the force of reason & confidence."[67] Varina's "ruinous condition," as Martha had reported in January 1795, was little improved after the couple's extended absence at Virginia's therapeutic springs and their failed effort at clearing the debt through land sales. So, the couple again would "spend some months" at Varina in early 1796 and Martha needed "articles" from the household's center at Monticello.[68] Young Jeff, his Grand Papa claimed, "often repeats that [his mother] told a story," when she left for Varina and reassured him she would come back.

"The future fortunes…of descendents"

Despite the felicitous life Jefferson portrayed to Eliza Trist, financial affairs continued to plague the "industrious farmer" and cast a net over the enslaved "souls" of his family. Still another creditor of the Wayles estate, Robert Cary & Company, was pressing for settlement, and co-legatee Francis Eppes had arranged in 1796 a three-payment agreement. Jefferson agreed to whatever could be arranged and offered to "give security too by a mortgage on negroes…the first mortgage [he] ever gave."[69]

Nor was his "tranquility…of mind" undisturbed by the "falsehoods and follies" of political intrigue. Aaron Burr's secretive visit to the reclusive farmer in the fall of 1795 and Jefferson's divisive letter to Mazzei earlier that year became issues in selecting Virginia's Presidential electors. Political opponents accused Jefferson of conspiring to subvert the Jay Treaty after its ratification. A "Freeholder" from James City County publicly charged that his responsibility for the Wayles debt held by European firms made him subject to foreign influence, and therefore, an unsuitable candidate. The charges regarding private debt and political scheming were of sufficient concern to produce two depositions denying the charges. One swore there were "no suits instituted" for debt in the U. S. District Court; another disingenuously swore that no "political character" was at the meeting of Messrs. Jefferson and Burr, only "some female relations…the gentleman of his family" and a neighbor.[70]

The discomfort of debt and the follies of politics were only exacerbated by the contrast to happy prospects anticipated by Maria's courtship. Her suitor had generously agreed to settle wherever it pleased his betrothed and her father. The notice of their marriage in early 1797 filled Jefferson with "inexpressible pleasure"; it relieved the "only anxiety…remaining" after Martha's "happy establishment" and her gift of an "inestimable friend to whom [he could] leave the care of everything" he loved. A near reverie fueled his imagination of a "fireside formed into a groupe, no member of which has a fibre in their composition which can ever produce any jarring or jealousies." There would be "[n]o irregular passions, no dangerous bias, which may render problematical the future fortunes and happiness of [their] descendents." The tranquil family could be "quieted as to [the children's] condition for at least one generation more."[71] It only remained to settle the newlyweds nearby at Pantops, but the "follies" of politics, a dispirited Randolph, and a daughter unsure of her father's affection would shatter this vision as well.

Republican Daughter and Wife

The complexity of being both a republican daughter and wife is aptly illustrated by Randolph's first run for office in the spring of 1797, just a few weeks after Martha's father assumed the vice-presidency. Jefferson arrived home from being sworn in early March expecting another family reunion, only to find Maria and Martha at Varina with the newly born Ellen, and Mr. Randolph in Richmond having Anne and Jeff inoculated for small pox. Her father was "impatient" to know if Martha had recovered from her illness, but he had "confidence in the dose of health…which Monticello" would give. Her presence, in turn, would dispel his emotional gloom.

> The bloom of Monticello is chilled by my solitude. It makes me wish the more that yourself and sister were here to enjoy it. I value the enjoiments of this life only in proportion as you participate them with me. All other attachments are weakening, and I approach the state of mind when nothing will hold me here but my love for yourself and sister and the tender connections you have added to me. I hope you will write to me: as nothing is so pleasing during your absence as these proofs of your love. Be assured my dear daughter that you possess mine in it's utmost limits.[72]

Being together in a particular place was essential to "enjoiments." Even the blooms of a Monticello spring could not solace the loneliness of being physically separated from "tender connections." Father's love for Martha was the sustenance of life itself; Monticello the place where life and love flourished; and while apart, it was their letters that reaffirmed the deep affection they shared. Martha was "perfectly miserable" at not being with her children during their inoculation. But she concurred with her father in projecting an intangible emotional state onto a physical place.

The anxiety I feel on their [the children's] account my Dear Father does not prevent my feeling most sensibly for the solitude and gloom of your present situation. I never take a view of your solitary fire side but my heart swells. However as nothing detains us now but the children I hope soon [to] be restored to your paternal embraces and dispel by the presence of your children the cloud which obscures the beauties of spring, no where so enchanting as at Monticello.[73]

In arguing for the new family's settlement at Edgehill in 1790, Jefferson had assured Randolph he "might get into the assembly for that county [Albemarle] as soon as you should please."[74] At this early juncture in their relationship, he probably was wholly unaware of his son-in-law's impetuous nature, even though the abrupt withdrawal from Edinburgh should have given ample pause for concern. Randolph ran for the House of Delegates in the spring of 1797, just a few weeks after Jefferson assumed the vice-presidency, but lost what was considered a sure election because he failed to follow the customary practice of campaigning at the Charlottesville courthouse during polling.

[It] gave much uneasiness and embarrassment to your friends to be unable to give any account of you. It made a serious impression even on the zealous; and I have this day written a circular letter, with the apologies your letter furnished, addressed to every militia captain for his company, which I hope will set the thing to rights.

Jefferson admonished the reluctant campaigner that he "should possess the affections of the people [rather] than that you should make use of them." The public's "esteem will contribute much to [his] happiness," but it is questionable whether office holding would do the same. The same day her father wrote to Randolph, Martha was encouraged to "come up" from Varina with Maria and little Ellen, leaving her husband behind. He would have the "pleasure of seeing" her and could "make better arrangements for [her] accomodation" during his absence in Washington.[75]

Perhaps, it was having "female relations" present during the Burr visit, or the debt from his wife's inheritance becoming an election issue. Possibly, five years in national politics had weakened the impenetrable barrier Jefferson had drawn mentally between private affairs and the public sphere, or he may have come to realize just how women might be a part of his oblique, non-confrontational style of political action. Regardless, the newly-elected Vice President wrote the sister-in-law of political nemesis Alexander Hamilton. The political "agitations of Europe have reached even us," he admitted to Angelica Schuyler Church, "and here, as there, they are permitted to disturb social life…we have not yet learnt to give everything to it's proper place, discord to our senates, love and friendship to society." He was confident her "temper and inclination" would follow the "happy privilege of the ladies, to leave to the rougher sex, and to the newspapers, their party squabbles and reproaches."[76] The ensuing years on the national stage would reveal whether Jefferson's neat, rhetorical division was more a work of imagination than a reality in the New Republic.

"Save us & our children from beggary"

Jefferson's victory would require a resumption of the defeated candidate's duties as executive overseer of the Monticello household. However, seven years of many "commissions," both large and small, had not added to Mann Randolph's confidence. "[H]aving in considerable degree a recurrence of [his] old nervous symptoms," he proffered his aid but disparaged his capacity:

> If I can in any way whatever be of use to you in your Albemarle or any other affairs I claim the service tho' I cannot help feeling that my frequent neglects and the weakness of my character should make me forfeit that honor.

The family's emotional dynamic at this time was aptly captured in the agitated closing penned by an anxious son-in-law:

> Tell my Dear Martha that I shall hasten as much as I can [to Monticello] without disabling myself from enjoying my family when I do meet it; the remembrance of the horrors of 94 and 95 makes me extremely cautious: I should shun them by embracing death if it could be done no other way. With the most sincere affection…[77]

Indeed, he had cause for "nervous symptoms"! In June 1797, British creditors were awarded $64,000 in a suit against Randolph Senior's estate with $42,000 assessed against the already heavily indebted properties of Mann Randolph and his brother William.[78] The marriage settlement of legacy debt on the Monticello household was continuing to derange its financial affairs.

Father's "marriage" letter to Martha in April 1790 emphasized the shared affection that bound the expanded family together and her spousal duty to "please" Mr. Randolph in everything. Maria, like her sister, was advised that "affections" and "harmony in the marriage state" were the principal features of family life that were accomplished by "a firm resolution never to differ in will." This was the imagined family Jefferson had so ardently described to young Patsy during their years in Paris. However, seven years of living with a hollow marriage settlement, demanding foreign creditors, wildly fluctuating commodity prices, and reliance on a dispirited son-in-law had added a critical consideration to household sustainability.

> [B]ut before I finish the sermon, I must add a word on economy. The unprofitable condition of Virginia estates in general, leaves it now next to impossible for the holder of one to avoid ruin. and this condition will continue until some change takes place in the mode of working them. in the mean time nothing can save us & our children from beggary but a determination to get a year before hand, & restrain ourselves rigorously this year to the clear profits of the last. if a debt is once contracted by a farmer, it is never paid but by a sale.[79]

If her father was to "open and resettle the plantation at Pantops" for Maria so they could be "all together" as planned, the household's economic situation and emotional dynamic would become even more entangled. Just as they had been parted only by the Seine in Paris, the family would be reunited at a place they conceived of as "Monticello." Their household, however, would span the Rivanna, reach to the banks of James in Henrico and Chesterfield, and stretch its resources nearly to the Blue Ridge in Bedford. The ebullient father knew well from experience the practical difficulties of nourishing affections and sustaining finances in such a situation.

"A Consular commission"

Jefferson's efforts for seven years to direct farming and domestic activities from afar through detailed instructions to overseers had cast Randolph into ambiguous roles. Neither master nor overseer, he was called upon to intercede during times of crisis, to be an intermediary without direct authority regarding overseers, and to undertake many private commissions in legal and financial matters. When overseer Clarke was late in shipping tobacco from Poplar Forest, it was Randolph who was to see to "getting it down." The shipment of trees and shrubs was to be planted in particular locations at precise spacing within a defined time period.

> I endeavored to arrange my matters so as to prevent your being troubled with them as I am conscious you have been. yet should anything unexpected embarras them I must just give you the Consular commission 'to see that the republic recieves no damage'.[80]

Then and over the next few weeks, Randolph was "troubled" with finding a book on drawing for builder Dinsmore; sending a diamond cutting tool to James Madison; locating "as soon as possible" someone to estimate the rent due on Mr. Eppes's "negroes" for the prior year; forwarding a chimney piece to Philadelphia via George Jefferson; and considering sale of Varina to someone from Europe who is looking for "fine tracts of land...on the James river, below the falls."[81]

The Randolph family stayed at Monticello following Jefferson's departure for Philadelphia in late 1798 and finally returned to their rented estate in early January until he returned. Shuffling between Belmont and undertaking the many commissions, Randolph reported: "Your affairs at Monticello go on as usual—I shall visit it frequently and interpose with authority if at any time that should be necessary."[82] But even John Harvie's Belmont just up the road was not close enough for Jefferson: "I wish you to be where you can be in greatest comfort yourselves. It would have been an additional gratification to me if the accommodations at Monticello could have been instrumental to it."[83]

Sustaining a Family Through Letters

Despite an orderly schedule and efforts to establish a "regular post" funded by the government, the demands of public office, house, and farm made it nearly impossible to maintain a ritual that bridged the fissure between a lived and an imagined family. Three letters exchanged between Martha, her husband, and Father in early 1798 typify the themes of affection, place, debt, and the political public sphere that permeated their family-of-letters during the entire decade. House construction, farm reformation, and ordering of domestic affairs that Jefferson had undertaken at his "retirement" in 1793 were exacting their toll on the family.

Expanding the Monticello household to include nearby residences for the girls was fraught with delay, shortage of money, and unfavorable weather. Maria's husband "despaired of settling at Pantops this year [1798] every person in his neighbourhood who had negroes to hire refusing to let them come up to Albemarle."[84] Neither were matters improving for Martha finally having a permanent home. At Belmont a few miles away from the mountain, she was physically closer to Monticello than at Varina, but still not near enough to enjoy the health benefits father in 1790 had averred for that "up country" place.

> The extreme dampness of the situation and an absolute want of offices of every kind to shelter the servants whilst in the performance of their duties, have occasioned more sickness than I ever saw in a family in my life. pleurisie, rhumatism, and every disorder proceeding from cold have been so frequent that we have scarcely had at any one time well enough to tend the sick.[85]

The Belmont house was more than just damp. "[T]he cellar after every rain is full of water." The situation threatened a relapse in Randolph's malady. His health had "suddenly begun to decline when [he had] considered it as absolutely confirmed and had assumed all the habits of full vigor."[86]

Projects for rebuilding the mountain-top house and re-forming the farm continued to resist the blizzard of written instructions from the absentee patriarch. Mr. Randolph bemoaned that "insubordination" at Monticello and "discontent" at Shadwell among the workers had "greatly cloged their operations." He had seven years' experience as "executive overseer," nevertheless remained uncertain about the extent to which he could "command the usual functions." He had not "hezitated to interfere [at Monticello and Shadwell] tho' without authority I have made known to all I had none that my interference if not productive of wholesome effects might be rejected."[87]

"Monticello shines with transcendent luxury"

Matters were no better for commencing construction at the Edgehill location. The soil was "so retentive of moisture," Randolph complained, "that our yard is mud to the ankles long after the red land has dried perfectly."[88] He foresaw "no hope of geting farther than one flank of my house next summer—that I must make a sacrifice in my crop to obtain and will, for one flank with a temporary roof must be our habitation next winter."[89] They had no money in Richmond to buy "a game of goose" that mother had promised the children. But there should be enough in Philadelphia, Martha thought, to "lay out" for that and some "plate, table spoons, tea spoons &c," despite "the many other urgent calls for money building [at Edgehill] will occasion." Almost eight years after marriage, Martha still did not have a home, other than a disheveled Monticello and a flooded Belmont, nor the rudimentary accoutrements. These privations paled in comparison to the company she longed for to complete her happiness: "I feel every day more strongly the impossibility of becoming habituated to your absence."[90]

Their complaints of primitive and unhealthy living conditions were just the opening Father needed to once again insist on their ultimate "plan." To draw her still closer, rescue her family from their unhealthy situation at Belmont, and to alleviate Mr. Randolph's riding to and fro, he urged:

> [S]urely, my dear, it would be better for you to remove to Monticello. the south pavilion, the Parlour & Study, will accomodate your family;...let me beseech you then to go there, and to use everything & every body as if I were there. I shall anxiously hope to hear that you adopt this plan. [91]

Martha obligingly voiced the affectionate sentiment her father desired and attached it to a specific place.

> Nothing makes me feel your absence so sensibly as the beauty of the season; when every object in nature invites one into the fields, the close monotonous streets of a city which offers no charms of society with in doors to compensate for the dreariness of the scene with out, must be absolutely intolerable: particularly to you who have such interesting employment at home. Monticello shines with a transcendent luxury of vegetation above the rest of the neighbourhood...[92]

She considered herself "blest" in her family at home, but Father was "still wanting to compleat [her] happiness." When they are united, "Monticello will be interesting indeed."[93] Reports of a late frost, the death of Aunt Fleming, Jeffy's two-mile walk to Mr. Sneed's school, and other details of her life had their desired effect: "[B]y kindling up all my recollections," Father replied, her letter "increases my impatience to leave this place & everything which can be disgusting, for Monticello and my dear family, comprising everything which is pleasurable to me in this world."[94] Yet, this pleasure would be enjoyed only intermittently over the next decade. So daughter and father would continue to rely of their epistolary ritual to share the details of separately lived lives, to affirm their mutual affection, and to longingly anticipate what they imagined would be their final reunion at a place called "Monticello."

An Imagined & Lived Family

A year into his vice-presidency in 1798, Martha's father eloquently explained how their letter ritual was a means of sustaining a family imagined as counterpoised to the family they were living apart. Father's situation was filled with "the worst passions," and Martha was experiencing "more sickness than [she] ever saw in a family."[95] Under such conditions, their letters were even more vital to sustaining the family they envisioned. Martha's writings altered his emotions and the mood of his situation. They stimulated "very great pleasure...especially when they express [her] affections," which he loved to hear repeated. They were "gleams of light, to chear a dreary scene, where envy, hatred, malice, revenge, & all the worst passions of men are marshaled to make one another as miserable as possible." He remembered an evening at her fireside and valued it "worth more than ages" in the political life he endured. Her father expectantly imagined a reunion at Monticello in the spring "with all the fondness of desire to meet you all once more, and with the change of season, to enjoy also a change of scene & of society."[96]

Immediately on arriving home in the spring, Maria's father wrote that her "sister came over with me from Belmont...[T]he family will move over the day after tomorrow....We want nothing now to fill up our happiness but to have you & mr Eppes here." But apparently two visits by Mr. Randolph in as many months were insufficient to look after enclosing a family space from the weather. "[S]carcely a stroke has been done towards covering the house since I went away," Jefferson bemoaned, "so that it has remained open at the North end another winter. it seems as if I should never get it inhabitable."[97]

Three months passed. Martha and family at last were ensconced at Monticello; Mr. Eppes was tending to affairs near Petersburg; and Maria was keenly aware her failure to write for so long gave her father "displeasure." It had not been from "forgetfulness," though a measure of "indolence" may have been operating, but rather the distance from their Mont Blanco residence to the Petersburg post afforded only "rare opportunitys." In the future, her letters would "prove...that tender love which I can never express which is interwoven with my existence." What continued to remain merely a hope was that her husband would

126

"build up there [at Pantops] & we shall then allways be one of the first to welcome your arrival." Maria had endorsed her father's claim that Monticello is more healthful than "down country," for the "sallow complexion of my neighbors & their own complaints…are sufficient proofs of the unhealthiness of the country" surrounding the tidal region near Petersburg.[98]

Deaths in the "Family"

The specter of death haunted the Monticello family in the year of its master's political "revolution," and reminded them just how tenuous were the ties of affection and bondage. First, there was news from Martha about casualties in the slave quarter. Her father's longtime personal slave, Jupiter, consulted with "a negro doctor," whose "dose" threw him into "convulsions" and brought his death nine days later. He "has fallen a victim to an imprudent perserverance [sic] in journeying," Jefferson wrote Randolph. "I was extremely against his coming to Fredsbg [Fredericksburg] with me."[99] He was "sorry," because even "with all his defects" Jupiter's death created a "void" in the household's "domestic arrangements." It would fall to Martha or Randolph to oversee bottling "cyder" and retrieving any keys entrusted to Jupiter.[100]

Maria's pregnancy had not been an easy one. Letters in the late summer and fall had repeatedly noted her poor health that had prevented their reunion on the Mountain top. In the throes of political maneuvering, Jefferson reminisced with Maria about the "happy domestic society when together at Monticello." For "no society gives me now any satisfaction," Maria's father wrote, "as no other is founded in sincere affection.…[M]y happiness rests solely on yours and that of your sister & your dear connections."[101] The following day, January 18th, Grand Papa learned that "fortune has at length crowned" John and Maria Eppes with a daughter born the last day of 1799.[102] The successful birth filled his heart with the "purest joy," and at the same time assuaged his "anxiety on that subject" arising from Maria's difficulties. News of the new baby girl was "a balm to the painful sensations of politics," Father confided to Martha. "I look forward with hope to the moment when we are all to be reunited again."[103] It was not to be.

Baby Eppes had died the day before on January 17th, and Maria was dangerously ill with inflamed breasts. "My heart," Martha sorrowfully told her father, "is torn by an event which carries death to hopes so long & fondly cherished by my poor sister."[104] He would not even attempt to console Maria, as "time & silence are the only medecines," but his "tranquility" depended on hearing often from her. "I feel inexpressibly," he disclosed, "whatever affects either your health or happiness. My attachments to the world and whatever it can offer are daily wearing off, but you are one of the links which hold to my existence."[105]

The "link" would remain in the letters they exchanged and not the physical proximity of Pantops. The Eppes family had chosen to develop their marriage portion some ninety miles distant at Bermuda Hundred in Chesterfield County; meanwhile Martha, pregnant and with four children, had moved from Belmont to Edgehill in late 1799 to be even closer to Monticello. Matters of correspondence would be improved at Bermuda Hundred, even though "the house was not in a very comfortable state" with carpenters still working and only two rooms completed. Maria was "in anxious suspence about the election" but would "endeavor to be satisfied in the happiness" a Jefferson Presidency would "give to so many." There could be "no greater felicity," however, than to be with dear Papa "forever."[106]

Household, Family & Public Sphere

Events late in the decade typify just how the household, family, and politics intersected through the effect of foreign relations on tobacco prices that, in turn, intensified the anxiety over both legacy debt and current expenses. The obstacles that foreign crises put in the way of family reunions at Monticello were corollaries to (and frequently the same as) those that left the household's financial condition suspended between hopefulness and disappointment. The political fever roused by the "war-men" in Philadelphia delayed Jefferson's reunion with his family in the summer of 1798; it also "induced" him to accept immediately $13 per hundred weight for tobacco, "as a war with France, or even the invasion of England may check the price for this summer."[107]

Jefferson was more sanguine the next year about potential downward pressure on tobacco prices as a result of foreign affairs. Despite increased domestic supplies from Georgia and South Carolina, he optimistically predicted the "price will be at it's maximum...whether that will be more than 13. D. I do not know, but I think it will." This confidence was predicated on British disrupting tobacco shipments from Spanish colonies, which would increase demand for Virginia leaf. What he had not figured, however, were the effects of America's non-intercourse law and the British shipping "monopoly."[108] By May 1799, he "was astonished at the stagnation of the price of tobo. in London."

He wrote George Jefferson, his Richmond commission agent. "I find I can clear 10 D."[109] It finally sold later that year for $7 with payments extended over ten months.[110] On 30 October 1799, Jefferson wrote to the lawyer handling the Wayles debt, Littleton Waller Tazewell, that he would once again be late in making his $1,000 installment. He felt "unlucky" in not selling earlier in anticipation of a price rise from $11. "[I]n the meantime it has so fallen as to give me little hope of a tolerable price unless the exportation to France should be permitted."[111]

In Randolph's mind, there were lifelong consequences to speculating on higher prices, as his father-in-law had recommended.

> I cannot express the feelings your kindness excites: I was really on the point of ruin from my own neglect: I knew all along that I should not have one moment when the Varina debt <u>did</u> come on me [for payment] & should have sold my Tob'o. in full time to meet it if I had acted wisely: but a great price for that crop rendered me perfectly easy for life & I risked ruin with the hope of obtaining it & I fear have procured embarrassment for life...My crop on hand I am compelled to sell immediately for I counted too much on high prices for produce & made contracts which I shall be rendered unhappy by, but I believe I may (if I do not lose my health,) by exertion get through without a sale; if the absolute necessity I shall now be under for years, of Selling my crops as soon as I can get them to market does not curtail too much my annual income.[112]

Matters had been only slightly better for his father-in-law. Even his disappointing returns were not reserved to pay on the Wayles debt due June 1; rather, they were diverted from creditors for payment to Randolph's Varina debts. After ten years of marriage and in his early thirties, co-mingled debt had made the young man even more financially dependent on his father-in-law. Both had delayed marketing crops based on Jefferson's optimistic discounting of domestic and foreign political events. "[T]hus ends this tragedy by which we have both lost so much," he summarily wrote his distressed son-in-law.[113] For young Randolph, however, it was not the end but an "embarrassment for life." "I would rather have lost the land," he disclosed, "if I had not considered my family: my own feelings would have sacrificed it.[114] Perhaps Jefferson's rescue of Varina was considering the family as he imagined it at Monticello. "I observe

Varina advertised. how does that matter stand?" Uncertainty in politics and markets was the enemy of ordered affairs and of the independent plantation household sheltering a family of affection.

"Sentiment of tenderness" & "Republican principles"

The order he had tried to put in his "affairs" in 1790 with the Farell and Jones agreement on the legacy debt from Wayles; the "bosom of family" he had struggled to place in the Monticello household; and the protection of "said Martha and her heirs" that was attempted with the marriage settlement incorporating a heavily mortgaged Varina were all devolving into a serious derangement of the household. Social and political affairs increasingly were injected into the intimate family sphere. Martha complained about "the concourse of strangers which continually crouded the house" before her father left for Washington to endure thirty-six ballots and be elected President in 1801. He reminded her that "to have the intercourse of soft affections hushed & suppressed by the eternal presence of strangers...[was] evidences of the general esteem which we have been all our lives trying to merit."[115] Enduring visitors, even at the expense of family "tranquility," "peace and harmony," was just one of the personal behaviors and dispositions contributing to the lifelong search for social esteem. In father's mind, after all, the lived family had become a party to his participation in the political public sphere. To Maria, her father claimed his happiness would be in "the moment" they could "all be settled together, no more to separate"; however, that condition could be secured only in the political public sphere.

> I feel no impulse from personal ambition to the office [Presidency] now proposed to me, but on account of yourself & your sister, and those dear to you. I feel a sincere wish indeed to see our government brought back to it's republican principles, to see that kind of government firmly fixed; to which my whole life has been devoted. I hope we shall now see it so established, as that when I retire, it may be under full security that we are to continue free & happy.[116]

Even when her father was home, Maria was "afraid I shall lament more than ever the distance which separates me from Monticello as I fear it will be an obstacle not allways to be surmounted."[117]

The one "truth" that sustained Martha and her father throughout their travails expanding the Monticello household, enduring Mr. Randolph's inconstancy, and painful separations was the deep and unassailable bond of affection they had formed many years prior and their expectation of some day expressing it in person at a place called "Monticello." As Martha starkly confessed:

> I feel every day more strongly the impossibility of becoming habituated to your absence—sepparated in my infancy from every other friend, and accustomed to look up to you alone, every sentiment of tenderness my nature was susceptible of was for many years centered in you, and no connexion formed since that could weaken a sentiment interwoven with my very existence.... believe me with every sentiment of tenderness, gratitude and respect your affectionate child...[118]

Until their reunion, a family-of-letters would have to suffice.

Chapter 7

"Dreary and monotonous":

The Quandary of Private Happiness & Public Duty

Just four months into her father's presidency, near full term again, mothering four children aged two to ten, and hostess to aunts and friends, Martha considered her life as plantation mistress "dreary and monotonous." In the summer of 1801, she was "crouded" once again with company. Maria was at Edgehill awaiting the birth of her second child; Mrs. Bache from Philadelphia and her family were staying until her husband returned. Martha delayed sending for Aunt Marks because the "family" already was too large to accommodate her. Given these domestic responsibilities, it was "utterly impossible" to go immediately to Monticello on her father's arrival. "[Y]et the idea of being so near you and the pleasure of seeing you sometimes," she wrote, "will enliven a time otherwise dreary and monotonous."[1] The "idea" of reunion, however, evoked emotions that were sometimes quite different from actually being together. Her father's arrival at Monticello was not "unmixed with pain." It demarked "a return to the world from which I have been so long been secluded," Martha anxiously disclosed, "and for which my habits render me every way unfit." But the "good" of seeing him every day would "render every other evil light."[2] The source of Martha's happiness tended to be a single person; her "pleasure" came from the very "idea" of being near her father and occasionally seeing him alone. Jefferson's consolation during their separations came from imagining himself in the tranquil "bosom of family," and his daughter "surrounded by the cares and the comforts of [her] family."[3] However, the practical realities of being a plantation mistress, mother, wife, and republican daughter were far removed from Father's imaginary "cares and comforts."

"Soft affections" & "circle of cabal"

The life of Martha and Mann Randolph from 1800 to 1809 would be directed and shaped by the patriarch's participation in public affairs, as the family they imagined receded always into some future, hoped-for time. Jefferson's imagination drew a broad and deep boundary between the state and society, public and private, political and domestic, female and male, a "circle of cabal intrigue & hatred and the "intercourse of soft affections."[4] Stirring a "revolution" ordered to republican principles and at the same time ordering Monticello's household affairs demanded that he abrogate in practice these strict separations. The household's emotional dynamics, economic well-being, and material comfort would be unalterably affected by Jefferson's election as President. Accompanying joyful births, mournful deaths, financial plights, and political triumphs, their letters constantly reminded each other just how interdependent the public and private spheres were and how contingent their well-being was.

The public sphere and affairs of state were routinely injected into the far-flung operations of the Monticello household and intruded emotionally, materially, and economically on domestic tranquility.[5] Father's correspondence provided a running commentary to the family on Administration policies, legislative actions, electoral politics, and foreign affairs. He described how these and other political activities might affect the family, the household, and their collective well-being. The family was called forth physically and in their imaginations to experience the world. Public and private, state and society, domestic and political were so intertwined in the Monticello household as to be practically indistinguishable.

A defining tension in the family from 1800 to 1809 was between Martha's responsibilities as a mother and plantation mistress on one hand and her father's drive for public esteem and desire to place her in Washington society on the other. Family members, especially Martha, ordered much of their lives around the President's coming and going through the cycles of legislative sessions: a springtime visit of a few weeks in April or May; a longer stay during the "sickly season" from sometime in July or August to late September.[6] In anticipation of his arrival in July 1801, Martha, eight months pregnant, was directed to "go over at once with [her] sister to Monticello and take up quarters"; she was to notify overseer Gabriel Lillie "to be collecting geese and ducks and to provide flour."[7] The household sent horses and phaeton to meet the President's homeward-bound retinue; ladies of the house knitted socks and sewed shirts for the President; and scurried to the mountaintop in anticipation of his arrival.[8]

All the while, the Randolphs diverted a substantial amount of time and personal resources from their own domestic and farming matters to Jefferson's business, social, and sometimes political dealings. He expected the family would follow him to Washington.[9] They were distracted from completing their Edgehill house, neglected their garden, and sidetracked from monitoring overseers at their Varina farm. Political contests delayed eagerly anticipated reunions and foreshortened visits, causing family members to lament their separation even more fervently. A stream of politically-connected visitors to Monticello intruded on even the brief times the family had alone.

"No republic," Jefferson wrote Noah Webster, "is more real than that of letters..."[10] Embedded in the family-of-letters Jefferson and others constructed was a republic of letters that engaged in a "rational discourse" and, not infrequently, conveyed emotional outbursts on affairs of state as well as society Historically, the wider "public sphere" was a discursive space intermediating between formally organized state entities and the communities, religious institutions, merchants, and similar elements of society. The phenomenon was marked by pamphlets, essays, broadsides, lectures, orations, social circles, street demonstrations, and even artistic productions that were created to shape public opinion and ultimately influence government policy.[11] The letter-writing ritual of the Jefferson-Randolph family brimmed with all manner of commentary and opinions on foreign relations, tariffs, taxes, military incursions, political shenanigans, local elections, and policy directions.[12] Family letters and print media formed a well-traveled bridge linking the world of political tumult with that of tranquil domesticity. Despite Jefferson's view that the "ladies" should leave "party squabbles" to the "rougher sex and to the newspapers," he did not insulate his daughter from either domestic or foreign political affairs nor hesitate to describe how they might personally affect her.[13] He speculated that some classmates from Panthemont may have been "butchered" on St. Domingo. Toussaint's "Patriotic party" on the island had captured 400 "aristocrats and monocrats" and proposed sending them to the United States. If the government could distribute them among the Indians, it "would teach them lessons of liberty and equality."[14]

In addition to letters, the Monticello household was regularly supplied Philadelphia's *Aurora* newspaper as well as the *Independent Chronicle* and *Constitutional Telegraphe* from Boston.[15] Martha was a consumer: "We had had thro the medium of the newspapers, news...which announce an actual commencement of hostilities on the side of the british which I am afraid will retard your return to us."[16] Publications would be frequently electrified emotionally with Jefferson's signature rhetorical flourishes: "Duer, the king of the alley, is under a sort of check...[The] fate of the nation seems to hang on the desperate throws and plunges of gambling scoundrels." These speculators were "like nine pins knocking one another down...[as if] the whole town [New York] had been burnt to the ground."[17] The printed words and inscribed emotions were punctuated with a reminder that the family's financial lifeline of tobacco production was threatened by speculations in land and government contracts awarded to Secretary Hamilton's associate, William Duer.[18]

"All my heart holds dear"

Over a year before his election to the Presidency and "crouded" with business, Maria's father had rhapsodized on their "happy domestic society...as no other is founded in sincere affection." In the political realm, passions without even a modicum of affection fueled controversies over Adam's Quasi-War with France, renewal of the bill prohibiting trade with France, Senate debate over levying taxes for a possible war, and other hotly contested matters in what was to be the waning months of a Federalist administration. Therefore, it was incumbent that he "write no letters the ensuing year for political reasons."[19]

"Politics are such a torment," Martha's father complained, "that I would advise everyone I love not to mix with them." He was "abandoning the rich, & declining their dinners & parties, and associating entirely with the class of science."[20] Meanwhile, Martha was living in a house filled with "smoke, rain & wind thro' badly furnished windows" and caring for three children suffering with "colds so bad as to create suspicions of the hooping cough." Writing late at night, she was "disturbed and allarmed" at her family's condition and sought the comfort of her Father's company. The despair was palpable: "Dear and respected Father hasten I entreat you, the blest moment which will reunite me to all my heart holds dear in the world."[21] Both the reunion and the savor of "true happiness" would be short-lived, however. Jefferson was anticipating the fall election and actively engaged in devising strategy and organizing political action at both the national and state levels.

"Leave me most at home"

On January 12, 1800, Jefferson wrote in cipher to Virginia Governor James Monroe that he had conferred with Aaron Burr on New York's process for choosing presidential electors. Republicans in that state, Pennsylvania, Virginia, and others were frantically pressing to change from selection by a state-wide "general ticket" or by legislatures, opposition federalists held sway. "[B]eing more chequered, & representing the people in smaller sections, [election by districts] would be more likely to be an exact representation of their diversified sentiments." "I ought in delicacy be silent on this subject," Jefferson confided. "[B]ut you, who know me, know that my private gratifications would be most indulged…which should leave me most at home." Nevertheless, Jefferson encouraged his political ally to share the letter with Madison and "to those possessing our joint confidence."[22] Madison's protégé, James Barbour, representative from Orange County in Virginia's House of Delegates, soon reported to Jefferson that the "lower house" had narrowly passed by five votes a bill for a "general ticket" but maintained the principle of districts by permitting only one elector from each. "This law excited the opposition more sensibly than any measure" this session.[23]

Over the three days following Barbour's letter, like-minded Virginians acted immediately to organize a proto-political party to take advantage of the new election law. Members of the Legislature created a state-level committee of five persons to coordinate "a general system of correspondence through the state for the purpose of giving effectual support to [their] ticket" of twenty-one presidential electors, each from a single district. In addition to the "central committee," Chairman Philip Norborne Nicholas reported that five-member subcommittees had been created in each county "to communicate useful information to the people…and repel every effort…to injure the ticket."[24]

Jefferson without delay lent his support to the nascent organization by providing "useful information" in the form of pamphlets "on a subject interesting to all the states" and eight dozen copies of another political tract that "should be sent to every county commee [*sic*]" in Virginia. The postal service Jefferson had pushed so ardently in the 1790s to sustain his family-of-letters had become by 1800 in his mind a political instrument of the Adams administration: "I dare trust nothing this summer through the post offices," he warned

Nicholas. So, political materials were being forwarded by a "private handle," and he was trusting the central committee chair with the "secret" of the pamphlets' origin.[25]

Not even dear Maria, who lay dangerously ill in early 1800 after childbirth, was spared Father's litany on how politics affected her life. "[T]he bill suspending intercourse with France…is in fact a bill to prohibit the exportation of tobacco & to reduce the tobacco states to passive obedience by poverty." If this legislation was not allowed to expire, he advised Martha, "our state would to better to drop the culture of tobo. altogether."[26] Mann Randolph was reminded that even more financial houses in New York, Baltimore, and Philadelphia had failed, largely as a result of Napoleon's European adventures. Consequently, "it is difficult to transfer money from hence to Richmond"—a matter so critical to meeting the demands by Randolph's creditors and to preserving a portion of his mortgaged legacy at Varina.[27]

Jefferson clearly was ordering his private affairs throughout 1800 in anticipation of the impending presidential elections. Before leaving the "paroxysms" of his Vice Presidential post in Philadelphia, he paid Gilbert Stuart $100 for the first of three life portraits the artist was to devise of the noted republican. He departed his "hateful labours" by stage on 15 May with a stop in Richmond to confer with Governor Monroe and make a payment on the Wayles debt; then on to Mont Blanco to collect dear Maria, who was physically recovered but still emotionally grieving from the loss of her child. Daughter and father visited their recently widowed aunt and sister, Mary Jefferson Bolling, at Chestnut Grove and Maria's in-laws at Eppington, finally arriving at Monticello on 29 May.[28]

Both Martha and her father would learn through two Presidential terms that society, the state, a republic of letters, and practical politics were part and parcel of a democratic polity that struggled to bind individuals' self-interest into collective institutional and social action. Fomenting the "revolution of 1800" (as Jefferson would later interpret his election) would be only slightly more difficult than living the unperturbed family life that Martha and he fancied.[29] The Monticello household, including his enslaved "family," made Jefferson's political life possible; an imagined family rendered it emotionally tolerable; and their letter writing was the ritual that sustained both.

"Counting chickens before they are hatched"

That fall's election returns were favorable to the north-south alignment that Jefferson, Burr, and others had engineered; but the two "republicans" claimed the same number of presidential electors and the matter devolved to the House of Representatives controlled by federalists. As his election remained uncertain in January 1801, Martha's father already was imagining her in the boil of Washington society and politics, just "three easy days journey" from Monticello.

> I should hope you & the family could pay an annual visit here at least; which with mine to Monticello of the spring & fall, might enable us to be together 4. or 5. months of the year. on this subject however we may hereafter converse, lest we should be counting chickens before they are hatched.[30]

Throughout his first term as President and two years into the second, Jefferson continued to urge his family to join him in the world of politics and Washington society. Unlike Monticello, Washington City of 1801 was "a mixture of the bad passions of the heart," filled with "federalists and most of them of the violent kind."[31] The "Essex school" was attempting to prevent Jefferson's election in the House of Representatives and "transfer the government by law to the Chief Justice or the Secretary of State."[32]

"The ladies of the place"

If Martha visited and followed the customs of Washington, however, she would not have the privilege of limiting her society to the "class of science," as her father had done in the waning months of his vice presidency, nor would she have been insulated from political affairs and social gossip. Jefferson's ardent partisan, Margaret Bayard Smith, had anxiously watched from the House gallery the thirty-six ballots of his election. She saw a "Heroic woman"—the wife of Representative Joseph Hopper Nicholson (MD)—rouse her "almost dying husband" in the anteroom to repeatedly guide his hand in writing the name "Jefferson." In Smith's opinion, this dutiful "American equaled in courage and patriotism the Roman matron." She knew how politics, family, and society intertwined in Washington City. Her newspaperman husband, Samuel Harrison Smith, had been a key political operative in convincing her federalist cousin, Congressman James A. Bayard, to cast a blank vote on the thirty-sixth ballot to elect Jefferson President over Aaron Burr.[33]

Margaret, like Jefferson, urged sisters-in-law Mary and Susan Smith to "participate in the pleasures of that delightful season" of a Washington springtime. The casual fashion of rural Virginia would hardly suit a President's daughter, but whatever her dress, it would be scrutinized by Washington's "ladies." Attending a Washington soirée on New Year's Day, 1801, Margaret Smith offered a critical appraisal of one female reveler: "There was a lady, too, who afforded us great diversion, I titled her, Madam Eve, and called her dress the *fig leaf*."[34]

On the last day of January 1801, Martha complained that "in a period of 2 months not one day could have been found to discharge so sacred and pleasing a duty" of writing to her father. Since he left Monticello, she had suffered a "derangement" of her stomach that she attributed to her "incipient pregnancy," "unable to digest anything," and "harassed to death by little fevers." Nine-year-old Jeffy had "cought (that filthiest of all disorders) the itch from a little aprentice boy in the family." Her mental state was agitated further by having been deprived of even "one sociable moment" with her father during his visit in December. The imagined family life for her was more fulfilling than the one they were forced to live as participants in the political public sphere. "I suffered more in seeing you all ways at a distance than if you had still been in Philadelphia, for then at least I should have enjoyed in anticipation those pleasures which we were deprived of by the concourse of strangers." Martha was "every day becoming more averse to company" and her only pleasures were performing the "duties" of educating the three older children. This, too, was "attended with more anxiety." Although Ellen was "wonderfully apt," Anne and Jeff were "uncommonly backward in everything" and "excite serious anxiety with regard to their intellect." Her oldest daughter appeared to "Learn absolutely without profit." While her son was "quicker" than she had "ever thought it possible," he was losing time at not being "placed at a good school."[35]

Later in the spring of 1801, the President wrote to his neighbor's wife: "Thomas Jefferson begs that either Mrs. Madison or Miss Payne will be so good as to dine with him today, to take care of female friends expected." The chief executive reported his enjoyment at having Mrs. Madison stay temporarily at the President's House, because it had "enabled [him] to begin an acquaintance with the ladies of the place, so as to have established the precedent of having them at [his] dinners." Her leaving "to commence housekeeping" left him without a female presence, making it "awkward" for the ladies to continue attending. "It would be the greatest comfort imaginable," he wrote to Martha, who was six months pregnant, "to have you or Maria here."[36] He invoked Washington's "ladies" to persuade Maria, five months pregnant as well. "It would make [the ladies of the Capital] as well as myself very happy could I always have yourself or your sister here," father wrote her in the spring of 1801, "but this desire, however deeply felt by me, must give way to the private concerns of Mr. Eppes."[37] He felt no compunction in offering a "promise" to "society" that one of his daughters would "pass the spring" and "the other the fall" in Washington City.[38] They may have been merely "three easy days journey" from that delightful society, but children's illnesses, pregnancies, death, and other necessities of private family life repeatedly thwarted the President's designs for almost two years.

"Could I be forever with you"

Upon learning of Maria's betrothal to Jack Eppes in 1797, her father had envisioned a "fireside" surrounded by a family without any "jarring or jealousies," "irregular passions," or "dangerous bias." The household would extend its reach from the mountaintop across the Rivanna to Edgehill and Pantops and down the James some ninety-miles to Varina and farther on to Bermuda Hundred in Chesterfield Co., VA at the storied river's confluence with the Appomattox. This constellation would create "the ineffable pleasures of…family society."[39] However, the election of 1800 would keep the family dispersed and only add to their feelings of separation.

Maria, like her sister, was suffering already from their father's absence. She was in "anxious suspence about the election" but resigned to its favorable outcome. "I shall endeavor to be satisfied in the happiness I know it will give to so many tho I must confess mine would be much greater could I be forever with you & see you happy I could enjoy no greater felicity." A few weeks later, she lamented the difficultly of regularly hearing from him, as his letters were "the greatest pleasure" she received and nothing else was "so valuable." Maria was emboldened to voice a suspicion that carried the seed of that "dangerous bias" her father had imagined would never erupt at Monticello.

> [S]ensible of the distance which Nature has placed between my sister & myself the tender affection I feel for her makes me judge what yours must be, and I rejoice that you have in her so great a source of comfort

& one who is in every way so worthy of you, satisfied if
my dear papa is only assured that in the most tender
love to him I yield to no one.[40]

This feeling of secondary status in her father's affections had surfaced
early in Maria's life, when the sixteen-year old wrote:

The more I see her [Martha] the more I am sensible
how much more deserving she is of you than I am, but
my dear Papa suffer me to tell you that the love, the
gratitude she has for you can never surpass mine; it
would not be possible."[41]

Then as in the instant case, her father's response did not exactly address
Maria's feelings of subordination: "On my part, my love to your sister
and yourself knows no bounds, and as I scarcely see any other object in
life, so would I quit it...whenever my continuance in it shall become
useless to you."[42]

Maria's sensibility found concrete expression in her request for
Monticello's harpsichord (rather than giving it to her Aunt Bolling),
because her "Piano will not hold in tune long." The quality of Maria's
harpsichord had been an artifact symbolizing the sisters' perceived
differences in status since 1798. Martha considered her younger
sibling's instrument a "charming one...tho' certainly inferior" to her
own. When a new "Forte-piano" arrived at Monticello in mid-1800, the
eldest daughter continued to insist her harpsichord with the "celestini"
stop was superior. Their father glossed his daughters' differences by
noting the "tone...will be found sweeter for a moderate room, but not
as good as [Martha's] for a large one."[43] Maria would not "yeild" to
Martha in feeling "the most tender love" to their father, but she was
anxious to accept an instrument her sister considered the least among
Monticello's collection.

Her father wanted to "fly from the circle of cabal, intrigue &
hatred" in Washington City, but Maria's letter had raised the prospect
his journey would not be to a place "where all is love and peace." He
reassured his daughter of his evenhandedness and invoked an imaginary
family to assuage her misgivings:

No, never imagine that there can be a difference with
me between yourself & your sister. you have both such
dispositions as engross my whole love, and each so
entirely that there can be no greater degree of it than
each possesses. Whatever absences I may be led into for

a while, I look for happiness to the moment when we can all be settled together, no more to separate.[44]

"A government truly republican"

Mann Randolph more accurately, colorfully, and with an unusual candor captured the tensions of separation his father-in-law was experiencing because of "the necessity of…sacrificing all private ease & comfort" in exchange for public office.

> [W]e know well that your mind does from nature exult in grand scenes, in ample fields for exertion, in extraordinary toils, as much as the finest animal of the most excellent race of our noblest Quadrupedes must do in the length of the Course.[45]

The posts along Jefferson's political course frequently were marked by the tensions of balancing his needs for public esteem, private honor, and family affection. (After all, life's happiness depended on it!) From mid-eighteenth century, the meaning of "private" had become increasingly narrowed to denote "family" affairs, intimacy, and independence; after the Revolution, it was used as an oppositional contrast to "government."[46] From early in his political career, Jefferson pleaded family affairs for declining or delaying public office. His imagination erected an impenetrable mental barrier between private domesticity and political life, yet life experiences and his actions fostered the interpenetration of state, public, private, and domestic. In 1801, the presidential candidate felt "worn down" and "surrounded by enemies & spies catching & perverting every word," as he endured the thirty-six ballots in the House. "I pant for that society where all is peace and harmony," he complained to Martha, "where we love & are beloved by every object we see.[47] Pant he might, but withdrawing to that "society" carried its own risks, as he had revealed to Maria some years earlier:

> The real difficulty is that being once delivered into the hands of others, whose feelings are friendly to the individual and warm to the public cause, how to withdraw from them without leaving dissatisfaction in their mind and an impression of pusillanimity with the public.[48]

Retiring from or even declining public service in Jefferson's mind could be a matter of honor just as acceptance of such positions offered the prospect of public esteem, yet both required separation from those he loved. The tension had been a long-standing struggle, since the days of the Revolution.

In August 1776, for example, he had rejected fellow Virginian Edmund Pendleton's suggestion of "engaging in the Judiciary" of the new Confederation because of the "indisposition of Mrs. Jefferson." Yet, by October he was busily engaged in drafting legislative proposals for the Virginia General Assembly to lay "a foundation for a government truly republican." Two of the 126 bills directly impacted the family. An 1821 reminiscence claimed that abolishing entails "would prevent the accumulation and perpetuation of wealth in select families"; and eliminating primogeniture "removed...distinctions which made one member of every family rich, and all the rest poor."[49]

The national government, however, would not relent in trying to cajole Jefferson into that "grand scene" Mann Randolph had described. Just one day after assuming his legislative post in Virginia on 7 October 1776, a letter from the President of Congress, John Hancock, informed him of his appointment, along with Benjamin Franklin and Silas Deane, as "Commissioner at the Court of France. This trio was "to negotiate such Business as the Congress shall entrust [them] with."[50] Congressman Richard Henry Lee urged acceptance by invoking symbols he well-knew would resonate with a fellow Virginian. The perilous times required men of "great abilities and unshaken virtue." He continued his appeal: "In my judgement, the most eminent services that the greatest of her sons can do America will not more essentially serve her and honor themselves, than a successful negotiation with France."[51] The words "eminent services," "honor," and "virtue" had, at least, a momentary effect on Jefferson. He underwent three days of "conflict," while Hancock's messenger waited for a response, but in the process posed a distinction between private affairs and his family:

> No cares of my own person, nor yet for my private affairs would have induced one moment's hesitation to accept the charge. But circumstances very peculiar in the situation of my family, such as neither permit me to leave nor to carry it, compel me to ask leave to decline a service so honorable and at the same time so important to the American cause.[52]

Whatever the "cares" of his person or "private affairs," the family in his mind was distinctly more compelling; nevertheless even a year later, Jefferson retained a lingering regret about his choice of family over service. "I wish my domestic situation," he wistfully wrote Franklin, "had rendered it possible for me to join you in the very honorable charge." But it was more than honor that he was missing. "Residence in a polite court, society with literati of the first order, a just cause, and approving god will add length to life for which all men pray."[53]

Five years later in 1781, he once again resisted (this time over a period of several months) an appointment to treat with Great Britain. Nothing would have been "so agreeable, Virginia's former Governor replied to Edmund Randolph,

> But I have taken my final leave of everything of that nature, have retired to my farm, my family and books from which I think nothing will ever more separate me. A desire to leave public office with a reputation not more blotted...will oblige me to emerge at the next session of our [Virginia] assembly and perhaps accept a seat in it."[54]

Pressed to attend the "next session" of Virginia's General Assembly while his wife was seriously ill, he decried that its demands were a form of "slavery." He had retired to a "family" that required his "attention and instruction," he pleaded to Monroe.[55] It was only with the death of wife Martha in September 1782 that he showed no compunction in quickly accepting an appointment as Peace Commissioner in Paris and later Minister Plenipotentiary to France in 1784. He demurred at accepting Washington's "call" in 1789 while he completed the details of Patsy's marriage settlement and entertained "gloom forebodings" that his service as Secretary of State might end with "criticisms and censures" by the public.[56] Before election as Vice President in 1795, he adamantly told friend Madison that considering public office was "forever closed," because he needed get his private "affairs into a clear state." And, so it had gone, even until century's turn when he proclaimed to Monroe he wanted to be "most at home," whilst conspiring to ferment his "revolution of 1800."

Little wonder that the uncertainties of reunion should lead Martha to complain to her father about the "concourse of strangers" interfering with their intimate times during following his election. It was the cost of public service for which there was no recompense.

> And to have that intercourse of soft affections hushed
> & suppressed by the eternal presence of strangers goes

very hard indeed; & the harder as we see that the candle of life is burning out, so that the pleasures we lose are lost forever. But there is no remedy.[57]

The crowds that had swarmed the mountaintop, he told Martha, were to be endured as evidence of the esteem the family had been "all their lives trying to merit."[58] It was just on such occasions that Jefferson plumbed the depths of his emotions and posited a sharp distinction between the intimate family life he imagined and the unsettled political life he actually was living. Even the physical isolation of a mountaintop refuge was insufficient to warranty the "private ease and comfort" of family intimacy from intrusions by either society or politics. Despite Martha's protestations, Father regularly invited the political world into their sanctuary, including foreign dignitaries, cabinet Secretaries and spouses, colleague Madison, and protégé William Short. Even "an elderly English gentleman...seeking an asylum in [their] quiet country" was thrust upon Randolph for guidance.[59]

Torn between his needs for public esteem, honor, and domestic felicity, Jefferson relieved the tensions by painting the political public sphere as a place of conflict, tumult, and self-interest and imagining himself at a place brimming with harmony, tranquility, and affection. Only in their imagination were the boundaries firmly fixed between family, society, and the state.[60]

"A few removals from office"

Martha's health and maternal duties were keeping her from Washington society, but her father was discovering that "family" affairs, nonetheless, could be injected into his public responsibilities. He was not replacing all office holders with Federalist sympathies, but "a few removals from office [would] be indispensable...chiefly for real malconduct, & mostly in the offices connected with the administration of justice." Among this apparently select group was Virginia's U.S. Marshal David Meade Randolph, husband of Mann Randolph's sister, Mary (Molly). He wrote apologetically to his son-in-law:

> One removal will give me a great deal of pain, because it will pain you also, but it would be inexcusable in me to make that exception. the prostitution of justice by packing of juries cannot be passed over.[61]

George Jefferson, the President's distant relative and Richmond business agent, was "very apprehensive" to even forward his relative's solicitation for an appointment in the republican administration, as it might be "deemed obtrusive and impertinent." Forwarding the request was a "disagreeable necessity," but the Richmond businessman believed John Jefferson's "capacity to fill some Office…would not stand the test of investigation." Moreover, simply the name "Jefferson" would incorrectly impute a close connection and only add to Federalist's gossip "that one who has acted with the greatest impropriety…will continue to hold his" office (namely, David Meade Randolph).[62]

At the same time Jefferson was tacking these courses between protégés, in-laws, and kin in the political public sphere, he was confronted with even more troublesome matters in his private family.

"An object of great anxiety"

Adding to both the dread and agonies of Jefferson and Mann Randolph was the unrelenting task of keeping creditors at bay. In October 1801, the President apologized for not keeping a promise to help his son-in-law repay the Gibson and Jefferson partnership which had rescued Varina from a sheriff's sale. "To be entirely clear of debt," he confided to Randolph, "is an object of great anxiety."[63]

Jefferson's road to freedom in 1800 led on from paths the household had followed during earlier flights from public office. The life transitions in 1790, 1793, and 1800 were accompanied with a "plan" to relieve the family of the emotional "torment" of debt and free them from being like a "species of property." In the newest scheme, income would come from rents on farms and a grist mill (yet to be built), profits from a nailery staffed with enslaved youngsters, and a government salary of $25,000.

Jefferson's insistence on managing the details of the plantation and Randolph's indifferent performance as "executive overseer" had made it difficult in the early 1790s for him to correct the "derangement" of his private affairs and wage his political contests with Hamilton in Philadelphia. The schedule of Congressional sessions, in particular, kept him away from Monticello at critical times in the seasonal cycle of tobacco production, and his responsibilities as head of a Department were pressing throughout the year. Consequently as early as 1793, Jefferson had considered "procuring tenants in Maryland for all [his] lands on the Shadwell side of the river" and hiring out "the negroes on the same lands for 25. Dollars."[64] These farmers had the skills to manage his new farming system that involved converting cropland from tobacco to wheat, orderly rotation of crops to replenish depleted soils, expanding animal production, and nail manufacturing.

Renting would not only free the household from day-to-day farm management but also transfer some of the risks of commodity production to tenants.

"Retirement" from 1793 through 1796, and thereafter, the lesser demands of the Vice Presidency seemed to have lessened the urgency to divest of farming duties. The "tragedy" he and Randolph experienced in marketing their 1799 tobacco, when prices plummeted as a result of foreign affairs, would bring renewed efforts to transfer the risks to tenants and diversify enterprises.

"Not fit to be a farmer"

Monticello's master was never further from his farms than the closest nib and inkwell. Jefferson's memory, as he claimed, may have forgotten the "minute" details of agriculture, but it did not deter the President from penning painfully detailed instructions to overseers, son-in-law, and his plantation mistress. He directed "Goliah & his senile corps to prepare...the garden"; ordered the wine "stored in the Dining room cellar, & that secured by double locks"; provided Randolph with the conditions for leasing Tufton farm; and bought "sheets, towels, counterpanes and tea china," groceries, tumblers, and wine glasses. Labor overseer Richard Richardson was reminded that "somebody should sleep so as to guard the house, perhaps...Joe, Wormely & Burwell" and they were to be in the "North square cellar." "Burwell should feed the horses, if a supply of forage is kept ready." Richardson was to "keep the key to the corn crib in the stable, and see that the corn is always locked up." And, of course, he was to write immediately after receiving a letter from Jefferson who in turn would respond on the same day; in this way, the plantation master would be "possessed of the progress of the several works & enable [him] to give directions."[65]

Despite close attention to farming operations over nearly a decade, the President finally enlisted Loudoun County agriculturist Stevens Thomson Mason to find prospective lessees from near the Virginia-Maryland border. "I am not fit to be a farmer with the kind of labour we have," he confessed to Mason, "and also subject to such long avocation."[66] Maryland farming, Jefferson thought, was "performed by slaves with some mixture of free labourers," so tenants from there would "understand the management of negroes on a rational and humane plan." It had been his intent since 1790 to concentrate farm production on "wheat and grazing: little corn, and less pork" and a strict crop rotation to improve and restore soil fertility.[67] Indeed, perpetual European conflict would keep commodity prices "high for years to come, especially bread," therefore the production of wheat could not be pursued "too boldly."[68] A corollary enterprise would be a grist mill. Early crops caused him to exalt that "100 bushels of wheat are as easily made as 1000 lb. of tobo."[69] These hopeful predictions were soon challenged in 1792, however, by the inexorable march of the Hessian fly that had "made an alarming progress to the Southward," arriving at Baltimore and abounding in Philadelphia. Added to natural depredations were uncertainties in the financial markets when the Philadelphia bank refused to discount merchants' bills for purchasing wheat and prices fell precipitously from $1.25 to $1.13 per bushel.[70]

A five-year lease was finally signed on 1 October 1799 with Craven Peyton for approximately 160 acres of the Shadwell tract at $160 per year in "gold or silver coin of the United States."[71] As he was preparing in early 1800 for the forthcoming election, Jefferson confided to Randolph: "My anxiety to get my lands rented is extreme."[72] He was able to further his plan by August in anticipation of continuing his "long avocation" by agreeing with Marylander John Craven to another five-year lease of £350 Virginia currency annually in exchange for 500 Acres and 45 slaves.[73]

At the beginning of the first Presidential term, Jefferson approached his longstanding plan with renewed vigor. It still envisioned a "manufacturing" or leased mill on the Rivanna River to produce flour for export; crop diversification to spread the risks of commodity production; and land, facility, and labor leases for sure money would further hedge uncertainties. Now, it seemed there was a more dependable windfall: a government salary of $25,000 would provide for his "maintenance," while "profits" from the new farm plan could lift the "burthens of debt."[74] He fancied that his Presidency would secure republican government for future generations of Americans as well as financial well-being for his progeny—for Jefferson an unusual convergence of private interests and public duty! The exercise of civic virtue in his mind had its "hateful labours" and "torments" but also, presumably, material rewards.

"A disagreable piece of business"

Public affairs and domestic responsibilities were getting in the way of honoring their family's letter-writing ritual. "My business is become so intense," Jefferson complained, "that, when post day comes, it is often out of my power to spare a moment." Grand Papa was especially anxious about the children's whooping cough, rightly so, given the family's tragic experience with Lucy Elizabeth. "There is no disease whatever which I so much dread with children."[75] Instructing three children, knitting socks for the President, coping with frightful whooping cough, purging worms, and late-term pregnancy were creating a deafening silence from Monticello. However, it was neither "inclination" nor "want of materials" that had prevented Martha writing her "Dear Father" for three months; rather, it was a deficiency of character—"a spirit of procrastination." Her "affections" and "thoughts" were constantly with him, she reassured, "and never without deeply regretting the unavoidable necessity of [his] spending so much time cut off from that society which alone gives charm to life." His daughter's "society" in the Monticello household had been stirred with the "disagreable piece of business" of mediating between her aunts and in-laws. Martha Jefferson Carr had attempted "many ineffectual efforts" to knit socks requested by the President, so his sister Lucy and Mann Randolph's sister Jane Cary made "united and importunate entreaties" to take over the task. Martha's only choice, she claimed, was to comply and "avoid hurting the feelings and perhaps giving offence to these ladies, even though the resulting stockings were not to her "satisfaction."[76]

Maria left Monticello in early November 1801 with baby Francis, whose whooping cough had placed him "in a very precarious state of being." Martha's daughters, Ellen and Cornelia, had been delirious with the same ailment, but the "crisis" seemed to have passed. Fatigued and disappointed at her father's "long silence," Martha wrote after 1 a.m.:

> My God what moment for a Parent. The agonies of Mr. Randolph's mind seemed to call forth every energy of mine. I had to act in the double capacity of nurse to my children and comforter to their Father. It is of service perhaps to be obliged to exert one self upon those occasions. Certainly the mind acquires strength by it to bear up against evils that in other circumstances would totally overcome it.[77]

Their separation into public and private spheres was shrouded under a pall of loneliness; burdensome responsibilities crowded out even the family-of-letters they had created for solace, and anxieties were suffered alone without the consolation of a spouse or even the "ladies" of Washington City. Yet Martha accepted that life's trials as well as its exultations were but part and parcel of being a republican daughter, mother, and wife.

Chapter 8

"No subject...so dear and interesting":

Dis-tending the Household & Re-forming the Family

Nearing the end of a first Presidential term in 1804, Martha's father recounted his "most fatiguing journey" to Washington over roads mired in a "heavy drizzle" of mid-May that soaked his "outer great coat twice." "I have written you this long chapter about myself," he confessed apologetically, "because I have really nothing else to write about." Perhaps, his uncharacteristic loss for words was a consequence of travel fatigue, a sense of emptiness from being separated once again, or the emotional strain of another family tragedy. He need not have been so regretful. "No apology can be necessary for writing lengthily to me about your self," Martha reassured. "I hope you are not yet to learn that no subject on earth is or ever can be so dear and interesting to me."[1] Martha, too, had not been well since they parted. Her stomach had cramped with violent "spasms" followed by an "insuperable distension of the breast" and a feeling of "suffocation." Mr. Randolph "affirmed it to have been hysterics," which she knew was wrong but nevertheless stood in "dread of another attack." Martha's racking ailment and Father's unrelenting fatigue were exacerbated by their silent grieving of another family loss. As they had some twenty years earlier, they were clinging to each other at a time of emotional turmoil.

Maria had left them; her frail newborn was tied to life by a raveling thread. Their efforts to reconstitute the Monticello household in Washington City over the prior four years had been obstructed by illness, pregnancies, inclement weather, and politics. Moreover, they had learned that the project was doomed, because domestic tranquility required a place, unlike the Capital, insulated from the conflation of society and politics. Politics and private life had become even more confounded by Mann Randolph's election to Congress and his Georgia Scheme that had threatened to isolate him even further from the "bosom of family." These emotionally exhausting experiences, a growing family of six children, and the increasing complexity of household production made it abundantly clear by the spring of 1804 that the devoted couple would be enduring another four years of separation, interrupted only intermittently by brief reunions. Small wonder they were feeling the fatigues and maybe even hysterics of balancing personal happiness with public duty.

"A little deception...for the scheme"—Georgia

The year 1802 had marked the beginning of a watershed for the Monticello household and its family. Some forty letters between family members from early March 1802 through April the following year recorded parallel dialogues moving figuratively and literally in opposite directions. One envisioned pulling the family together and contracting the Monticello household by land sales; the other, keeping them apart for longer periods and extending the household even further geographically. Martha, Maria, and their father planned, delayed, and planned again their much anticipated reunion at the President's House. While they labored to end their separation, Randolph was plotting to disjoin them even further by "removing all his slaves" to the Mississippi territory and establishing a "Cotton plantation."

For over a decade, Thomas Mann Randolph had been dashing between his Varina farm and Monticello trying to erase his legacy debt and at the same time dutifully respond to the many "commissions" his father-in-law commanded. He "exactly attended" to sawing scantling for re-building the house; transmitted Jefferson's instructions to overseers, workman, and slaves; carried financial papers to Richmond; arranged for getting crops to market; negotiated leases with tenants; entertained foreign dignitaries; and simultaneously was asked to keep daily weather records, study the opossum, read law, and provide regular reports on the progress of plantation affairs.[2]

Whether from being overextended, indifferent, incapable, resistant, or for whatever reason, Randolph frequently did not fulfill his father-in-law's orders. "I am ashamed," he wrote, "that we will scarcely have a double quantity of the White Wheat...as there was then no prospect of the garden being inclosed in time to sow it."[3] After a "journey of 300 miles," the weary traveler still proffered his deference:

"I am sorry it is not in my power to give you such an estimate of the probable product of your harvest this year as might be satisfactory."[4] Randolph frequently resorted to words like "ashamed" and "sorry" when his actions did not meet what he perceived were Jefferson's expectations.

Randolph's full-time attention to farming had been no more successful in lessening his debt than Jefferson's absentee management and government salary had improved his solvency. He had followed his father-in-law's lead in tobacco price speculation, diversified into wheat production, and leased his land to increase income. Still, he had been forced to borrow from Jefferson to preserve Varina in 1800 and faced the prospect of further obligations in 1801 by a gift of additional land at Poplar Forest.[5] By the spring of 1802 with the likely prospect of seven more years of "commissions," a harried thirty-four-year-old Randolph with five children finally decided to take independent and decisive action in his farming and financial affairs.

"I communicate to you early a plan I have formed for the more profitable employment of my slaves," Randolph confided, "lest coming to you by report you might suppose the removal was meant to extend to my family allso." Apparently, he did not consider Jefferson's offer of "6 or 800 or 1000" acres in Bedford County just ninety miles away from Monticello a sufficiently profitable prospect to relieve his debt. A "large Cotton plantation" in the "Mississippi territory," which he would visit "at least once in two years," offered "the certainty of immense gain." His approach to the plan was one that should have given pause (but apparently did not) to someone, like Jefferson, who had so fervently entreated his grandchildren just a few days before "never...to tell a story."[6] The children's father proposed "a little deception...for the scheme absolutely hangs upon it." First, the slaves were to be led "to believe that the whole family may come after two crops." "[M]y slaves are willing to accompany me any where," he confidently wrote, "but they know well I should be little with them while the family is at a distance...besides their attachment to Martha would make their departure very heavy." Second, Randolph proposed to ensnare the children in his deception and spread it beyond the Monticello household: "[T]he children are encouraged to talk of it and the neighbours permitted to believe that emigration is our design."

"Whose happiness fortune has thrown upon my will"?

Randolph used "family"—both black and white—as a rhetorical strategy to falsely reassure Jefferson its "bosom" was secure at

Monticello; to justify his proposed "deception" on the basis of the slaves' attachment to their owners; to mislead his neighbors through the children; and to envisage his concern for the next generation. Moreover, among the reasons he claimed for undertaking the scheme were concerns for his "Negroes" and their "connexions." His "feelings" for them had not been "blunted by dreams of wealth." Rather,

> I have encouraged my fancy to irritate & quicken [my feelings] yet they join with cool reasoning to determine me on this step: they urge me strongly to remove these persons, whose happiness fortune has thrown upon my will, to a mild climate & gentle labor, with all their connexions I do or can in any way command, rather than to keep them at extreme hard labor & great exposure here or to trust them to the mercy of strangers...or very little & only at times within my control.

Martha would be "tortured" by his absence and the children [had] "declared...they could not leave Grandpapa." Nevertheless, there were more compelling family commitments that intersected with his debts and were his "first wishes"—namely, "to endow two sisters and to be prepared to give [his] Son the most complete education by attending institutions of learning and traveling abroad."[7]

He did not consider it necessary to "trouble" Jefferson with the "obvious" reasons for his "scheme" but proceeded to review them anyway. Their farms yielded more from rent and suffered fewer depredations with tenants than overseers. There was "little hope of profit from the culture of Tobacco," and the transition to animal agriculture and wheat "cannot be successfully pursued by means of Slaves...who are little worth for care & judgement" of livestock. Finally, there was "the risk of loss from large slave establishments after the West India manner."

Throughout his letter, Randolph conflated sentiment and reason, black and white, family and neighbors, being away and being within the circle. Just a month earlier, he had declared:

> The good temper and promising qualities of the children, their steady health, fine growth & progress in their education which she [Martha] directs & labors with all her powers makes her feel and declare herself frequently to be as happy as any person on earth.[8]

He must not have been privy to Martha's "anxiety" in 1801 over Anne and Jeff being "uncommonly backward in everything," her considering the life of a plantation mistress "dreary and monotonous," or the burden of being a "comforter" to a distraught father whilst nursing their seriously ill children.[9] Yet now he acknowledged she would be "tortured" by his absence, while the children declared their fealty to Grandpapa. He had struggled with managing Varina, a mere sixty miles from Edgehill, but energetically considered undertaking a new form of agricultural production some 1,400 miles distant. His plan was one of impetuous haste: "disposing by lottery" his Milton property, leave in April or May for Natchez, return no later than the "middle of July," and "move all [his] Slaves out...on the 1st day of November next." All the while, Varina, Bedford lands, Edgehill, and of course, Monticello would be left in the care of the President's epistles to barely literate overseers during a critical period of wheat harvest and tobacco cultivation. His "scheme" threatened to dissolve unilaterally the Monticello household that had been so assiduously constructed with so much effort, money, and personal sacrifice over the prior decade. Randolph's principal rationale hinged on two matters he knew full well would resonate in Jefferson's mind—family and debt.

By 1802, he must have been aware that it was Martha's "study to please him in everything" but also, that such devotion was secondary to love for her father, whose company was essential to her happiness.[10] Mann Randolph had been superseded by Jefferson and alienated from Randolph Senior in the Edgehill negotiations so Martha could be near her father. Besides a legacy of debt, Randolph's father bequeathed a message of the son's inadequacy by naming him co-executor but not guardian of his minor sisters, Harriet and Virginia. This slight he petulantly considered "an unaccountable and mortifying omission," since he and his brother, William, were "by Nature pointed out for this trust and by custom regarded the most proper persons. It wears the appearance of a suspicion of inability."[11] A biennial, arduous, and dangerous journey through Indian country to Natchez, extended separations from his family, and respite from multitudinous little "commissions" may well have seemed more congenial than his ambiguous position in the Monticello household and second place in his wife's heart.

"Practicable and adviseable"

Perhaps knowing well his son-in-law's inconstancy, Jefferson's immediate reply was not to dissuade him from relocating but, rather, to suggest alternative places that might be more suitable, feasible, healthy, safe, and profitable. He even mildly suggested an interest in a "Southern enterprize" and passing "every winter under the orange trees," if his "negroes could be persuaded." Over the ensuing months, Jefferson offered financial support, political influence, and information to further the "scheme," modified, of course, to his liking.

Jefferson was typically oblique and simultaneously directive in his response, penned just two days after learning of the "scheme." He was "very glad" to know Randolph's intentions, because "no resources within [himself] or without…could have supported [him] under the idea of a separation." He professed "not to be qualified" to advise him or to have "much information on the subject," but proceeded to mingle reasons pro and con and state a belief that "something of the kind is practicable and advisable"—just not in Mississippi. "I know that cotton is the most profitable production of the U.S." But the "powerful" Chickasaw, Choctaw, and French nations present a potential threat to the "little helpless speck of a settlement thrown off at such a distance from support." The Choctaw can bring 8,000 "warriors into the field" against a meager 800 from the 8,000 "souls" in the Mississippi territory. Louisiana will be in the hands of "the most turbulent spirits of the French Army." On the other hand, "a labourer there will make 300 D. worth a year." He suggested Randolph could travel through Kentucky via the Ohio and Mississippi rivers, rather than Tennessee as proposed, although the climate along this route is "unsafe for strangers," even in April, and he has "information" of "400 boatmen and seamen" dying every year from disease.

> Attending to the importance of this enterprize on your future affairs, and believing as I do that something of the kind is practicable and adviseable, I should think it prudent to take a comparative view of the circumstances under which other places offer themselves with a view to the same rich culture. Georgia certainly presents itself under some very advantageous aspects.[12]

In that state, land was cheaper and more abundant, climate healthier, commerce "not dependent" on any "foreign nation"; the country was "strong growing stronger," the trip "by sea quite trifling," and the communities were "made up of Virginians," who would be "trustworthy friends" and facilitate financial transactions with Richmond. Perhaps most importantly for Jefferson's personal needs, Randolph could visit his "possessions in Georgia spring and fall," just the seasons Father had been pressing Martha to join him in Washington.

Without Randolph's assent, Jefferson drew on his political connections to actively seek information to further *his* plan. "Mr. Baldwin and Gen. Jackson of Georgia…say that a labourer tends 5 acres of cotton a year:…lands are from 1 ½ to 6, 8, or 10 D. the acre…. They consider 300 D. [the hand] as what may be calculated on." Congressman Milledge of Georgia "will be able to give…more particular information."[13] He later arranged for these distinguished politicians to visit Edgehill in the spring on their return to Georgia.

"The children grow daily and improve in mind proportionally I hope," Randolph reported on March 13th. "[T]hey do not appear to be naturally deficient and their Mother's diligence[,] constancy and art surely never was surpassed."[14] Domestic affairs might be felicitous, but the prospective émigré was being pressed to adopt his father-in-law's terms. Congressman Milledge's information on land and slave prices, cotton husbandry, preferred locations in the State, and typical returns were detailed by Jefferson to Randolph on March 20th. Land with a "tolerable dwelling house and improvements" could be had for "6 Dollars"; each hand cultivated eight acres, but a total of twenty was required to grow corn for food. "A good negro labourer, young, will sell for from 550 to 600 D.," Milledge calculated and recommended that "there should not be more than 18 to 25…on one plantation." Submerged in Jefferson's favorable report, however, was a caution that, given Randolph's prior performance, should have been cause for concern to two farmers who routinely had miscalculated farming profitability: "He [Milledge] thinks the culture of the cotton requires nicer management and skill than tobacco does."[15]

Except for "horizontal plowing," Randolph's suggestions for changing farming practices were commonly met with a counterproposal from his father-in-law. For example, he had acquiesced to Jefferson's proposal in the early 1790s to transition from tobacco to wheat, but by 1792 considered it of "no importance compared with the one [they] have to make with regard to Indian corn." He was "determined to drop immediately the culture of [Indian] corn on [his] lands" and advised his father-in-law to do the same. Jefferson agreed corn was a "very hurtful culture" but hesitated eliminating it entirely because of his "negroes…attachment to it as a food."[16] Jefferson's rhetorical style makes it impossible to determine whether he was simply engaging in give-and-take or genuinely disapproving of Randolph's suggestions. Given the son-in-law's feeling of subordination and inclinations to overt deference (and frequently silent resistance), he most likely interpreted the alternative as disapproval. Such ambivalence was a feature of his responses to Jefferson's Georgia proposal over the ensuing months. Indian corn became the central argument Randolph deployed in initially opposing the alternative.

"Anxious thought"

Randolph "expected with impatience and received with great pleasure the information and opinions" that Jefferson had provided. He had been in "constant anxious thought on the subject" of emigration. The deferential son-in-law claimed he had already considered Georgia for its "geographic & political situation" as well as "climate." Randolph mildly resisted, however, by claiming that Indian corn was "more necessary even than mild treatment, moderate labor or a warm climate to Virginia Negroes." Georgia "pine land" (which Jefferson had already recommended against) would yield no more corn than Virginia's "old fields," whereas the "rich loam of the Mississippi insured abundance allmost without labor." Moreover, "It would be long & severe to our negroes to get accustomed to the substitutes for Corn bread which...are used in Georgia." Then he reversed positions! Until Jefferson informed him, he was unaware that Mississippi was "less productive in Cotton," and he had "erred in Supposing New Orleans to be the best market." These were "mistakes," so he arrived in his "anxious thought" at a compromise that accommodated both of their concerns for abundant Indian corn:

> It will be wise to make my first journey to georgia where perhaps I may meet with a tract of Cotton land at a low price with some river Swamp-land adjoining which is capable of being reclaimed from the tide with mud banks at no great expence: such land I know from experience to be the most productive of Indian Corn of any whatever, and to bear it annually without exhaustion.

Randolph ended his already contorted letter with a perplexing flourish of political ideology and concern for foreign relations. Reclaimed swamp and Indian corn would be "infinitely preferable" to having the "French for neighbors." If that country retakes possession of Louisiana,

after its immense Sacrifices and when there is leisure &
quiet for arranging & confirming the conquests of
Liberty by the establishment of a genuine free polity, my
affections will abandon the nation as my Sympathy does
now their aims in the war of St. Domingo.[17]

Continuing to marshal arguments for what, in his mind, was a
settled plan, Jefferson ignored matters of Indian corn, foreign relations,
and the fact his son-in-law had not yet consented to abandon
Mississippi. He forwarded a note from Meriwether Lewis on a tract of
land for sale. The government was considering internal improvements
to "open a road from Kentucky and Tennessee to head waters of
Savannah" that would make it a favored port over New Orleans. His
"chair" would be available for Randolph's visit financed by "draughts"
on Jefferson for money along the road.[18] "The plan is now arranged as
follows," Maria's father wrote:

> Mr. Randolph…goes to Georgia to make a purchase of
> lands, and Martha and the family come back with me
> and stay till his return [in late July;] Monticello for the
> months of Aug., and Sep. I cannot help hoping that
> while your sister is here you will take a run…I have
> enquired further into the best route for you…[19]

Only the tendentious Father knew that *his* plan—expressed in
early 1801—was to have both daughters and their children in
Washington during the spring and fall and at Monticello in the summer,
when he was home; the Georgia "scheme" fortuitously offered the
prospect of realizing an objective long-thwarted by pregnancies,
whooping cough, measles, and worms. Martha, similarly, was informed
of Father's "expectations as to [her] motions" during Randolph's
journey, but also was conferred an elevated position in the Monticello
household:

> I have desired Lilly to make the usual provision of
> necessaries for me at Monticello, and if he should be at
> a loss for the particulars to consult with you. My orders
> as to the garden were to sow and plant as usual, and to
> furnish you with the proceeds. Order them therefore
> freely: you know they will do nothing if you leave it to
> their delicacy.[20]

In the past, the task of directing overseers had been delegated
to Martha's husband, but this subtle shift in position would become

more prevalent as Randolph became increasingly unavailable to Monticello's household and family.

"The idea of their being blockheads"

Martha's husband initially planned to leave on his southern reconnaissance in April, but with the family's impending visit to Washington, "a few weeks sooner or later would make no material difference with him," Martha advised her father. Besides, his "anxiety to conduct such a family of little children thro the difficulties of the journey [to Washington] would naturally induce him to postpone his" to the south. Although nine-year-old Jeff was "reading latin with his Papa," that would soon end, if the Georgia scheme came to fruition; therefore, the youngster's mother was "seriously uneasy at his not going to school." Martha herself in 1783 was about Jeff's age, when her father had imagined a "fourteen to one" probability she would marry an intellectual "blockhead."[21] That was not the case. However, if Randolph was in Georgia for extended periods, "the education of her family" would, as Jefferson had speculated years earlier, depend on "her own ideas and direction without assistance"—except, of course, Grand Papa's.

Martha was "indebted" for her father's letter expressing his "surprise" that "in so short a time [Ellen] learned to read and write"; she had been encouraged to carry on, even before getting into "two syllables." Anne was progressing in her translations with "tolerable facility," but still Mother's "anxiety about them frequently [made her] unreasonably apprehensive."

> Unreasonably I think for surely if they turn out well with regard to morals I <u>ought</u> to be satisfied, tho I <u>feel</u> that I never can sit down quietly under the idea of their being blockheads.[22]

Like her father, Martha could not abide "blockheads"; unlike him, she was conflicted about whether the moral sense was pre-eminent in the pantheon of accomplishments fostering private esteem, public honor, and affection from others. Despite this possible difference in priorities (or perhaps because of it), an anxious and "unreasonable" mother knew well the sentiment most important to Father and closed by entreating: "Believe yourself <u>first</u> and unrivaled in the heart of your devoted child."

Martha and her father would remember in their joint letter to Nathaniel Burwell in 1818 that she had been prepared with a "plan of reading" and convent school to educate her daughters and, perhaps, her sons, "should their fathers be lost, or incapable, or inattentive."[23] They may have been reflecting on their experiences over the prior sixteen years. A prospective spring and fall in Georgia, as Jefferson envisioned, would result in the children's father being "lost" (just not dead) and his attention to family seriously distracted.

"I am looking forward with impatience to the moment when I can embrace you in all my affection and the dear children," Jefferson wrote. "It already occupies much of my thoughts as the time approaches." He left Washington on 5 May 1802, two days after the Seventh Congress rose for its summer recess. His "embrace" of family was a mere twenty-one days, but an efflorescent Monticello springtime rewarded him with "cherries ripe May 9, peas the 12th, strawberries the 14th."[24] The enjoyment of such beauty and the "bosom of family" undoubtedly were palliative to the "thralldom" of debt that his government salary, rentals, and farms had done little to relieve.

"Suppose about..."

Before his flying trip to Monticello in May, Jefferson had prepared an accounting of income and expenses for the first year of his presidency, 4 March 1801 to 4 March 1802. The results were not encouraging! On the expense side, operating the President's House in humble republican fashion had required $16,798 (excluding wines); Monticello, $4,385; and "family aids" just over $1,000. He had, in addition, paid down debts of about $3,900 incurred prior to the election; acquired land, carriage, and horses for slightly more than $4,700; and paid workmen on the house, $2,076. The total of this commingled list and other minor items was $33,635, but in his estimation the carefully kept records did not include money owed tenant Craven for corn nor accounts with local stores for "necessaries for negroes & house." The income account, in light of these expenses, did not look favorable to furthering Jefferson's objective of leaving public office free of debt. There was a government salary of $25,000 on which he was so optimistically relying, tobacco sales at $2,974, and "profits of nailery, suppose about $533.33." Most ominously, there also was a "debt contracted with J[ohn] Barnes" of $4,361 at his Georgetown mercantile house. Although income was less than expenses, even including the new loan, "yet it is exact enough to give general ideas."[25] The cost of exercising republican civic virtue was proving to involve more than painful separations from loved ones and the frustration of managing the farms through intermediaries who would "do nothing if you leave it to their delicacy." After a year in office, Jefferson by this rough accounting had incurred more loans ($4,361) than he had cleared ($3,918).

The President returned to his official duties on May 30ᵗʰ. He immediately renewed his insistence that Martha join him and advised on the schedule for her letter writing and that of the postal service. "It is now time for you to fix a day for my having you met at Mr. Strode's, and it would be well if you could do it so that a postday should intervene, and give me an opportunity of acknoleging the reciept of your letter so that you may be sure it has not miscarried."[26] Once again, nature intervened to extend their separation.

Measles were afoot in the Monticello neighborhood. To prepare for Maria's "coming up" immediately from Bermuda Hundred, her father directed that "should the nail boys or any others have it, they [will] be removed to the plantation instantly on your arrival." She and Francis, then, would be at Monticello "in perfect security."[27] Maria and little Francis were "very sick" with "constant fevers" that the frail mother attributed to teething and "nursing him in [her] weak state of health." She hoped Francis would "mend daily" now that she had "procured a healthy nurse for him."[28] "As it is," Father responded to the disappointing news from Edgehill and Eppington, "We must agree to the fall visit; and as Maria will be at Monticello, I trust she will come with you."[29] In the meantime, Martha straightaway undertook her new position as interlocutor with the overseer as well as continuing to see after the house and performing her duties as a republican daughter:

> I will send over to Lilly immediately to let him know your orders upon the subject [of removing the nail boys]....I do not know if I gave you a list of the things most wanting in the house. I do not exactly recollect what they were but sheets towels counterpanes and tea china were I think foremost on the list. Your linen has not arrived or it would have been made up before your return.[30]

"Whatever you may call for"

Neither public nor private family financial affairs were proceeding to Jefferson's liking over the summer and fall months. "A view of the consumption of butcher's meat from Sep. 6. 1801 to June 12. 1802" revealed that the expenses of his "outfit" in Washington— including eleven servants—were unabated. They were consuming an average of seventeen pounds daily (about one and one-half each) and the "masters," almost twenty-one. Just one week in July required over $243 for salaries, provisions, wood, and wine, which represented twenty-four percent of the net returns from the 1801 Poplar Forest tobacco the President had received in the prior October.[31]

The family in Virginia also continued to draw on his resources. Brother Randolph Jefferson was advanced $100. Niece Polly Carr, daughter of Jefferson's widowed sister Martha, was forwarded "33.33 D...towards hire of her negro." "I enclose you 100 Dol[lars] for the expences of yourself, Maria and all your party," he generously offered. "Mr. Randolph would do well to exchange the bills for gold and silver which will be more readily used on the road." What was more, both daughters were encouraged to call "freely" on their father's account with commission agent George Jefferson in Richmond. "It was never my intention," he clarified, "that a visit for my gratification should be at your expence."[32]

"A special liscence...for my slaves"

For whatever reasons, Randolph's hasty ardor to depart had cooled somewhat by the fall of 1802. His concerns were not Indian corn, deceiving neighbors, or reclaiming swamplands in Georgia. Rather he was coping with how to adjust practical matters of a private, slave enterprise with the politically-inspired changes in the structure of the Atlantic trade. Perhaps he was discouraged by obstacles that had been erected by the states of the Upper South in reaction to an approaching Constitutional ban on the importation of slaves. The solution was to invoke his father-in-law's political connections for personal ends by seeking a special license to transport his enslaved family through South Carolina.[33]

Without such politically-arranged dispensation, the financially strapped Randolph would be required to take a "circuitous rout" with "much greater difficulty and costs." There was no one in Washington with information on the laws of South Carolina, so Jefferson sought advice from the Carolina "Gamecock," Thomas Sumter, who had been newly-elected to the Senate in December the previous year. It was just "an innocent passage" of slaves, Jefferson argued, that could be warranted by either a bond or an escort "appointed by the authorities of the state." Cleverly mixing private needs and political concerns, the President also asked his fellow Democratic-Republican's "opinion on this question" of removing South Carolina Federalists from office, though wholesale replacements were against his "inclination," because "justice" and "tranquility of our country" were better served by filling vacancies as they occur.[34]

Randolph appeared to be under an irritable impatience. "I did not doubt that [information on South Carolina] might be obtained at Washington." On learning the passage through the State was "practicable," he snappishly told Jefferson, "I could have made the application and arrangment myself." His father-in-law had been "in daily expectation of receiving notice of the day on which [he and Martha] would set out" for Washington. Implying he doubted Randolph's safe chaperone of the family, Jefferson directed him to engage a guide, as "the road is so difficult that nobody unacquainted can possibly find it." Randolph's reply did not indicate the family's plans for Washington, but firmly informed Jefferson, "By the 1st Jan. the latest day of my departure, I am sanguine I may obtain assurance of the safety of my property" transiting through South Carolina. The scheme had originally been proposed by Randolph for reasons of family and debt, so Jefferson interpreted the project as part of *his* scheme for gaining solvency:

> If I can in any way aid your views in Georgia, explain it freely, as nothing will gratify me more than to do so, believing that I cannot serve my family more solidly than by clearing the old debts hanging on us. I am straining every nerve to do it: and hope to accomplish it by the time my term of service expires.[35]

The offer was soundly and hastily rejected!

> I feel the warmest gratitude for your offer to aid my views in this journey: there cannot I hope arise a necessity for that beyond what you have done allready by making me acquainted with Mr. Milledge. If I should make a purchase of Land on installments I can give Virginia lands of value along with the Slaves I settle as a pledge.[36]

Where was his collateral in "Virginia lands"? His Varina farm still was under a mortgage cloud, Milton property was to be disposed of by lottery, and Jefferson's proposed Bedford gift had not been made. In addition, Randolph, along with his brother William, as executors of Randolph Senior's will, had been held personally liable in 1797 by the U. S. District Court in Richmond for $42,000 of $65,000 that the estate owed to British creditors.[37]

A frustrated Randolph had been detoured from Mississippi to Georgia, was being asked persistently to remove his family from Edgehill to Washington, was obliged to rely on Jefferson's political connections, and now was made an instrument in his father-in-law's plan of "clearing the old debts hanging" on them. His bold and decisive effort to finally achieve some independence at age thirty-four, once again, was being subordinated to the needs of Martha and her father. It was simply too much!

"Silly bird...in the company of the Swans"

For Randolph, there was more than "dreams of wealth" at stake in the "Georgia scheme." It went beyond "mild climate & gentle labor" for his slaves. There was even more than endowing sisters Virginia and Harriet or affording Jeff a "complete education" and "traveling abroad." After eight months, his emotions finally erupted to disclose the torment he sought to escape.

> The last passage of your letter which seems to embrace me within the narrow circle of your family affects my heart deeply, but there is a mixture of pain with the emotion; Something like shame accompanying it and checking the swell of tenderness, from consciousness that I am so essentially & widely different from all within it, as to look like something extraneous, fallen in by accident and destroying the homogeneity. I cannot like the proverbially silly bird feel at any ease in the company of the Swans. Yet I can, alone, or surrounded with any number nearly the same social & intellectual level with myself be as happy and as benevolent as any being alive. The sentiment of my mind when it contemplates yourself alone is one, of the most lofty elevation and most [unmixed?] delight. The rapture of my fancy when it takes in view your extraordinary powers and considers the manner in which they have been, with unceasing and unvarying force for so many years employed and directed, is too strong for a man of less enthusiasms to feel. The feelings of my heart, the gratitude and affection it overflows with when I attempt to estimate the value to the whole human race, as an example; the precious worth, to all who live under it, as the benignant sky which covers them; of the incredibly,

inconcievably excellent political system which you have with much more hinderance [and] opposition than aid, created, developed, matured, and at last I think permanently established; will no doubt yet render absolutely eternal by some additional arrangements which will make it, like the work of the Allmighty, go, by laws enacted at its [conception?], as long as the people which form it shall endure. The feelings of my heart when I make these reflexions are such as a disposition of weak benevolence could never generate. I find I am writing a Rhapsody but I was kindled and I have not now time to write again or alter. With Sincere & ardent affection…[38]

Randolph suddenly and directly struck at the very foundation of Jefferson's life and self-fashioned identity. Maria and Martha were the "links" that held their father to "existence." Being together was the "only times that existence [was] of any value." For Maria, her "tender love" for Father was "interwoven with [her] existence." Martha unequivocally asserted that "no connexion" formed since their seven years away from Monticello, "could weaken a sentiment interwoven with [her] very existence." "I was never so sick to the heart as of the scene in [Philadelphia]," Jefferson longingly complained to his son-in-law in 1798, "and never felt the endearments of my family so necessary for my existence." These deep, abiding sentiments were symbolized by letters but only found full expression and satisfaction when Father and daughters gathered harmoniously around the Monticello fireside.[39]

He had told Martha on the occasion of Maria's betrothal: "I now see our fireside formed into a groupe…No irregular passions, no dangerous bias, which may render problematical the future fortunes and happiness of our descendants." It was this hopeful vision that sustained her father in Washington politics amid "jealousies," "hatred," "rancorous and malignant passions."[40] Now a presumed member of this imaginary, tightly bound "groupe" was charging alienation, exclusion, and most treacherously, the impossibility of ever entering the "narrow circle" because he was "so essentially & widely different." His self-indictment claimed to have destroyed the family's "homogeneity"—the "harmony" his father-in-law contrasted so sharply with political life. Randolph's "passions" were so very "irregular," so confounded. The "tenderness" in his heart was smothered with "shame" for having wreaked such devastation on the family. The emotional tension was painful! By their own trumpeting, the "Swans" happiness was only "complete" when they were together; the "silly bird's," only when separated physically and emotionally from them, as he would be in Georgia or elsewhere. Happiness, the ultimate purpose of life for individual family members, could only be reached through diverging paths.

Randolph considered himself below their "social and intellectual level" and even more subordinated to Jefferson's lifelong practice of civic virtue. Against this melancholy of living on the fringes of an affectionate family, Randolph's imagination ("fancy") incited him to a "rhapsody" on Jefferson's "lofty elevation" in the public sphere. His father-in-law was near the "Allmighty," he had "extraordinary powers," and he promulgated eternal verities so "the whole human race" could live under an "incredibly, inconceivably excellent political system." Nonetheless, this deification consoled the distressed "silly bird" by discovering within himself the quality of benevolence both men considered vital to private honor.

While in public office, Jefferson was delaying his "happiness," he reminded Maria, "to the moment when we can all be settle together, no more to separate." Father claimed to have considered the Presidency in part for the sake of Maria, Martha, and those "dear" to them. He simply wanted to bring the government "back to it's republican principles."[41] He salved his present discomfiture by fancying a future life with those he loved. Randolph's agonized lament coupled with his "scheme" menaced this hopeful prospect and wedded his esteem to Jefferson's public, rather than private, life.

Jefferson's response to Randolph's anguished letter was an awkward combination of mild rebuke, expressions of gratitude, holding up himself as an exemplar, and tying their emotional relationship to material support. Although he valued Randolph's "affection...in the highest degree," the young man's self-image cast a pall over their happiness that "can be made perfect only by a mutual consciousness of mutual esteem." Jefferson notably ignored Randolph's feelings of alienation from the "narrow circle" and of subordination to the "Swans" it encompassed. Rather, he focused on merging the two men's beings and interests. Jefferson always considered his son-in-law a "part" of himself, but material conditions have impeded expressions of the heart:

> If any circumstance has given me more pain than all
> other things, it has been the old embarrasments hanging
> on me and preventing my being as useful to you as my

heart made me wish to be. In matters of interest I know no difference between yours and mine.[42]

While Randolph might feel alienated, Jefferson pledged that his own "feelings and desires" had been unwavering: "They have never permitted me to doubt a return of the same affections." The son-in-law was directed to look to Jefferson's steadfast attachment as the balm for his anxiety:

> I hope therefore you will feel a conviction that I hold the virtues of your heart and the powers of your understanding in a far more exalted view than you place them in; and that this conviction will place your mind in the same security and ease in which mine has always been.[43]

Mann Randolph's letter had begun by asserting he could have arranged the South Carolina transit himself. He announced a firm departure date just two months away and rejected an offer of financial assistance from his father-in-law. These were simply prelude, however, to voicing the emotional turmoil he was experiencing. His complaint opened by referencing the "narrow circle of your family." Jefferson reinforced that perception, first, by directing his response only to his relationship with the son-in-law, and second, by subtly posing his own emotional fidelity and "exalted view" of Randolph as the quintessence that should be emulated. There was little question in either's mind who was "head" of a growing family and patriarch of the Monticello household.

The threats to Jefferson's "security and ease" of mind apparently were not in doubting his son-in-law's attachment but in getting Martha and children to Washington. "Your letter of the 29th has relieved me from the great anxiety I had felt on your previous silence about your journey." Written on the same day as his reassurances and remonstrance to her husband, Jefferson was concerned if Mrs. Madison would choose the proper color for Martha's wig and whether "sister Marks" had received her "necessaries" from Higginbotham's store in Milton.[44]

"We are in earnest"

After nearly two years of false starts, Martha and Maria finally departed Monticello on Wednesday 17 November 1802, on a four-day journey to spend a few winter weeks in the midst of Father's annual legislative campaign. "[T]his is a flying visit," Martha forewarned her father, "only to shew that we are in earnest with regard to Washington."[45] Maria had a different interpretation of their trip:

> I lament sincerely that it has not been possible for us to go sooner, as the visit will be scarcely worth making for so short a time and should prefer waiting till the spring and returning there with you as we could then remain with you some time but my sister will not agree to put it off any longer.[46]

Jefferson advanced Captain Lewis $40 and Martha $200 for travelling expenses; Mr. Barney received "50.D. [for a] carriage & horses to Strode's," as Mr. Eppes's was "much out of repair" and the Randolphs' was "absolutely not in traveling condition."[47] Mann Randolph had been "summoned to Richmond," so Jack Eppes saw them to Strode's in Culpeper County, where they were met by the President's emissary, Meriwether Lewis.[48] Martha carried Peter Hemings's receipt for muffins,[49] as her father had directed, but refused his request to bring five children, "considering the lateness of the season and the bad weather."[50] Indeed, the "first ice" had formed in Washington on 1 November and the thermometer dipped to 29 degrees on the 4th.[51] Daughters and grandsons Jeff and Francis (13 months) greeted their dearest Father and Grand Papa on Sunday, November 21st for what must have been a joyous reunion so long in the making.

His daughters had requested "2 wigs the colour of the hair enclosed [in Martha's] letter and of the most fashionable shapes." Such trim was "universally worn" and would relieve them of "dressing" their own hair, a task in which Martha and Maria were not "adepts." Mrs. Madison was enlisted to have milliner Mary Ann Pic make two such adornments for "38.D."[52] During Martha's and Maria's seven-week stay, their father drew on his commission agent, John Barnes, to pay Stille ordinary "15.D. subscription to balls" and McLaughlin ordinary "10.D. subscription to Geo. town balls." The Washington Jockey Club races, just west of the President's House on 30 November and 1 December, were a meager $2.25, assuming Jefferson sustained his abhorrence of gambling. Entertaining 125 "gentleman" from December 7–19, however, was more extravagant, requiring fifty bottles of "Champagne."[53]

"Beaming with intelligence, benevolence and sensibility"

Maria's natural endowments, embellished with fashionable wigs and presented in a diffident style, were favorably received by at least one "Roman matron" of Washington society. "Mrs. Eppes is beautiful, simplicity and timidity personified when in company," Margaret Smith apprised sister-in-law Susan, "but when alone with you of communicative and winning manners." Martha, on the other hand, "is rather homely, a delicate likeness of her father, but still more interesting" than her sister. Father's "plan of reading" and "considerably different" education for his eldest daughter were more on display in a Washington milieu than the rural isolation of Monticello with Mesdames Nicholas or Gabriel Lilly:

> She is really one of the most lovely women I have ever met with, her countenance beaming with intelligence, benevolence and sensibility, and her conversation fulfils all her countenance promises. Her manners, so frank and affectionate, that you know her at once, and feel perfectly at your ease with her....She has that rare but charming egotism which can interest the listener in all one's concerns. I could have listened to her for two hours longer...

Smith and the Virginians already had exchanged five morning visits in the first month of their stay, because they were "heartily tired" of evening "entertainments."[54]

Father saw his daughters, grandsons, and son-in-law Randolph across the Potomac at the George Town "ferrge" on January 5 (cost $2.83). The family experienced a "disastrous journey" in blustery winter weather over rutted and muddy Virginia pathways before arriving at Edgehill five days later. Baby Francis was showing symptoms of measles, fifteen-month old Virginia did not recognize her Mother, and Martha's "dear friend" Eliza Trist was in residence. Maria was suffering a "depression of spirits" from leaving her father behind and "heart ache" from "the recollection of the heavy expense this journey has been" for him. "[I]nexperience in some respects," she confessed, "was greatly the cause of my own part of the great abuse of your indulgence towards us."[55] "Indeed I suffer for you in imagination beyond anything I had long felt," Father lamented to Martha. "I felt my solitude too after your departure very severly."[56] Their parting would be brief, as he set out a month later on 7 March for a short three-week visit, during which he attended to various financial affairs.

A $1,300 note was given to tenant Craven Peyton for his secret purchases on Jefferson's behalf of Henderson's lands around Milton. Poplar Forest had yielded over 51,000 pounds of tobacco in 1802, but 6,500 pounds were the overseer's share, and provisions cost £212–8–3 or slightly over $700 dollars. This outlying plantation also had produced among other items 2,825 pounds of "bacon & dried beef," 44 gallons of brandy, 135 pounds of soap, and 268 pounds of butter. Later that year in July, the crop sold for $3,425—over one-third or which was disbursed to clear Peyton's note.[57]

Randolph had been diverted from Mississippi, in part, due to the Chickasaw nation standing between the United States and Natchez. On the same day Jefferson was expressing feelings of "solitude" to Martha, he secretly shared with Congress his views on the Indians. They were "the most friendly tribe without our limits, but the most decided against the alienation of lands." The President's scheme was to convince Congress "how desirable it [was] to possess a respectable breadth of country" on the Mississippi by exploring the Missouri River.[58] His alternative for Randolph's scheme had been in abeyance since before Martha's visit. From Sumter's letter in late November, Jefferson did not "think the aspect flattering" for securing passage for his son-in-law's "negroes" with a bond or official escort. A carelessly "mislaid" letter from South Carolina Governor John Drayton three days later relayed that there was "no prospect of getting [Randolph's] negroes through." Like much political intelligence, General Sumter three weeks later offered a contrary opinion, assuring that "there would be no doubt of the success of an application to the legislature." By mid-January, at least the legal hurdles were removed: "The S. Carolina assembly have [sic] amended their law so as to permit negroes to be carried through their state," Jefferson reported. "Yours therefore will meet with no difficulty."[59]

During late winter and early spring of 1803, both daughters again were pressed to enter Washington society, and Congressional elections promised to add their husbands, as well, to the "rancorous" clamor of the City's partisan politics. Jack Eppes's election to Congress in 1802 stirred Father's "hopes" that Maria would come in the winter and later "find it convenient to accompany [her] sister in the spring" of 1804. The serious illness of incumbent William Branch Giles relieved her father from suffering "the imputation of being willing to lose to the public so strong a supporter, for the personal gratification of having yourself and Mr. Eppes with me." The Georgia scheme and Congressional elections, however, were a prickly private and political matter in the case of Randolph. He was less direct with Martha but no less adamant, given their emotional bond. Jefferson bought "a beautiful blue Casimer, waterproof" coat for her husband, presumably still thinking he planned a southern reconnaissance trip.[60]

Intersecting Spheres

Without consulting the President, Randolph inserted himself into the political public sphere by suddenly deciding to run against a staunch Jefferson ally. Samuel Jordan Cabell had been active during the election crisis of 1801, according to Jack Eppes, "lying two nights on a blanket to make [Jefferson] President." Unaware the nascent public servant was abandoning his Georgia scheme to pursue his boyhood dream, Jefferson reassured Cabell of his neutrality in the election.[61] On 29 April 1803, Randolph reported that his "struggle with Colo. Cabell has terminated in [his] favor…after nine days continuance." The margin was a slim thirteen votes of over 1,800 cast, and rumors circulated that his opponent would contest the outcome. After exhaustively detailing negotiations over the purchase of cherry logs and almost as an afterthought, Randolph informed Jefferson:

> I expect to be disappointed entirely now in my Georgia scheme…I am inclined at present to dispose of such of the Negroes, destined to settle in Georgia according to my late scheme, as are of bad character, either here or there, and to reserve the others for improvements.

Then, in a closing that fully revealed his awareness of the family's triangulated emotional dynamics that had spawned his scheme in the first place:

> I mention this that you may know I shall be at home to take care of the children, if you should yet desire Martha to come to Washington; though your own return being now not very distant I have a hope you may not be so anxious for it; though I am ready to forward [her] journey and shall part with her cheerfully.[62]

The disappointed émigré had returned to the ambivalent deference that concealed his relationship with Jefferson behind a fog of comity. While hoping Father would not "be so anxious" for a visit, he nonetheless agrees "cheerfully" to part with her. The Georgia "scheme" had threatened to separate the conjugal unit, at least spring and fall each year and, in her husband's opinion, would have "tortured" Martha. With his son-in-law gone, her father had interpreted it as an opportunity to be with her more frequently and exclusively.

A scheme Jefferson considered "practicable and advisable" a year before he now doubted "whether it would be profitable...on the whole to scatter...property so much." Nine months of supporting the move with information, political influence, and the offer of money were cast away with a litany of reasons for discontinuing the scheme: "To the pecuniary inconveniences too must be added those of an annual journey, long absences from your family, and risk to your own health. On the whole therefore I am glad you decline it." The "most profitable" cotton and the opportunity of "clearing the old debts" were subordinated to Randolph's "health," "travel," and "long absences." The "Swan," however, now knew the real reasons for the flight of the "silly bird." "With respect to Martha's visit, I could not possibly propose or consent to it, if it were to separate the family. I could not, to gratify myself, wish to do what I know must produce both pain and injury to them." Martha had become a token shuttled mentally across the checkered emotional landscape between Monticello's patriarch and its most dutiful pawn. She was "considerably advanced in pregnancy," Randolph disclosed near the end of May. "[O]n that account chiefly I am pleased with your relinquishing her visit...for the stage carriages all jolt severely."[63] (Pregnancy had not been an explicit consideration by Randolph in the early months of 1801, when both Martha and Maria were more "advanced" than at this time.)

Randolph would not be required to "take care of the children," so could recover his self-confidence as well as attend to Cabell's challenge to the "most disagreeable" election. Randolph confessed he would not have "felt the smallest mortification, if it had terminated unfavorably," as he had expected. With no acknowledgement of disturbing Jefferson's political alliance, he felt "a heavy anxiety [from] the consciousness of wanting the qualities and acquirements necessary for passing through [the office] with honour."

> I knew well when I determined on the undertaking that if I succeeded I should enlarge my circle of thought and action far beyond my power to fill, but I thought it possible by industry, in time, to travel through it without disgrace and I even hoped I might at last move in it so as to give some satisfaction.[64]

While his Georgia scheme was being delayed in October 1802 by state law, Randolph had woefully acknowledged that he was "extraneous" to the "narrow circle" of family and not equal to its intellectual and social standing. As the possibility of a "Cotton plantation" and "dreams of wealth" diminished, he regressed to his boyhood dream of a political life where he could "enlarge [his] circle of thought and action." But even this alternative was shrouded in self-effacement and low expectations. He was not seeking the "grand scenes" or "extraordinary toils" he attributed to his father-in-law or even of "passing through with honour." No! He merely wanted to do it "without disgrace," with "some satisfaction."[65] Even these modest goals beyond the "narrow circle" would elude him, as would breaching the affectionate bond between Martha and Father.

Neighborhood Chicanery

Regardless of the election's outcome (which was not settled until March 1804), Mann Randolph would not want for work. The mill portion of Jefferson's plan to achieve solvency was being threatened by competitors. One of the Henderson heirs (whose land Jefferson had been secretly buying though Craven Peyton) was proposing to sell four acres on the Rivanna for a mill site. Such a move was a "gross deception," because a dam of sufficient height would overflow not only the Henderson's mill site but also "injure" Randolph's "seat on the opposite side" of the river. "As you are interested in this matter," Jefferson rhetorically directed Randolph, "would it not be well for you to act in concert with Mr. Peyton" to gain approval under their auspices for a mill on Jefferson's tract. This would reduce the value of John Henderson's four acres and its vacant mill that could then "be bought for the price of the irons and scantling."[66] Perhaps from his "tragic" experience marketing wheat in 1800 and the most recent disappointments regarding Georgia, Randolph did not seem inclined to follow his father-in-law's advice. He had not consulted Peyton and even was "considering" selling his "seat in north Milton" to the prospective competitors to Jefferson's mill. Randolph foresaw a sale as serving the "due interests" of his "successors" (children) and an opportunity to provide "a considerable quota of labor at the seasons when [his] force…at Varina ought to be withdrawn."[67] Such a move in Jefferson's opinion might add value to Henderson's remaining lots "which would forever put it out of my power to get rid of him as to the rivalry" by surreptitious purchases.[68] If his neighbor persisted, Jefferson threatened to degrade the property's value by taking down the dam that was on a lot Peyton owned on his behalf. Since he had undertaken to buy Henderson's land secretly, Jefferson was completely dependent on Randolph and Peyton for carrying out this bit of chicanery to further one the central elements of his plan for reducing debt.

After two years maintaining a Presidential "outfit" and aware that income from all sources was on a rough parity with current years' expenses, Jefferson was less sanguine about reducing the household's debt with his government salary. Still in mid-1803, he oddly clung to his original plan for achieving solvency.

> My great object at present is, within the course of my present term of office to get compleatly thro' the old debts of Mr. Wayles's estate and my own. I hope I shall do it by the aid of this and the next years crop, and what sparings I can put by from my salary, tho' they are very small.... [I]t is quite as much as I can hope, if by the end of my second term of office (which will certainly be my last) I can see all of us out of debt, and my mill and farms in such a state as to supply the expences of living to which the course of my political life will expose me I fear unavoidably.[69]

If free of debt, Jefferson speculated, "all my desires will be crowned with contentment to myself, and I hope...to carry into retirement the contentment of the public."[70] Balancing accounts, political interests, and family dynamics would prove a Herculean task.

A "Merry" Affair

Jefferson in 1788 from the safety of Paris could idealize to Anne Willing Bingham a distinction between European "Amazons" and American "Angels," whom he claimed were content "to soothe and calm the minds of their husbands returning ruffled from political debate." But by 1797, the "agitations of Europe," the newly-elected Vice President confided to Angelica Schuyler Church, had reached the American shores to "disturb social life." The tumble of political life did not leave "discord to senates, love and friendship to society."[71] The women of Washington City were integral to the social scene and fully capable of stirring the cauldron of partisan dissension.

Martha's father used these very same "agitations" and "discord" to conjure an image of Monticello "in the only scene where...the sweeter affections of life have any exercise." By drawing sharp contrasts between their separately lived situations, he also intended to enhance Martha's sense of emotional wellbeing:

> For you to feel all the happiness of your quiet situation, you should know the rancorous passions which tear every breast here, even of the sex which should be a stranger to them. politics & party hatreds destroy the happiness of every being here. they seem, like salamanders, to consider fire as their element. I am in hopes you make free use of the garden & any other resources at Monticello.[72]

Amid partisan politics in a city thriving on gossip, even social conviviality could be breached by matters of protocol. The President early in his administration allowed guests to enter the dining room *pell mell* and select seats without distinction as to rank, gender, or other markers of inequality. This practice, he later claimed, was to convey that in the New Republic "social circles all are equal, whether in, or out, of office, foreign or domestic: the same equality exists among ladies as among gentlemen."[73] Such a radical republican ideal did not comport with the manners that British minister Anthony Merry was accustomed to in his home country of Lords, Knights of the Realm, and other finely gradated ranks. This seemingly minor social peccadillo became a political *causa celebris* taken up by the Federalists and sustained with a boycott of official social events by the Merrys and Spanish envoy extraordinary Marqués de Casa Yrujo.[74]

Political fallout from the Merry affair even clouded the signal triumph of Jefferson's first term and moderated his urgency for the company of Martha and Maria. Congress planned a dinner to celebrate the acquisition of Louisiana, but would "invite no foreign ministers," he wrote Martha, "to avoid questions of etiquette in which we are enveloped by Merry's and Yrujo's families."

> As much as I wished to have had yourself and sister with me, I rejoice you were not here. The brunt of the battle now falls on the Secretary's ladies, who are dragged in the dirt of every federal paper. You would have been the victims had you been here, and butchered the more bloodily as they would hope it would be more felt by myself. It is likely to end in those two families putting themselves into Coventry until they recieve orders from their courts to acquiesce in our principles of the equality of all persons meeting together in society,

and not to expect to force us into their principles of allotment into ranks and orders.[75]

In Paris, Jefferson could cloister his teen-aged daughter against the influences of countrywomen Mrs. Robert Montgomery, Mrs. Robert Barrett, or the *salonnières* Houdetot and Necker, whose company he so enjoyed. If they bent to Father's entreaties to visit the new Nation's capital, however, Martha and Maria would be subject to the same critical scrutiny and social demands as other women of the city. Ambassador Merry's wife, for example, merited both criticism and praise in the eyes of the Americans. She was "very fat and covers only with fine lace two objects which could fill a fourth of a bushel," Rosalie Stier Calvert informed her mother in Europe."[76] Margaret Bayard Smith gauged "brilliant and fantastic" the Englishwoman's diamond studded combs, earrings, and necklace that was "displayed on a bare bosom." But such lavish, fashionable attire did not compare with the display of a European's courtesan-like spouse, Mrs. Jerome Bonaparte (née Elizabeth Patterson). "Mobs of boys have crowded round her splendid equipage," Smith informed sister Jane. "Her dress was the thinnest sarcenet [silk]…; her back, her bosom, part of her waist and her arms were uncover'd and the rest of her form visible."[77] Her other qualities were celebrated with even fainter praise from Rosalie Calvert, who tagged her "a most extraordinary girl, given to reading Godwin [Mary Wollstonecraft] on the rights of women, etc., in short, a modern *philosophe.*"[78]

Rosalie's niece and Martha Washington's granddaughter, Nelly Custis Lewis, contributed a different peek on Mrs. Merry by finding her "manners extremely affable and friendly," and would "be very much pleased to cultivate her acquaintance." Her physical endowments went unmentioned.[79] (This fashion exceeded the "sloven and slut" appearance young Patsy had been sternly rebuked for in 1784.) The Muse in land speculator Thomas Law was aroused sufficiently by the spectacle to spawn a ditty of Betsy Patterson Bonaparte which Aaron Burr shared with the newlywed and found its way into the rounds of elite circles:

Well! What of Madame Bonaparte
Why she's a little whore at heart
Her lustful looks[,] her wanton air
Her limbs revealed[,] her bosom bare
Show her ill suited for the life
Of a Columbians modest wife

Wisely she's chosen her proper line
She's formed for Jerome's concubine.[80]

The women of Monticello would likely have agreed with Margaret Smith's opinion of Washington City: "There is no place in the United States where one hears and sees so many strange things, or where so many odd characters are to be met with."[81]

Drawing more family members to the Washington scene would not only open private affairs to public attention but also underscore how exercising civic virtue only exacerbated the family's pain from emotional and physical separation. When son-in-law Eppes was beginning his Congressional term in 1804, Maria lay dangerously ill from the pregnancy of their third child. Her "spirits are bad," sister Martha wrote despairingly, "partly occasioned by her situation...and partly from the prospect of congress not rising till April...[C]ertainly her mind would be more at ease could he [Eppes] be with her."[82] If not with him in Washington City, Maria's father still hoped that in the last months of pregnancy she would have the "resources of courage, not requiring the presence of anybody." He looked forward to March. They would begin preparing a house site at Pantops and building her "hen-house" for "two pair of beautiful fowls" he had received from Algiers.[83] "Low in spirits and health," it was only the "anticipation" of her reunion with Dear Papa and Mr. Eppes that sustained Maria in the "tedious interval." Being with them "would compensate for any suffering." Meanwhile, she begged he honor a promise to have a picture drawn by St. Mémin. "If you did but know what a source of pleasure it would be to us while so much separated from you," Maria pleaded from her lying in. So many years without a father present to share so many births, deaths, illnesses, and even a few moments of uncheckered happiness had deflated Maria's expectations to a mere facsimile: "It is what we have allways most wanted in our lives."[84]

With neither the promised likeness nor the company of the President nor Mr. Eppes, Maria gave birth five days later on 15 February and was offered "a thousand joys...on the happy accession to her family." Accompanying the congratulations was an excuse; if only Congress had recessed in time, they would have been with her "at the moment when it would have been so encouraging to have had friends around."[85] The family's exuberance was fleeting, as Maria's health continued to decline. Mr. Eppes hurried to her side, her father held back by public duty. In a state of "terrible anxiety," he hastily wrote: "Nothing but impossibilities prevent my instant departure to join you. But the impossibility of Congress proceeding a single step in my absence presents an insuperable bar."[86] Mary Jefferson Eppes died on 17 April, survived for a time by her newborn namesake, a two-and-a-half-year-old son, and Congressman John Eppes.

"Not...a scruple in sacrifising them"

Grieving Maria's recent death and near the end of the first Presidential term, the emotional intensity of extended separations had increased to the point that father and daughter were finding more and more solace in their imagined future. It was Martha who articulated a reconstructed family and unequivocally pledged her eternal devotion solely to the one she held dearest:

> I do not hesitate to declare if my other duties could possibly interfere with my devotion to you I should not feel a scruple in sacrifising them, to a sentiment which has litterally "grown with my growth and strengthened with my strength,["] and which no subsequent attachment has in the smallest degree weakened. It is truly the happiness of my life to think that I can dedicate the remainder of it to promote yours. It is a subject however upon which I ought never to write for no pen on earth can do justice to the feelings of my heart.[87]

Their letters over the preceding years were interpreted as tokens of affection and had offered a modicum of compensation for lack of propinquity. Now with only two members of the original Jefferson family remaining, the heart could not find its way onto paper.

Chapter 9

"A harbour from the cares and storms of life":

Republican Wife, Daughter, and Mother

"Horrors of a trial so severe"

By the fall of 1804, the "unlimited calumnies of the federalists" had "obliged" Martha's father to stand for another election. Nevertheless, his "heart" was not dedicated to another session of Congress nor the election.

> My passion strengthens daily to quit political turmoil, and retire into the bosom of family, the only scene of sincere and pure happiness. One hour with you and your dear children is to me worth an age past here.[1]

The Washington society he initially had enjoyed in 1801 and relentlessly encouraged Martha and Maria to attend was judged "remarkably dull" in December 1804. There were "very few ladies" and no actors for the theatre. Such amusements could no longer compensate for the "bosom of family" that Martha enjoyed. "You are happy to need none of these aids to get rid of your time and certainly they are poor substitutes for the sublime enjoiment of the affections of our children and of our cares for them."[2]

Father had been absent since early October, enduring the social boredom of Washington City and expecting her in early January. Her husband had arrived there on Sunday, November 4th to complete his first term in the Eighth Congress, would return home briefly to campaign, and return to Washington in mid-January. All the while, Martha was home managing domestic chores, stretched between

Edgehill and Monticello, dealing with overseer Lilly, a runaway slave, and six children, aged one to twelve years. Alone in mid-February 1805, she was stricken with "an hysteric fit" similar to what she had experienced a few weeks after Maria's death the prior year.[3] Her symptoms then were a "cramp in the stomach…with a desire to puke…a difficulty of breathing amounting allmost to suffocation…and the affection of the speech." She "thought [herself] dying" during the most recent occurrence and hinted that it was preceded by a "complaint…brought on by the <u>cold</u>."[4] April on the mountaintop brought an end to Martha's "cough" and "sentiment of debility or languor," Randolph reassured Jefferson. "Her appetite and digestion are both right and her spirits as good as ever." Nonetheless, it was four months later and two months pregnant that she decided to "resume her housekeeping in person" in the midst of an outbreak of mumps among the children.[5]

Since the earliest days of his Presidency, Jefferson had insistently urged Martha and Maria to visit for extended periods during the wintertime social and legislative "season." The daughters had been able to make only one "flying trip" in the winter of 1802–03. A confluence of political, financial and health concerns dampened Martha's enthusiasm for another reunion in Washington. Following the attack of "hysterics" in early 1805, her health had been delicate through much of the year. She fearfully wrote a month before leaving Edgehill:

> Nothing but my present situation could justify my leaving home at a time when it is so little convenient to Mr. Randolph…[M]y courage shrinks from the horrors of a trial so severe under the most favorable circumstances but rendered infinitely more so in this instance from the uncertainty of my accustomed medical aid and the want of a female friend, Jane being a fellow sufferer.[6]

Martha's "present situation" also included the prospect of being home alone once again while her husband began his second Congressional term—a circumstance much like Maria's before her death in 1804.

Despite these reservations, she dutifully begin preparing for the visit by requesting that her father ask Mrs. Madison to buy "a set of combs for dressing the hair, a bonnet shawl and white lace veil, for paying morning visits" as well as "2 lace half handerchiefs." He forwarded the request to Mrs. Madison in Philadelphia, gave his daughter $100 for travel expenses, and told her to expect everything to be furnished, "so that the visit may not at all affect Mr. Randolph's pecuniary arrangements."[7] On 2 December 1805, Martha and newly re-elected Congressman Randolph arrived at the President's House, where just seven weeks later their eighth child was born and honored with the name of Grand Papa's closest associate, James Madison. Neither her spirits nor those of her father were buoyed by Randolph's political antics later that spring that potentially threatened to make him permanently "unavailable" to her and the family.

"Lead and steel"

In January, Jefferson had proposed to a closed-door session of Congress that the United States purchase West Florida from Spain for $2 million, thereby removing another foreign nation from the continent. His "wise and frugal" administration wanted to fund the acquisition with the salt tax originally enacted for military actions against Barbary pirates. The opposition countered with an amendment introduced by House Ways and Means Committee chair John Randolph of Roanoke to repeal the tax. When a tax opponent's floor speech became inflammatory, Mann Randolph and several others loudly shouted for order, eliciting a quick reaction from his rhetorically skillful cousin. The Roanoke branch of the family asked:

> But what has thrown us into this heat? Is it the dinner we have just eaten? I hope no honorable gentleman, who has heretofore kept the noiseless tenor of his way, because we have adjourned for half an hour, has permitted his passions to indulge in an asperity not shown on any former occasion. I did hope that whatever contumely or hostility may have been manifested during the earlier period of the sessions, we would have thrown in the last moments of it, neither the splenetic temper of age or youth; but that we should have parted like men not ashamed of what we had done, or afraid to meet the public award.[8]

Repeal of the tax failed by 40 to 47, but Albemarle nonetheless took up "contumely" as referencing him and rubbed rhetorical "salt" in his cousin's defeat. He charged the gentleman from Roanoke with making more "noise" this entire session of Congress than was useful for orderly proceedings, his talents had become "perverted," and he was "bankrupt forever as a popular statesman." Mann Randolph acknowledged his "inferiority" in matters of intellect, but John was his lesser "in the point of true patriotism." This self-deprecation was more than rhetorical artifice. Albemarle had not entered on public life brimming with self-confidence, and unlike brother-in-law John Eppes, was not a particularly active Member. Following his narrow victory for a first term, Randolph confessed to "heavy anxiety [over] the consciousness of wanting the qualities and acquirements necessary for passing through with honour." If successful, however, he knew that he would "enlarge [his] circle of thought and action far beyond [his] power to fill." This self-doubt was clear in his "apology" to the House.

Self-effacement, however, did not cause him to shrink from an ominous challenge to his cousin.

> The gentleman made use of the term "contumely." To this and other offensive terms, with an allusion which, as to me, is as unjust as it is insulting....[T]his gentleman is apt to indulge himself, while he has the shield of the dignity of this House,...in language...which would be inadmissible in society...I never will, unprovoked, seek a quarrel with any one;...but I have always thought and always shall think, that lead and even steel make very proper ingredients in serious quarrels...[9]

Perhaps, Mann Randolph had used the half-hour dinner break to indulge his "passions," but it had not lessened their ardor. The challenge had been offered; Roanoke readily accepted; and the cousins appointed their seconds. However, the challenger was assured through his cousin's second that the remarks were directed at William Findley. Randolph consulted Members and found not a single one considered him the object. Albemarle retook the floor to admit using "severe and harsh language," but he had been under the belief that "expressions of a disrespectful nature" had been "dropped" on him by John Randolph of Roanoke. Mann Randolph had self-effacingly expressed to his father-in-law in 1803 that he merely wanted to "travel through [elected office] without disgrace"; now he thought even this modest objective threatened by the words "noise" and "contumely" hurled at him by a distant relative.

> By a rapid movement of my mind, I came to a resolution not to go home with such a load on my feelings...that the treatment I had received was in the face of a company of a hundred men, who were to

disperse to-morrow, and spread my disgrace through all quarters of the Union.[10]

To his "mortification," some Congressmen speculated that his speech was "a studied attack" on John Randolph for his vocal opposition to the Administration throughout the First Session. In other words, he was being accused of using a public forum to further private, not partisan, interests—taking up for his father-in-law! "I could not have done so with honor, unprovoked, for private reasons," he declaimed. "I have never imagined such a design, nor could I to answer that end have used such language." He considered the umbrage a private and personal matter, but for others it could play just as well in the public, political arena as a defense of his near relation.

Clarifications, veiled apologies, and a Congressional recess did not end the matter, however, because newspapers in Washington and Richmond took various sides on which of the irascible Randolphs had first left the field of honor.[11] Rancorous speeches on the floor of the House and journalistic punditry paled in comparison to the torments, fears, and anxieties that the "rapid movement" of Randolph's mind had visited upon the family.

"[W]here the future happiness of our whole family, or their future misery unmixed and unabating, are hanging in even suspence," Jefferson reminded Randolph, "it must be justifiable to urge our rights to a due share of weight in your deliberations." The anxious patriarch pleaded with "an aching heart" that his impetuous son-in-law limit any public response to simply correcting matters of fact "without colouring, without reflection, without any expression of feeling." In emotive language seldom used by Jefferson, he described the stakes in the conflict:

> How different is the stake which you two would bring into the field! On his side, unentangled in the affections of the world, a single life, of no value to himself or others. On your's, yourself, a wife, and a family of children, all depending, for all their happiness and protection in this world on you alone. Should they lose you, my cares for them, a poor substitute at any time, could continue, by the course of nature, but for a short time. Seven children, all under the age of discretion and down to infancy would then be left without guide or guardian but a poor brokenhearted woman, doomed herself to misery the rest of her life. And should her frail

frame sink under it, what is then to become of them? Is it possible that your duties to these dear objects can weigh more lightly than those to a gladiator?[12]

The "thinking part of society," "the valuable part of society," that part of society "whose esteem we value" condemned dueling as an "imaginary honour," as tearing "asunder all the ligaments of duty and affection," and consigning to "misery and ruin innocent and helpless families." Jefferson confessed his "anxiety in this case was extreme:"

It flows from a sincere and warm affection for you, and from that devotedness to the happiness of my daughter and her children, without which there can be none for me. I see all this depending on your prudence and self-command...[13]

If past experience was an indicator, Randolph's "prudence and self-command" were slender threads, indeed, for securing the family's "happiness and protection." Jefferson was warranted in closing his letter "with sincere prayers that this calamity may be averted." If Mann Randolph could just prudently state the facts of the Congressmen's dispute "without expression of feeling," that disturbance would be quelled."[14]

By mid-July, Jefferson claimed that "general opinion" held the entire imbroglio "may stop where it is now with entire honour" to both parties. With words that must have stung so sensitive a family member, Jefferson had concluded that his son-in-law had been "mistaken in supposing [Roanoke] meant to try any experiment on [his] sensibility." An end to the matter brought "peace of mind and happiness" to the family.[15]

Amid the temperamental Randolph's brouhaha and Martha's absence from his daily life, Jefferson found his "confinement" in Washington each day "more disgusting." He hoped to "preserve a steady course for two years," carry into retirement the "good will" of his constituents, and "restore" himself to the only place he was happy—"domestic scenes."[16] His son-in-law's petulance would seriously disturb the "steady course" and *ersatz* domestic scene at the President's House, just as he had riled the People's House.

"Jarring and jealousies"

Having avoided another Randolph-induced crisis, a depression clouded Jefferson's spirits by the fall of 1806: "...[T]he loansomeness of this place is more intolerable than I ever found it. My daily rides too are sikening for want of some interest in the scenes…: and indeed I look over the two ensuing years as the most tedious of my life."[17] Before leaving office, his son-in-law heaped further discomfiture on his spirits by striking at Jefferson's ideal of a fireside without "jarring or jealousies," "irregular passions," or "dangerous bias."[18] He did a "Randolph," as the family came to call the behavior with respect to his son Jeff, viz., "having once let his imagination convince him of a thing however improbable, he would continue to think it though his own senses were to tell him the contrary."[19]

Angered that Jefferson had invited John Eppes but not him to an event at the President's House, Congressman Randolph abruptly moved in mid-February 1807 to a boarding house run by Frost and Quinn at the other end of Pennsylvania Avenue.[20] His letter of complaint caused Jefferson to suffer a "pang" and to "hastily and crudely" throw his "feelings on paper" but omit "thousands…which are inexpressible." True, he confessed to his brooding son-in-law, Eppes alone had been invited, but reminded him that his memories of deceased Maria and attachment to everything she loved were "too sacred a cast to inspire any umbrage." Randolph had alluded to "other acts indicating a preference" for Eppes, but his "overwhelmed" father-in-law was not aware of any and "was conscious they have been misconstrued" by the complainant. He urged upon Randolph his feelings of "warmest affection," regard for his "virtues," and estimation of his "qualifications." Still, it was their "connection through the dearest tie"—daughter and wife Martha—that would make "separation…a calamity." Umbrage and separation endangered the family that father and daughter had been imagining for years:

> Ardently longing for the moment when I can retire to the bosom of my family, when I was hoping to receive from their love something which might warm the chilling and dreary feelings of age, if the curtain is to be dropped between that consolation and myself, then indeed all is lost for me! I have not one glimmering of comfort in this world left; if the last ties of nature which hold to the human are to be torn from mine, I sincerely wish that the hour which closes the career of my public duties, may close that of my life also.[21]

The political public sphere had penetrated to the very heart of the intimate private family. In a moment of crisis when their entire family construct seemed near destruction, death was its antipode, not public life! More than "jarring and jealousies" among brothers-in-law, however, were contributing to the Randolph's "state of disquietude."

Randolph's quick response on 18 February apparently claimed he was alienated from his father-in-law's affection—just as he was from the "family circle" of "Swans" in 1802. In addition, political affairs in his opinion had been forcefully injected into this family division by rumors he was "joining the Federalists to censure [Jefferson's] public conduct." On the question of affection, Jefferson pled himself "guilty of an error" in not conveying that he loved him like a "son." As to the charge of political disloyalty, "there is some enemy," the President alleged, "who has endeavored to sow tares between us." "[N]o mortal ever presumed to say to me one word disrespectful or disapproving of you," Jefferson declared on his honour, "and not a word or thought of that character ever escaped from me to any mortal." Given a "mutual understanding" was hopefully the result of these reassurances, "what has past is never more to be recollected."[22]

The Virginia farmers reached sufficient rapprochement the following week they could ride in a cold rain to buy thorn plants for a Monticello fence and share the consequent misery of severe colds. Yet, Randolph would not consent to "return to his former room" at the President's House, where he would be "so much more comfortable," and his presence would make Jefferson "extremely happy."[23] There was a flurry of messages to Martha on her husband's lingering illness. On Monday, March 2: "He is considerably reduced and weakened." Friday: "I left him at 4. P M with not much fever, entirely at ease and in good spirits." Improvement continued over the weekend: "Mr. Randolph is entirely well...[and] he moved here on Saturday." The worst of the Randolph's physical crisis was over in slightly more than a week, but Jefferson's "periodical head-ache" continued on him from "9 or 10 in the morning till dark," perhaps exacerbated by the impending conspiracy trial of Aaron Burr docketed for 30 March. He alerted Martha: "There may be a possibility of something connected with this circumstance arising which might detain me a little."[24]

Such were the traveling conditions in late March of 1807 that Martha advised her father and husband to avoid them, as they were both recovering from serious illnesses. The roads between Washington City and Monticello were "in a state not to be conceived." Nephew Samuel Carr tried "putting 9 horses to one waggon," but still had to unload and pry out "2 of the horses who mired." Martha's primary concern now, however, appeared not to be miry roads but knurly family relations.

Knowing well their pattern of deference and condescension and her husband's recent snit, she became Randolph's interlocutor:

> Mr. Randolph's fear of detaining you may make him venture upon it [the trip] sooner than prudence would authorise....I mention this merely to put you both entirely at your ease. I know he would rather be left than detain you one moment, or set off himself sooner than entirely prudent.[25]

After years of experience in their triangulated relationship, Martha skillfully presented a strategy that melded potentially different interests into a joint action—just the political acumen Jefferson so frequently attempted. If not fully recovered, Randolph would defer to remain behind, rather than delay Jefferson; should Jefferson decide to forego his son-in-law's company on the return to Monticello, he would only be doing Randolph's will, rather than condescending to an act of benevolence. Martha's contorted rationale was presented in the context of a husband-father relationship that had become quite prickly earlier in the year, even to the point of threatening a rupture. The family she imagined would prevail after 1809 required at least a modicum of civility. Health and weather had improved sufficiently by April 7th that the ailing republicans could set out directly for Monticello.

The family's emotional and physical crisis had nearly split them asunder. However in its throes, Randolph wisely "decided absolutely not to offer again for Congress." The whole affair reinforced for Father just how much his happiness had become entwined solely with Martha's. "Is there anything here I can get or do for you? It would much add to my happiness if I oftener could know how to add to your convenience or gratification." Martha, too, made clear just where her future happiness lay.

> I make no exception when I say the first and most important object with me will be the dear and sacred duty of nursing and chearing your old age, by every endearment of filial tenderness....Every age has it pleasures, with health I do not know whether youth is to be regretted....[Cicero] has certainly seen it [old age] in it true light, as a harbour from the cares and storms of life to which the turbulence of the passions expose us in youth.[26]

"Pray take care of yourself," Martha urged her father in anticipation of his retirement from political life in 1809. "I look forward to the 2 remaining years with more anxiety than I can express." Her emotions had reached a fever pitch by 1809, when she wrote: "My heart beats with inexpressible anxiety and impatience."[27]

"Inexpressible anxiety and impatience"

Apprehensively enduring the final two years of separation and suffering the hateful labors of public service, daughter and father began to plan for living the family they had only imagined for so many years. The accumulation of people, places, things, and political baggage over two decades compounded the difficulties of creating a new life for themselves. The political detritus of eight Presidential years and four in the vice presidency; Randolph's unexpected entry into politics and his unpredictable "spirits"; Maria's death and John Eppes's remarriage; children venturing forth from the security of the Monticello household; and other life-changing events would make difficult a move to the long-fancied "fireside," "tranquility," "solitude," and "ineffable pleasures…of family society." It was even unclear just who would be living in the household. Anne Cary, the Randolphs' eldest daughter, was married in September 1808 and left Edgehill "in a state of extreme dejection at the separation from her family." However, her husband, Charles Bankhead, informed Jefferson the next month their intent was to return "until the population of the hive shall force a swarm or the concourse of [law] clients call for and afford a separate establishment."[28] The eldest son, Jeff, had left for Philadelphia to further his education. The Monticello household might be contracted by land sales to pay down debt and expanded with new enterprises.

The Plantation Mistress

From a newly married, seventeen-year-old in 1790 trying to clarify daughter-father-husband-wife relationships and struggling to get the "boys in tolerable order," Martha developed into her father's plantation mistress and had become a confident overseer of her domestic domain by 1809. Also after Randolph entered the Ninth Congress in 1803 and was no longer available for his father-in-law's myriad "commissions," she increasingly assumed more of a role as intermediary, interlocutor, and commentator on other household functions beyond her gendered "domain." Overseer Gabriel Lilly was resisting Jefferson's directive to sell corn, Martha reported, because he considered it necessary for the horses. A Monticello workman who had been double paid absconded to Kentucky. Jefferson's lack of money to fully pay for "negro's" hired from the Smiths of Louisa County required their return a half-year before the lease was up. In no uncertain terms, she opposed merchant David Higginbotham's suggestion that her father assume the debts of Monticello blacksmith, William Stewart, whose household goods had been "attached during the time of his supposed flight." "Humanity," she asserted firmly, "cannot be interested in the fate of a man so well able to provide for himself."[29] Most significantly for Martha's changing responsibilities was the "servant" John. This recalcitrant engaged in "depravity" of all sorts, "throwing everything into confusion, encouraging the hands to rebellion and idleness…I really believe him," Martha charged, "to be a most determined villain equal to any crime on earth."

The range of topics on which she offered advice and the manner in which they were expressed denoted a growing comfort in her role as confidante and mistress of her Father's "great estate." She candidly criticized her father's plans for paying off debt; forcefully rejected his suggestion to engage Aunt Marks as a helper; was an intermediary between Father and overseers when Randolph was "unavailable"; and felt unrestrained in assessing the skills and personal characters of the grist mill tenant, Shoemaker, the enslaved John, or others connected with the household.

But the domestic scene for almost fifteen years hardly had been what her father promised! Most importantly, however, Martha nearing age forty voiced with unwavering clarity the priorities for their future life together. Nowhere was this more obvious than in their correspondence discussing past disappointments, present unhappy conditions, and the future they imagined together, as they tried to untangle the web of comingled debt and negotiate family priorities for the retirement years.

In the waning months of the second term, Martha was living in a state of "anxiety" amid "desolation" in the extended Randolph family, and Jefferson was finding his political life "nauseating and intolerable."[30] Both expressed deep disappointment over the past, especially the compounding of debt. The future they were trying to imagine, while it envisioned them together on the mountaintop, was more modulated and less rapturous than they had described for impending "retirements" in 1793 and 1799. While engaged in distasteful political "occupations," Father and Martha could imagine the "blessings of domestic society"; in retirement, the family no longer would be able to ignore the financial winds that had fanned the "cares and storms of life." Anything was possible in their imagination; now they must deal with the practical requirements of living a family life together. They discussed modifying living arrangements, assignment of household responsibilities, Randolph's role in the family, and most critically, the priorities for using their resources.

Configuring the "bosom of family"

For almost two decades Martha's letters had served "like gleams of light, to chear a dreary scene" of the political public sphere.[31] Now, Martha and Father were anticipating their final reunion, "the blessings of domestic society," and were confronted with rendering hopes into realities. The "retirement" of 1809, like prior ones, was accompanied with increasing anticipation; their long separations, unpredictable reunions, and exposure to public scrutiny would finally end, or so they hoped. Just before Jefferson arrived home in March, Martha confirmed her pledge "to manage so large an establishment...with feelings which [she] never could have in [her own] affairs." However, their planning over the prior fourteen months for a new life was carried out under the cloud of debt. "I have now the gloomy prospect," Jefferson forewarned his daughter in early 1808, "of retiring from office loaded with serious debts, which will materially affect the tranquility of my retirement." In response, she unequivocally voiced her priorities and "conjured" him not to consider the children's future but only concentrate on securing his own "tranquility."[32] "Nobody was ever more determined than I was to leave [Washington] clear of debt," he noted with disappointment, "but trusting to estimates made by my head...I omitted till to late the taking an accurate view of my calls for money."[33] It was a seemingly insuperable obstacle to realizing the imagined life of "ease, domestic occupation, and domestic love and society."[34] Despite the household's desperate financial situation, however, Martha was undeterred in claiming he was the first consideration.

Jefferson had discovered by early 1802 that consumption and investment expenditures were exceeding his income from all sources. After March 1803, he was "trusting to estimates made in [his] head," even though the smallest expense each day was carefully recorded in his Memorandum Book.[35] In retirement without a guaranteed government salary, Jefferson was confronted with repaying $10,000 in bank loans incurred during his Presidency, the remaining Wayles legacy debt, money advanced by tenant Craven Peyton for secret land purchases, large balances in accounts with merchants in Charlottesville and Milton, and more.[36]

"A gloom over my spirits"

The family's indebtedness had only increased by years in Washington supporting a suitable Presidential outfit, rebuilding the Monticello house, and continuing to buy land surrounding Monticello. Under these conditions, the private "burthens of debt" had not been lifted by a public salary of $25,000.[37] In January 1808, he bemoaned to Martha: "I never in my life have been so disappointed as in my expectations that the office I am in would have enabled me from time to time to assist [Mr. Randolph] in his difficulties." Then, almost as if their situation was too unsettling to even consider, Jefferson chose to imagine the future rather than live in the present: "However, not being apt to deject myself with evils before they happen, I nourish the hope of getting along."[38] The penurious future he described "cast a gloom over [Martha's] spirits" to such an extent that she was moved to forcefully question his latest plan for liberation. Since their time in Paris, Jefferson had looked to his crops to pay debts and, after years of shortfalls, still considered Monticello and Tufton farms capable of supporting them. Martha voiced a candidly different opinion. "The impossibility of paying serious debts by crops, and living at the same time, has been so often proved," she asserted, "that I am afraid you should trust to it."[39]

Jefferson's 1809 scheme for retiring debt remained much the same as 1800—mill and farm rents along with profits from nail-making—but now there was no $25,000 government salary. Other features in the latest "plan" carried significant implications for the configuration of the household and composition of the family. He expected Martha and her family would live at Monticello, with the Tufton farm providing the sole "maintenance" for what, in Jefferson's mind, was their "joint family." Mr. Randolph would manage the farm, but his financial obligations—extending far beyond those of the Monticello household to siblings and in-laws—would be partitioned from those of "Dearest Father," his "affectionate daughter," and the children they ultimately would raise together. (Earlier, he had conveyed a somewhat different message to Randolph regarding both selling property: Whether proceeds "go to pay your debts or mine is perfectly equal to me, as I consider our property as a common stock for our joint family.")[40] Land in Albemarle and Bedford owned by Martha and her father would go to placing "all the children in independence."

Accepting Martha's claim that crops alone could not pay off debt, her father proposed that three "detached tracts" in Albemarle would be sold to pay *Randolph's* Varina obligations, not the $10,000 in bank loans he claimed were a consequence of his public service. For these obligations, he persisted in relying on crops at Poplar Forest ($5,000), but proposed selling Natural Bridge ($1,600–2,000), a detached tract of 400 or so acres in Bedford, and parting with much of the Henderson land along the Rivanna that he had been secretly buying for several years.[41] These speculative financial calculations, however, were the least of the changes being considered by Martha and her father during the last year of the presidency.

"A certain evil for a very uncertain benefit"

Shortly after Maria's death, her sister had declared to their father that if any other "duties" interfered with her devotion to him, she "should not feel a scruple in sacrifising them."[42] Knowing her father was "gloomy" about "serious debts," expressing guilt over her own "wanton" spending, and isolating her husband's financial problems from the rest of the family, Martha also raised serious objections in the summer of 1808 to "incurring so great an expense without any certain benefit" for son Jeff's education. He was almost fifteen when his mother considered:

> His education is too back ward I am afraid to enable him to profit by any instructions conveyed by <u>lectures</u> and his indolence so great as to render it doubtfull whether he can be trusted to himself as much as he would be in the situation *in vue*. I believe that a good <u>common</u> school is the only one that would answer for him as yet. Of Course My Dear Father it would <u>be</u> <u>wrong</u> to incur a certain evil for a very uncertain benefit and perhaps the danger of giving expense for one who certainly has very little prospect at present of anything more than bare competency.[43]

When just ten years old, Jeff's mother had considered him "uncommonly backward…than many others who have not had half the pains taken with them." Her expectations had been "so little sanguine" that she was surprised when he proved "quicker" than she thought possible. His Grand Papa held a "good opinion" of grandson's "dispositions" but had not formed one with respect to his "genius." The following year of 1802, Martha allowed as how she could never be satisfied with the notion her children were "blockheads."[44] In both instances, she was concerned that her son was "loosing time" by not attending a proper school, even though, when he was twelve, she had "received the most flattering accounts from [his] Master as a boy of uncommon industry and application."[45]

As early as 1807, Jefferson had contacted Caspar Wistar in Philadelphia describing what he wanted fifteen-year-old Jeff to study and requesting information on the cost of board, professors' fees, etc. Nevertheless, he was still uncertain of his grandson's intellectual talents.

> Whether he possesses that lively imagination, usually called genius, I have not had opportunities of knowing. But I think he has an observing mind & sound judgment. He is assiduous & of the most amiable temper & dispositions. As he will be at ease in point of property, his education is not directed to any particular possession, but will embrace those sciences which give to retired life usefulness, ornament or amusement.[46]

Interestingly, Jefferson some seventeen years earlier had recommended to Jeff's father that he read the law as a necessary supplement to a farmer's income and as preparation for public office. Grand Papa in 1807 was imagining his progeny "at ease in point of property," so he should study botany, natural history, anatomy, and possibly surgery. "For a country gentleman," he claimed the following year to Jeff's father, "I know no source of amusement and health equal to botany and natural history." He might add "a course of surgery, as entirely subordinate to the others, and merely as a convenient acquisition for a country gentleman."[47] Though pressed with debts threatening to disturb the "tranquility" of his retirement, Grand Papa insisted he could pay fifty dollars a month without "inconvenience," and Mr. Randolph should entertain no thoughts of "declining" the offer.[48]

Martha was "very happy" with reports in the fall of 1808 from Philadelphia friend Dr. Benjamin Rush regarding Jeff's intellectual progress. She considered him "anxious to learn, rigidly correct in his morals and affectionate" but was concerned about an emotional legacy he might harbor. "I see enough of the Randolph character in him to give me some uneasiness as to the future." Just what were the qualities of a "Randolph character"? Mother's list was presented in terms of what she did not want her son to become: "indolent, impatient of reproof and at times irritable"; "Jealousy and suspicion"; indulging "mean and little passions." These behaviors simply were not "customary for genteel society." (This could well have been a description of her husband in the Randolph cousins' brouhaha, the quarrel with John Eppes, his Georgia scheme to move his "negroes," or the Edgehill land purchase conundrum.) Associating with "virtuous and well bred" company would develop "good manners," which Mother believed "more important in forming character than good sense and reflection." Louis Dubroca "proves that the various little rules of etiquette which though scrupulously observed have been though light of as <u>ceremonies</u>," she argued, "are really derived from the amiable and virtuous feelings of the heart." [49] Martha's "pedagogy" hearkened more to the eighteenth-century country-gentleman ideal of sociability than to her father's notions of physical, mental, and moral "accomplishments" as the path to private esteem, public honor, and others' affection. Nevertheless, Grand Papa immediately responded to Mother's concerns a week later with a lengthy letter to her son describing the social "dangers" he faced in Philadelphia (especially those due to Jefferson's political past) and advising him on how to avoid these "patients of Bedlam" and "fiery zealots." [50]

Mother and Grand Papa were uncertain about Jeff's "genius" or dispassionate "judgment," but both considered him eager to learn and affectionate. They could appreciate from their nearly twenty years with his father, however, that a propertied country gentleman in a genteel plantation culture could ill-afford to be seen as suspicious, jealous, irritable, impatient, and passionate. Such character traits not only upset social harmony but also, as they knew so well, disturbed family tranquility. If "good company" in Philadelphia could be a palliative, then Mother could rest easy that the benefit was worth the expense.

"My land will insure them food & raiment"

Martha declared that Father's thought of preserving Bedford lands for the children should be quickly abandoned, if their sale could relieve him from the "pressure of debt." The priority for their future, Martha stressed, was his "tranquility."

> The children are all young <u>their</u> habits are yet to form and upon those only will depend their happiness that, moderate desires, youth, and health can not fail to insure as far as they will be capable of enjoying it and wealth itself could do no more. [51]

She had come to accept what her father had argued many years earlier in *Notes on the State of Virginia*. Children's happiness, he had written, does "not depend on the condition of life in which chance has placed them [or] circumstances in which they find themselves but on good conscience, good health, occupation, and freedom in all just pursuits."[52] Martha's main concern was not the children's future but her father's "comforts...which habit [had] rendered necessary to [his] health and ease."

Martha strangely claimed responsibility for her father's financial straits but denied any responsibility for those of her husband. Their shared "gloom" in 1808 over debt and its effects on the future she attributed to "having so wantonly so cruelly added to [Father's] embarrassments by the expense of [her] last visit to Washington" some three years earlier in the winter of 1805–06.[53] Indeed, she had requested "a fashionable wig...a set of combs for dressing the hair, a bonnet shawl and white lace veil...[and] 2 lace half handerchiefs," all of which cost her father a mere sixty dollars; other recorded items totaled only about $465.[54] It was not, as Martha claimed, the "cost" to his retirement of replacing what she had "so wantonly squandered in going to live with...[her] Dear Father." The modest outlays for her visit seem even more trivial when set against two $4,000 notes Father renewed with the Bank of the United States during her stay, or two renewed with the Bank of Columbia for $1,000 each.[55] Rather, the self-professed "wanton" seemed chagrined that her husband could not provide financially for his family. She had lamented at the time: "Nothing but my present situation [pregnancy] could justify my leaving home at a time when it was so little convenient to Mr. Randolph as [to] induce me to saddle you with any part of the expense."[56] Martha now confessed:

> It was never our intention to burthen you with the maintenance of our large family. Mr. R. has entered into no new engagements [debts] the consequences of the old are yet at issue and upon the event will rest the situation of our children. Let it come to the worst my land will insure them food and raiment.[57]

Mann Randolph was called upon in early 1808 to settle the affairs of David Randolph—sister Mary's husband, the former U. S. Marshall removed by Jefferson, and eager disseminator of the Hemings and Walker gossip to New England. "The ruin of the family is extending itself daily," Martha fretfully wrote. "The desolation which surrounds us has kept us both in a state of great anxiety which the present appearance of affairs is not likely to dissipate." Brother William was "ruined"; cousin Archie, who had been involved in the Bizarre affair, was "without shelter for his family"; Will Fleming Randolph, yet another cousin, was "a cripple for life" after shooting himself in the leg while defending his home from a sheriff's foreclosure. Martha and her husband had already mortgaged Edgehill in 1807, Varina debt remained unpaid, and Father was in strained circumstances. Could their lives be far from "desolation"? Randolph had resisted his family's "solicitations"—which was easy in the absence of money—but also had the "prudence" not to sign more "security slips" with his family's creditors.[58] Martha's father had,

> always apprehended that Mr. Randolph would be in great embarrasment between the imprudencies of some members of his father's family, and the necessity of taking care of a large one of his own, and knowing his liberal dispositions I thought it possible that present pressure might sometimes prevail over a prudent foresight of the future.[59]

Jefferson's most severe and devastating criticism of Randolph's character then was presented obliquely in the form of a catechism on teaching children "the wisdom, the honor, and the blessed comfort of living within their income." They only have to look at "their nearest acquaintances" to learn the folly of living "a few years of splendor above their income, to have their property taken away for debt when they have a family growing up to maintain and provide for." Moralizing and direct evidence, however, cannot assure good fortune for future generations.

> Still there is another evil against which we cannot guard, unthrifty marriages; because characters are not known until they are tried. But even here, a wife imbued with principles of prudence, may go far towards arresting or lessening the evils of an improvident management.[60]

Certainly, the legacy debt heaped on Martha and her husband had created an "unthrifty marriage"—despite Jefferson's carefully drafted marriage settlement. Randolph's "improvident management" of their Varina and Bedford farms had added to the pile. But "prudence" by a "wife"—like Martha—potentially might slow or reduce the accumulation of financial obligations, some of which were imposed by the Randolph family's "imprudencies." A decade later in 1818 and in even deeper financial troubles, father and daughter would advise Nathaniel Burwell that "order and economy" in both the house and farm were essential to avoiding "ruin…and children destitute of the means of living."[61]

Martha was separating her future financial interests from those of her husband, as Father had implied in his letter of 5 January, and moreover eschewed any personal responsibility for the Randolphs' plight. "It is some comfort to reflect that whatever may happen his children and myself have never contributed. Our expenses have been regulated by the most rigid economy." An empty marriage settlement and an adverse court decision had saddled the Randolphs' with legacy debt; but, so too, their paltry condition stemmed from being the "link of love" between family members that Father had urged much earlier in the cases of Gabriella Harvie and Nancy Randolph. Feelings of attachment and a sense of duty—laudable in the abstract—had carried a steep price—financially, emotionally, and maritally. As they were planning one last reunion atop their Mountain refuge, letters from January 1808 to March the following year make clear the "Swans" were casting their financial lot together—as they had their emotional one in the 1790s—and isolating the "silly bird" to manage "his own difficulties."

"Any little commission"

Despite the looming "desolation" in Martha's extended family and Father's estimation of Mr. Randolph's situation, she did not hesitate to recommend her husband for work at Monticello. A freshet had washed away one-half of the dam serving the newly leased grist mill that Jefferson was figuring to support his retirement "tranquility." "Mr. Randolph begs particularly that you will transmit your orders about the repairs to <u>him</u>," Martha relayed. "He has nothing to do, having two overseers to overlook his business…he thinks Bacon has not understanding and Shoemaker wants honesty to do it properly." After a rancorous conclusion to an undistinguished public career, Randolph's wife was looking to resituate him in the Monticello household. "I know it will give him real pleasure to receive any little commission from you," she encouraged her father, "and it cannot possibly put him to the least inconvenience." On the same day Jefferson reassured Martha her last Washington trip had "scarcely added…to expences," he accepted her offer of Mr. Randolph's services and seemingly reinstalled him as proto-patriarch and executive overseer: "I shall write to Bacon by this post to conform to your directions," Jefferson informed his son-in-law.[62] Unlike the period before Randolph's entry into politics, however, there were no references in their 1808 correspondence to crops, wheat sales, financial affairs, the nailery, house construction, or the mill dam. With one exception noted below, Jefferson's letters were confined to reporting on impersonal and emotionally neutral matters from the public sphere, domestic politics, and foreign affairs. The exception suggests a change in the emotional dynamics and social relations within the Monticello household in which Randolph was bypassed in directing the overseer's work. "I charged Bacon very strictly to keep the water of the Canal always running over the waste, as Shoemaker has made the want of water the ground of insisting on a suspension of rent, and will probably continue to do it."[63] The void between Jefferson and Randolph was filled by Martha.

"Pardon me if I tease you"

The epistolary record beginning in January 1808 portrays Martha as an intermediary between husband and father. (This was the same period in which they were discussing the Randolph family's "desolation," the protection of their own lands over Randolph's, funding Jeff's education, and retirement plans generally.) She acknowledged that her "situation" as a "link" in the kinship network compelled her to forward requests for patronage appointments, though it made her uneasy. More importantly, at least in the case of the obsequious Richard Hackley, Father used his daughter's position in the family to advise sister-in-law Harriet's husband how to lobby for the consulship at Cadiz, Spain. "You will be sensible," he advised Martha, "that the communication to him must be made with caution so as not to commit my name....Mr. Hackley may be told...the dispositions of the Executive are extremely favorable to him...."[64] Martha did not hesitate to solicit directly an appointment for her nephew, Beverley, when his parents were "reduced to absolute want" and his mother was establishing a Richmond boarding house to support her family. "You were never backward in the cause of humanity," she wrote the Secretary of State's wife, Dolley Madison. The children of David Meade and Mary Randolph were reasonably provided for. "There remains only Beverley...[and] the object is to obtain for him, if possible, an under clerkship in one of the offices..."[65] She used her father's position as President to ask that he dine with yet another Beverley Randolph, son of another bankrupt brother-in-law: "Any little attention from you being particularly grateful to the family."[66]

In the same letter lamenting her "wanton" spending in the winter of 1805–06, Martha reported: "Mr. Hackley has written Mr. Randolph to know with certainty what he can count upon." The husband of Randolph's sister Harriet claimed that Jefferson had promised him a consulship in Cadiz, Spain, but a competitor for the position had "found powerfull friends to support his claim" for the office. Further, Mann Randolph "begged" the President through Martha to recommend his second cousin for a midshipman's appointment. "Pardon me if I tease you," she demurred. "It is my misfortune to be so circumstanced as not to be able to avoid it allways as much averse to it as I am."[67] Early in 1809, Martha expressed her continued uneasiness with her interlocutor position.

> I enclose you another letter My Dearest Father, irksome
> as it is for me to add to your vexations of the kind Mr.
> R. thinks he cannot refuse without danger of giving
> offense [to] friends who think they have a claim upon
> him.[68]

Whatever the annoying letter, she still was placed in the situation of doing Mr. Randolph's bidding on another matter: "Mr. Hackley also wrote to beg him to mention his name to you."[69] "Mr. Randolph begs the favor," "Mr. Randolph has been applied to," and "Mr. Randolph thinks it probable" were refrains in Martha's 1808 letters.[70] Her father through Martha responded with "Mr. Randolph can answer"; but finally on 2 January 1809, he wrote directly to his son-in-law denying a request from a "Mr. Stith" that Randolph had forwarded and repeating what he had already written Martha regarding other requests. The epistolary logjam was broken.

Just four days later, Randolph breached his silence to ask, not unexpectedly, a favor regarding a prospective buyer for debt-laden Varina and to reveal his own debt-reduction plan.

> Finding my debts increase every day by the means I am
> forced to use for the satisfaction of demands, I have
> determined (& Martha heartily concurs with me) upon
> relieving myself at once from insufferable torment by a
> sacrifice of this property [Varina] …We shall then have
> our other property clear & by taking advantage of
> markets, should commerce be restored, may derive a
> greater income from it than we ever have from the
> whole. I consider it much better to sell this property
> than my slaves, which I must otherwise dispose of, for

without them the land here would be worth nothing to us and as I have raised many of them myself...[71]

But Randolph was to first learn through his wife that he was "misinformed" about the prospective buyer. Over a week later, his father-in-law conveyed his approval for selling land rather than "labourers," even offered his "detached" Albemarle tracts for sale to meet Randolph's "most pressing calls" and to forestall parting from those he had "raised." Jefferson, also, revealed his financial plans for retirement in which his son-in-law would be a pivotal figure. Although he failed to mention everyone living in the Monticello house, the Tufton farm was seen as a major contributor to its support:

> But I know nothing of management. I have ever been unwilling to trouble you with my affairs, knowing that your own required your whole time. Yet when Craven's farm [Tufton] returns on my hands, it's yield will be so important that I shall be obliged to ask some aid from you in it's direction. It will not be long before Jefferson can aid us both.[72]

Randolph's response has been lost, but Jefferson on 31 January again reassured that his "aid and counsel in the management of the farms...will become essential."

> My whole life has been passed in occupations which kept me from any minute attention to them, and finds me now with only very general ideas of the theory of agriculture, without actual experience; at a time of life, too, when the memory is not so retentive of observation as at an earlier period.[73]

"Disagreeable as it is to tease"

Martha bore no reservations about the necessity of or her capacity for effecting the domestic economies necessary to improve their financial position. She had firmly stated in 1808 her low opinion of crops as a reliable income source, so was "thoroughly convinced of the necessity" for "retrenching all possible expense" as Father had proposed. However, she still was adamant that even these actions had one and only one purpose: "Your comfort My Dearest Father must however be the only criterion. Any encroachment upon that were it productive of millions to the children would be distracting to me."

Expressing confidence and firm resolve in lifting the household's debt, Martha did not hesitate to proffer her opinion on a critical matter of business, though "disagreeable as it [was] to tease." Rental income for the toll mill had been a critical part of her father's debt reduction plan in 1800. The scheme had been set back by freshets, threatened with competitors, and delayed by workmen's indifference, until the mill was finally rented in 1807 to Jonathan Shoemaker and son Isaac. Millers on the Rock Creek in Washington, the Shoemakers had never made a payment on their $1,250 annual lease. In many ways just as troublesome were claims that farmers' wheat had been processed, sold, and the proceeds not received.

"I am afraid you will be much disappointed in your expectations from Shoemaker," Martha warned two weeks before Father arrived home. Son Isaac was "not a man of business" and he struck "bargains...ruinous to himself." There was not "one spark of honesty," so no one will "trust him with their grain." Moreover, she wrote, "I am afraid you have been deceived in the character of his Father. There are strong doubts of his honesty in the minds of many here." There was no chance of recovering the money through the son, whom Martha considered a "rascal" and "personal enemy." "If the bargain was made with the Father perhaps you may secure yourself though even that is doubted." Martha had gleaned intelligence from the neighborhood on the character, business acumen, and milling skills of the Shoemaker family, but the conclusions and opinions were clearly her own. "You may depend upon it that I have not exaggerated the reports and I have reason to believe them too well founded." Though the entire matter was a "disgusting subject" for her, Martha did not hesitate to suggest a tactical response to Father, which he executed soon after returning. Business matters were impinging seriously on much-valued neighborhood comity and the "trust" Jefferson had placed in the miller's "good faith." After three weeks at home, he had not been to the Shadwell mill, but "facts" had come to him from "such persons as cannot be doubted."[74]

Even more vehemently than when first proposed in the 1790s, the newly-installed and confident plantation mistress rejected any suggestion that another free white woman, even a family member, could meddle in her domain. Having Aunt Marks come live with them in order to effect domestic "economies" was neither "desirable" nor "proper." She was,

> totally incompetent to the business...[and] has neither
> head nor sufficient weight of character to manage so

large an establishment as yours will be. I shall devote myself to it and with feelings which I never could have in my own affairs. And with what tenderness of affection we will wait upon and cherish you My Dearest Father...[75]

"The rest of our difficulties," she asserted, "we will talk over together." Signed: "your truly affectionate child."

"Divide the confusion"

The household's structure and the family's internal configuration would continue to undergo change during these years of a third retirement. Monticello would be contracted with the sale of "detached tracts," the Natural Bridge ornament, and, perhaps at last, even Varina. The principal interface with the external world would be through the household's master, eliminating the need for an "executive overseer." The household's financial understory would return slowly to private hands—merchants, commission agents, neighbors, and friends—fleeing the dreadful clutches of the banks. Debt—the "torment" and "burden" of life—along with business affairs generally would be more frequently removed from the privacy of gentlemanly agreements to the publicity of chancery courts.

Martha and Father's imaginary family was bound together by affection and located on a secluded mountaintop; the one they lived in retirement would continue to be strained with emotional tensions and ever-changing membership. Just a few months to never being separated again, Jeff could have been found in Philadelphia preparing himself to be a "country gentleman" on Grand Papa's plantation. Martha's eldest, Anne Cary, had left Monticello after her marriage in late 1808 to live with Mr. Bankhead's parents "down country" in Port Royal, Virginia. Randolph's sister, Virginia, who been had taken in after her father's death, moved away. Martha was concerned that what appeared to be "fairest prospects" in marriage for daughter Anne and sister-in-law Virginia would become a "sad experience." (She, after all, had experienced "unthrifty" marriages.") Martha's life course from grieving child to republican daughter and plantation mistress had revealed that private esteem, public honor, and living among those whom you loved were insufficient to ensure happiness. With resignation to the uncertainty and "instability of human affairs," she harkened to those days at Panthemont where she learned from the ancient Solon "that no

Man can be pronounced a 'happy one before his death'…and so too many of us have experienced."[76]

Chapter 10

"Elate from Monticello":

Living Family Life on the Mountain

Shared grief in 1782 and recurring separations had tempered the affectionate bond between Martha and Father. Their attachment deepened and intensified in those early years together in Philadelphia and Paris isolated from family and friends. To counteract the agony of repeated separations over twenty years, they created a ritual and artifacts—a family-of-letters—in which they could imagine an idyll of tranquility and solitude amid a loving family atop a mountain. To live this family, however, had required adding to an already burdensome debt and extending the plantation household to the foot of the Mountain and beyond. Affection/family, separation, plantation household, place, the public sphere, and debt would continue as comingled themes in the years following 1809, until Martha's death on 10 October 1836.

However, there seemed no prospect that the Monticello household would want for a "bosom of family" when Grand Papa returned. In the early months of retirement, Martha's old Washington acquaintance, Margaret Bayard Smith, reported a touching scene at Monticello. Incapacitated from "excessive inflammation and pain" in an injured eye, Martha excused herself from dining with her visitor on a summer's evening in 1809. Later in her bedchamber, Mrs. Smith was "delighted" to witness Father's "tender attention…as he sat by her and held her hand, for above an hour."[1] At age thirty-six, Martha still had six children at home, ranging in age from under one year (Benjamin Franklin) to Ellen (12) and arrayed in between were Cornelia (9),

Virginia (7), Mary (5), and three-year-old James Madison; in nine months, another would arrive. During 1809, seventeen-year-old Jeff was brought from Philadelphia closer to home at Louis Hue Girardin's school in Richmond, where he would continue his preparation for becoming a "country gentleman."[2] The following year, he would return to help with the farms, mills, and nailery. Anne hoped to rejoin the "hive" when husband Charles Bankhead began his study of law in the South Pavilion. Little wonder that a month before Father's arrival Martha could complain that her letter was "written in the midst of the children with never less than three talking...which is sufficient apology for the many inacuracies in it for they really distract me with their noise and incessant questions."

Though the bevy of "swans" was migrating home by 1809, the "silly bird" would begin almost immediately to separate himself. Randolph figured only briefly in his father-in-law's plans for clearing debt, was increasingly absent pursuing other interests, and by the early 1820s was estranged physically and emotionally from the family he referred to as "Monticello." His daughters' education was left to their mother and grandfather in subjects of no use in the evolving cultural milieu in which they would live. His eldest son was educated intentionally as a "country gentleman" under Grand Papa's direction in preparation for replacing his father as executive overseer of the household. The order of generations and family roles had become a jumble.

But the bosom of family did not settle for long on the Mountain or cluster around its feet over the next quarter century. Only Jeff planted himself steadfastly at Edgehill as Grand Papa's executive overseer. Ellen married a Boston merchant in the Far East trade, endured his long absences, and brooded on what had been lost. Jefferson's social capital did not return enough 60-day bank loans, merchants' credit, nor advances from friends or relatives to save Monticello from the auctioneer's cry. Martha, however, did skillfully invest Father's political capital to secure temporary work from the War Department for Mann Randolph; a State Department appointment for son-in-law Nicholas P. Trist; a position for her son Meriwether Lewis to reside with and study law under her cousin Judge Dabney Carr; a surgeon's mate appointment for son Benjamin Franklin; and an apprenticeship in the Navy for youngest son George Wythe. A relieved and grateful mother informed Nancy Morris that "the memory of My dear father still sheds it's blessing."[3]

If the past was any guide, Martha likely expected that with Father's retirement further disruptions would arise from the "concourse of strangers" she had complained of in 1800. But now after two presidential terms, she could better appreciate her father's view that "to have the soft affections hushed & suppressed by the eternal presence of strangers…[was] evidences of the general esteem"; along with private honor and being loved by others, it was an essential part of completing her happiness.[4] The dutiful republican daughter was eager to be installed as Monticello's mistress.

> To divide the confusion of your arrival and my moving and thereby lessen it I think I shall go to Monticello the 9 or 10th. It will give me time to fix myself before the arrival of your waggons and servants which will naturally occasion some bustle in the family. Adieu My Very Dear Father your Devoted child…[5]

The "confusion" of Father's arrivals—as well as his departures, absences, and impulse to civic virtue—had shaped Martha's life for twenty years. But his life in the "world" also had provided her with the experiences necessary to be the plantation mistress of a "great estate"; to endure the "crouds" demanded by hospitality in a genteel household; to mediate the inconstancy of a self-debased husband and the condescension of a father-in-law's equanimity; and to imaginatively fashion an existence until she could be with the one who made her "life compleat." Now the challenge for the plantation mistress was to gather the "bosom of family" whilst "nursing and chearing" Father's old age in their mountaintop "harbour."

Monticello—both the place and the household—had long been held out as exemplary in health, fruitfulness, tranquility, and most of all, love. There were the extraordinary efforts to achieve propinquity like Patsy, Polly, and Father had enjoyed briefly in Paris. When after a decade Martha finally had crept to the foot of the Mountain, her Edgehill house was open to the elements, cooled by wintry drafts, filled with smoke, and an incubator for all matter of illness. "It would be better," her father advised, "for you to remove to Monticello….I should think mr Randolph would find less inconvenience in the riding…than in the loss of his own and his family's health." Maria had been "sincerely delighted" at her sister's unpleasant arrangements and would "rejoice" if it truly forced her return to Monticello.[6]

Anticipated and experienced reunions at Monticello were palliative to the emotional pangs of separation to such an extent that an internal sentiment became attached to an external object—the top of a mountain—never to be uprooted. "With infinite pleasure I elate once more from Monticello," Martha effused as she awaited Father's return. Simply being home was not enough for him, however: "The bloom of Monticello is chilled by my solitude….I value the enjoiments of this life only in proportion as you participate them with me." For Martha on the other hand, the "bloom" evoked a sense of loneliness: "Nothing makes me feel your absence so sensibly as the beauty of the season." Spaces and objects of the place stimulated memories to sooth the pain of separation. "My affections, my thoughts are however perpetually with you, incessantly hovering over you," Martha reassured after three months without writing Father. "There is no scene in your solitary establishment in which they have not visited you."[7] Martha's imagination fed by her emotions could conjure a spectral imminence but, so too, did her father: "It has always been my wish and expectation," he informed her in 1808, "that when I return to live at Monticello, Mr. Randolph, yourself and family would live there with me."[8] Affection, happiness, tranquility, and a host of warm sentiments were planted at a place which family members in the years after 1826 would mentally husband into a memorial and even a near-sacred ground.

Through it all, debt was their widest lens for interpreting life and viewing the world around them. The family's finances limited what education Martha's daughters could pursue. The lack of money constrained her father's plans for the mill, nailery, and farms whose produce was to erase debt. Grand Papa's desire to retain Monticello and Martha's commitment to his happiness compelled them to publicly air the family's private affairs in seeking legislative authority to gamble their future on a land lottery. Indebtedness alone had been embarrassment enough, but it was made acutely painful by trumpeting it throughout the Old Dominion. Further mortification was occasioned by an open, public conflict between Martha's husband and son over the sale of Edgehill to satisfy creditors.

Debt would ultimately consume the entire household, cleave the family from the mountain, and separate them from each other to Washington City, Boston, Florida, Cuba, and Switzerland. There were no relatives to take them in, no farm to generate even a meager subsistence, and they chose not to use their knowledge and skills to remain independent by opening a school. Ironically, it was the political public sphere that rescued the private family from beggarly poverty. Their most valued treasures—privacy, independence, tranquility, optimism, and, yes, Monticello—were ransomed for a modest security, a future of ennui, and for Martha, homelessness.

Just as the Mountain had slowly and inexorably slid down its slopes into the meandering Rivanna and beyond its place, the Monticello household began to disassemble and disperse as well. The affection that Mother and Grand Papa had rooted there—"the scene of whatever happiness [they] had ever known"—was passed to the daughters.[9] Mama and Grand Papa had nurtured them to an insular family life of intellect and affection—of head and heart—that irrevocably unsettled them and complicated their adjustment to the "world" outside. Their succor was to transfigure a lost house into a "temple," his bedroom into a "sanctum," and bestow "sacredness" on the patriarch's "character."[10] The relics from their family-of-letters were read as inspirational liturgy: "We will never despair, we will never be cast down by difficulties," Cornelia proclaimed while copying Grand Papa's letters for publication. "We will bear ourselves bravely & be cheerful in the midst of misfortunes, & if we are thrown upon our own resources we will find them in ourselves."

They lost a place but regained a family-of-memory.

As events unfolded from 1809, and life did not mirror what had been imagined, Martha and her father began to concoct "The Jefferson Family Story." Themes and story lines were arranged to make meaning of their lives together, to self-fashion identities, and to shape the historical narrative.[11] The protagonist was "Jefferson, the Republican and Kindly Master." Opposing him were "Incompetent Overseer," a "Dishonest Relative," and "Plantation Slavery." Supporting roles were devised for the "Irascible Mr. Randolph," the "Stalwart Jeff," and a "Dutiful Republican Daughter" turned "Plantation Mistress."

Affection was the one emotion family members returned to again and again to sustain themselves though life's triumphs and defeats, fears and hopes. They cared deeply for each other—worried during sickness, encouraged each other to accomplishments, modulated their complaints with thankfulness, and silently endured thankless tasks. Attachment to each other and to their place was the family's anchor in the "cares and storms" of life blown to the shoals by debt and exposure to the political public sphere.

Martha, the newlywed in 1790, had been unequivocal in openly declaring that love for Father was first in her heart, so much so, debt and family dissention were endured in return for seating herself at the foot of the Mountain. Some years later, the mother of three petulantly reminded him exactly why this was so: Father had "separated" her at "infancy" from "every other friend"; "every sentiment of tenderness" had been focused only on him, and no subsequent relationship could "weaken a sentiment interwoven with [her] very existence."[12] She reaffirmed four years later that this love and tenderness would overcome "scruple" to sacrifice all other "duties," including those of a wife and mother. Years of separation, longed-for reunions, and living through letters only excited these sentiments and intensified the need for physical proximity, until they could never be subordinated to family or to clearing the debt, but only to preserving for a few more years their time at Monticello. If Father's happiness was situated at that place; if it provided the venue for garnering "social esteem"; if it was where he imagined his loved ones were, then she was willing to sacrifice everything—Bedford lands, the children's education, Edgehill, Randolph's inheritance, and even her future. She doubted they could support such a large establishment with only the Tufton farm, the mills, and a turn to wheat but demurred, nonetheless, to stay at Monticello. Even when there was no one with which to share an imagined future, she would draw on memories of her happiest years in Paris, of evenings at their fireside, of days visiting Poplar Forest neighbors. Martha would never again be separated from "Dearest Papa," whether living or dead.

Or, so they imagined.

"We shall all see better days…"

Martha miscarried at the fourth month in July of 1811, contracted "dyssentarry," and was incapacitated for six weeks. "I have had more ill health this summer than common," she sighed. Too, the children had been sick. "[M]ore ill health in the family than in all times of the year before." She knew the household's financial situation remained precarious. The Bedford wheat crop was stuck at the mill because a dam had been lost and their account with merchant Higginbotham was growing. Little surprise she comforted her friend Eliza Trist with words just as applicable to herself:

> Indeed there seems to be so much of chance in our fates that I never feel secure in any circumstances and I hope I never shall again despair. Happy are those who never abused their prosperity nor deserved their adversity. I trust we shall all see better days yet.[13]

Her physical well-being, financial security, and social standing were repeatedly assaulted by intractable debt, her husband's inconstancy, and the Randolph family's imprudence.

A few weeks before returning permanently to Monticello, Jefferson informed Randolph that he would be a pivotal figure in farming operations. The Tufton farm "will be so important that I shall be obliged to ask some aid from you in it's direction." Two weeks later on 31 January 1809, Randolph was reassured that his "aid and counsel in the management of the farms...will become essential."[14] However, Randolph would become increasingly separated from household and family affairs in parallel with an acceleration in the downward spiral of his financial condition. His father's legacy was burdensome; Varina's debt continued to bear heavily, even after its "rescue" by agent George Jefferson. Younger sisters Virginia and Harriet had been forced from their Tuckahoe home by their step-mother and become Randolph's charges. So too, sister Anne Cary (Nancy) frequently received support from her brother after she had clashed with stepmother Gabriella Harvie Randolph, fled to sister Judith's, and suffered the ignominy of the Bizarre scandal. In 1807, a deed of trust for $5,600 on Edgehill had been made with George Hay, the son-in-law of James Monroe. The 840 acres in Bedford from the marriage settlement were sold in 1810 for $8,400.[15]

Throughout his life just as he seemed on the brink of success, doing a "Randolph" had sabotaged every effort. There was Edgehill with his Father in 1791; the Georgia scheme in 1802; in 1803, the run against Jefferson staunch political ally, Samuel Cabell; a dispute with cousin John Randolph in 1806; and the snit with brother-in-law Eppes at the President's House.[16] Though Randolph in 1807 had "decided absolutely not to offer again for Congress," he did two years later and was roundly defeated for his old seat held by Wilson Cary Nicholas.[17] Still seeking public esteem, he contemplated entering the State Senate race in 1810 only to withdraw in favor of Joseph C. Cabell. Just a half-year after offering in 1809 to help Jefferson with management of the farms, he wrote his youthful protégé, Francis Walker Gilmer:

> [T]he great exercise I necessarily take in the daily visit to my farm and the inspection of it may have unfitted my mind for correspondence, as I feel it does for conversation, by the languor it leaves even during the time of rest....I find myself sometimes from the same cause neglecting the most urgent business.[18]

Eliza Trist, Martha's "dear friend" from Philadelphia days now resident in Albemarle County, kept that friendly city appraised of the family's affairs. "Mr Randolph is surmounting his difficulties and appears much more happy," she wrote to Catherine Wistar Bache in Philadelphia as 1810 drew to a close. If her account is to be believed, he once again had "come to a determination to take his Negroes to the Mississippi to sell" but had been dissuaded when Jefferson told his daughter "that it wou'd never do to destroy the goose...[and] he had better dispose of the land" in Bedford county.[19] But the situation at Monticello was not as rosy as Eliza led Catherine to believe.

Forty-five years old with nine children from ages three to twenty-two, Martha's husband chose in March of 1813 to become a Colonel in the U. S. Army, commanding of the 20th Infantry Regiment. "Our Martha has had a poor time," Father wrote Eliza Trist in early 1814, "since the birth of her new daughter, harassed with lingering fevers which have greatly debilitated her." The children were "serenading" the house with whooping cough. By the way, Jefferson wrote: "Mr. Randolph will probably leave us in the spring to try another [military] campaign, tho' he does not seem decided."[20] The outcome was decided for him when his threat to resign, if not returned to the field of battle, was readily accepted.

Home on winter leave from Ontario, Colonel Randolph was directed to undertake a recruitment effort at Leesburg but pleaded "impediments not of a private nature" that delayed his reporting to duty.[21] (These "impediments" may have been his appointment by President Madison as federal tax collector.) Adjutant-General de Walbach unexpectedly accepted his feigned "resignation." The Colonel later appended an explanatory note to de Walbach's letter: "I determined to go on immediately to the lines & wrote to request such an order intimating that I had rather resign than be recruiting."[22] Adding to this dismissal was his replacement in 1815 by Jeff as executive overseer of the Monticello farms.

"A hard fate"

When daughter Anne and sister-in-law Virginia wed in 1808, Martha had been concerned about "unthrifty" marriages. Her worry was prescient. Anne continued to live with in-laws at Port Royal, pending payment of husband Charles Bankhead's debts. What with his excessive drinking, "hers has been a hard fate, but thank God the property is secured to herself and children." Martha's other sister-in-law, who like Virginia had been pushed from their Tuckahoe home by stepmother Gabriella Harvie Randolph, was suffering an equally ignoble fate. The husband of Harriet Randolph Hackley had "defrauded his creditors...[and] is devotedly attached to a Spanish woman."[23]

John Randolph of Roanoke, however, was "preeminent in wickedness" in Martha's estimation; he publicly reopened in 1815 the Bizarre affair from two decades past. These and other misfortunes underscored just how tenuous was social esteem, so highly valued and long sought by her father. Martha's disgraced sister-in-law, Anne Cary (Nancy) Randolph, had reprised to husband Gouverneur Morris the scurrilous story that in the 1790s she had conceived a child by her guardian and brother-in-law, Richard Randolph, and the two had committed infanticide. Now married to the wealthy businessman and able politician from New York, she was confronted with even more defamatory charges by Richard's brother, John. She had lived in Richmond as a "common prostitute," he claimed; had tried to "seduce" her nine-year-old nephews, Judith's sons; and had a "connection with a black man." Emboldened by her newfound social status and independence from genteel Virginia culture, Nancy mounted a vigorous and semi-public defense with a circular letter mailed to key members of the Virginia elite in the midst of John Randolph's campaign for re-election.

Martha had been a naive newlywed in 1793 and could "blush for so near a connection" when called by defense counsel John Marshall to acknowledge her suspicions of Nancy's pregnancy and to admit having provided her with a potentially abortive concoction, gum guaiacum. Now over twenty years later, the Randolph clan had once again flouted genteel decorum by opening the most private matters to public display, affronted the social esteem of the Monticello household, and sought to breach a rift in the family. But more troubling was John Randolph publicly implicating Martha as evidence of Nancy's debauched character. Monticello's mistress shared her quandary with "dear friend" Eliza Trist.

> J. [John] Randolph says in his letter that the granter of the annuity meaning we presume Mr [Thomas Mann] Randolph was so well convinced of her [Nancy's] infamy before she left Virginia that he would not let his wife [Martha] associate with her. if my testimony would be of the smallest advantage to her I would write to her to contradict that part of the charge. but her husband takes up the cudgels so vigorously in her defence and asserts so roundly that she never decieved him that it would be useless for me to say anything and she might look upon it as an attempt to propitiate her now that she is in prosperity. she still speaks very badly of me &

says that I intercept the letters she has written to her brother because he has been too lazy to answer them. for I believe every feeling of resentment has subsided as entirely in his breast as I call heaven to witness it has in mine. and this moment if I thought my writing would even give her pleasure and much more if I believed it would benefit her I would write to her immediately to contradict as far as it is in my power the infamous falsehoods John Randolph has propagated about her.[24]

The rakish New Yorker, who brought Nancy Morris wealth and respectability, died just a few months later on 6 November 1816. The "resentment" obviously had not left Martha's breast. She trenchantly informed her father that Morris's death

> will be irreparable to his wife by lessening the <u>little</u> consequence that I am afraid she had...I wrote to her upon the occasion although we had not previous corresponded, but the poor creature she is surrounded by enemies and never in more need of a support of her family than at present.

Martha overcame her compunction sufficiently in subsequent years so that Nancy—disgraced but now restored—became a confidante. She may not have wanted to "propitiate," but a recurring complaint to her New York in-law was the differences in their financial positions and the effects of poverty on the life of her Virginia relatives.[25]

There were more serious family problems closer to home. Anne's husband, Charles Bankhead, continued the drinking and abusive behavior that, when mixed with the Randolph temperament, was a nearly lethal dose. Unfortunately, the matter could not be confined to the privacy of family, for Eliza Trist spread it into Philadelphia society by gossiping with Catherine Bache: "Bankhead has turn'd out a great sot always frolicking and Carousing at the Taverns...and Mr R. is so much involved [in debt] that 'tis thought he can never be extricated from ruin."[26] Martha angrily told her father that "sending him [Bankhead] to the mad house [was] but a temporary remedy....[T]he best way would be to hire a keeper...and let him finish himself at once.[27] He still was not finished three years later. Just as Jefferson was being informed of the *coup de grace* administered by Jeff Randolph's in-law, banker Wilson Cary Nicholas, he learned from Martha that Ann and Charles "have jointly with Capt. Miller rented a small farm 3 miles from Doctor Bankhead's." Martha was "delighted" the Captain would live with them "for they will always require a protector. Mr. Bankhead has begun to drink again."[28] He had also been stirring the family cauldron, according to Eliza Trist, by sending an offensive letter to Jeff's wife, Jane. "What gave rise to his doing [this] I cant conceive." Like the family's Bizarre story many years before, the accounts differ on just who started the fight between Jeff, brandishing a "Horse whip," and his brother-in-law thrusting with "large clasp knife." Regardless, the result was a bloody-headed Bankhead, a Randolph laid low with stab wounds, and a family further divided. Mann Randolph interceded at the young couple's Carlton farm, ordering its overseer to ignore Bankhead's directions.[29]

Neither Randolph's $4,000 job as Federal tax collector, the mill leased with cousin Thomas Eston Randolph from Jefferson, nor his Governor's salary of $3,333 were sufficient to ameliorate the Randolph family's financial situation.[30] By 1817, it was necessary to borrow from the Bank of the United States, using Edgehill and over fifty slaves as collateral with son Jeff and Sam Carr as endorsers.

Randolph's mill venture, which had been a key element in Jefferson's pre-retirement plans for achieving solvency, only compounded the financial problems of the Monticello household. "In consequence of a considerable loan from me to Mr. [Mann] Randolph," Jefferson coyly informed Eston, "it is understood that he is responsible to you for the whole rent as usual." The renters estimated in 1815, they would "sustain a considerable loss...certainly not less than $600." Jefferson could not postpone lease payments the next year, "having exhausted all other funds, even of credit." Mann's indebtedness to Eston would accumulate to $8000 and only be settled with the sale of Edgehill in 1825.[31]

Another toll of juggling debt among banks, in-laws, and employees was separating the Randolph's enslaved family from them. "Maria, daughter of Iris, born at Edgehill" was conveyed in the fall of 1818 to Monticello's overseer, Edmund Bacon, in exchange for $500 and payment of a note he held on Randolph. The following spring, an urgent call on Randolph by "Bank of the U. S., and Bank of Virginia...forced" him to "offer the little girl at Edgehill" to Bacon. Four-year-old "Edy, daughter of Fennel," was traded for $200 cash.[32]

At fifty-one, Martha's husband returned to political life as Albemarle delegate in 1819, was elected governor for three successive years, but ended this career disastrously by publicly attacking the Council of State with whom he shared executive power. Randolph wrote both the *Richmond Enquirer* and the *Compiler* asking they publish his address to the Legislature beginning his third term. "The Governor of Virginia for the last five years," he carped, "has been no more than a reading and signing clerk to the Council & of much less weight in the government than their recording clerk." Randolph vowed to "never...lose an occasion of giving his testimony against the usurpations of the Council, which deprive the Governor, of all his constitutional importance in the Government."[33] This impetuous public display of the Council's internal conflicts alienated once and for all even his long-suffering political allies.

"Coup de grace"

On August 7th 1819, a letter arrived at Poplar Forest informing Ellen, Cornelia, and their Grand Papa that Wilson Cary Nicholas had "placed his estate in the hands of trustees to be sold for the payment of his debts." Unfortunately, Jefferson had entered a desperate, Faustian bargain with his in-law and President of the Bank of United States in Richmond. He endorsed $20,000 in notes, in exchange for a $3,000 loan to pay a thirty-year-old obligation in Amsterdam that had resulted from commingling personal and government draughts while in Paris. Nicholas approved the loan but with a proviso: "Will you do me the favor," he asked Jefferson, "to endorse for me, two notes for ten thousands each?...[Y]ou can never suffer the slightest inconvenience from ever complying with it." [34] Ellen was so "shocked" to learn of the trustees' sale she could not "recover her spirits." She wrote Mama that "ours is but a shattered bark to breast the waves which have overwhelmed so many goodly ships in our view." Perhaps, she hoped vainly:

> [A]fter struggling all our lives with debt & difficulty, we
> may be reserved as another proof of the capriciousness
> of fortune, who sometimes takes pleasure in elevating
> the long-depressed in the midst of the fall and the ruin
> of her former favorites.[35]

The Nicholas imbroglio became in Jefferson's mind the "*coup de grace*" to his intractable debt dating back, at least in this case, almost four decades.

Monticello's Mistress

Martha's position in the household had become elevated sufficiently by the 1820s that she could intervene forcefully in family disputes and serve as her father's surrogate with visitors. She confessed to Nicholas Trist that her time was "frittered away [in] a series of trifling occupations, each one apparently of little importance [but] en masse indispensable to the comfort of the family....[A] defect of both education and character...disposes me too much to loiter and enjoy society." She clearly had been involved in less "trifling" discussions about Father's "hobby" of his old age—the University. She effused that it would be "different from all others...on the continent,""6 hotels...and the board required not to exceed 100$," "manual exercise will be a regular branch of their education." "The neighbourhood will undergo great changes...We have every reason to believe the society of the neighbourhood will be very good." Like her Father, this was obviously the one bright light amid the "encreasing derangement of Mr. Randolph's affairs" that would drive them to "ruin."[36]

Genteel hospitality was Martha's forte and enjoyment of society her feigned "defect of character." Mother protested to her recently married daughter: "I have literally not one quiet hour from 5 in the morning my usual hour of rising, till 10 at night, when we generally retire." With Lafayette's visit and the University's Board of Visitors, they "had more company [that] summer than usual." Nonetheless, she was her father's voice to visitors crowding Monticello.

> I have had more to say to them in consequence of My dear father's indisposition, and I certainly have saved him a great deal without giving offense which the denial of the heads of the family would in most instances have done.

Monticello's mistress found time, however, to vigorously insert herself and resolve family disagreements. Virginia had to be supported in her desire for a piano, "against the prudence of the Tufton family." "I imposed silence," Martha wrote to Ellen, "by declaring them incompetent to the business, having no ear [for music] they could form no just calculations on the subject" of whether a piano was desirable. Jeff, who was by this time the financial manager for the entire household, laughingly acquiesced to Mother, Virginia, and Nicholas "not following his advice, but as usual he thought everybody in the wrong who differed with him in opinion."[37] This attitude, which the family called "a Randolph," had been a recognized disposition of his father for many years.

"No extravagance of ours"

In 1824, Mann Randolph passed on to his son the only legacy he had left—debt. The $23,000 owed creditors which Jeff Randolph assumed was backed by a deed of trust on Edgehill, Varina, and forty-nine "negroes."[38] He sold Varina in early 1825, much to his father's relief, but his proposed disposal of Edgehill was the first spark of what would become a firestorm enlightening a curious public to the family's financial plights. It was more than a simple real estate transaction to solve a financial problem. This turn of events had major ramifications for an insecure Mann Randolph who lived in a genteel plantation culture where masculine identity was dependent on private esteem, public honor, and the exercise of republican civic virtue. Edgehill was the last parcel enfranchising Randolph in a state whose constitution limited voting to property-holding males. It would also remove the last symbol and public display of treasured independence, even though it had been created in the shadow of Monticello. And finally, selling Edgehill irretrievably inverted the cultural order of generational dominion by placing the disheartened farmer under Jeff's financial care. As Jefferson and the plantation's mistress had advised Nathaniel Burwell in 1818, "the order and economy of the house are as honorable to the mistress as those of the farm to the master and if either be neglected ruin follows, and the children destitute of the means of living."[39] Knowing Martha's self-doubts about her domestic capacities and inclinations, there is little wonder that she was struggling with interpreting this course of life events—to make meaning of her experiences.

"We are irretrievably ruined," a dejected Martha informed her well-situated New York in-law. But why? How must she interpret this unfortunate turn of affairs? It was "securityships for which money was borrowed upon usurious interest" that diverted the couple's income for "the payment of other people's debts." Absent these self-inflicted wounds, they "might have lived in affluence and laid by every year something for [their] children." No mention of her husband abandoning the flour mill operation to Eston's hands and leaving nine children in Martha's while the forty-five year-old went off to war; she failed to recount Secretary Barbour's patronage for the border survey and Mann's stormy, public conclusion; his dalliance in sending tobacco to market was forgotten; and a host of other misjudgments that Mann

Randolph had made over the years. Nancy Morris would have been well aware that much of the supposed income diversion was to herself, her sisters, and other Randolph relatives. In the context of how Martha had been reared, these acts demonstrated her husband's moral sense—his succor of others' distresses, that most important marker of personal character; but it was developed to the point of excessive disinterest that her father considered a vice of the southern character. Was it neglect of domestic "economy" or that of the farm that had precipitated the "ruin"? Honor hung in the balance, and Martha needed a resolution. "I have the comfort of knowing that no extravagance of ours has occasioned or even <u>accelerated</u> the mischief," she forcefully concluded to the woman who had been dishonored, impoverished, rejected, and defamed only to resurrect herself as a wealthy Mrs. Gouverneur Morris. (A similar message in more detail had been conveyed sixteen months earlier to her son-in-law, Nicholas Trist.) This theme of enduring self-sacrifice to the point of economic ruin would become the central theme of "The Jefferson Family Story" she and Father constructed for posterity. The sale of Edgehill was stopped by "an injunction which Mr. R—obtained," a beleaguered wife reported to Nancy. "I see no advantage in putting off the evil day for come it must."[40]

Unlike his father-in-law, Mann Randolph's *coup de grace* in his mind was not signing "securityships for others"—that was what honorable gentlemen did—but, rather, being denied the last vestige of republican civic virtue, social esteem, and self respect. His political career ended in 1825 as it had started in the 1790s with a sound defeat of three to one. The disappointment was exacerbated by the tension between father and son that erupted into a public spectacle. An appearance before a chancery court judge had corrected some "<u>misstatements</u>" critical of Jeff made by his father and had resulted in a postponement of the Edgehill sale until December of 1825. Martha wrote to Ellen:

> The only good effect of such a measure will be to spare the family the scandal of such a rupture...But you know the parties too well to hope for anything like cordiality on one side [Thomas Mann Randolph]. decency of deportment is all the most sanguine can expect... [T]hings have gone off much better than I dared to hope, and when this business is finally settled we shall be relieved.[41]

Martha by 1825 had clearly taken the side of her son and had come to view her husband as a somewhat pitiable character. Her "most sanguine" hope proved to be just that, as the "rupture" continued to widen between Randolph (who now signed his letters with "Sr.") and whomever he included under his moniker "Monticello."

Husband, son, and even a Randolph nephew fueled the family's emotional conflagration. Students at Jefferson's "hobby" had rioted, challenged professors, caroused drunkenly, and caused bodily harm. Wilson Jefferson Cary, son of Virginia Randolph, was among the culprits involved in the brawl and was expelled. "Your dear Grand father is not so well," Martha fretted. "The fatigue of the last week has thrown him back a good deal and obliged me to encrease his nightly dose of laudanum to 100 drops; though suffering much pain yet he is not as feeble I think as when I wrote last."[42]

Martha's sense of uncertainty and acknowledgement of life's contingencies can be appreciated in the face of myriad disruptions to family harmony, security, and privacy, but she still could conjure a positive future. In a "fit of moralizing," she urged her newly-married daughter in the fall of 1825 to remember that "nothing is perman[ent] neither joy nor sorrow."

> Every sorrow takes off to a certain degree the keen edge of our sensibilities and consequently every succeeding one finds us, if not better able to bear, yet with diminished sensibility to the evil. a most wise dispen- sation, for we always retain enough to enjoy the good in store for us, and it is no loss to have less for the cares incident to every situation in life.

She sorely needed this "moralizing" uplift herself! The person who made her happiness "compleat" was in rapidly declining health; a husband still lived but had departed the family; daughter Anne was preyed on by an alcoholic husband; Edgehill gone; and her second daughter had moved to far off Boston. According to Mary, aged twenty-two, the family was living "among fallen fortunes…in the midst of the clouds that darken round [them] so thick as sometimes to shut out even the hope of better days."[43] Mary's father had been unable to parlay farms, flour mill, tax collector position, the Governor's office, or federal appointments into financial solvency or his daughters' portions. Grand Papa had shuffled merchant's accounts, bank loans, personal notes, and farm receipts until his credit worthiness was worn as thin as his frock.[44]

The Edgehill sale in January 1826 had "fallen very short of the payment of the debts," when Martha wrote Nancy Morris. Her husband had so poorly subdivided the property that "it was cried 4 hours at 16 $ with no bidders, so Jeff finally offered $17 for the whole. Martha complained her "relinquishment of dower in 2 great estates" was a poor bargain for "old Scylla, Priscilla and Betsy with her children, Critty's 3 little orphan girls and an Orphan child of Molly Warrens, making in all 3 women old and infirm and 8 little children." But her sister-in-law and Nancy's sister, Jane, had fared much better, because her husband, Thomas Eston Randolph recovered $8000 owed him by Mann from the defunct grist mill partnership. "[H]ad the sale of Edgehill been postponed, the house from over [their] head would have gone and I believe everything else besides." Nancy's brother would always have a home, Martha assured, but his prospects actually were little better than cousin Eston's.

> My dear father wrote most kindly and pressingly to him to live with us altogether, for of late years he has spent most of his time at his plantations, but his independence of spirit will not permit him to stay where he could be doing nothing for himself or his family, his spirits are gone and he is completely overwhelmed.[45]

Even while Father was pressing, Martha was aware that there might not be a Monticello for her husband to come home to.

"Keep our affairs unblended"

Her father's letters urging Randolph's return were solicitous at the same time they made clear the financially distressed farmer must rely on his own devices. Jefferson could not help with saving Edgehill because his resources were being husbanded "for the support of the family." Just as Randolph's last asset was placed on the auction block in the summer of 1825, Jefferson wrote: "Your situation is painful, but neither novel nor unfrequent....Restore yourself to the bosom of your family and friends; they will cherish your happiness as warmly as they ever did." He encouraged his son-in-law to use his education, books, and restored physical health to await the "call into public service."[46] What Jefferson would never know was that Randolph would not recover his physical or mental health, the voters "confidence" in his "talents," or the "bosom of family."

The mixed messages in Jefferson's letter a month later on July 9th could not have been heartening to Martha's troubled husband. He confronted Randolph with the opinion his financial difficulties had been "brought on...by too liberal a disposition to engage <u>yourself</u> for others." Faint praise, indeed, a character deficiency! It was a vice of Virginians, Jefferson had told Chastellux, to be "disinterested" to the point of "ruin."[47] Late in his Presidency, Jefferson had pledged to Randolph that he considered their property as "a common stock for our joint family." He similarly had written Martha in 1809: "Indeed I know no difference between his affairs and my own."[48] Now, however, one Virginia farmer was ruined, another was on the brink, and the years had not been kind to their relationship. It was on "mature consideration" that Jefferson had not intervened to relieve his difficulties.

> I thought the best service I could render...would be to keep our affairs unblended, that, if any misfortune should happen to yours, mine might be a resource for the maintenance and care of the family.

Still, Jefferson beseeched him "to return, and become again a member of the family." Interestingly after so many years, he could not understand why his disaffected son-in-law might not wish to consider Monticello "home" and act as though it was his "own house." His physical separation was precipitated by emotional estrangement, feelings of being an inferior "silly bird," a sense of being so different from others in the "narrow circle" of family.[49] His passion was certainly "loud and imperious," As he had confessed to his journal.[50] Again, Randolph did a "Randolph." He later revealed the most intimate details of the family's emotional life by publishing in Richmond's *Enquirer* these two letters entreating his return to the family as a counter to rumors he was estranged from that very person whose overtures he refused. He appended notes denying or explaining his separation from Monticello. Adopting the third person voice, he wrote: "After the sale of his farm...he did not enjoy company, which Mr. Jefferson always had. He did not choose to meet the supercilious looks of Mr. J's guests." Another read: "T. M. R. spent every day in his house at North Milton, but every night, without hindrance from high water or very heavy rain, at Monticello." Grand Papa was undoubtedly correct that the children and young adults of the Randolph family were "distressed" and had experienced "grief" by his "withdrawal."

Mother was suffering, too, and her "sensibilities" had been dulled even more, until she could not even imagine better times. "My life of late years has been such a tissue of privations and disappointments," she lamented to Nancy early in 1826, "that it is impossible for me to believe that any of my wishes will be gratified, or if they are, not to fear some hidden mischief flowing even from their success."[51] There was a not so "hidden mischief" in Father's financial condition that he would attempt to solve with a scheme that might "spare the family the scandal" but, nonetheless, expose the most private and intimate matters to public scrutiny.

"Inspiration from the realms of bliss"

From 1790 at each inflection in his life course and anticipated retirements, Jefferson had a plan to achieve solvency. He renegotiated the Wayles's legacy debt; reduced tobacco, added wheat production, and diffused his risks by cash renting farms; built mills to add value to commodities; expected his Presidential windfall of $25,000 yearly to be the family's bail; planned to sell "detached" land tracts"; and "reducing [their] establishment to the style of living of a mere private family." Martha was "thoroughly convinced of the necessity" for "retrenching all possible expense," but even in 1809 there were ample reasons for her to be skeptical of these arrangements.[52] Fifteen years later, life experiences had dulled not only the "keen edge" of her sensibilities but had whittled away the capacity to even imagine a better future. Only inspiration remained.

The "lottery scheme was an indication of just how desperately her father was clinging to his beloved Monticello. It was conceived in a dream and hastily pursued without informing the family. Jefferson knew the stakes of requesting that Virginia's legislature authorize the sale of tickets for a chance to win part of Monticello and preserve the remainder for his heirs. Private affairs would be fully opened to public scrutiny; treasured independence would be compromised; the pretense to unvarnished civic virtue exposed; and, if it was denied, the bedrock of his republican ideology—citizens' benevolent impulse—would be called into question. The scheme demonstrated just how intertwined were the family's debts, their mutual affections, fear of impending separations, an attachment to place, and hunger for privacy.

There were alternatives to preserving Monticello—all of them rejected, because the deep, abiding affection Martha and Jeff felt for the patriarch attached them emotionally as well to that mountaintop place. Selling the Bedford property was deemed to entail "a sacrifice [in price] so great as to defeat the object" of settling some of the debt. Grandson Francis, dissatisfied with the fanciful octagon house at Poplar Forest, offered to exchange that property for either $5000 or land. Monticello would be sold. This particular plan, Martha wrote Ellen, devised that,

> we should go to Bedford, retaining only the necessary furniture for that house, and a small but effective household of servants and sell the whole property here and as many negroes as would pay the debts—it was a most bitter sacrifice to us all.[53]

Jeff and Martha hesitated to share their proposal with her "dear Father"; their personal "sacrifice" paled against the thought that he would be "turned out of his house and deprived in his old age of the few pleasures he was capable of enjoying." They considered his attachment to Monticello so resolute that "his few remaining years would be embittered and shortened" by a separation. However, the approach of the creditors was as inexorable as the ebb of life—the race was between death and foreclosure.

> [T]he crisis was at hand, things could no longer go on in the train they were, the consequence of a delay would have been <u>complete</u> ruin a few years later, when we should no longer have possessed a home to shelter us. it was paying too much for the priviledge [sic] of living a few years longer at Monticello.[54]

But for Martha, her children, and Father, it was the *emotional*, not financial, toll they felt most keenly. By 1826, the family could not enjoy, as they had so often in prior years, the spring-time reawakening of the orchards, emerging crocuses, return of the bluebird, and myriad rhapsodized features of their mountaintop.

They may have become reconciled to the reasonable necessity of leaving Monticello for a more modest establishment at Poplar Forest; but their affections compelled them to choose "<u>complete</u> ruin." Jeff was "so much agitated" by the plan. "The rest of the family even down to the little children was really as if a recent death had taken place." For Grand Papa, the "shock was...dreadful" and he concluded "his death would be an advantage to his family." Gloom, anguish, death, mortification, shock, and "a deadly blast of all peace of mind" were among the fog of words family members used to describe their sentiments at the prospect of leaving Monticello. Separation from that place evoked the emotional equivalent of parting with each other grimly presaged by Father's failing health. However, they "became reconciled" and were "trying to look forward to plans of future comfort and improvement." Then, an epiphany struck!

> [L]ying awake one night from painful thoughts, the idea of the lottery came like an inspiration from the realms of bliss to My father. the moment it was light he got up and sent for Jefferson who immediately saw in all it's bearings the immense advantage of the scheme. property enough sold at a fair value to pay his debts, a maintenance for the family, the means of educating the boys, and a <u>home</u> for myself and children that might be unprovided for, and last tho not least, the undisturbed possession of Monticello during his precious life.[55]

Rejecting Poplar Forest in favor of Monticello was a pivotal choice whose consequences set Martha adrift with children in tow up and down the Atlantic coast, moving from house to house, always without a home for the remaining decade of her life. Their head reckoned a "bitter sacrifice" of Monticello, a "small" Poplar Forest household, and selling "negroes," but the heart succumbed to a fanciful scheme whose "price" would be breaching the wall separating private and intimate family affairs from the public sphere and politics especially.

The morning-after effects of Jefferson's vision from the "blissful realm" was anything but idyllic. The agony of debt was emotionally unbearable. It was a constant reminder of dependence on and subjugation to creditors; it amplified the uncertainties of plantation agriculture; and debt threatened his material and symbolic legacy to future generations. However, there was more to "debt" than the inconvenience of nagging creditors, the grief of losing a magnificent home or even the most likely prospect of "children destitute of a means of living"—though these were prominent features of Jefferson's identity. As evidenced by his reasoned apologia in the lottery essay and his letter begging editorial support from publisher Ritchie (which was to become his obituary), the toll of "debt" was being collected from the very core of Jefferson's self-fashioned identity, his lifelong pursuit of happiness, and the republican political ideology he had embraced. Certainly, the practical aspects of meeting financial obligations—selling land, reining in personal consumption, and constricting the household—circumscribed material independence. But more significantly, his life's purpose was part of the stakes and public esteem, if the plan failed, might be the ante. Both Jefferson's personal identity and political ideology were threatened by his lottery scheme.

The most immediate threat was the unvarnished exposure of private and even intimate affairs to public scrutiny and possible derision. The lottery would abrogate Jefferson's binary of "hateful labours" and "bosom of family," of "tumult" and "tranquility," which had sustained their imagined family construct and facilitated his devotion to civic duty. The dichotomy, also, had been a way of inflating civic virtue: the more "hateful" the service to others, the greater the sacrifice, the more honorable was personal disinterestedness to benefit the collective good. The lottery, as argued by Jefferson, converted private interest into a public obligation in "payment" for service—the very antipode of republican civic virtue. If the wall between public and private was breeched by voluntarily exposing your private affairs, then the sacrifice—the honor—was diminished.

Jefferson had written from Paris that debt held by European merchants had made planters a "species of property"; if so, then his financial obligations were resulting in the same condition—only closer to home. If the natural right to choose "pursuits" was curtailed, where was independence? Personal freedom? The lottery scheme was an open admission by Jefferson and the family that they were no longer free to pursue what interested them, but were compelled to trade treasured independence for dependence on the public's good will. The debt that for decades had weighed on his spirits was, in the final months of life, striking at the very meaning of life for Thomas Jefferson, so much so, he offered to end his existence as palliative for the family's suffering.

"But what is chance?"

"Thoughts on Lotteries" was an essay to himself written sometime in February 1826, justifying a decision that crossed the fine grains of his identity and political philosophy. It took the form of a legal brief citing precedent, countering imagined objections, and asserting principles on which his case for a lottery should be judged. Parts and themes of the essay surfaced in letters to Madison, Monroe, and publisher Ritchie that same month.

Jefferson attempted to deflect any criticism from his imaginary antagonist that his lottery scheme was "gambling" with the contorted claim that all of life was a game of chance—farming, ocean navigation, hunting, cards, dice, insurance, raffles, &c. "[E]very one has a natural right to choose for his pursuit such one of them as he thinks most likely to furnish him subsistence." But there are two criteria for judging these choices by right: Do they "produce something useful to society?" Will they "endanger the well-being of the individuals" or their families? For someone who had told his teenage daughter that card playing was unseemly in "genteel people," it is not surprising that "cards, dice, billiards, &c." were classed along with "insanity, infancy, & imbecility" as warranting suppression of "the pursuit altogether, and the natural right of following it."[56] As Jefferson's mental adversary might have predicted, lotteries to clear otherwise intractable debts were deemed socially useful by saving <u>creditors</u>; moreover, they would not "endanger others," because tickets were purchased by the "willing only" who can "risk the price."

Jefferson's based his claim for a lottery on his sixty years of public service, but length of service was only a device for opening the door to a staged review of the past. He interpreted his life as saving the Republic from Federalists; prohibiting importation of slaves; obliterating the distinction between "nobles and plebeians"; elevating daughters to receive inheritances equal to sons; and sending forth into the world from the University of Virginia the republican light of the Old Dominion kindled in the sons of "sister States" and stoked to create "indissoluble bonds" of "fraternal affections." Abandoning all dissimulation, Jefferson declared to his imaginary opponent: "I claim some share in the merits of this great work of regeneration....And what remuneration do I ask? Money from the treasury? Not a cent....My request is, only to be permitted to sell my own property freely...To <u>sell</u> it, I say, and not to <u>sacrifice</u> it, not to have it gobbled up by speculators to make fortunes for themselves."

The lottery essay relied on precedent as its principal argument form.[57] Jefferson equated purchasing a lottery ticket to "a tax levied...with their own consent." The majority of citations related to raising money for schools, bridges, navigation, roads, towns, and counties, not for the relief of an individual. So domestic and public spheres had to be conflated in Jefferson's argument, thereby abrogating a distinction that for decades had framed his notions of family and personal independence itself. The imagined family that emotionally sustained him in public life and the lived family to which he fled for emotional restoration were both thrown into the world for deliverance from ruin.

In fearful desperation, the shy, self-effacing persona typical of his public displays was abandoned entirely in this argument with himself. Will the lottery scheme "lead to evil" by setting a precedent? Certainly not, Jefferson argued, for he was unique among public servants! "Have they, as in this case, devoted three-score years and one of their lives, uninterruptedly, to the service of their country?" In addition to sheer number of years, there are qualitative features any future claimant should have to meet. "Have the times of those services been as trying...their trial of equal importance...the share they have borne...equally marked?" Then, the distressed patriot, Father, and Grand Papa unabashedly claimed to never have had nor likely would have an equal: "The single feature of a sixty years' service, as no other instance of it has yet occurred in our country, so it probably never may again." As Jefferson closed his internal argument with a make-believe opponent, "Sixty years" morphed into a third person ("it") with possessions he had so persuasively recognized some fifty years before: "It...asks but a simple permission, by an act of natural right, to do one of moral justice."

"To spend for their credit"

In earlier years, Jefferson consistently claimed he only wanted to leave public office with the approval of the people, after restoring government to sound republican principles. The hospitality Monticello showered on all comers—relatives, friends, and strangers—was reciprocating the social esteem the household had spent a lifetime pursuing. He told French merchant Stephen Cathalan in 1807 there was "one other consolation that after 40 years of service to [his] country,"

> I retire poorer than when I entered it. Not that I have anything to reproach them [citizens] with. They have always allowed me as much as I thought I deserved myself. But I have believed it my duty to spend, for their credit whatever they allowed me and something more. No servant ever retired better satisfied with his employers.[58]

The reputation he had built became a temporary obstacle to raising money. Upon learning of a proposal before the Virginia legislature authorizing a land lottery, Jeff relayed disheartening news: "A panic seised [sic] the timid and indecisive among his friends as to the effect it might have upon your reputation." Jefferson, who had warned Jeff while in Philadelphia of gambling's dangers, was delayed in gaining legislative approval, because "the policy of the state had been against lotteries as immoral."[59] The legislature had struck at the core of Jefferson's own internal struggles, if the lottery was interpreted as gambling. Their rejection, he disclosed to Ritchie was "great & painful,"

228

and to Madison he admitted to a "mortification."[60] "I had so far overvalued myself," he confessed to his grandson, "as to have counted on it with too much confidence." The failure to gain approval was a "deadly blast of all peace of mind."[61] More so than for himself, Grand Papa expressed concern for the family's future. Though serendipity can easily be mistaken for prescience, it was poignant that Jefferson early in his Presidency had clipped a poem, "The Beggar," whose themes would be echoed during these final months of his life, read in part:

> Pity the sorrows of a poor old man!
> Whose trembling limbs have borne him to your door,
> Whose days are dwindled to the shortest span,
> Oh! give relief ____ and heav'n will bless your store.
> …
> Your house erected on the rising ground,
> With tempting aspect drew me from my road,
> For plenty there a residence has found,
> And grandeur a magnificent abode.
> …
> (Hard is the fate of the infirm & poor!)
> Here craving for a morsel of their bread,
> A pamper'd menial forced me from the door,
> To seek a shelter in an humbler shed.
> …
> A little farm was my paternal lot.
> Then like the lark, I sprightly hail'd the morn;
> But oppression forc'd me from my cot,
> My cattle died, and blighted was my corn.
> My daughter, once the comfort of my age!
> Lur'd by a villain from her native home
> Is cast abandon'd, on the world's wide stage,
> And doom'd in scanty poverty to roam.[62]

Much like this poor, old beggar, Jefferson confided that his "spirits" were laid low by "disease, debility, age and embarrassed affairs," but his agony was erupting as well from the very nature of the family he and Martha had created.

> My dear and beloved daughter, the cherished companion of my early life, and nurse of my age, and her children, rendered as dear to me as if my own, from having lived with me from their cradle, left in a

comfortless situation, hold up to me nothing but future gloom.[63]

He would "not care were life to end," except Mann Randolph's "unhappy state of mind" left Martha without any recourse but her father. The family's "affectionate devotion to me," he wrote Jeff, "makes a willingness to endure life a duty as long as it can be of any use to them."[64] Their affection for Father and Grand Papa held them to the Mountain; his for them, to life itself.

Jeff vainly tried to lift the spirits of his "dear Grandfather" in the face of maybe losing the lottery vote. "We shall never think of difficulties or loss of property as an evil," he wrote from Richmond. "My own trials and struggles with the world have been so salutary…not to be dismayed at any difficulties…[C]hildren that make the poverty of rich men, make the wealth of the poor ones."[65] In these last months and facing the prospect of losing Monticello, Jefferson returned to what he had for decades considered and advocated as the *sine qua non* of happiness—honor, esteem, beloved by others—and counted these among his blessings:

> Uninterrupted health, a competence for every reasonable want, usefulness to my fellow-citizens, a good portion of their esteem…the world which has sufficiently honored me, and above all, a family which has blessed me by their affections."[66]

Enough minds in Virginia's legislature were finally persuaded to approve a special lottery for Jefferson, perhaps even accepting his argument that an unprecedented act was appropriate for a life of exceptional public service.

"A Great Man has fallen in Israel!"

"There is no longer any doubt," Monticello sadly reported to Boston at 9:15 a.m., July 4th. "He has been dying since yesterday morning…[and] we were in momentary fear that he would not live, as he desired, to see his own glorious fourth."[67] Later that day, the punch bowls of Richmond would be brimming, arms raised to stirring salutes, and mouths opened in mellifluous toasts, but the Nation had not unfolded its purse to reward years of civic virtue, as had been hoped from the "realms of bliss." In three days, a bold headline in Ritchie's *Enquirer* declared the historical and cosmic significance that Virginians attached to both Jefferson's life and death. "What a wonderful coincidence!" Editor Ritchie proclaimed. "Fifty years from the Declaration of Independence…this great man…has breathed his last. No other Euthanasia could have been wished to him!"[68]

The Editor—to compensate for what he considered his "deficient" paean to Jefferson—presented "a curious and authentic Memoir" that was called forth by "a particular occasion." The "curious" document was provided the *Enquirer* by a "friend" and was put "in that touching style for which the author was so remarkable." Jefferson had not only prescribed his own epitaph—"Author of the Declaration of American Independence and the statute of Virginia for religious freedom, and father of the University of Virginia"—but bequeathed an interpretation of his life in an unusually devised autobiography. His lottery essay content, appended with letters to Madison, Monroe, Loyall, and Ritchie, contained the central themes of what would become his life's historical narrative—"The Jefferson Family Story."

Over the coming weeks, months, and even years, an emotional farrago tumbled through the hearts of the Monticello family. Grief, loneliness, fear, and ennui competed with hope, caring, warm memories, and anticipation. As Monticello was wrenched from hands, their hearts sanctified the place and deified its creator. Mother welcomed an escape to Boston from "the bitter anguish of seeing…the sanctum of his bed room violated by the auctioneer."[69] Ellen asked Mother for "any anecdote" revealing the "perfection of his private character…[provided] it would not be violating it's sacredness."[70] Using the house for any purpose other than a home would seem to Cornelia "like prophaning a temple."[71] The family's consecration was echoed by the world outside, as well. Almost before Richmond's Fourth-of-July punch bowls were dry, the literati were waxing poetic about the place called "Monticello." Poetess Sigourney was moved to console the "philosophick maid" enshrined in "Monticello's sacred shade."

> Turn from your mountain heights and weep
> Thou philosophic maid!
> …
> From Monticello's sacred shade
> So long they lov'd abode
> Where in harmonious sway
> Wisdom with the Graces trod
> Turn pensive Muse away.[72]

The family and near connections were beginning to disperse as the spot to which they were so attached began slipping from their grasp. They only had a tenuous, heavily mortgaged hold on Edgehill. Jane Randolph, Mann's sister, had left the neighborhood and opened a school near Francis Eppes in Bedford County. The Monticello family's grief was intensified because they had no central location for situating their sentiments. Affection, separation, family, place, and debt were bound in such a Gordian knot as to defy untangling.

Chapter 11

"Never ashamed of an honorable poverty":

Fashioning a Legacy

In late September 1826, just a few weeks after Jefferson's death, Beach Lawrence posed a question to Joseph Coolidge that others were asking and that to this day continues to puzzle historians. As relayed by Ellen to "Dearest Mother":

> [H]ow it came that having received from his father a large property, marrying an heiress & receiving for many years a regular salary from the public Treasury, he should have in his latter years fallen into the distress which induced him to apply for permission to sell his estate by lottery.[1]

"The Jefferson Family Story"

The first draft of the "answer" had been constructed by Jefferson in his "Thoughts on Lotteries" and letters to editor Ritchie of the *Richmond Enquirer*, Madison, and Monroe. Martha's answer to Beach Lawrence in 1826 repeated and embellished for dissemination to a wider public the themes of "The Jefferson Family Story" her father had introduced over the years. The family's response was finally canonized in 1856 by Ellen's retelling and elaboration for Henry Randall's *Life of Thomas Jefferson*. Others unknowingly contributed to the narrative through their life experiences that were observed by the authors and used to explain away unflattering inconsistencies.

Bits-and-pieces of the "Story" had been seeded from the very early days of Jefferson's entry onto the public stage, but they only coalesced into discernible themes in the final months of his life. Father had artfully reassured Maria in 1801 that he chose public office not for "personal ambition" but for the sake of his daughters and future generations.[2] Many years away from home until 1809 had robbed him of "actual experience" of farming, and he claimed to be "ignorant…in the management of a farm."[3] Despite these demurrals, however, Jefferson had been deeply involved in every aspect of farming operations over the entire period. He prescribed crop rotations, distributed workers between enterprises, bought raw materials, arranged the shipping, marketed flour, nails, and tobacco, and performed a host of other management functions.[4]

Another plotline, added in 1819, attributed their financial condition to "3 years of war…4 years of [overseers] Goodman and Darnell" and "impoverishment of…fields by constant culture without any aid of manure." He ominously offered a draconian choice to Poplar Forest overseer Yancey:

> We must either attend to the recruiting our lands, or abandon them and run away to Alibama [sic], as many of our countrymen are doing, who find it easier to resolve on quitting their country than to change the practices in husbandry to which they have been brought up.[5]

The truculent farmer for whatever reason had delayed eight years putting Jeff in charge of both enterprises. "I have for some time been become sensible that age was rendering me incompetent to the management of my plantations," he confessed in his mid-seventies to Joel Yancey. "Failure of memory, decay of attention and a loss of energy in body and mind convince me of this; as well as the vast change for the better since my plantations here have been put under the direction of my grandson."[6]

But as each of his debt reduction plans of 1793, 1800, and 1809 had failed, and when Jeff's farm management could not undo Grand Papa's financial missteps, the loss of household, place, and home became increasingly unavoidable. The family was impoverished after decades of devotion to civic virtue, dangerously near forfeiting heralded independence, "children destitute of a means of living," and threatened with detaching their affection from Monticello to disperse over the world. The themes and story lines had to be arranged to make meaning of their lives together, to self-fashion identities, and to shape the historical narrative.[7]

By February 1826, the topics of public service and debt in "The Jefferson Family Story" had been fully developed and were told to four correspondents strategically situated to carry them forward. To

Delegate George Loyall in the Virginia legislature, even after the lottery had been approved:

> Every owner of a Virginia estate, knows how prone they are to mismanagement and ruin, even when distant alone [is considered.] How much more so when long & necessary absences of the master are added to distance, and still more when his line of life adds invincible ignorance to his intermissions of attention....[Then] an overwhelming stroke fell on me from a friend.[8]

"To keep a Virginia estate together," he informed protégé James Monroe, "requires in the owner both skill and attention; skill I never had and attention I could not have." Similarly to editor Ritchie, he beggared "want of skill in the management of our land & labor."[9]

Jefferson attributed his dire situation to a host of factors beyond his control. As he recounted to correspondents, agriculture that had been for many years in a state of "abject depression"; "calamitous fluctuations in the value" of money; planters "abandoning farms no longer yielding profit and moving to the Western country"; and a "long succession of unfruitful years, long-continued low prices, [and] oppressive tariffs levied on other branches [of commerce] to maintain that of manufactures." If Jefferson's reports were correct, land prices had declined sharply. In 1819 at the height of the Panic, he noted that a tract near Poplar Forest had brought $100 per acre and was desperate enough to offer 200 acres of Poplar Forest for a reduced price of $50–60.[10] Between a thirty percent decline in flour prices and tobacco selling for under $5 cwt., Jefferson estimated his crop receipts would be off about $3000. The forced sale of the Randolph's Edgehill in early 1826 realized $17 per acre—"a price no one else would have given"—only because Jeff bought the property.[11]

So in Jefferson's mind, inflation, migration, weather, and government policies (under the stewardship of loyal Jeffersonians) all converged so "property [had] lost its character of being a resource for debts."[12] Though painted in broad strokes, this picture of economic conditions following the War of 1812 and re-establishment of the U. S. Bank accurately summarized real world conditions, even if not the proximate cause of his penury.[13]

Jefferson's internal soliloquy hearkened the past to secure the future, when it pleaded for "those who have trusted my good faith" and appealed for the opportunity to "honestly and honorably" pay them. Land and honor were no longer sufficient collateral, because the institutional structure of America's economy and financial sector had changed to a more businesslike approach in which productivity, returns, and profits were supplanting honor, rank, and esteem as measures of solvency. Notes between gentlemen over time had become bonds to commission agents, factors, and merchants that, in turn, were increasingly transformed into loans of fixed and short terms from banks whose sole measure was repayment capacity. This was precisely how the patriarch's finances had evolved. Jefferson knew this so well from his "*coup de grace*" administered by Nicholas—in-law and bank president. Interest of $1,200 annually on these two notes, he disclosed to Madison, "was absorbing so much of my annual income…that the maintenance of my family was making deep and rapid inroads on my capital."[14]

Financial travails of the tattered gentility, despite recovery from the Panic of 1819 generally, were well-known among the revelers in Richmond on the day of Jefferson's death, but the gloom enshrouding Monticello had not yet descended to the fall line of the James. Patriotic enthusiasm (and perhaps the punch) left no room for troubling thoughts as Virginia's notables unwittingly were offering a final salute to their Founder. Jefferson's nephew, Court of Appeals Judge Dabney Carr, presided over a gathering of fifty or sixty gentlemen at Mitchell's Spring, where the assembly heard again the inspiring words of the *Declaration*.[15] Their twenty-four toasts that day saluted "Washington: A patriot, statesman, and hero." "Thomas Jefferson: In the full fruition of liberty," was hailed for "his disinterestedness, his patriotism, his wisdom." One salute the late Monticello patriarch could have unequivocally endorsed was to "The University: Owing its existence to the liberality of Virginia, and fostered by the author of the Declaration of Independence, it must become the nursery of genuine republican principles."

At Baker's Spring, praises included much the same congeries of memories, events, icons, and political uplift; however, toast number nine echoed a familiar Jefferson refrain: "The general diffusion of knowledge: An enlightened public mind, the best security for the permanency of civil and religious liberty." Missing from the legacy, however, was Editor Ritchie's speculation that "Mr. Jefferson has left behind him a pretty considerable Memoir of his own Life and Times." If he meant an orderly biography carefully chronicling bold revolutions, foreign entanglements, and political intrigue, the Editor and others would be sorely disappointed. Richmond's worthies staged the performance, but Jefferson had written the script as well as constructed the themes for his life's narrative.

Greedy Overseers & A Kindly Master

Extracts of Jefferson's public life from "Thoughts on Lotteries" were available to Beach Lawrence from the *Enquirer*'s obituary, but the discrete private scenes remained to be written. The Coolidges were to "select what would be proper to communicate and what to withhold from the publick," Martha advised. Having "long basked in the sun shine of his affections," she wondered how her answer could "not look like partiality?" Nonetheless, the themes from Father's lottery essay were repeated: physical and mental debility by 1809; Nicholas's *coup de grace* in 1819; and "depredations" arising from long absences in public service. She, also, expanded the drama and accented the "Story" with sub-texts.

To "long absence" from Monticello, she added "greedy overseers." This reconciled Father's explanation with the fact that Mann Randolph had been explicitly engaged to intermediate, look over, and report on plantation operations. Her father's "load of debt contracted by his overseers" she located primarily between 1792, when he first "retired from publick life…almost entirely free from debt," and 1809, when he arrived at Monticello without the management or technical skills to run a plantation. Martha expanded the "Story" with the Wayles's inheritance, paid three times over, the last (she claimed) with a sale of "100 negroes." A lost family "secret" was revealed as well (perhaps unwittingly), viz., heirs to John Wayles's estate personally became liable for its obligations by voluntarily deciding to distribute its assets before it was probated. This debt, too, was credited to the legatees' desire to rescue a Wayles's estate "so badly managed."

"Fears of negroes overworked"

An antagonist/protagonist plotline was added by combining the "overseer" thread with what might be called "the kindly master." Despite a crop of 90,000 pounds of tobacco in 1798 and almost 30,000 in 1823 from Poplar Forest alone, Martha told Ellen her Grand Papa after 1790 had "prohibited the culture of tobacco as a <u>crop</u>, because it was such hard work for the negroes."[16] Second, she reinforced the lottery essay's claim that "a Virginia slave estate" goes to "ruin" without "the most unremitting and judicious attention and good management." And finally: "[H]is fears of having his negroes over worked and ill treated furnished his overseers with an excuse for doing nothing," because "their own wages...[came] out of the principal even where they made nothing." This, in spite of her father drawing on tenant Craven Peyton, and overseers Bowling Clarke and Edmund Bacon for credit. Martha creatively filled "gaps" in the published obituary to make a unitary story that attributed her family's indebtedness, first, to the system of agricultural production and, second, to people they hired to attend to farming operations. But why was Father gone? They were the same answers Martha and Maria had been given during the "revolution" of 1800. "[T]he violent political struggle between 2 great parties that divided the Union," Martha recalled, "drew him most reluctantly, I do aver, from his retirement."[17]

"Cannot reside at Monticello again"

Suffering the chill of her first Boston winter, a weakened, disheartened, and grieving daughter lamented: "[T]he doors of our beloved home have been closed forever upon My devoted family." A "state of doubt and uncertainty" about her long-term living arrangements had produced in Martha a "complete prostration of health, strength, and spirits." Mary sadly informed Ellen that the family's "prospects look as gloomy as they well can, the success of the lottery is extremely doubtful." Should the lottery fail, "mama's plan [was] to issue proposals immediately for keeping a school which [would] be opened as soon as she returns from Boston." Mary planned to spend the winter "applying myself...to those things which will best fit me for bearing my part."[18] The family was mourning the loss of a beloved and, if the lottery failed, maybe a place as well.

As they fearfully awaited the patriarch's passing in 1826, "Th. M. Randolph Senior" had not seen fit to cross the Rivanna, ascend the mountain, and bid his final adieus. His precipitous behaviors from Edinburgh to Edgehill spoke volumes—sometimes in a booming voice, at others in a sad, pitiful whimper. He could reveal himself cryptically though veiled musings in a "Notebook," confidential letters to a much younger Francis Walker Gilmer, and jottings on the margins of private letters ill-advisedly published for the world to read. His father-in-law's death and his own depleted spirit finally opened his angry and caring heart to the family. "I do not consider myself a member of the family at all," he stridently asserted to son-in-law Trist, "and cannot reside at Monticello again."[19] Mary at twenty-four and Septimia at thirteen became their father's confidantes, his son, a target of fury.

Father may have left her without home, household furnishings, or money, but Martha would effectively use his intangible, but no less esteemed, reputation to provide for her family. By the fall of 1826, Randolph, Sr. once again was employed in a government position. Martha had invoked her father's reputation to arrange through their neighbor and Secretary of War, James Barbour, a position to survey the Georgia/Florida border [20] "It is true the situation is a temporary one," Barbour wrote Martha, "but I hope by or before its completion to be able to place him in some permanent employment." The Secretary expressed his "many strong personal obligations" to Jefferson, so "to repay the debt in part by acts of kindness to his Descendants is most grateful to my heart."[21]

Nancy, Jane, Virginia, Mary, and Harriet—all sisters of Mann Randolph—had been displaced from their homes and households for one reason or another. Nevertheless, they found a variety of ways to support themselves, their children, and occasionally their husbands. Harriet (Mrs. Richard) Hackley had opened a young ladies' academy in Richmond to maintain herself and children after her husband's questionable business interests failed and he abandoned the family for another woman. Aunt Mary (Molly), had closed her Richmond boarding house, moved to Arlington, Virginia, but continued to support her family by writing what became a highly popular cookbook, *The Virginia Housewife.*[22] Virginia (Mrs. Wilson Jefferson Cary) , also, took up the pen to become an enterprising author and received $1000 for her first volume. And Nancy, pilloried and flushed from Virginia plantation society, had married well in New York and personally fought the legal battles to secure her husband's bequest.[23] All the Randolph women lived in a culture that inscribed a constellation of spheres on the basis of gender, rank, and lineage. Their independent actions were confronting long-standing social expectations of a home-bound, diffident belle feigning intellectual limits, physical weakness, and emotional sensitivity to the needs of men. Political revolution, economic exigencies, and social mores were gradually eroding this eighteenth-century elite ideal of a genteel lady.

Martha did not relish the "drudgery" of starting a school which her education afforded; but Father had imbued the emotional qualities to sustain a hopeful outlook even while suffering in grief. Six months after his death, she wrote from Boston to daughter Mary: "[W]hen we meet it will be, I hope, to show ourselves worthy of our origin. Through life I have had a bright example [her father] of fortitude, cheerfulness, and dignified resignation to unavoidable evil."[24] She was less cheerful when writing her wealthy relative in New York that same month. Martha despondently judged the lottery a failure, even while Jeff was busily trying to gain approvals for ticket sales in other states. The family's circumstances were "entirely desperate" in her opinion and only the "profits of a school" would be available to maintain herself and seven children age eight to twenty-five. Personal and real property would be sold to pay debts. "But for me," Martha complained to Nancy, "nothing will remain but an education given in happier days and for very different purposes."[25]

But the family's prospects looked "much brighter" by the spring of 1827. It seemed that the lottery would go forward to pay old debts and "the generosity of South Carolina" had provided a gift of $10,000 for future income. These two measures together, she wrote Nancy,

> will save me from the horrors of keeping a boarding school…which in the country where I should have had the trouble of boarding with all it's teasing consequences, in addition to tuition, would have been a very severe trial in my feeble state. I can conceive of none more so.[26]

Randolph continued at his North Milton hermitage and urged their daughter Mary to report the latest "intelligence from Boston."[27] He departed 14 January 1827 on the Georgia-Florida boundary survey arranged by Martha and returned 2 June 1827. When Barbour did not respond to his report, he considered himself "dismissed" and once again imprudently vented his spleen in Charlottesville's *Central Gazette*, and an extract was picked up by the *Richmond Enquirer*, 6 July 1827. His biographer summarized this final job as follows: "At any rate, the brief interlude of responsible behavior did not survive the shock of disappointment, and the black, depressing moods and the violent, unreasoning rages of the past returned with increasing intensity."[28]

"Where I wonder shall we go"

With Mama in Boston, Mary, Cornelia, and Virginia bore their final days at Monticello with "much trouble and little comfort" as they prepared to "shut up the house." Physical illness and emotional fatigue overtook them. "We cannot bear to leave the scene of whatever happiness we have ever known," Mary mourned. Their future was to be "thrown upon their own exertions to earn by the drudgery of a school a scanty precarious subsistence." How could they complain, she asked, when others like Aunt Jane, their father's sister, were "suffering under similar or worse misfortunes?"[29] How, indeed?

Other Randolphs associated with the Monticello family were less fortunate and could no longer truck on their good name or illustrious lives to solve financial woes. Deeds of trust were falling to the auctioneer's gavel. Tobacco merchant Nathaniel E. Venable (1791–1847) and his business partner advertised the "trust sale" of 600 acres near Farmville, Virginia, to liquidate a deed of trust dated 29 September 1821 bearing signatures of Thomas Beverly Randolph, his wife Maria, and a Martha Randolph. Thomas's sister, Lucy Bolling, had wed Mann Randolph's brother, William, and they too were being foreclosed on 419 acres lying along the Appomattox River that had been purchased from Richmond businessman Henry Heth and a Martha Randolph around the middle of June in 1817.[30] A sister of Mann Randolph, Jane Cary, and her husband Thomas Eston Randolph had been "steadily advancing" toward financial "ruin."[31] Rather than cling to the Ashton plantation near Monticello, they however relocated to New London outside Lynchburg. "House rent" and "provisions" were "cheap" and "a good female school" they planned to open, Martha wrote Ellen, "will command every young lady within 10 miles around or more."[32]

Cornelia, with Virginia's encouragement, spoke to her sister Ellen through a poet's voice to express the family's uneasiness with separating from Monticello and their anxiety over where they would go. Everyone, except Mama, wanted to leave the state. "[W]hether to Louisiana or Vermont, to the west or the east, when people's inclinations are so different & yet all wish to hang together, is hard to say....I hope what Virginia & the poet say is true."

> Oh! deem not that the tie of birth
> Endears us to this spot of earth,
> For where so e'er our steps may roam,
> If friends are near, that place is home,
> No matter where our fate may guide us
> If those we love are still beside us.[33]

Just a few weeks after Grand Papa's death, Cornelia was hopeful that sentiment united people and transcended place, that true affection knew neither metes nor bounds nor emanated from inspiring vistas. Yet, she was uncertain: "I think one reason mama objects to going to Boston is that she fears she shall only return to these scenes to pack up to leave them forever; if we do leave this place where I wonder shall we go." By year's end, she pronounced "the bitterest of our grief is over, & for my part, with the dismal future constantly before me…I care not what trade I follow…Any place is better than this state." Cornelia discerned the connection between their financial plight, where they were, and the need to engage a "trade." "Why should we dread a school so much?" she asked Ellen. "It will keep us employed busily…Keeping house is as hard & as disagreable work. And I am quite sure that we shall not fail from want of exertion."[34]

"Affection the only thing left"

Affection, place, and debt were fused into an emotional jumble for the ever more volatile Randolph, as well. By August 1827, he pleaded with thirteen-year-old Septimia to "write often" because her "affection [was] the only thing left" and "the only satisfaction in life." As for son Jeff, however, Randolph charged: "[He] has made it his first interest to defame, depreciate, and ruin me in reputation as well as fortune." His son had displayed the "keenest avarice" and his daughter-in-law (Jeff's wife) spewed "the most vulgar and disgusting malignity" that resulted in his "total ruin." Randolph could not counter depredations inflicted by Jeff and Jane because he "was completely paralysed in [his] defense by the strength of [his] attachment" to Martha. Yet when she had not used their customary language in a letter, he inferred that his wife was "desirous to live apart" and had plotted to secure for him a "miserable post" as Indian agent in the "extreme Northwest." He considered her a co-conspirator in his financial downfall. His wife could have "prevented all that has happened of altercation & litigation" over the Edgehill property. "[S]he had been artfully persuaded that if I were completely sacrificed," he alleged to his thirteen-year-old daughter, "her Father could be saved, and she had brought her mind to wish that sacrifice."

Perhaps these allegations were not unreasonable conclusions in light of his father-in-law's refusal just before his death to comingle their financial plight. Martha had a reputation to maintain. She rejoined vehemently in denying husband's charge that Randolph Senior and Francis Eppes had been "tricked by the Monticello family" in the marriage settlements for herself and Maria. (Their father had prudently written these agreements to clearly confer the assets on his daughters and their heirs.) With "6 children…unprovided for [and] 4 of who are going to school," she would be "in miserable circumstances" without $20,000 in donations from two states. "We are obliged from poverty to keep few servants," she wrote Nancy from Edgehill. "Your means are abundant to supply every comfort, amongst which I reckon <u>servants</u> <u>first</u> & foremost...[35]

The devastated father-husband-planter in his anguish had forgotten Martha's decision was made decades before, when she pledged her love to Father, and had been openly confirmed by the "silly bird" twenty-five years earlier, when he knew he could never live among the bevy of "swans."

> But I cannot live alone, I cannot give up George and yourself, if I am compelled to live separate from her....I have loved your Mother, and her only, with all my faculties for 35 years...I have loved her most when she was sick...But I never have been rich, and have allways been compelled to work too hard to devote all my time to her comfort, which I most gladly would have done...I have spent nothing on myself, and I have disipated [sic] no property."[36]

"Damn it, let it go!" Jeff angrily declared. His lobbying for lottery legislation initially had been opposed by the very legislature in which Jefferson had ably served and the same public body that had heaped encomiums on him when he "retired" in 1783. By March 1827, Maryland had prohibited the Jefferson lottery; New York threatened the same. Sales elsewhere were tepid.[37] Grand Papa may have been right in claiming to Ritchie that "agriculture property had become no resource for the payment of debts." If so, why would someone even "run small risks for the chance of obtaining a high prize" whose profitability was questionable?[38] Coolidge advised Trist that money could be had in Boston for five percent but "'twould be a vain attempt" to pledge for security "personal property in land or slaves." New England demanded bank stock or "security of that sort."[39] Jefferson had continued to believe, even with his lottery scheme, that land *per se* had value independent of its productivity. Indeed for most of his lifetime, land and slaves had been a marker of rank that was combined with a culture of personal honor to undergird the private financial dealings that was the South's "bank". The "right" person's signature was not quite as good as gold, but no one deigned ask its value, though frequently not worth the paper. Randolph and his father-in-law had commented that land without slaves was worthless, but they forgot that slaves with unproductive land were "certain ruin." Martha in her time of acute need was required to forego the independence and domestic privacy Father and husband so cherished and cast her lot, not with a lottery exchanging land for money, but on the charity and benevolence of America—that is, a hope that their moral sense would lead them to "succor the distress of others."

"My heart often turns toward home"

Mary, influenced perhaps, by her Mother's attitude, admitted she "always had a lurking hope that the school might be eventually found to be unnecessary." She confessed to having done nothing over the prior winter to prepare herself for teaching. "Even the next six months" were so uncertain that Mary felt "so entirely unsettled, so totally without interest." She was grieving the loss of her past so much that ennui—that "canker of human happiness"— and lethargy were clouding her future:

> [M]y heart often turns towards home, the only spot I can yet consider as such, and every member of the dear circle by which it was once filled, with an insupportable longing and I sigh to remember that it is now only in my dreams that I can ever hope to live over again those scenes of past happiness.[40]

Cornelia was no less attached to Monticello than Mary or Mama, but she used her feelings to construct a memory. A springtime walk on the mountaintop in 1827 was one of her "greatest pleasures," because "the place is so lovely & in this beautiful season too, that if it was not for our affection to it would be a pleasure to come." The house was refreshingly cool, compared to Tufton; "old remaining chairs, & marble tables...set in order" welcomed them, and the "robin sung his sweetest song" just as on the day Ellen was wed. Memories of those times were bittersweet—stirring a "mixture of pleasure & pain."[41]

Virginia experienced no pleasure, only sorrow on ascending the Mountain. She bemoaned to Ellen and Joseph: "It will grieve you both very much to hear of the depredations that have been made at Monticello by the numerous parties who go to see the place." These curious marauders carried off Mama's "yellow jessamines, fig bushes, grape vines." Jeff's house at Tufton was only a "temporary resting place." "I long for a home once more where I may make permanent arrangements & plans for my convenience & comfort...I look towards Monticello as to an object that I doat [sic] on & have lost forever."[42]

Mother and Grand Papa had for years imagined their happiness could only be complete if they were together on Monticello; Mary's future happiness was only in her "dreams" of the "dear circle" on the

Mountain; Virginia grieved of her loss of a home, while Cornelia was moved by the place's natural beauty and pleasurable memories.

Martha's gracious letter thanking South Carolina for a $10,000 donation was read by the citizens of Portland, Maine in their *Eastern Argus*; those of Salem in the neighboring state learned of it from the *Essex Register*; word was spread by *The Rochester Telegraph*, *Newport Mercury*, and *Pittsfield Sun*.[43] Along the Atlantic seaboard, the public was informed that "many persons...have been of the belief that Mrs. Randolph's situation in life did not call for the laudable donation." There should have been little doubt, however, once they saw Martha's plaintive account to E. S. Davis of Abbeville, South Carolina, that appeared in the *Columbia Telescope*:

> Dear Sir: I should not have been thus remiss in returning you my thanks for your kind attention, in forwarding the South Carolina resolutions, but for the delay occasioned...by some days detention of your letter in Albemarle, and also the circumstance of its finding me confined to my bed with a severe in disposition, which left me in a state of great debility.
>
> I will not do myself the injustice to attempt any expression of my deep feelings of gratitude to the generous hearts whose liberality have given support to my old age: to understand them, it is only necessary to know, that it found me prostrate in heart and spirits, in poverty, and with eight children unprovided for, five of them still of an age to go to school.[44]

It seems most family members were considering themselves dependent on the $1,200 income from this donation and an equal amount from Louisiana. Martha numbered "family" as sixteen: "3 of them boys going to school and 10 that have no other source of income," including the children of her deceased daughter, Anne Cary Bankhead. With "rigid economy," she thought the annuity would permit them to "live in real poverty" but with "a degree of comfort."[45]

"We have quite a school here"

Jefferson's public service made possible Martha's "considerably different" learning experiences. She complained of being educated to become the "heiress of a great estate" but ill-prepared for such a role by learning "music, &c, &c," rather than sewing and other tasks of a plantation mistress. His retirement made Latin, French, Moliere, Plutarch, Livy, and other subjects of classical learning obligatory for her daughters, Ellen, Anne Cary, Cornelia, and Virginia. Ironically, they would bemoan how the needle, company, visiting, sending out the meat cut-up, and other duties befalling the carrier of the keys were obstacles to developing the accomplishments they were encouraged to learn.

Such intellectual "ornaments" along with the harpsichord, fine needlework, and a sprightly dance step would have made them most agreeable drawing room company for the gentlemen, but with few exceptions their female counterparts would have been bemused, at best, by their "manly" accomplishments. Perhaps most tragically, the daughters were acutely aware their education was erecting a social wall that few peers—female or male—would scale; that housekeeping "drudgery" was their fate in the isolated and deeply gendered plantation culture in which they were confined. While cared for and deeply loved, they also were bound inevitably by this affection to the place most cherished by Mother and Grand Papa, but where their "accomplishments" had little or no utility other than being pleasant companions.[46] What if the household is "lost," the land sold, the home abandoned, and the family dispersed?[47] Not all women, including the Randolphs, could be nestled in the "bosom of family" their entire lives and oversee a "refuge from the cares and storms of life" for the head of the household. The Randolph sisters joined the lost generation of revolutionary daughters (like their Mother) who were intellectually gifted but lacked an outlet for their accomplishments beyond the drawing room, the nursery, and being pleasant companions for men.

The internal tensions between gender expectations, household demands, and self-image had been palpable for years. "I wish I could become a well educated woman, or had no ambition to be so," Virginia had confided to her betrothed, Nicholas Trist. Her "impatient and despairing temper" combined with an "almost unconquerable indolence," she self-deprecated, "were insurmountable "obstacles."[48] But also, her "occupations at present" were not "calculated to sharpen wit, or raise spirits" because she was "constantly employed at [her] needle."[49] Mary, aged 17, threatened to "learn latin in a fortnight to…surprise" Virginia, but wondered whether such a fanciful learning schedule "would be compatible with [her] house keeping duties" or feeding the "school boys."[50] As Virginia described in the winter of 1822:

> We have quite a school here of late. The boys spend this
> month at home saying their latin lessons to Grand Papa,

and learning French with Mama. Ellen [Bankhead] has also begun French...D. O. Carr has been here for a week past to carry on his Italian studies...[51]

If the "drudgery" of housekeeping chores, personal dispositions, and hearing the boys' lessons did not obstruct learning, then the hospitality required by women of a genteel household did—even at Grand Papa's retreat. A student's life, Ellen speculated from Poplar Forest, "Must be the most innocent and happy in the world."[52] However, she lamented to Mother: "If instead of traveling about the country...I could only stay at home, and improve myself in a language, the knowledge of which promises to open to me so wide a field of enjoyment."[53] Twenty-year-old Cornelia also found visiting at least three days per week interfered with her books. "[B]esides all the time taken up by the act of dressing and visiting," she complained to Virginia, "I really am so stupid and so much fatigued."

"Nothing but a woman"

Grand Papa had made it clear to their mother at age eleven that his love for her was conditional. "If you love me then, strive...to acquire those accomplishments...which go far towards ensuring you the warmest love of your affectionate father."[54] Ellen realized at an early age the conundrum erected by these conditions in a plantation culture. A student, she speculated, is "innocent and happy;" "free of nervous anxieties, feverish hopes & groundless fears." "[T]he pursuit of knowledge unlike other pursuits is subject to no disappointments... every step counts, where every advancement is secure..." However:

> [I]f I had been a man...I would have been just such a one, I think, but being a woman and not a rich woman, I must be content with peeping every now and then into a region too blissful for my inhabitance, and after...a short interval...return to the vanities, follies[,] cares and pleasures of ordinary life.[55]

The felicitous life and confident sense of self that derived from "accomplishments" were not in Ellen's opinion available to a "woman." Mary soon discovered the same limitations on her sex, while lurking around the periphery of the institution Grand Papa considered one of his life's signature accomplishments. "I have been several times to the little library at the University," she wrote sister Ellen and, "sighed to think that through the severity of the restrictions I could derive no other advantage from it."[56] The matter of learning's utility for women had not improved emotionally for Ellen either. Reading John Locke's *Essay on Human Understanding*, she lamented that she had in the past only read what "amused" her and what would prepare her to be a "companion for...intelligent and well-informed persons in whose society [she] most delighted." She had been unaware as a youth that the "proper and healthy employment of the mind was to think." Alas, the opportunity for improving the mind had been lost with time. "I am nothing but a woman," she censured, "and could promise myself no competent reward for so much trouble."[57]

Monticello was almost gone in 1828. Ellen was approaching thirty-two years of age; married to a man engaged in international trade. Financially secure, living in Boston, a mother, and perhaps stricken by her own father's impending death, Mrs. Joseph Coolidge resorted to a "personal note" to relieve the "sad thoughts" that she confessed often oppressed her. So many years after Poplar Forest summers, fireside discussions with Grand Papa, and eight-hour days conquering Latin, Ellen attributed her demons to just those times when family and friends showered uncritical attention and unconditional affection. Mentoring by America's *philosophe* aided by a learned mother had failed to provide "wholesome discipline." Rather, they had lauded to the skies," "lavished...every species of kindness," and made her the "darling of all." These very "instructors" and "flatters of [her] family," however, represented such a high "standard of moral & intellectual worth" Ellen always felt that she "fell far short."[58] The middle-aged woman remembered a family that for her was <u>too</u> affectionate, that set <u>too</u> high a mark, that had contributed to her oppressive and "sad thoughts" as an adult.

What she had been expected to learn was of little use for a woman in the world beyond family intimates, even in a Boston, a Washington, or bustling Richmond. Virginia, Mary, and Cornelia—while varying in their "powers"—were faced with the same predicament. They were made acutely aware of their intellectual potential but soon discovered that being accomplished had slight purchase beyond Monticello's hearth; and, even there, keeping the fires stoked and hospitable entertainment took precedence.

The Monticello household placed demands on every family member—women and men, young and old, free and enslaved—but especially on the daughters straddling their mother's requirements for domestic help and Grand Papa's insistence on their becoming accomplished beyond what was useful outside the confines of his "essay in architecture." The daughters' thirst for learning had been roused. When their intellectual accomplishments did not meet expectations, Virginia, Anne, Ellen, Cornelia, and Mary frequently attributed it to their personal deficiencies, domestic chores, or the demands of household sociability. The women of Monticello had learned languages, history, writing, music, the ornaments, and other subjects necessary to teach an advanced "English" curriculum and earn a living independent of Jeff, Grand Papa, or Mann Randolph. Sadly, they had not been prepared emotionally or socially for such a departure from their family ideal. Ultimately, precious independence was surrendered to charity from South Carolina, Louisiana, selling altered copies of the patriarch's written relics, and from accommodating relatives.

The expectations of them were high, but they had limited opportunities to speak Latin and French, to discuss the moral sermons of Sterne, or to titter at the wry humor of *The Spectator*. The household that had defined and constrained their development was no longer available to display their accomplishments. The family that had bestowed unalloyed affection was dead or dispersed to separate lives. They were left with the memory, a moldering shrine, and an inspiring story, all the while suffering the pain of being "nothing but a woman."

"Painfull to me in a family"

Thomas Mann Randolph, Senior (as he now signed himself) revealed his innermost anguish, suffering, and distress just before his death in 1828 as he returned to live in the one-room and cellar of Monticello's North Pavilion. He required "undisturbed solitude" and being "completely separate" from the family, he wrote to son-in-law Trist. A dejected Randolph recalled his life as forty years of misery. The isolation was required by a "state of Mind so influenced by no very pleasing associations with Monticello during the last short interval of my residence there, almost constant from Dec. 1789." His aching heart was "cherishing a most sincere and genuine affection" for the family; he earnestly wished for "their welfare and happiness."

The anguish of a broken husband and father was palpable from his words: "Indeed I must acknowledge that it is painfull to me in a family, because it constantly recalls past scenes which it is better for me to forget." He had neither a remembered, imagined, or lived family! The "tranquility" that was to have been the hallmark of a Monticello household had become incompatible with the affectionately bound family it was supposed to protect from the "world." "I must live by myself to be tranquil, and tranquility is indispensable to be as I am now manifestly in the decline of life."

Private honor—a consequence of "accomplishments" in Thomas Jefferson's mind—was lost; its companion, public esteem, long since vanished. Politically disenfranchised by the sale of his properties, Randolph asserted his "political rights" by mingling with "the crowd on all public occasions." It is a "heartless intercourse," he bemoaned, but "all other social feeling is for ever lost." The one condition he could not endure was exactly the one he tragically had been in all his life— dependence! "Nor shall my spirit ever bow to it," he scrawled truculently, though his fortunes, his confidence, his sense of self had succumbed long ago.[59] He had left Monticello but like others in the family could not separate his mind or emotions from the place.

"Honorable poverty"

While Ellen from a bourgeois Boston house could bemoan the effects of her upbringing, Cornelia in sight of a decaying mansion was confronted with the necessity of refashioning herself. After deaths and being "driven from the home...all the other evils of poverty are nothing," she reminded Ellen.

> I have given up all ambition & all pride, & put down the dusting brush or the needle, smooth my hair & come out to receive company feeling as much a lady as I have done when I laid my book or drawing for the same purpose.

Cornelia was separating from her former persona at the same time she was parting with the place the family associated with affection and happiness. This sentimentalist of her Grand Papa's legacy chose a literary voice to describe the beauty of dis-ordering a space that had been so carefully crafted by the ardent gardener's hand. Monticello "never looked so lovely & the house never so beautiful as now," Cornelia effused. "The very luxuriance of wild things growing up in the yard has a beauty in it, the thickening shade of the unpruned trees closing round the house as if to conceal it from prophane eyes...I had rather the weeds & wild animals...should grow in and live in the house it self." [60]

By 1828, Cornelia's mother was voicing a similar stoic denouement to those dark days immediately after that sorrowful July Fourth. Martha had skillfully used the legacy of her father's esteem and political connections to secure sixteen-year-old Meriwether Lewis a place reading law with her cousin Judge Dabney Carr. She had arranged her husband's commission to survey the Georgia-Florida boundary through neighbor James Barbour. (Later, son George would receive an early entry into naval service through similar channels.) She, at last, was preparing to leave the Monticello environs for Washington City to become once again the mistress of a household, if not a plantation one.

"How can I express my gratitude," she asked a Washington friend and ardent admirer of her father, "for your kind and very efficient exertions in our favour, and which no doubt have had their full weight in the appointment Nicholas has obtained." Margaret Bayard Smith's intervention with Secretary of State Henry Clay on behalf of young Trist promised Martha "a life of ease, leisure, and charming society." This situation was much preferred "to the fatigue, anxiety, confinement, and bustle of a school to which I had great doubt as to my competence either in mind or body." An experienced Washington matron would understand Martha's donning the mantle of "republican daughter" and graciously accepting the consequences of exercising civic virtue.

> I never had, and never shall have, the folly to be ashamed of an honorable poverty. it is the fruits, and the price we have paid, for a long and useful life devoted to the service of his country....but I never regretted the sacrifice he made. his country had a right to his services and if a few must suffer for the advantage of the many it is a melancholy necessity, but I see no help for it.[61]

The next several months were a bustle in preparing to leave. A parcel of some 579 acres lying around the town of Milton and along the Rivanna was sold in January to Martin Dawson; it brought in $2,992.25 at $5.17 per acre. The last Monticello library left the Mountain by wagon in mid-February to be loaded on a steamboat at Fredericksburg and shipped to Washington for sale. The first volume, first edition of the family's publishing venture was printed by R. Carr and Co. in Charlottesville: *Memoir, Correspondence and Miscellanies from the Papers of Thomas Jefferson*, edited by Thomas Jefferson Randolph. With Virginia's husband in Washington and young Francis Eppes soon to depart for Florida, the cousins "all went up to Monticello" in early May 1829, and they agreed to a "compact" that they would "meet there after death."[62]

"Mistress of a home"

Other family members, also, were abandoning Virginia in 1829 for more attractive prospects. Martha's nephew and his wife (Francis and Elizabeth Eppes) along with Eston and Jane Randolph's older children left New London, Virginia, for the Florida panhandle in May 1829. The new Eppes-Randolph home was far different than the fanciful octagon they had just left in Bedford County or the Palladio-inspired mansion they frequently visited. It was "roomy and airy, & quite good looking for a log pen," Aunt Jane's daughter reported. "The floor of our loft (Mary's and mine) is not nailed down, and the seams gape rather more widely than is pleasant." Surrounded by "superb oaks covered with the long moss" and a "fine crop of cotton," Harriet "never imagined anything so beautiful and graceful."[63]

Martha, too, was finally to take her leave of the Monticello environs in mid-October of 1829. "[A]gain I shall be a mistress of a home, though a rented one," Martha informed Nancy Morris. "[A]nd where I have to learn the art of supporting a large family in genteel society, upon very limited means." And it was her house: "Nicholas & Virginia, Browse, & Burwell, will all live with me, each furnishing their portion to the general expenses."[64]

The Monticello diaspora arrived in time for Washington City's social season, twenty-four years after Martha's last soiree into fashionable society. She may have recalled the anxiety she felt in 1806 leaving Monticello to complete her pregnancy in a strange city without the aid of the women who customarily attended her. Martha remembered clearly that city life was distinctly different than the isolation of central Virginia.

> We are getting through our most important work & first visits which ought not to wait, and which still coming in with the 2ds & 3ds of the more active, & parties, keep us closely employed, about trifles it is true, but important matters in the fashionable world in which we at present move. ...

> We do not feel at home yet, and our thoughts and hearts are often with you taking our seat at your chearful fire side; but I believe that I have upon the whole done for the best and although the girls Mary & Virginia & Septimia, are constantly regretting [missing] the quiet of the country, yet I am sure I can live cheaper here than in

Virginia, and that we may here enjoy society without expense which there you can not.[65]

Furnishing her modest, rented home in Washington City had cost more than expected, but Martha assured her "dear Son" that expenses would not exceed income of $1,200 from the $20,000 donated by Louisiana and South Carolina when added to proceeds from sale of Father's papers. Expressing the unwarranted optimism characteristic of Father, "I hope to live enough with in to be able to discharge our debts." Jeff was under "a strange misapprehension," Mama pointedly told him, when he alleged "the girls took everything worthy of retention." She proceeded to inventory each item every family member held as a memento; included were the relics from a "large trunk" she could not part with containing Father's "old gloves, old shoes, leather straps broken...old rusty tin boxes & & &." Seeing them gave her "pain," yet she could not "destroy" them.[66]

Martha would never feel "at home" again as she roamed for the next six years between that little rented abode in Washington's genteel society, a Boston townhouse, rented rooms in Cambridge, an Edgehill crowded with children and visitors, back to Washington, and on to New England, until she returned to the foot of her beloved Mountain in the spring of 1836.

Even that was better emotionally than staying in place. Mama was "much agitated" while at Edgehill in 1831 and "hearing that the bargain about [the sale] of Monticello had been concluded with Dr. Barclay." "I have felt all along that any place was better for us than this neighbourhood," Cornelia lamented, "where we are in full sight of Monticello & where we are constantly hearing those things that fill us with regret & bitterness & the very beauty of the country adds to it."[67] Separation, however, could no more erase the memory of Monticello than it could recollections of those days "wandering over the world," or the brief intervals of reunion, or the "compleat happiness" of being together with Father.[68]

Not since those sorrowful days of 1782–84, before leaving for Paris had Martha led such an itinerate life style; the interim had rooted her affection to a place in Virginia where she could longingly anticipate reunions with Father, and hasten to the mountaintop on his arrival. "After once having known the happiness of a comfortable home of our own," she wrote from Boston to a daughter, "how bitter is the moment that drives us from it, and how little interest has any other spot after it!" Always before she had been able to imagine how it would be when the family celebrated its reunions; now the future was impossible to conjure.

> A mere resting-place for the while where everything is confined to the present; no future which brings anything but a change of place, nothing to amuse the heart or interest the fancy. If ever I can afford it I will have a permanent residence somewhere, a home, in fine, —a feeling I never shall know in a rented house."[69]

By the following year, even her "bright example of fortitude, cheerfulness, and dignified resignation" was failing her. A veil of gloom was drawn over Martha's perspective on life. Even Nicholas Trist's consulship in Cuba was clouded with a misapprehension; the position's financial "profits have been extravagantly exaggerated," the weather was uncomfortable, expenses sizeable, and, most importantly, the family must be left behind. Son Meriwether Lewis was engaged, but "he poor fellow has nothing, and she...is also poor." Even good fortune could not brighten Martha's spirits, nor could imagining a future. She was infected with ennui—that "canker of human happiness" Father had warned of.

> I have learnt to expect nothing, nor anticipate evil. for there is such absolute uncertainty in the most plausible calculations, that I never look 3 months ahead in the land of mist. much evil that I have anticipated has never happened, or if it did proved a blessing and many blessings that I never could have forseen have befallen me. at the same time that I have been disappointed where I had most reason to hope.[70]

Trist's appointment to a consulship in Cuba, though a good turn of fortune for the struggling family, again uprooted his mother-in-law from Washington to the Coolidge's Boston house in fall of 1835. Martha's last letter to the spurned and redeemed Nancy Randolph Morris reflected her ambivalence toward life. "This dispersion of my children," a homeless Mother sighed, "is as painful as it is mortifying."[71] Enfeebled in the "winter season of life," Martha considered her "strength and usefulness...gone," having been "a close prisoner to the house since early November." To avoid "encouraging gloomy anticipations," however, she averred the pleasures in old age included "dear children the <u>first</u> and <u>greatest</u> of blessings, fine weather, books, flowers." Besides dearest Papa, there was one loss suffered by the former mistress of Monticello that could never be recovered.

> [O]h if I should ever again be fortunate enough to have a <u>home</u> I should hardly think I had a right to complain; but we are too many to live with any family,…when Mr Coolidge returns I must try once more to accomodate my expenses to my means, and go to house keeping upon such a scale as I can afford, small enough God knows, but not too small for happiness and respectability.[72]

Monticello—the house, the place, the salon—had been conceived on a large scale, elevated to the heights, and crowded with a "concourse of strangers," friends, and relations as "evidences of the general esteem" that the family had been "all [their] lives trying to merit."[73] She was intensely loved by others and had lived an "honorable poverty" but struggled to achieve without a home the "general esteem" Father had deemed essential to happiness. Longing for the place never subsided in Martha's heart nor could the ache be extinguished in the hearts of her daughters. Ellen did not even know when she would return to America from Geneva, Switzerland; nonetheless, almost two decades after leaving Monticello, she wrote Jeff's wife:

> How I wish I could pass this summer in Virginia, dear Jane; I long to re-visit home, to see my native mountains, to breathe the fragrance of the yellow jessamine, hear the cry of the Whip-poor-will, and find myself once more in the midst of friends. I should so much enjoy talking over old young times with Jefferson & yourself, when, with us all, life was young & promised to be happy.[74]

Death and debt unmoored Martha from Monticello to follow her children from place to place, wherever necessity carried them, but never to a home—not even Edgehill—where she returned temporarily that spring of 1836.

"Thy pure devotions flame"

The tragedy of Thomas Mann Randolph was that in more reflective moments he was acutely aware of his emotional pitfalls. "Certain temperaments are little prone to passion: how fortunate are men of such constitutions!" Randolph confided to his Notebook. "Whenever I find myself very strongly impelled to any act, a doubt whether it be right allways arises. The voice of reason is low and persuasive that of passion loud and imperious."[75] Asserting righteous outrage at a word like "contumely" and similar bombasts in his opinion arose from self-doubt, from uncertainty about how others would judge his behavior, from confusion over right and wrong.

In his final days, the distressed and failed planter called son Jeff to his bedside and begged for "mutual forgiveness," spoke favorably of his "adored wife," and affectionately of each child. "His blessing, as he said himself [was] all that he had to leave, he left to us all," Martha shared with Ellen. He sought to "atone for the errors, blunders he called them, of his past life…by his death bed sufferings." He laid his transgressions on "the violence of his passions" overwhelming "the dictates of his head." Former Monticello overseer and Randolph's creditor Edmund Bacon recalled: "Before he died his mind became shattered, and he pretty much lost his reason."[76] Indeed, Martha allowed as how her husband had "it much at heart to prove the soundness of [his head] at all times" in his final days. Despite Mann Randolph's dying remorse, "the same suspicion, impatience, and propensity to argue…shewed it self as strong as in health."[77]

Martha's reflections on her late married life were given even fuller voice following the death on 20 June 1828 of Thomas Mann Randolph:

> Every unkind feeling has been buried in the grave of the sufferer; no longer an object of terror or apprehension, he became one of deep sympathy, or rather commiseration and kind feeling; and affection it self could not have watched with more attentive and patient kindness over every motion forward; but the habits of intercourse with his family were so completely broken, the bonds of affection so much weakened by the events of the last years of his life, that after the first burst of grief was over, tranquility was soon restored. nor was the void occasioned by his loss long percepbible [sic]. he had not been an inmate for years, no chair at table, recalled him at meals, no part of the house was associated with his idea, and we could not but acknowledge that all was for the best; for I think with you, that returning health would have brought with it

the same passions and jealousies, and that confidence so completely destroyed could never have revived.[78]

Devotion anchored Martha and Father to the mountaintop and on that perch they nurtured the fledgling intellectual, moral, and physical capacities of Anne, Ellen, Cornelia, Virginia, and Mary for a life as the "bosom of family" in a plantation household. As Ellen advised biographer Randall: "[I]n order to understand him, you must understand those by whom he was surrounded."[79] Cornelia grasped fully the social-emotional dimension of personal accomplishments that Grand Papa considered essential to achieving life's ultimate purpose. Ellen clearly seized the mental domain as a realm in which her accomplishments would make her beloved by those among whom she lived. Because they so powerfully held each other for so long and through so much, Mama and Grand Papa knew that happiness was living with the whole person, remembering triumphs and anxieties, and imagining how it might be. But as Ellen noted, they were a high standard to which she could only aspire and which few attain.

For Martha and Father, Monticello had been a place with the power to give life anew; the site where memory, imagination, and living merged into a single reality. After enduring years of separation after separation, she refused that final parting in 1826 and continued to use the Mountain to plumb a bountiful memory to make her happiness "compleat" with an imagined reunion. Martha left us a piece from an unknown author in Father's Commonplace Book that sparks a curiosity about what she was praising. A place? A person? A way of life? Perhaps all three?

I will still think of thee, as in times gone by when I looked from the terrace of Monticello and thought "all the kingdoms of the world and the glory thereof" lay spread before me. Every feature of that landscape has its own spell upon my heart, can bring back the living, breathing presence of those long mingled with the clods of the valley, can renew (for a moment) youth itself. Youth with its exquisite enjoyments, its ardent friendships, and Oh! dearer than all, its first, purest, truest love![80]

Even the sudden death of son James in 1834, just a few days shy of twenty-eight, was an occasion for remembering another leaving.

"How much more cruel the loss would have been had we had the comfort of his society and associated his image with every object around," a dispirited mother wrote. "I unfortunately know from bitter experience."

At the foot of her beloved Mountain in the Edgehill house she had abandoned to be still nearer to Father, Martha once again made her happiness complete by joining him on 10 October 1836. Granddaughter Sarah Nicholas Randolph many years later conveyed the family's story of these final hours. Impending separation from children and place had "saddened" her summer, as she prepared a return to Boston, because Virginia, Cornelia, and Septimia planned to join Nicholas Trist in faraway Havana, Cuba. Amid such anxiety and stress, the family was not surprised by a bout with Mama's "periodical headache." Crying "'My God, what a pain!' as she pressed her hand to her head," Martha Jefferson Randolph died in the arms of her son Jeff.[81]

Material and psychological tensions between the family of memory, imagination, and life would continue beyond the grave in the poetic epitaphs daughter and father left for each other and in "The Jefferson Family Story" they had constructed for history.

The "sacred charge" Father had assumed in 1782 and nurtured for the next forty-four years warranted more than a mere plagiarized copy of Sterne's "time wastes too fast" that had been his valedictory to her Mother. Dearest Papa penned an original adieu for their last separation:

Life's visions are vanished, its dreams are no more;
Dear friends of my bosom, why bathed in tears?
I go to my father, I welcome the shore
Which crowns all my hope or which buries my cares.
Then farewell, my dear, my lov'd daughter, adieu!
The last pang of life is in parting from you!
Two seraphs await me long shrouded in death;
I will bear them your love on my last parting breath.[82]

His Dearest Patsy assuaged her loneliness over the next ten years, as she had done through those many decades of separation, but the memory bore no hopeful imagery of reunion.

Thence may thy pure devotions flame
On my forlorn, descend;
To me thy strong aspiring hopes
Thy faith thy fervors lend.

Let these my lonely path illume,
And teach my weakened mind
To welcome all that's left of good,
To all that's lost resigned.

Farewell! with honor, peace, and love
Be thy dear memory blest!
Thou hast no tears for me to shed,
When I too am at rest.[83]

Sources

Abbreviations

CSmH: The Huntington Library, San Marino

DLC: Library of Congress, Washington

FLP: Family Letters Project, Thomas Jefferson Foundation, Charlottesville

MHi: Massachusetts Historical Society, Boston

MoSHi: Missouri Historical Society, St. Louis

NHi: New York Historical Society, New York City

PPAmP: American Philosophical Society, Philadelphia

TJF: Thomas Jefferson Foundation, Charlottesville

ViHi: Virginia Historical Society, Richmond

ViU: University of Virginia, Charlottesville

ViW: College of William and Mary, Williamsburg

Short Titles

JMB: *Jefferson's Memorandum Books,* 2 vols. eds. James A. Bear, Jr. and Lucia C. Stanton (Princeton, NJ: Princeton University Press, 1997).

JFL: *The Family Letters of Thomas Jefferson,* eds. Edwin Morris Betts and James A. Bear, Jr. (Charlottesville, VA: University Press of Virginia, 1986).

Papers: *The Papers of Thomas Jefferson,* 38 vols. through 2011, eds. Julian Boyd, et al. (Princeton, NJ: Princeton University Press, 1950–).

Papers, RS: *The Papers of Thomas Jefferson: Retirement Series,* 9 vols. through 2011, eds. J. Jefferson Looney, et al. (Princeton, NJ and Oxford, UK: Princeton University Press, 2004–).

Works: *The Works of Thomas Jefferson* (Federal Edition), 12 vols. ed. Paul Leicester Ford (New York: G. P. Putnam's Sons, 1904–05), http://oll.libertyfund.org/ .

Writings: *The Writings of Thomas Jefferson* (Library Edition), 20 vols., eds. Andrew A. Lipscomb and Albert E. Bergh (Washington, D. C.: The Thomas Jefferson Memorial Foundation, 1903).

Selected References

The following is a condensed list from over 300 references used in researching and writing this book. They include background to biographical and political details of Martha and her father's lives as well as the six themes prominent in their letters. Access dates to web sources are indicated in parenthesis following internet addresses.

Adams, William Howard. *The Paris Years of Thomas Jefferson.* New Haven, CT: Yale University Press, 1997.

Allgor, Catherine. *Parlor Politics in which the Ladies of Washington Help Build a City and a Government.* Charlottesville, VA: University Press of Virginia, 2000.

Bear, James A., Jr. *Jefferson's Cannons of Conduct.* 73 vols. Vol. 8, *Monticello Keepsake Collection.* Charlottesville, VA: Thomas Jefferson Foundation, Inc., 1964.

————. *Jefferson's Advice to His Children and Grandchildren on Their Reading.* Charlottesville, VA: The University of Virginia, 1967.

————, ed. *Jefferson at Monticello.* Charlottesville, VA: The University Press of Virginia, 1967.

————. "Thomas Jefferson and the Ladies." *Augusta Historical Bulletin* 6, no. 2 Fall (1970).

Bear, James A., Jr., and Lucia C. Stanton, eds. *Jefferson's Memorandum Books: Accounts, with Legal Records and Miscellany, 1767–1826,* vols. 1 and 2. *The Papers of Thomas Jefferson, Second Series.* Princeton, NJ: Princeton University Press, 1997.

Bergh, Albert Ellery, ed. *The Writings of Thomas Jefferson.* Washington, D. C., 1907.

Berkin, Carol. *First Generations: Women in Colonial America.* New York: Hill and Wang, 1996.

Betts, Edwin Morris, and James A. Bear, Jr., eds. *The Family Letters of Thomas Jefferson.* Paperback edition. Columbia, MO: University of Missouri Press, 1966; Charlottesville, VA: University Press of Virginia, 1986.

Bloch, Ruth. "Inside and Outside the Public Sphere." *William and Mary Quarterly,* 3rd Series 62, no. 1, Forum: Alternative Histories of the Public Sphere (2005): 99-106; available from http://www.historycooperative.org/journals/wm (October 12, 2005).

Boyd, Julian P., Lyman H. Butterfield, Mina R. Bryan, and et al., eds. *The Papers of Thomas Jefferson*. 39 vols. thru 2012. Princeton: Princeton University Press, 1950–.

————. *To the Girls and Boys: Being the Delightful, Little-Known Letters of Thomas Jefferson to and from His Children and Grandchildren*. New York: Funk & Wagnall's, Company, Inc., 1964.

Brooke, John L. "Reason and Passion in the Public Sphere: Habermas and the Cultural Historians." *Journal of Interdisciplinary History* 29, no. 1 (1998): 43-67; available from http://www.jstor.org/ (October 19, 2005).

————. "On the Edges of the Public Sphere." *William and Mary Quarterly*, 3rd Series 62, no. 1 (2005); available from http://www.jstor.org/ (October 23, 2005).

Brown, Kathleen M. *Good Wives, Nasty Wenches, and Anxious Patriarchs: Gender, Race, and Power in Colonial Virginia*. Chapel Hill: University of North Carolina Press, 1996.

Burstein, Andrew. *The Inner Jefferson: Portrait of a Grieving Optimist*. Charlottesville: University Press of Virginia, 1995.

————. *Sentimental Democracy*. New York: Hill and Wang, 1999.

————. "Jefferson's Rationalizations." *The William and Mary Quarterly*, 3rd Series 57, no. 1 (2000): 183-197; available from http://www.jstor.org/ (February 1, 2006).

Clinton, Catherine. *The Plantation Mistress: Woman's World in the Old South*. New York: Pantheon, 1982.

————. "Equally Their Due: The Education of the Planter Daughter in the Early Republic." *Journal of the Early Republic* 2, no. 1 (1982): 39-60.

Coolidge, Ellen Wayles Randolph. Correspondence of Ellen Wayles Randolph Coolidge, 1810–1861 Special Collections, University of Virginia, Charlottesville, VA. Accessions 38-584, 9090, 9090-cL.

Crawford, Alan Pell. *Unwise Passions: A True Story of a Remarkable Woman and the First Great Scandal of Eighteenth-Century America*. New York: Simon & Schuster, 2000.

deMause, Lloyd, ed. *The History of Childhood*. New York: The Psychohistory Press, 1974.

Edgehill-Randolph Papers, 1725–1826, Accession #5533. Albert H. and Shirley Small Special Collections Library, University of Virginia (ViU), Charlottesville, VA.

Ellis, Markman. *The Politics of Sensibility: Race, Gender, and Commerce in the Sentimental Novel*. Cambridge, UK: Cambridge University Press, 1990.

Fiese, Barbara H., and Arnold J. Sameroff. "The Family Narrative Consortium: A Multidimensional Approach to Narratives."

Monographs of the Society for Research in Child Development: The Stories That Families Tell: Narrative Coherence, Narrative Interaction, and Relationship Beliefs, 64, no. 2 (1999): 1-26; available from http://www.jstor.org (July 10, 2007).

Fliegelman, Jay. *Prodigals and Pilgrims: The American Revolution Against Patriarchal Authority*, 1750–1800. Paperback ed. New York: Cambridge University Press, 1984.

Ford, Paul Leicester. *The Works of Thomas Jefferson* (Federal Edition) G. P. Putnam's Sons, 1904–05.

Fox-Genovese, Elizabeth. *Within the Plantation Household: Black and White Women of the Old South*. Chapel Hill, NC: University of North Carolina Press, 1988.

Fraser, Walter J., Jr. R. Frank Saunders, and Jon L. Wakelyn, eds. *The Web of Southern Social Relations: Women, Family & Education*. Athens, GA: The University of Georgia Press, 1985.

Ganter, Herbert Lawrence. "Jefferson's 'Pursuit of Happiness' and Some Forgotten Men." *The William and Mary Quarterly*, Second Series 16, no. 4 (1936): 558-585; available from http://www.jstor.org (January 14, 2003).

Gilreath, James, ed. *Thomas Jefferson and the Education of a Citizen*. Washington, D.C.: Library of Congress, 1999.

Goodman, Dena. "Enlightenment Salons: The Convergence of Female and Philosophic Ambitions." *Eighteenth-Century Studies* 22, no. Spring (1989): 329-50; available from http://www.jstor.org/ (October 7, 2005).

————. "Public Sphere and Private Life: Toward a Synthesis of Current Historiographical Approaches to the Old Regime." *History and Theory* 31, no. 1 (1992): 1-20; available from http://www.jstor.org (October 23, 2005).

Habermas, Jurgen, Sara Lennox, and Frank Lennox. "The Public Sphere: An Encyclopedia Article (1964)." *New German Critique*, no. 3 (1964): 49-55; available from http://www.jstor.org (October 19, 2005).

Hoffman, Ronald and Peter J. Albert, eds. *Women in the Age of the American Revolution*. Charlottesville, VA: The University Press of Virginia, 1989.

Isaac, Rhys. *The Transformation of Virginia*, 1740–1790. New York: W. W. Norton & Company, 1982.

————. "Stories and Constructions of Identity: Folk Tellings and Diary Inscriptions Revolutionary Virginia." In *Through a Glass Darkly: Reflections on Personal Identity in Early America*. Edited by Ronald

Hoffman, Mechal Sobel and Fredrika J. Teute, 206-237. Chapel Hill, NC: University of North Carolina Press, 1997.

Jefferson, Thomas. *Notes on the State of Virginia.* Edited by Frank Shuffleton. New York: Penquin Books, 1999.

Kerber, Linda. "The Republican Mother: Women and the Enlightenment—An American Perspective." *American Quarterly* 28, no. 2 (1976): 187-205; available from http://www.jstor.org/ (December 9, 2007).

———. "Separate Spheres, Female Worlds, Woman's Place: The Rhetoric of Women's History." *Journal of American History* 75, no. 1 (1988): 9-39; available from Kerber, Linda, Nancy F. Cott, et al."Beyond Roles, Beyond Spheres: Thinking about Gender in the Early Republic." *William and Mary Quarterly*, 3rd Series 46, no. 3 (1989): 565-585; available from http://www.jstor.org/ (October 23, 2005).

Kierner, Cynthia. *Beyond the Household: Women's Place in the Early South, 1700–1835.* Ithaca, NY: Cornell University Press, 1998.

———. *Scandal at Bizarre: Rumor and Reputation in Jefferson's America.* New York: Palgrave Macmillan, 2004.

———. *Martha Jefferson Randolph, Daughter of Monticello: Her Life and Times.* Chapel Hill: University of North Carolina Press, 2012.

Klein, Lawrence E. "Gender and the Public/Private Distinction in the Eighteenth Century: Some Questions about Evidence and Analytic Procedure." *Eighteenth-Century Studies* 29, no. 1 (1996): 97-109; available from http://must.jhu.edu/journals/ (March 5, 2005).

Langhorne, Elizabeth. *Monticello: A Family Story.* Chapel Hill, NC: University of North Carolina Press, 1989.

Lewis, Jan. *The Pursuit of Happiness: Family and Values in Jefferson's Virginia.* New York: Cambridge University Press, 1983.

———. "The Republican Wife: Virtue and Seduction in the Early Republic." *The William and Mary Quarterly*, Third Series 44, no. 4 (1987): 689-721; available from http://www.jstor.org/ (January 23, 2004).

———. "Jefferson, the Family, and Civic Education." In *Thomas Jefferson and the Education of a Citizen*, edited by James Gilreath, 63-75. Washington, D. C.: Library of Congress, 1999.

Lipscomb, Andrew A., and Albert E. Bergh, eds. *The Writings of Thomas Jefferson.* Library Edition. 20 vols. Washington, D. C.: The Thomas Jefferson Memorial Association, 1903.

Looney, J. Jefferson, et al., eds. *The Papers of Thomas Jefferson: Retirement Series.* 9 vols. through 2012. Princeton, NJ and Oxford, UK: Princeton University Press, 2004– .

Malone, Dumas. *Jefferson and His Time*. 7 vols. Boston: Little, Brown and Company, 1948–1981.

———. "Polly Jefferson and Her Father." Virginia Quarterly Review 7, January 1931): 81-95; available from http://pao.chadwyck.co.uk (December 9, 2007).

McCrudden, Carrie. "Childhood at Monticello: Ages Twelve and Under, Slave and Free Children." In Thomas Jefferson Foundation Special Collections Research Report, 228. Charlottesville, VA: Thomas Jefferson Foundation, 1992.

Mann, Bruce. *Republic of Debtors: Bankruptcy in the Age of American Independence*. Harvard University Press, 2002.

Murray, Melissa E. "Analysis of Female Education at Thomas Jefferson's Monticello." In Thomas Jefferson Foundation Special Collections Research Reports, 85. Charlottesville, VA: Thomas Jefferson Foundation, 1995.

Onuf, Peter S., ed. *Jeffersonian Legacies*. Charlottesville, VA: University Press of Virginia, 1993.

Peterson, Merrill D., ed. *Visitors to Monticello*. Charlottesville, VA: The University Press of Virginia, 1989.

Randolph Family Papers, 1829–1978. Tallahassee, FL: State Library and Archives of Florida. Available from http://www.floridamemory.com/ (November 8, 2007).

Randolph, Sarah N. *The Domestic Life of Thomas Jefferson*. Reprint of 1871 edition published by Harper, New York. Charlottesville, VA: The University Press of Virginia, 1978.

Revell, Katherine G. "Jefferson and Women: Source Compilations for Specific Women and Selected Topics." In Thomas Jefferson Foundation Research Reports. Charlottesville, VA: Thomas Jefferson Foundation, 1995.

Rice, Howard C. *Thomas Jefferson's Paris*. Princeton: Princeton University Press, 1976.

Rogoff, Barbara. *The Cultural Nature of Human Development*. New York: Oxford University Press, 2003.

Scharff, Virginia. *The Women Jefferson Loved*. New York: HarperCollins, 2010.

Shuffelton, Frank. "In Different Voices: Gender in the American Republic of Letters." *Early American Literature* 25, no. 3 (1990): 289-304; available from http://pao.chadwyck.com (December 9, 2007).

———. "Binding Ties: The Public and Domestic Spheres of Jefferson's Letters to His Family." In *Thomas Jefferson and the Education of a Citizen*, edited by James Gilreath, 28-47. Washington, D. C.: Library of Congress, 1999.

Smith, Ann Macon, and Ann Lucas. "Family Correspondence (1826–1833)." In Thomas Jefferson Foundation Research Reports, 119. Charlottesville, VA: Thomas Jefferson Foundation, 1991.

Smith, Daniel Blake. *Inside the Great House: Planter Family Life in the Eighteenth Century Chesapeake Society*. paperback ed. Ithaca, NY: Cornell University Press, 1980.

———. "The Study of the Family in Early America: Trends, Problems, and Prospects." *The William and Mary Quarterly*, Third Series 39, no. 1 (1982): 3-28; available from http://www.jstor.org/ (March 11, 2004).

Smith, Daniel Scott. "Female Household in Late Eighteenth-Century America and the Problem of Poverty." *Journal of Social History* 28, no. 1 (1994): 83-107; available from http://www.jstor.org (June 6, 2006).

Somers, Margaret R. "What's Political or Cultural about Political Culture and the Public Sphere? Toward an Historical Sociology of Concept Formation." *Sociological Theory* 13, no. 2 (1995): 113-144; available from http://www.jstor.org/ (October 18, 2005).

Sowerby, E. Millicent. *Catalogue of the Library of Thomas Jefferson*. 5 vols. Washington, D. C.: Library of Congress, 1952–1959.

Spruill, Julia Cherry. *Women's Life and Work in the Southern Colonies*. Chapel Hill, NC: University of North Carolina Press, 1938.

Stone, Lawrence. "Past Achievements and Future Trends." *Journal of Interdisciplinary History* 12, no. 1 (1981): 51-87; available from http://www.jstor.org/ (April 20, 2005).

Stowe, Steven M. "The Not-So-Cloistered Academy: Elite Women's Education and Family Feeling in the Old South." In *The Web of Southern Social Relations: Women, Family, and Education*, edited by Jr. Walter J. Fraser, Jr. R. Frank Saunders and Jon L. Wakelyn, 90-106. Athens: The University of Georgia Press, 1985.

———. *Intimacy and Power in the Old South: Ritual in the Lives of the Planters*. Baltimore, MD: The Johns Hopkins University Press, 1987.

Stuart, Andrea. *The Rose of Martinique: A Life of Napoleon's Josephine*: Grove Press, 2003.

Sturtz, Linda L. "The Ladies and the Lottery: Elite Women's Gambling in Eighteenth-Century Virginia." *Virginia Magazine of History and Biography* 104 (1996): 165-84.

Tauber, Gisela. "Reconstruction in Psychoanalytic Biography: Understanding Thomas Jefferson." *Journal of Psychohistory* 7, no. 2 (1979): 187-207, copy of article in files of Thomas Jefferson Foundation.

―――. "Thomas Jefferson: Relationships with Women." *American Imago* 45 (1988): 431-47, copy of article in files of Thomas Jefferson Foundation.

―――. "Notes on the State of Virginia: Thomas Jefferson's Unintentional Self-Portrait." *Eighteenth-Century Studies* 26 (1993): 635-48; copy of article in files of Thomas Jefferson Foundation.

Taylor, Olivia. "'Edgehill' 1735–1902." In *The Magazine of Albemarle County History*, 61-67, 1972.

The Thomas Jefferson Papers, 1606–1827. Library of Congress (DLC), Washington, D.C. http://memory.loc.gov/ammen/collections/jefferson and microfilm, Series 6.

Thomas Jefferson Foundation. "Subject File: Ordinaries, Inns & Taverns." n.d.

―――. Information Files and Long Files. n.d. Charlottesville, VA.

―――. "Research Reports Subject File: Places/Taverns." n.d. Charlottesville, VA.

Wagoner, Jennings L. "'That Knowledge Most Useful to Us': Thomas Jefferson's Concept of Utility in the Education of Republican Citizens." In *Thomas Jefferson and the Education of a Citizen*, edited by James Gilreath. Washington, D. C.: Library of Congress, 1999.

―――. *Jefferson and Education*. Monticello Monograph Series. Charlottesville, VA: Thomas Jefferson Foundation, 2004.

Wallace, Beth Kowaleski. "A Modest Defense of Gaming Women." In *Studies in Eighteenth-Century Culture*, edited by Ourida Mostefai and Catherine Ingrassia, 21-40. Baltimore: Johns Hopkins University Press, 2002.

Wayson, Billy L. "'Considerably different…for her sex': A Reading Plan for Martha Jefferson Randolph." In *The Libraries, Leadership, & Legacy of John Adams and Thomas Jefferson*, edited by Robert C. Baron and Conrad Edick Wright. Golden, Co: Fulcrum Press, 2010.

―――. "Thomas Jefferson and Affairs of the Heart." In *A Jefferson Compendium*, edited by Francis Cogliano. New York: Wiley-Blackwell, 2011.

Wilson, Douglas L. *Jefferson's Literary Commonplace Book*. Princeton: Princeton University Press, 1989.

Wister, Mrs. O. J., and Agnes Irwin. *Worthy women of our first century*. Philadelphia: J.B. Lippincott & Co., 1877.

Wogan, Miriam C. "The Working Women of Monticello: A Study of the Lives of Women in the Monticello Household, 1810–1826." In *Thomas Jefferson Foundation Research Reports*. Charlottesville, VA: Thomas Jefferson Foundation, 1991.

Woyshner, Christine. "The Education of Women for Wifehood: Coverture, Community, And Consumerism in the Separate Spheres." *History of Education* 43, no. 3 (2003): 410-428; available from http://www.historycooperative.org/ (January 5, 2004).

Yazawa, Melvin. *From Colonies to Commonwealth: Familial Ideology and the Beginnings of the American Republic.* Baltimore: John Hopkins University Press, 1985.

Zagarri, Rosemarie. "Morals, Manners, and the Republican Mother." *American Quarterly* 44, no. 1 (1992): 192-215; available from http://www.jstor.org/.

————. "The Rights of Man and Woman in Post-Revolutionary America." *William and Mary Quarterly*, 3rd Series 55, no. 2 (1998): 203-30; available from http://www.jstor.org/ (May 1, 2005).

Endnotes

Introduction

[1] Martha Jefferson Randolph to Thomas Jefferson, Bellmont, 12 May 1798, *The Family Letters of Thomas Jefferson*, eds. Edwin Morris Betts and James Bear, Jr. (Columbia, MO: University of Missouri Press, 1966; reprint Charlottesville: The University Press of Virginia, 1986), 160-61. Hereafter cited as Betts and Bear, *JFL*. Spellings in the original documents have been largely maintained with some minor exceptions like compound words ("every thing") and without the usual "*sic*".

[2] Thomas Jefferson to Martha Jefferson Randolph, Philadelphia, 17 May 1798, Ibid., 161.

[3] Jan Lewis, "'The Blessings of Domestic Society': Thomas Jefferson's Family and the Transformation of American Politics," *Jeffersonian Legacies*, ed. Peter S. Onuf (Charlottesville, VA: The University Press of Virginia, 1993), 138.

[4] Thomas Jefferson to Thomas Mann Randolph, Philadelphia, 1 January 1792, *The Papers of Thomas Jefferson*, eds. Julian Boyd, et al., 39 vols. to 2012 (Princeton: Princeton University Press, 1950–), 23:7-8. Hereafter cited as *Papers*.

[5] Thomas Jefferson to Martha Jefferson Randolph, Philadelphia, 15 January 1792, Ibid., 23:44-45.

[6] Thomas Jefferson to George Washington, Monticello, 14 May 1794, Ibid., 28:74-75.

[7] Thomas Jefferson to Wilson Cary Nicholas, Monticello 19 October 1795, Ibid., 28:512.

[8] Martha Jefferson Randolph to Thomas Jefferson, Bellmont, 22 January 1798, Ibid., 30:43-44.

[9] Martha Jefferson to Thomas Jefferson, Bellmont, 12 May 1798, Ibid., 30:346-47.

[10] Thomas Jefferson to Martha Jefferson Randolph, 8 February 1798, Ibid., 30:91-92.

[11] Martha Jefferson Randolph to Thomas Jefferson, Edgehill, 31 May 1804, Ibid., 261-62.

[12] Thomas Jefferson to Martha Jefferson Randolph, Washington, 5 January and Martha Jefferson Randolph to Thomas Jefferson, Edgehill, 16 January 1808, *The Family Letters of Thomas Jefferson*, eds. Edwin Morris Betts and James Bear, Jr. (Columbia, MO: University of Missouri Press, 1966 ; reprint Charlottesville: The University Press of Virginia, 1986), 319-20 and 322-23, respectively. Hereafter cited as Betts and Bear, *JFL*.

[13] Martha Jefferson Randolph to Thomas Jefferson, Edgehill, 2 March 1809, Ibid., 386-88.

[14]*Eastern Argus*, vol. III, issue 272, page 2, 18 May 1827, as forwarded from the Columbia, SC, *Telescope* http://infoweb.newsbank.com/ (December 14, 2007).

[15]Cornelia Jefferson Randolph to Ellen W. Randolph Coolidge, New London, 11 December 1826, FLP (ViU), http://familyletters.dataformat.com (April 18, 2007).

[16] Virginia Scharff, *The Women Jefferson Loved* (New York: HarperCollins, 2010) provides a general introduction and summary of some of these relationships without distinguishing Jefferson's acknowledged gradations of "affection," relating this impulse to the Scottish moral sense philosophy he espoused, or probing the subtleties of novelist Lawrence Sterne's influence on Jefferson's expressions of attachment in frequently oblique, *double entendre* ways.

Chapter 1: "Time Wastes too fast"

[1] "Lines Copied from Tristram Shandy by Martha and Thomas Jefferson, *Papers*, 6:196. Wife Martha's hand begins the quote, but her husband takes up and finishes. Laurence Sterne was a favorite of Jefferson, and this slightly altered quote is from *The Life and Opinions of Tristram Shandy, Gentleman.* Jefferson advised his nephew Peter Carr: "The writings of Sterne particularly form the best course of morality that was ever written" (Thomas Jefferson to Peter Carr with Enclosure, Paris, 10 August 1787, *Papers*, 12:14-19).

[2] Martha Wayles (1748–1782) was the daughter of Martha Eppes and lawyer John Wayles. She married Bathurst Skelton at eighteen and delivered one son before her husband died. Son John died at age three, six months before she wed Thomas Jefferson.

[3] *Jefferson's Memorandum Books: Accounts, with Legal Records and Miscellaney, 1767–1825*, The Papers of Thomas Jefferson, Second Series, 2 vols., eds. James Bear, Jr. and Lucia C. Stanton (Princeton: Princeton University Press, 1997), xlvii-xlviii. Hereafter cited as Bear and Stanton, *JMB*. The son died on 14 June 1777.

[4] Ibid., 1:502 records Lucy's birth. For the details of invasion as recalled by the Governor Jefferson, see "Diary of Arnold's Invasion and Notes on Subsequent Events in 1781, 1796[?], *Papers*, 4:258-77. The family left Richmond on January 4th; Arnold entered the next day, and was gone by 7 January 1781. Tuckahoe was owned by Jefferson's boyhood friend and near relative, Thomas Mann Randolph, Sr., and he had lived there from aged two or three until nine, when his father managed the estate. On June 4, 1781, Jefferson noted (*JMB*, 1:510): "British horse came to Monticello." The family had already evacuated and by mid-June was safely at Poplar Forest some 90 miles from Monticello.

[5] Bear and Stanton, *JMB*, 1:428 (Wythe and Ludwell), and 1:426 (shoes and toys). Wythe was attending the Continental Congress and upon his return the Jefferson family moved to an apartment building ("tenement"). Jefferson's desperate pleas from Philadelphia to hear from his family staying at the Eppes' plantation, the "Forest," were clear in his letter to Francis Eppes, 7 November 1775 (*Papers*, 1:252): "The suspense under which I am is too terrible to be endured. If anything has happened, for god's sake let me know it."

[6] Bear and Stanton, *JMB*, 1:431. Tom Garth leased part of Monticello and Shadwell for several years; served as steward from sometime in 1776 to 1782; and sold him the Lego farm in 1775 (*JMB*, 1:253n71)

[7] Thomas Jefferson to John Page, Philadelphia, 30 July 1776, *Papers*, 1:483.

[8] Bear and Stanton *JMB*, 1:425, 1 October 1776, and 1:429, 6 December. The latter was most likely Dr. James McClurg (1746–1823), graduate of William and Mary and Edinburgh, a noted physician, and delegate to the Constitutional Convention in 1787.

[9] Thomas Jefferson to John Hancock, Williamsburgh, 11 October 1776, *Papers*, 1:524.

[10] Bear and Stanton, *JMB*, 1:447.

[11] Thomas Jefferson to James Monroe, Monticello, 20 May 1782, *Papers*, 6:184.

[12] Marquis De Chastellux, *Travels in North America in the Years 1780, 1781 and 1782*, Introduction and Notes by Howard C. Rice, Jr., trans. (Chapel Hill: The University of North Carolina Press for the Institute of Early American History and Culture, Williamsburg, VA, revised translation, 1962), vol. 2, 391.

[13] "Lines Copied from Tristram Shandy by Martha and Thomas Jefferson, *Papers*, 6:196.

[14] See Jan Lewis, *The Pursuit of Happiness: Family and Values in Jefferson's Virginia* (New York: Cambridge University Press, 1983) [hereafter cited as *Pursuit*]; Gordon S. Wood, *Radicalism of the American Revolution* (New York: Alfred A. Knopf, 1992); Jay Fliegelman, *Prodigals and Pilgrims: The American Revolution Against Patriarchal Authority, 1750–1800* (New York: Cambridge University Press, 1984 paperback); Jack P. Greene, "The Social Origins of the American Revolution: An Evaluation and an Interpretation," *Political Science Quarterly*, 88, no. 1 (1973), 1-22, http://www.jstor.org/, (March 23, 2005); and Rhys Isaac, *The Transformation of Virginia, 1740–1790* (New York: W. W. Norton & Company, 1982).

[15] Jan Lewis, *Pursuit*, passim.

[16] Gordon S. Wood, *Radicalism*, 163, 5 and passim. See also Jan Lewis, "The Blessings of Domestic Society: Thomas Jefferson's Family and the Transformation of American Politics," *The Jeffersonian Legacies*, ed., Peter S. Onuf (Charlottesville, VA: University Press of Virginia, 1993), 109-146.

[17] Markman Ellis, *The Politics of Sensibility: Race, Gender, and Commerce in the Sentimental Novel* (Cambridge, UK: Cambridge University Press, 1990), passim.

[18] Herman R. Lantz, et al. "The Changing American Family from the Preindustrial to the Industrial Period: A Final Report," *American Sociological Review*, 42:3 (June, 1977), 406-21 and 411 specifically.

[19] Daniel Blake Smith, *Inside the Great House: Planter Family Life in the Eighteenth Century Chesapeake Society* (Ithaca, NY: Cornell University Press, paperback edition 1980), hereafter cited as *Great House*.

[20] John F. Walzer, "A Period of Ambivalence: Eighteenth-Century American Childhood," in *The History of Childhood*, ed. Lloyd deMause (New York: The Psychohistory Press, 1974), 351-382.

[21] Smith, *Great House*, 40 and 46; and Carole Shammas, *A History of Household Government in America* (Charlottesville, VA: University of Virginia Press, 2002), passim. Some argue this change in child-rearing practices occurred as late as the 1830s; see Philip J. Greven, Jr., *Child-Rearing Concepts, 1628–1861: Historical Sources* (Itasca, IL: F. E. Peacock Publishers, Inc., 1973), 4-5. See also: James Allison, *Constructing and Reconstructing Childhood: Contemporary Issues in the Sociological Study of Childhood* (London: RoutledgeFalmer, 2nd edition, 2003); Philippe Aries, *Centuries of Childhood: A Social History of Family Life*, trans. Robert Baldick, (New York: Vintage Books, 1962); Lloyd deMause, ed. *The History of Childhood* (New York: The Psychohistory Press, 1974); and Colin Heywood, *A History of Childhood: Children and Childhood in the West from Medieval to Modern Times* (Cambridge, UK: Polity Press, 2001).

[22] Melvin Yazawa, *From Colonies to Commonwealth: Familial Ideology and the Beginnings of the American Republic* (Baltimore: The Johns Hopkins University Press, 1985), 111-12.

[23] Benjamin Rush, *Essays, Literary, Moral and Philosophical* (Philadelphia, second ed., 1806), pp. 6-10, 12-13, 15-20 in *American Higher Education: A Documentary History*, Vol. 1, Richard Hofstadter and Wilson Smith, eds. (Chicago: The University of Chicago Press, 1961), 170-74.

[24] Linda Grand DePauw, "The American Revolution and the Rights of Women: The Feminist Theory of Abigail Adams" in *The Legacy of the American Revolution*, eds. Larry R. Gerlach, et al.(Logan, UT: Utah State University Press, 1978); Philip Hicks, "Portia and Marcia: Female Political Identity and the Historical Imagination, 1770–1800," *The William and Mary Quarterly*, 3rd Series 62, no. 2 (2005), 265-294, http://www.historycooperative.org/, (February 1, 2006); *Woman in the Age of the American Revolution*, Ronald Hoffman and Peter J. Albert, eds. (Charlottesville:

University Press of Virginia, 1989); Linda Kerber, "The Paradox of Women's Citizenship," *American Historical Review* 97 (1992), 349-78, http://links.jstor.org/ (October 23, 2005); "The Republican Mother: Women and the Enlightenment—An American Perspective," *American Quarterly* XXXVIII (1976), 187-205; "Separate Spheres, Female Worlds, Woman's Place: The Rhetoric of Women's History," *Journal of American History* 75, no. 1 (1988), 9-39, http://links.jstor.org/, (April 21, 2004); Linda Kerber, Nancy F. Cott, Robert Gross, Lynn Hunt, Carroll Smith-Rosenberg, and Christine M. Stansell, "Beyond Roles, Beyond Spheres: Thinking about Gender in the Early Republic," *William and Mary Quarterly, 3rd Series* 46, no. 3 (1989), 565-585, http://links.jstor.org/, (October 23, 2005); Cynthia Kierner, *Beyond the Household: Women's Place in the Early South, 1700–1835* (Ithaca, NY: Cornell University Press, 1998); Jan Lewis, "The Republican Wife: Virtue and Seduction in the Early Republic" *The William and Mary Quarterly, Third Series* 44, no. 4 (1987), 689-721, http://www.jstor.org/, (January 23, 2004); Mary Beth Norton, *Liberty's Daughters: The Revolutionary Experience of American Women, 1750–1800* (Boston: Little Brown, 1980); Frank Shuffelton, "In Different Voices: Gender in the American Republic of Letters," *Early American Literature* XXV (1990); Lorena S. Walsh, "The Experiences and Status of Women in the Chesapeake, 1750–1775," In *The Web of Southern Social Relations: Women, Family, and Education*, Walter J. Fraser, Jr., R. Frank Saunders, Jr., and Jon L. Wakelyn, eds. (Athens: The University of Georgia Press, 1985), 1-18; Rosemarie Zagarri, "Gender and the New Liberal Synthesis" *American Quarterly* 53, no. 1 (2001), 123-130, http://www.jstor.org/, (October 23, 2005) and "Morals, Manners, and the Republican Mother," *American Quarterly* 44, June (1992), 192-215.

[25] Thomas Jefferson to Angelica Schuyler Church, Philadelphia, 24 May 1797, *Papers,* 29:396-97: "You will preserve, from temper and inclination, the happy privilege of the ladies, to leave to the rougher sex, and to the newspapers, their party squabbles and reproaches." This is just one illustrative statement among many in Jefferson's letters referencing gender and the public sphere.

[26] Election Return for Delegates from Albemarle County, *Papers,* 6:174. He consented to re-enter political life to answer charges of misfeasance during British invasion of Virginia .

[27] Thomas Jefferson to Benjamin Harrison, Charlottesville, 13 April 1782, Ibid., 175-76.

[28] Bear and Stanton, *JMB,* 1:518-19.

[29] Thomas Jefferson to James Monroe, Monticello, 20 May 1782, 6:184 ff. While Martha lay "very dangerously ill," he was pressed by James Monroe and others to assume his seat in the House of Delegates and defend his performance as Governor during the British invasion of Virginia.

[30] James Monroe to Thomas Jefferson, Richmond, June 28, 1782, *Papers,* 6:192.

[31] Bear and Stanton, *JMB,* 1: 519-21. Jupiter was an enslaved person who was Jefferson's personal servant.

[32] Ibid. 1:521.

[33] "Lines Copied from Tristram Shandy by Martha and Thomas Jefferson, *Papers,* 6:196.

[34] Henry S. Randall, *The Life of Thomas Jefferson* (New York: Derby & Jackson, 1858), 1:382. Hereafter cited as Randall, *Life.* These remembrances were written many years later by Martha in response to an inquiry from St. George Tucker for his biography, *Thomas Jefferson, Third President of the United States,* 2 volumes (Philadelphia: Carey, Lea & Blanchard, 1837). Tucker had been appointed by Jefferson to Professor of Moral Philosophy at the University of Virginia.

35 Thomas Jefferson to Elizabeth Wayles Eppes, [3? October 1782], *Papers,* 6:198. Mrs. Francis Eppes was the half-sister to Jefferson's wife and one of her nurses in her final illness.
36 Thomas Jefferson to Chastellux, Ampthill, November 26, 1782, *Papers,* 6:203-04.

Chapter 2: "Educated as the heiress"

1 Martha Jefferson Randolph to an unnamed daughter, December 12, 1826, excerpted in Sara N. Randolph, "Mrs. Martha Jefferson Randolph," *Women of Our First Century,* eds. Mrs. O. J. Wister and Miss Agnes Irwin (Philadelphia: J. B. Lippincott & Co., 1877), 55.
2 Mary Jefferson (b. 1 August 1778) was called "Polly" by her family and, after her return from France, also by "Maria" which had been ascribed by her schoolmates at Panthemont. The aunt was Elizabeth Wayles Eppes (Mrs. Francis) and half sister to Jefferson's wife.
3 *A View of North America...in the years 1774, 75, 76, 77, and 78...*(Glasgow: William Smith, 1781), 18-20, http://galenetgalegroup.com/ (November 14, 2007).
4 Bear and Stanton, *JMB,* 1: 524-27 and *Papers* 6: 226. Her daughter Eliza House (Mrs. Nicholas)Trist would become a lifelong friend of the Jefferson family and reside at Monticello in later years.
5 Respectively, James Madison to Thomas Jefferson, *Papers,* 13 May 1783, 6:268-69; 6 May 1783, 6:264-65; and 22 April 1783, 6:262,
6 Respectively, Thomas Jefferson to James Madison, Tuckahoe, 7 May 1783, Ibid., 6:265-67; Monticello, 17 June 1783, Ibid., 6:277-78; and From Wakelin Welch, Sr., with Jefferson's Account with Robert Cary & Co., Ibid., 6:272-73. The amount is read as "118 pounds, 1 shilling, 4 pence"
7 Thomas Jefferson to Horatio Spafford, 14 May 1809, *The Papers of Thomas Jefferson, Retirement Series,* eds., J. Jefferson Looney, et al., 9 volumes to 2012 (Princeton, NJ: Princeton University Press, 2004–), 1:196-198. Hereafter cited as *Papers, RS.*
8 Bear & Stanton, *JMB,* 1:537. The Confederation Congress, which had been meeting in Philadelphia, adjourned to Princeton when soldiers mounted a public demonstration to demand back pay for Revolutionary War service. Jefferson took his seat at Princeton on 4 November 1783 but Congress adjourned the same day to reconvene at Annapolis three weeks hence (Dumas Malone, *Jefferson the Virginian* [Boston: Little, Brown and Company, 1978], 403-04).
9 Thomas Jefferson to James Madison, Monticello, August 31, 1783, *Papers* 6:336.
10 James Madison to Thomas Jefferson, Philadelphia, September 30, 1783, Ibid., 6: 341-42.
11 Sarah N. Randolph, "Mrs. T. M. Randolph," *Worthy Women of Our First Century,* eds. Mrs. O. J. Wister and Miss Agnes (Philadelphia: J. B. Lippincott & Co., 1877), 54. Hereafter cited as Randolph, *Worthy Women.*
12 Francis Hopkinson (1737–1791) held a variety of governmental posts in the colonial, state, and national governments, including the 1776 Continental Congress, the Constitutional Convention in 1787, and judge in the Federal Court from 1789 (George E. Hastings, *The Life and Works of Francis Hopkinson* [Chicago: University of Chicago Press, 1926], passim). Rittenhouse (1732–1796) built America's first observatory, served as first director of the U. S. Mint, followed Franklin as President of the American Philosophical Society, and was a frequent correspondent with Patsy's father (*American National Biography On-line,* http://proxy.monticello.org [11 July 2009]).

Elizabeth Fox-Genovese, *Household*, 113.

Daniel Blake Smith, *Great House,* 58: "The most powerful ways in which girls learned sex-role behavior was through observing and helping in the daily chores of the plantation." In modern terms, this is labeled "situated learning."

Dumas Malone, *Jefferson the Virginian* (Boston: Little, Brown and Company, 1978), 403-04.

See Billy Wayson, "Considerably different...for her sex": A Reading Plan for Martha Jefferson Randolph," in *The Libraries, Leadership & Legacy of John Adams and Thomas Jefferson*, eds. Robert C. Baron and Conrad Edick Wright (Golden, CO: Fulcrum Publishing, 2010), 133-158. This essay discusses Jefferson's reading list for young girls in the context of his pedagogical theories drawn from Enlightenment principles of epistemology, notions of human development, and Scottish moral sense philosophy.

Sowerby #4346

Sowerby #4347.

Thomas Jefferson to Marbois, Annapolis, 5 December 1783, *Papers,* 6:373-74. Marbois was Secretary to the French Legation and the one whose inquiries resulted in Jefferson's *Notes on the State of Virginia.*

Barbara Rogoff, *The Cultural Nature of Human Development* (New York: Oxford University Press, 2003), 3 ff. John Hardin Best has argued that education history of the South especially must take this perspective to adequately describe how so much learning occurred with so little schooling. He wrote: "The education of the South arose from nonformal sources, from the southern culture, traditions, and institutions more fundamental than mere schools....This kind of history is complex, convoluted, and difficult to do" ("Education in the Forming of the American South," *History of Education Quarterly*, Vol. 36, No. 1 [Spring, 1996], 47 and passim.).

Thomas Jefferson to John Adams, Monticello, October 28, 1813, *AJL,* 387-392

Thomas Jefferson to Chastellux, Paris, 2 September 1785, *Papers,* 8:468.

Thomas Jefferson to Martha Jefferson, Aix en Provence, 28 March 1787, *Papers,* 11:250-53.

Carol Berkin, *First Generations: Women in Colonial America* (New York: Hill and Wang, 1996), 143.

Elizabeth Fox-Genovese, *Inside the Plantation Household: Black and White Women of the Old South* (Chapel Hill, NC: University of North Carolina Press, 1988), 116. Hereafter cited as *Household.*

Thomas Jefferson to Nathaniel Burwell, Monticello, 14 March 1818, *The Works of Thomas Jefferson*, collected and edited by Paul Leicester Ford (New York: G. P. Putnam, The Knickerbocker Press, 1905, Federal Edition), 12:90-93, http://olldownload. libertyfund.org/ (June 4, 2003).

Thomas Jefferson to Nathaniel Burwell, Monticello, 14 March 1818, *A Jefferson Profile As Revealed in His letters*, ed., Saul K. Padover (New York: The John Day Company, 1956), 297-99. For discussion of how the novel served southern females, see Catherine Kerrison, "The Novel as Teacher: Learning to be Female in the Early South," *The Journal of Southern History*, 69:3 (August 2003), 514-48.

The Definitive Treaty of Peace between the United States and Great Britain, Article 4 provided that creditors "shall meet with no lawful impediment to the recovery of the full value in sterling money, of all bona fide debts heretofore contracted." Southern planters, like Jefferson, who were indebted to British creditors and had withheld payments during the War or paid with depreciated currency could now be pursued legally to make good on their obligation (*Papers,* 6:456-61).

[29] Abstract of Probate Book 5, page 151 Louisa County, Virginia, http://trevilians. com/probate/will4.htm#296 (May 22, 2010). Cocke was a pious reformer of Patsy's generation who pamphleteered against tobacco, decried alcohol consumption, and in 1833 released some of his enslaved for transport to Liberia (*"Dear Master": Letters of a Slave Family*, ed. Randall M. Miller (Athens, GA: The University of Georgia Press, Brown Thrasher Edition, 1990), 25-27 and 39.

[30] Bruce Mann, *Republic of Debtors: Bankruptcy in the Age of American Independence* (Cambridge, MA: Harvard University Press, 2002), 4, 6-33.

[31] US Department of Commerce and Labor, Bureau of the Census, "Heads of Families—Pennsylvania," and "Heads of Families—Virginia," Heads of Families at the First Census of the United States Taken in the Year 1790, Pennsylvania (Washington, D. C.: Government Printing Office, 1908), 10 (PA), 8 & 10 (VA), http://www2.census.gov/prod2/decennial/1790 (November 3, 2004).

[32] *The Pennsylvania Gazette*, February 5, 1783, http://etext.virginia.edu/ (December 2, 2004).

[33] Ibid., January 1, 1783.

[34] Thomas Jefferson to Martha Jefferson, Annapolis, December 22, 1783, *Papers*, 6:417.

[35] George Everett Hastings, *The Life and Works of Francis Hopkinson* (Chicago: University of Chicago Press, 1926), 34.

[36] Thomas Jefferson to Martha Jefferson, Annapolis, November 28, 1783, *Papers*, 6:359-60.

[37] Shuffleton, *NSV*, 154; Thomas Jefferson to Peter Carr, Annapolis, 11 December 1783, *Papers*, 6:379-80 and Paris, 19 August 1785, Ibid., 8:405.

[38] Susan Kern, *The Jeffersons at Shadwell* (New Haven: Yale University Press, 2010) provides a thorough description of these early years by creatively synthesizing literary and material evidence.

[39] Henry S. Randall, *The Life of Thomas Jefferson* (New York: Derby & Jackson, 1848), 1:11. Peter Jefferson managed for seven years the deceased William Randolph's Tuckahoe plantation, where Jefferson attended a school. Peter (1708–1757) and Jane Randolph Jefferson (1720–1776) had ten children; six daughters and two sons survived to adulthood.

[40] *Jefferson's Letters*, "Notes for an Autobiography, Monticello, January, 1821, ed. Wilson Whitman (Eau Claire, WI: E. M. Hale and Company, n.d.), 340-42. Hereafter cited as Whitman, "Notes."

[41] Thomas Jefferson to Thomas Jefferson Randolph, Washington, Washington, 24 November 1808, Betts and Bear, *JFL*, 362-65. Jefferson was age fourteen in 1757 and his mother did not die until 1776. His father's will had appointed five executors or "guardians" and John Harvie [Sr.] of Belmont was principally responsible for managing the estate until Jefferson attained his majority in 1764 (Dumas Malone, *Jefferson the Virginian* [Boston: Little, Brown and Company, 1948], 437-39).

[42] Shuffleton, *NSV*, 154

[43] Imitation or emulation had been a long-standing instructional method in the form of copy books, oratorical competitions, and memorizations. In late eighteenth-century France, for example, it was considered a natural sentiment that was "a generous, ennobling passion, productive of integrity and virtuous ambition." However, it was reinterpreted after the French Revolution as a way of reconciling civic virtue and individual self-interest in the public sphere and resulted in organized groups such as the Société Libre d'Émulation in Paris. See Nira Kaplan, "Virtuous Competition

Among Citizens: Emulation in Politics and Pedagogy During the French Revolution," *Eighteenth-Century Studies*, 36:2 (2003), 241-48; http://muse.jhu.edu (February 1, 2006).

[44] Thomas Jefferson to John Harvie, Shadwell, 14 January 1760, *Papers*, 1:3.

[45] *Report of the Commissioners*, 4 August 1818, in *The Portable Thomas Jefferson*, edited with an introduction by Merrill D. Peterson (New York: Penguin Books, 1977), 345.

[46] Thomas Jefferson to Martha Jefferson, Annapolis, January 15, 1784, *Papers*, 6:465.

[47]Thomas Jefferson to Martha Jefferson, Annapolis, 15 January 1784; 18 February; 19 March 1784; and 17 April 1784, Ibid., 6:380-81, 465-66, and 7:110.

[48] Shuffleton, *NSV*, 154

[49] Francis Hopkinson to Thomas Jefferson, with "A Literary Christmas Gambol," Philadelphia, 4 January 1784, *Papers*, 6:443-47.

[50] Eliza House Trist to Thomas Jefferson, Philadelphia, 13 December 1783, microfilm Southern Women and Their Families, Parts 4-6, reel 1, Nicholas P. Trist Papers (UnC), transcribed by author.

[51] Thomas Jefferson to Martha Jefferson, Annapolis, 22 December 1783, *Papers*, 6:416-17. Kate Haulman, "Fashion and the Cultural Wars of Revolutionary Philadelphia," *The William and Mary Quarterly, 3rd Series* 62, no. 4 (2005): 625-662, http://www.historycooperative.org/ (February 1, 2006). The eighteenth-century meaning of "slut" was a critical term denoting a woman who disregarded standards of cleanliness and modest dress without sexual connotations.

[52] Thomas Jefferson to Francis Eppes, Philadelphia,10 November 1783, *Papers*, 6:349-50.

[53] Lee to James Warren, 12 March 1783 as cited in Kate Haulman, "Fashion and the Cultural Wars of Revolutionary Philadelphia," *The William and Mary Quarterly, 3rd Series* 62, no. 4 (2005): 625-662, http://www.historycooperative.org/ (February 1, 2006).

[54] Hastings, *Hopkinson*, 30-39. Over his lifetime (1751–1797), Winchester was a New Light Calvinist, a Baptist, and ultimately a Universalist. He led evangelical revivals in the northeast, England, and among slaves in South Carolina; pastored churches in Philadelphia and Connecticut; and founded congregations in Massachusetts and London (Peter Hughes, "Elhanan Winchester," *Dictionary of Unitarian and Universalist Biography* (Unitarian Universalist Historical Society, UUHS, 1999–2006), http://www.uua.org [May 28, 2006]).

[55] Thomas Jefferson to Martha Jefferson, Annapolis, 22 December 1783, *Papers*, 416-17.

[56] Thomas Jefferson to Peter Carr, Paris, 10 August 1787, Ibid.,, 12:15. Among many other references to exercising moral sense, see especially Thomas Jefferson to Robert Skipwith, Monticello, 3 August 1771, Ibid., 1:76-81.

[57] Thomas Jefferson to Thomas Law, Poplar Forest, 13 June 1814, L&B, *Writings*, 14:138-144.

[58] Thomas Jefferson to Peter Carr, Paris 6 August 1788, *Papers*, 13:470-71 and 19 August 1785, Ibid., 7:405-08. For the "head & heart" construct of the human being, see Thomas Jefferson to Maria Cosway, Paris, 12 October 1786, Ibid., 10: 443-53.

[59] Thomas Jefferson to Robert Skipwith, with a List of Books for a Gentleman's Library, Monticello, 3 August, 1771, Ibid., 1:76-81.

[60] Thomas Jefferson to Charles Brockden Brown, Philadelphia, 15 January 1800, Ibid., 31:308.

[61] Thomas Jefferson to Martha Jefferson, Annapolis, November 28, 1783, Ibid., 6:360.

[62] Thomas Jefferson to Martha Jefferson, Paris, March 6, 1786, Ibid., 9:318.

[63] Thomas Jefferson to Martha Jefferson, Annapolis, 28 November 1783,Ibid., 6:360. The Eppes and Skipwith aunts were half-sisters to Patsy's mother; Aunt Carr, her father's sister.

[64] Thomas Jefferson to Martha Jefferson, Annapolis, 18 February 1784, Ibid., 6:543-44; 18 February 1784, Ibid., 543-44; and 4 April 1784, Ibid., 7:62

[65] Thomas Jefferson to Francis Eppes, Philadelphia, 4 March 1783, Ibid., 6:253.

[66] See James L. Goldon and Alan L. Goldon, *Thomas Jefferson and the Rhetoric of Virtue* (Lanham, MD: Rowman & Littlefield Publishers, Inc., 2002), 120-124; Andrew Burstein, *The Inner Jefferson: Portrait of a Grieving Optimist* (Charlottesville, VA: The University Press of Virginia, 1995), 116-49.

[67] Hugh Blair, *Lectures on Rhetoric and Belles Lettres* (London: A. Strahan, 1790, fourth edition), Vol. I, 66ff, http://www.rc.umd.edu/ (May 22, 2006).

[68] Thomas Jefferson to Martha Jefferson, Annapolis, 28 November 1783, *Papers,* 6:359-60.

[69] Thomas Jefferson to Martha Jefferson, Annapolis, 15 January 1784, Ibid., 6: 65.

[70] Thomas Jefferson to Dr. John Manners, 22 February 1814, L&B, *Writings,* 14:97-98; and Thomas Jefferson to Edward Everett, 24 February 1823, Ibid., 15, 414.

[71] Thomas Jefferson to Martha Jefferson, Annapolis, 17 April 1784, *Papers,* 7:110-111.

[72] Jan Lewis, "'The Blessings of Domestic Society': Thomas Jefferson's Family and the Transformation of American Politics," in, *Jeffersonian Legacies,* ed. Peter Onuf (Charlottesville, VA: University Press of Virginia, 1993), 129 and 138.

[73] Thomas Jefferson to Martha Jefferson, Annapolis, 15 January 1784, *Papers,* 6:465-66.

[74] *The Pennsylvania Gazette,* 18 June 1783, http://etext.virginia.edu/ (1 December 2004) Typographical styles of the period are retained in the citations from this source.

[75] DuSimitière's Design for a Coat of Arms for Virginia, [August, 1776], *Papers,* 1:510-11.

[76] Bear and Stanton, *JMB,* 1:539; "John Bentley," *Dictionary of Canadian Biography Online,* http://www.biographi.ca/ (22 September 2010).

[77] Thomas Jefferson to Martha Jefferson, Annapolis, 11 December, 1783, *Papers,* 6:380-82; 18 February 1784, Ibid., 6: 543-44; 19 March, 1784, Ibid., 7:43-44;

[78] Francis Hopkinson to Thomas Jefferson, with "A Literary Christmas Gambol," Philadelphia, 4 January 1784, Ibid., 6:443-47.

[79] Thomas Jefferson to Martha Jefferson, Annapolis, 19 March 1784, Ibid., 7:43-44.

[80] Thomas Jefferson to Martha Jefferson, Annapolis, 4 April 1784, Ibid., 7:62.

[81] Marquis De Chastellux, *Travels in North America in the Years 1780, 1781 and 1782* (Chapel Hill, NC: The University of North Carolina Press, 1963), a revised translation with Introduction and Notes by Howard C. Rice, Jr., 1:145.

[82] *The Pennsylvania Gazette,* 1 May 1782, http://etext.virginia.edu/ (December 1, 2004).

[83] Ibid., 10 November 1784; Francis Hopkinson to Thomas Jefferson, Philadelphia, 18 November 1784, *Papers,* 7:534-35.

[84] Thomas Jefferson to Chastellux, Paris, 2 September 1785, Ibid., 8:468.

[85] Thomas Jefferson to William Short, [30 April 1784], Ibid., 6:148-49. He was appointed on 7 May 1784.

[86] Bear and Stanton, *JMB,* 1:548-49.

[87] Ibid., 553n54; "Notes on Commerce of the Northern States," *Papers,* 7:323-55; Thomas Jefferson to G. K. van Hogendorp, Cul-de-sac Tetebout, Paris, 20 November 1784, Ibid.,545-46.

[88] Bear and Stanton, *JMB,* 1:551-52, footnotes 46 and 48.

[89] Philadelphia citations from Anonymous, *A View of North America…in the years 1774, 75, 76, 77, 78* (Glasgow: William Smith, 1781), 18-20, http://galenetgalegroup.com (November 14, 2004); Boston cites from L'Abbé Robin, *Nouveau Voyage dans*

l'Amérique Septentrionale en l'année 1781 (Paris, 1782) as cited in Henry T. Tuckerman, *America and Her Commentators with a Critical Sketch of Travel in the United States* (New York: Antiquarian Press, Ltd., reprint 1961, 1ˢᵗ edition 1864), 76-80.

⁹⁰ M. le Comte de Ségur, *Mémoires,* (Paris, 1825), tom I, 412-13 as cited in Tuckerman, Ibid., 117. Ségur (1753–1850) was a French diplomat who served as ambassador in St. Petersburg, Berlin, and Vienna, as well as a colonel in Rochambeau's Expeditionary force during the American Revolution. Caspar Wistar recommended and provided to Jefferson Ségur's *History of the Principal Events of the Reign of Frederick William II, King of Prussia* (Wistar to Jefferson, 22 March 1804), and this English translation was regularly on Jefferson's recommended reading lists (Sowerby #129). Twenty years earlier, the admittedly partial Englishman Andrew Burnaby proffered a similar prophesy after traveling the "middle colonies" in 1759–60: "In short, such is the difference of character, of manners, of religion, of interest, of the different colonies, that...left to themselves, there would soon be a civil war."'" He characterized southerners, like Jefferson did to Chastellux, "haughty," "jealous of their liberties," "indolent," and "unenterprizing"; Bostonians, formal, "precise," and industrious. *Travels...*(London: T. Payne at Mews-Gate, 1798), 121, 119, and 27, http://galenetgalegroup.com/ (November 12, 2004).

Chapter 3: "Judge of my situation"

¹ Bear and Stanton, *JMB*, 1:554.

² Martha Jefferson to Eliza House Trist, Panthemont, [24 August 1785], *Papers* 8:436-39. Spelling of the original retained.

³ Ellen Wayles Randolph Coolidge Letterbook, 1856–1858, transcript from files of Thomas Jefferson Foundation dated 4 September 1992, original manuscript ViU accession 9090.

⁴Bear and Stanton, *JMB*, 1:555; Martha Jefferson to Eliza House Trist, Panthemont, [24 August 1785], *Papers* 8:436-39.

⁵ William Howard Adams, *The Paris Years of Thomas Jefferson* (New Haven, CT: Yale University Press, 1997), 37ff. Hereafter, Adams, *Paris.* Howard C. Rice, Jr. *Thomas Jefferson's Paris* (Princeton, NJ: Princeton University Press, 1976), 3-13. Hereafter, Rice, *TJ Paris.* The Halle Aux Blés was a 120 feet diameter structure topped by a dome some 100 feet above the ground.

⁶ "A Bill for the More General Diffusion of Knowledge," was one among 126 introduced on 18 June 1779 in the Virginia General Assembly. Jefferson served on the drafting committee but claimed full credit for this particular Bill #79 as well as three others he considered central to establishing a "government truly republican": abolishing entails, eliminating primogeniture, and "A Bill for Establishing Religious Freedom" (*Papers,* 2:305ff). Education was very much on Jefferson's mind at this particular time. The proposals were still pending when the family left for Paris and Jefferson was revising his *Notes on the State of Virginia* that detailed his views on age-specific learning.

⁷ Bear and Stanton, *JMB*, 1:557-559. Jefferson used "f" to denote the livre monetary unit whose denominations were livre= 20 sous and a sou =12 deniers (*Bear and Stanton, JMB*, 1:556n).

⁸ Martha Jefferson to Eliza House Trist, Panthemont, [24 August 1785], *Papers* 8:436-39.

⁹ Ibid.

¹⁰ Thomas Jefferson to James Maury, Paris, 24 December 1786, Ibid. 10:628.

[11] M. de La Forest, *Méthode d'Instruction pour ramener les Prétendum Réformés a l'Église Romaine* (A Lyon: chez Amié de la Roche, 1784); Sowerby #1540. The flyleaf is dated "March 21, 1787" and signed "M. Jefferson panthemont." The family story was recorded by Sarah Nicholas Randolph in *Domestic Life of Thomas Jefferson*, 146. Jefferson's correspondence with the Dugnani is in L&B, XIX, 254-55 and the entire episode is discussed in *Papers* 14:356 footnote and Bear and Stanton, *JMB*, 1:730, footnote 47.

[12] William Short to Thomas Jefferson, Paris, 26 March 1787, *Papers*, 11:239-41. The italics are in the original.

[13] Dugnani to John Carroll, Paris, 5 July 1787, *John Carroll of Baltimore*, ed., Annabelle M. Melville, (New York: Charles Scribner's Sons, 1955), 102, from the Carroll Papers in the Department of Archives and Manuscripts, Catholic University of America as cited in *Papers*, 14:356n.

[14] Ellen Wayles Randolph Coolidge, "Recollections of Martha Jefferson Randolph," FLP (ViU), http://familypapers.dataformat.com, (April 11, 2007).

[15] The abbess, who descended from the politically powerful d'Oglethorpe family, was installed 21 February 1743. Unless otherwise noted, information on the history of Panthemont ("Pentemont") and environs is taken from the definitive published work by Howard C. Rice, *Thomas Jefferson's Paris* (Princeton, NJ: Princeton University Press, 1976), 64-68 and passim; and "Notebook A10:Paris—Left Bank: Faubourg Saint-Germain," Thomas Jefferson Foundation, Howard C. Rice Collection; additional details of curriculum, expenses, etc. can be found in Bear and Stanton, *JMB*, 1:560-61n84 and 1:730-31n47.

[16] A partial list of her "friends" at the convent can be found in *Papers* 18:480n. A ms copy of the complete list is in the files of the Thomas Jefferson Foundation.

[17] Rice, "Notes," citing Marquise de Ségur "L'Éducation des Jeunes Filles au XVIIIe," in *Esquisses et Récits, Calmann-Lévy* (Paris: 1908). The Panthemont "élèves" (students) dined mid-day at 11:00 AM and the Abbess at 1:00 PM. (Partial transcript of Ellen Wayles Randolph Coolidge diaries, 1838–39, vol. II, Thomas Jefferson Foundation files; original ms Massachusetts Historical Society [MHi] ms N-1027 on microfilm P-364.) Hereafter cited as Coolidge, *Diaries*.

[18] Coolidge, *Diaries*.

[19] Martha Jefferson to Eliza House Trist, Panthemont, [24 August 1785], *Papers* 8:439-39.

[20] General information for this section was drawn from Howard C. Rice, passim, and William Howard Adams 37 ff. For the details of expenditures during this period, see Bear and Stanton, *JMB*, 1:557-72. Simon Vouet (1590–1649) was a French painter in the Baroque period who painted many religiously themed pieces.

[21] Thomas Jefferson to Monroe, Monticello, 20 May 1782, *Papers*, 6:184.

[22] Thomas Jefferson to James Madison, Paris, 25 May 1788, Ibid., 13:301-03, and Bear and Stanton, *JMB*, 1:564n1 and n2, 550n39. One author has estimated the British pound sterling as equivalent to about 23.17 *livres tournois* during the 1780s (Robert D. Harris, "French Finances and the American War, 1777–1783," *Journal of Modern History* [June 1976], 233-258, 247 n 41). A similar exchange in New England in 1781 was reported by Abbé Robin, *New Travels Through North-America: In a Series of Letters* (Philadelphia, 1783), 16. (Both citations from http://www.hudsonriver valley.net/AMERICANBOOK/18.html (July 3, 2009). Using these current exchange rates, a rough equivalency was $4.86 to £1 or *livre* 23.143 or approximately $1 to *livre* 4.76. However, none should be compared with modern day values.

[23] Thomas Jefferson to James Monroe, Paris, 11 November 1784, *Papers* 7:508-513 and 17 June 1785, Ibid. 8:230.

[24] Francis Eppes to Thomas Jefferson, Eppington, 16 September 1784, Ibid., 15:615-16. Farell and Jones were Bristol merchants holding the debt inherited from his father-in-law, John Wayles. With no bankruptcy law, creditors received priority in court settlements based on when they filed liens; so, a filing could spawn a rush of suits.

[25] James Currie to Thomas Jefferson, Richmond, 20 November 1784, Ibid. 7:538-39. Currie (1745–1807) studied medicine at Edinburgh, immigrated to Virginia, and began practicing near the Medical College of Virginia across from Richmond's City Hall (C. B. Cosby, "James Currie and Hydrotherapy," *Journal of the History of Medicine and Allied Sciences* [Summer, 1950], 280-88, [July 3, 2009]).

[26] Adams, *Journal*, January 27th [1785], 45.

[27] Thomas Jefferson to Francis Eppes, Paris, 5 February 1785, *Papers* 7:635-6.

[28] Ibid.

[29] Francis Eppes to Thomas Jefferson, Eppington, 14 September 1785, Ibid., 15:623-64.

[30] Thomas Jefferson to William Short, 13 April 1820, Jefferson Papers (DLC) transcribed by Gerard W. Gawalt, http://memory.loc.gov (February 3, 2007). Commenting on a "Syllabus" that he had prepared (i.e., "The Jefferson Bible"): "I read them [Jesus' doctrines] as I do those of other antient and modern moralists, with a mixture of approbation and dissent."

[31] Rice, *TJ Paris*, 66. Josephine de Beauharnais (Rose) left Panthemont in 1784, just before Martha arrived (Andrea Stuart, *The Rose of Martinique: A Life of Napoleon's Josephine* [New York: Grove Press, 2005], 73, 64, and passim).

[32] Thomas Jefferson to John Banister, Jr., Paris, October 15, 1785, *Papers* 8:638. Accompanying this letter was an outline on which Jefferson had written "on sending American youth to Europe" that appears to have been for an essay. Considered in the context of the Banister letter, it gives an indication of the contrasting elements he would use to compare French and American cultures, e.g., government, manners, language, marriage, and dogs.

[33] Thomas Jefferson to Charles Thomson, Paris, 11 November, 1784, Ibid. 7:519.

[34] Thomas Jefferson to John Banister, Jr., Paris, 15 October 1785, Ibid., 8:635-638.

[35] Thomas Jefferson to Walker Maury, with a List of Books, Paris, August 19, 1785, Ibid. 8:409-412.

[36] Thomas Jefferson to John Banister, Jr., Paris, 15 October 1785, Ibid., 8:635-638.

[37] Ibid., 10:453-54 footnote.

[38] Underlying the seemingly flippant letter to Bingham was a much deeper emotional impulse labeled "sentiment" or "sensibility" in this period. Considered a refined character trait of being attentive to one's own and others' internal feelings, it was expressed frequently in Jefferson's interactions with women with whom he was socially intimate. See Billy L. Wayson, "Thomas Jefferson and Affairs of the Heart," in *A Jefferson Compendium*, ed. Francis Cogliano (New York: Wiley-Blackwell, 2011).

[39] Thomas Jefferson to Anne Willing Bingham, Paris, 7 February 1787, Ibid., 11:122-124. Anne Willing Bingham (1764–1801) was born into a prosperous merchant family in Philadelphia and married into an equally wealthy one at age 16. She and husband William spent 1783–86 visiting the capitals of Europe and dined frequently with Jefferson and the Adams family while in Paris.

[40] Dena Goodman, "Public Sphere and Private Life: Toward a Synthesis of Current Historiographical Approaches to the Old Regime," *History and Theory*, 31, no. 1

(1992),18-20; "Enlightenment Salons: The Convergence of Female and Philosophic Ambitions" *Eighteenth-Century Studies* 22, (Spring 1989), 329-50; and Steven D. Kale, "Women, the Public Sphere, and the Persistence of Salons," *French Historical Studies*, 25, no. 1 (2002) 115-148, http://muse.jhu.edu/journals (October 19, 2005).

[41] Jefferson's liaison with Anglo-Italian artist Maria Cosway (Mrs. Richard) has been the subject of exhaustive writing (and speculation) and will not be elaborated here. They met in mid-August 1786 shared outings in Paris and vicinity until her departure on October 5th, which in his words left him "more dead than alive." Among many accounts of their relationship are Carol Burnell, *Divided Affections: The Extraordinary Life of Maria Cosway: Celebrity Artist and Thomas Jefferson's Impossible Love* (Switzerland: Column House, 2007); John Kaminski, ed., *Jefferson in Love: Love Letters Between Thomas Jefferson & Maria Cosway* (Madison, WI: Madison House Publishers, Inc., 1999); John Kukla, *Mr. Jefferson's Women* (New York: Alfred A. Knopf, 2007): Helen Dufrey Bullock, *My Head and My Heart: A Little History of Thomas Jefferson & Maria Cosway* (New York: G. P. Putnam's Sons, 1945); and *Papers*, 10:443-55.

[42] TJ to James Madison, Paris, 30 January 1787, *Papers* 11:95.

[43] Anne Willing Bingham to Thomas Jefferson, [Philadelphia, 1 June 1787], Ibid., 11:392-94.

[44] Thomas Jefferson to Anne Willing Bingham, Paris, 11 May 1788, Ibid. 13:151-52.

[45] TJ to George Washington, 4 November 1788, Ibid. 14:328-32; actually written 4 December. The reforms circulating in late 1788 were to expand the powers of the (States-general) relative to Louis XVI and grant the "people" (*Tiers-état*) representation equal to the clergy and nobility.

[46] Thomas Jefferson to Martha Jefferson, Paris, 4 November 1786, Ibid., 10:507 and 15 October 1786, Ibid., 10:499; and Montgomery, 13:165n66. Nathaniel Barrett was a representative of Boston merchants in Europe.

[47] Thomas Jefferson to Dorcas Montgomery, Paris, 19 November 1786, Ibid., 10:543-44 and 13:165-66n. At the bottom of this letter is a cryptic notation that associates three women: "Mrs. (*Cosway*), (*Church*) Montgomery." He also returned Montgomery's letter "which you prohibit me from mentioning to others." She may have been part of some of the events Jefferson and Cosway participated in between early August and October, 1787. His letters to her are polite or limited to legal affairs but never convey the whimsical and flirtatious tone of those to Church, Bingham and Cosway.

[48] William Short to Thomas Jefferson, Paris, 6 April 1787, Ibid., 11:274-77. The phrase "on the *tapis*" can be translated literally as "on the table," meaning raising the subject for discussion.

[49] Judith Randolph to Martha Jefferson, Tuckahoe, 5 June 1789, Southern Women and Their Families, Parts 4-6, reel 1, Nicholas P. Trist Papers (UnC). Transcription by the author.

[50] Thomas Jefferson to Abigail Adams, Paris, 21 June 1785, *Papers*, 8:239-42. The Countess d'Houdetot presided over a *salon* north of Paris where she lived with her husband as well as her lover, the poet and philosopher St. Lambert. It was considered almost as influential as those overseen by Mesdames Necker and Helvétius, also Jefferson's regular acquaintances. Webster notes that the Madame had "inherited the materials from which it was composed from Madame de Terrier and Madame Geoffrin," who were two of the original Paris *salonnières*.

[51] Bear and Stanton, *JMB*, 1:598. As noted below, Patsy's father encouraged her to learn sewing as a pastime with "dull company" on an American plantation, since card playing and gambling were not appropriate for "genteel" ladies.

[52] From *Private Correspondence of Daniel Webster* (1:364) a "memorandum" by Webster describing his visit to Monticello (Dec, 1824). Ford, *Works*, 12:273, http://olldownload.libertyfund.org/ (May 29, 2006). For a thorough description of *salonnières* and their influence, see Dena Goodman, *The Republic of Letters: A Cultural History of the French Enlightenment* (Ithaca, NY: Cornell University Press, 1994). Suzanne Curchod Necker (1739–1794) was born to a Calvinist family in Switzerland, moved to Paris in 1764, and her Friday afternoon *salon* met until 1790.

[53] Thomas Jefferson to John Jay, Paris, 17 June 1789, Attachment, *Memoir, Correspondence and Miscellanies from the Papers of Thomas Jefferson*, ed., Thomas Jefferson Randolph (Charlottesville, VA: F. Carr, and Co., 1829.), 2:479. The French language text is in *Papers*, 15:191-93.

[54]Randolph, *Worthy Women*, 21; and Thomas Jefferson to William Temple Franklin, Paris, 7 May 1786, *Papers*, 9:466-67. Anne Louise Germaine Necker, Baronne de Staël-Holstein (1766–1817) was the wife of the Swedish Ambassador, Eric Magnus, Baron de Staël-Holstein. She became a noted fictional author (*Delphine*, [1802] and *Corinne* [1807] and literary theorist. Her writings on the latter subject included *A Treatise of Ancient and Modern Literature* and *The Influence of Literature upon Society*. Politically active, Mde. Staël was banned from Paris in 1803 by Napoleon. (Encyclopedia Britannica's Guide to Women's History; http://search.eb.com/women/article-6866 (April 13, 2007).

[55] M. LaBorde de Méréville to Martha Jefferson, 21 January 1789, *Papers* 14:478. LaBorde had been offered, but refused, in 1787 a powerful position as director of the Royal Treasury (TJ to André Limozin, Paris, 21 August and 9 September 1787, *Papers* 12:70 and 110; Thomas Jefferson to Martha Jefferson, Paris, 4 November [1786], Ibid. 10:507, [October 1786], Ibid., 499, and 14 June 1787, Ibid. 11:472). Dorcas Armitage Montgomery was a Philadelphian who had gone to France in 1781 for her son Robert's education. She was a friend of the Bache family and correspondent with Franklin Ibid. 13:165-66n.

[56] Thomas Jefferson to Martha Jefferson, Paris, 16 June 1788, Betts & Bear, *JFL*, 44-45. Madame de Corny (nee Marguerite Victoire de Palerne) was married to Dominique-Louis Ethis de Corny, Lafayette's former aide-de-camp and commissary general for the French expeditionary force in 1780. Polly's father claimed to have considered Mde. de Corny as her escort from London to Paris in June 1787 (*Papers*, 11:509-10). However, the next year he intentionally or unintentionally did not respond to de Corny's request "to visit [his] daughters and to take them out of the convent sometimes," while he was in Amsterdam from March 4 to April 23, 1788. Their father may have been concerned about her intention to take them to the traditional Holy Week celebrations at Longchamp that included Catholic religious observances, horseracing and, according to William Short *peu du monde* (trans.: not very nice or intelligent people). Short had earlier reported the debate between Mesdames de Tott and de Tesse regarding the appropriateness of attending the events and their advice that Mde. Lafayette's "piety would have been shocked" at an invitation to accompany him to Longchamp (Respectively, Short to Jefferson, 26 March 1787, *Papers*, 11: 239 and 4 April 1787, Ibid., 11:268). The footnote to this letter indicates that Patsy attended "La Toison d'Or (The Golden Fleece), also known as Médée a Colchis." From 1634, this was a common operatic and musical subject in France by several librettists and composers with variants on these names. They probably attended a 1786 version by Philippe Desriaux and Johann-Christophe Vogel (See Paolo Russo, trans. Mary Ann Smart, "Visions of Medea: Musico-Dramatic Transformations of a Myth," *Cambridge Opera Journal*, Vol. 6, No. 2 [July, 1994], 112-124, specifically 114-15).

57 *Jefferson's Literary Commonplace Book*, ed., Douglas L. Wilson (Princeton, NJ: Princeton University Press, 1989), 73, n 132.

58 Randolph, *Worthy Women*, 21.

59 Respectively, "Notes of a Tour of English Gardens," *Papers*, 9:369-75; and Beth Kowaleski Wallace, "A Modest Defense of Gaming Women," *Studies in Eighteenth-Century Culture*, eds. Ourida Mostefai and Catherine Ingrassia (Baltimore: The Johns Hopkins University Press, 2002), Vol. 31, 21.

60 Anne Willing Bingham, Philadelphia, [1 June 1787], *Papers*, 11:393-4.

61 Bear and Stanton, *JMB*, 1:683 records his subscription to this fashion magazine. By the late 1780s color and cut of clothing and hair styles were used to communicate political sympathies: red, white, and blue were the mark of a "democrat"; and less fervent citizens might choose a bi-color and signal their political ambivalence with black pants and stockings ("en demi-detuil" or semi-mourning fashion).

62 Eliza House Trist to Thomas Jefferson, 13 December 1783, microfilm Southern Women and Their Families, Parts 4-6, reel 1, Nicholas P. Trist Papers (UnC), transcribed by author; Thomas Jefferson to Martha Jefferson, Annapolis, 22 December 1783, *Papers*, 6:416-17; Martha Jefferson to Eliza House Trist, Panthemont, [24 August 1785], Ibid., 8:436-39.

63 Thomas Jefferson to Martha Jefferson, Paris, 14 June 1787, Ibid. 11:472.

64 Bear & Stanton, *JMB*, 1:730-743 [19 April to 26 September 1789]. Amounts are in livres. "Lawn & cambrick" [cambric] are both a type of linen cloth.

65 *NSV, Query XVIII*, 168. As Father would learn when Patsy challenged him later in her stay at Panthemont, learning was more than Titus Livy and painting pretty landscapes. Dining at the Abbesses table provided ample opportunity to discover alternatives constructions of family, experience diverse gender roles, etc. See Barbara Rogoff, et al. "First Hand Learning Through Intent Participation," *Annual Review of Psychology*, 54, 175-203, available from http://arjournals.annualreviews.org (June 3, 2006).

66 Thomas Jefferson to Elizabeth Wayles Eppes, 22 September 1785, *Papers* 15:624-25.

67 Thomas Jefferson to Francis Eppes, Paris, 30 August 1785, Ibid., 15:621-22. His first letter to Eppes on the subject was 11 May 1785 (8:141, an entry in SJL.): "I must have Polly."

68 Thomas Jefferson to Mary Jefferson, 20 September 1785, Ibid. 8:532-33.

69 Francis Eppes to Thomas Jefferson, Eppington, 14 September 1785, Ibid. 15:623-24.

70 Francis Eppes to Thomas Jefferson, Eppington, 31 August 1786, Ibid., 15:631-32 and 23 May 1786, Ibid., 628. Isabel was an enslaved woman whom the Eppes family intended to accompany Polly.

71 Francis Eppes to Thomas Jefferson, Eppington, 11 April 1785, Ibid., 15:625-26 (received 29 June 1786).

72 Mary Jefferson to Thomas Jefferson, Eppington, ca. 22 May 1786, Ibid. 9:560-61 and ca. 31 March 1787, Ibid. 11:260-61.

73 Martha Jefferson to Thomas Jefferson, Panthemont, March 8, 1787, Ibid., 11:203-204. Patsy is referring to the bishop ("eveque") from the city of Narbonne built by the Romans and located in southern France on the Languedoc Canal. He was a member of the clerical estate in the Assemblée des Notables that had been called together by Louis XVI to deal with the fiscal crisis facing the *ancien regime* that was due, in part, to France's financial support of the American Revolution. A thorough discussion of the French bishops' difficult political position in which they tried to reconcile secular

principles of liberty, equality, and fraternity with Catholic teachings is presented in Ruth Graham, "The Revolutionary Bishops and the Philosophes," *Eighteenth-Century Studies*, Vol. 16, No. 2 (Winter, 1982–1983), 117-140. Claude-Bénigne Balbastre (1724 or 27–1799), Patsy's tutor, was organist at Notre-Dame cathedral, harpsichordist at the Royal Court, and teacher of Marie-Antoinette.

[74] Thomas Jefferson to Martha Jefferson, Aix en Provence, March 23, 1787, *Papers*, 11:250-252.

[75] Thomas Jefferson to Martha Jefferson, Annapolis, November 28, 1783, Ibid., 6:360 and Thomas Jefferson to Peter Carr, Paris, August 19, 1785, Ibid., 15:405-408.

[76] Thomas Jefferson to Martha Jefferson, Paris, March 6, 1786, Ibid., 9:318.

[77] Thomas Jefferson to Martha Jefferson, Aix en Provence, March 28, 1787, Ibid., 11:250-252. Jefferson's emphasis on "habit" was one of his approaches to inculcating values, behavioral patterns, and ideas, generally.

[78] Shuffleton, *NSV*, 154.

[79] Martha Jefferson to Thomas Jefferson, Panthemont, 9 April 1787, *Papers* 11:282-82.

[80] Ibid.

[81] Thomas Jefferson to Martha Jefferson, Aix en Provence, 28 March, 1787, Ibid., 250-52.

[82] Thomas Jefferson to Chastellux, Paris, 2 September 1785, Ibid., 8:468.

[83] Martha Jefferson to Thomas Jefferson, March 25, 1787, Ibid., 11:238-39.

[84] Thomas Jefferson to Martha Jefferson, Toulon, April 7, 1787, Ibid., 11:277-78.

[85] Martha Jefferson to Thomas Jefferson, Panthemont, April 9, 1787, Ibid., 11:281-82. This likely is a reference to the husband of Lafayette's mistress. Jefferson wrote two weeks later from Aix-en-Provence: "I do not know whether to condole with, or to congratulate the Marquis [Lafayette] on the death of M. de [Simiane]. The man who shoots himself in the climate of Aix must be a bloody minded fellow indeed" (to William Short, Aix en Provence, 27 March 1787, *Papers* 11:246-47). "Thaubeneu" was Sister Taubenheim who handled administrative affairs for the convent.

[86] William Short, Jefferson's private secretary, "conjectured" the failure to inform L'Abbesse was "intentional" (William Short to Thomas Jefferson, Paris, 6 April 1787, *Papers* 11:274-77).

[87] Thomas Jefferson to Martha Jefferson, Marseilles, May 5, 1787, *Papers* 11:348-49.

[88] Martha Jefferson to Thomas Jefferson, Panthemont, 3 May 1787, Ibid., 11:333-34. Louis-Charles-Auguste Le Tonnelier, Baron de Breteuil; De Polignac was governess for the children of the royal household (Betts and Bear, *JFL*, 39 fns 3 and 4.)

[89] Thomas Jefferson to Martha Jefferson, Nantes, 1 June 1787, *Papers* 11:304-5.

[90] Thomas Jefferson to Martha Jefferson, [Canal of Languedoc], May 21, 1787, Ibid., 11:369-70.

[91] Thomas Jefferson to Martha Jefferson, Annapolis, December 11, 1783, Ibid., 6:380-81.

[92] *Thomas Jefferson's Farm Book*, ed. Edwin Morris Betts (Charlottesville, VA: University Press of Virginia, 1987), 27. A table labeled "number of souls in my family in Albemarle" for 1776 includes both 34 "free" and 83 "slaves."

[93] Respectively, Abigail Adams to Thomas Jefferson, London, 27 June 1787, *Papers* 11:502-03; 6 July 1787, Ibid., 11:550-53; and 10 July 1787, Ibid., 11:572-74. Maria ("Polly") was born 1 August 1778, nearly six years Martha's junior.

[94] Abigail Adams to Thomas Jefferson, London, 26 June 1787, Ibid., 11:501-02.

[95] Abigail Adams to Thomas Jefferson, London, 6 July 1787, Ibid., 11:550-53.

[96] Thomas Jefferson to Abigail Adams, Paris, 1 July 1787, Ibid., 11:514-15 and 6 July 1787, Ibid., 11:572, respectively.

97 Martha Jefferson to Thomas Jefferson, Paris, 27 May 1787, Ibid., 11:380-81 and 9 April 1787, Ibid., 11:281-82; Thomas Jefferson to Martha Jefferson, Languedoc, 21 May 1787, Ibid., 11:369-70.

98 Thomas Jefferson to Elizabeth Wayles Eppes, Paris, 28 July 1787, Ibid., 11:634-5.

99 Thomas Jefferson to Francis Eppes, Paris, 16 December 1788, Ibid. 14:357-59 and to Elizabeth Wayles Eppes, Paris, 15 December, 1788, Ibid. 14:355-56. Jefferson later diagnosed these ailments as "typhus" or "nervous fevers" and recommended in later years the course of treatment they received to many others (Thomas Jefferson to James Madison, Monticello, 13 January 1821, *The Republic of Letters,* ed., James Morton Smith [New York: W. W. Norton & Company], 3:1828–29.)

100 Thomas Jefferson to John Jay, Paris, 19 November, *Papers* 14:211-215; to John Adams, 5 December, Ibid., 332-336; to Elizabeth Wayles Eppes, 15 December, Ibid., 14:355-357; and to Nicholas Lewis, 16 December 1788, Ibid., 14:362-63.

101 Thomas Jefferson, "Answer to Additional Queries," [ca. Jan.-Feb., 1786], Ibid., 10:27. Jean Nicolas Démeunier had written a chapter on the United States for the revised *Encyclopédie Méthodique* and requested the American Minister answer several questions. He followed closely Jefferson *Notes on the State of Virginia* in the final edition.

102 Bear and Stanton, *JMB*, 1:730.

103 The religious manual was M. de La Forest, *Méthode d'Instruction pour ramener les Prétendum Réformés a l'Église Romaine* (A Lyon: chez Aimé de la Roche, 1784) recorded in Sowerby #1540.

104 Randolph, *Worthy Women,* 20.

105 *Thomas Jefferson's Granddaughter in Queeen Victoria's England: The Travel Diary of Ellen Wayles Coolidge, 1838–1839,* eds. Ann Lucas Birle and Lisa A. Francavilla (Boston and Charlottesville: Massachusetts Historical Society, Thomas Jefferson Foundation, 2011), 159.

106 Respectively, Bear & Stanton, *JMB,* 1:743; Nathaniel Cutting, "Extract from the Diary of Nathaniel Cutting at Le Havre and Cowes," [28 sep.–12 Oct. 1789], *Papers,* 15:490-499. Hereafter cited as Cutting, *Diary.* Captain Cutting was from Massachusetts but was engaged in the export/import business at Havré.

107 Cutting, *Diary,* 15:496-97, 98.

108 Ibid., 15:498.

109 Martha Jefferson Randolph, "Reminiscences of TH.J by MR," [ca. 1828–30], *Papers,* 15:560-61n.

110 Nathaniel Cutting to Martha Jefferson Randolph, 30 March 1790, Ibid., 16:207n.

Chapter 4: "Boys in tolerable order"

1 Thomas Jefferson to George Washington, Paris 4 [December] 1788, Ibid., 14:332; to Francis Eppes, Paris, 15 December 1788, Ibid., 357-59; to Elizabeth Wayles Eppes, Paris, 15 December 1788, Ibid., 355-56.

2 Thomas Jefferson, "Notes for an Autobiography, Monticello, January, 1821," *Jefferson's Letter's,* ed., Willson Whitman (Eau Claire, WI: E. M. Hale and Company, nd), 360. Hereafter, Willson, *Letters.*

3 Thomas Jefferson to James Monroe, Monticello, 20 May 1782, Ibid., 6:184 ff. While Martha lay "very dangerously ill," he was pressed by James Monroe and others to assume his seat in the House of Delegates and defend his performance as Governor during the British invasion of Virginia.

4 Martha Jefferson Randolph to Thomas Jefferson, 16 January 1791, Ibid., 18:499-500.

5 Thomas Jefferson, "Notes for an Autobiography, Monticello, January, 1821," Willson, *Letters*, 360.

6 Kathleen M. Brown, *Good Wives, Nasty Wenches & Anxious Patriarchs: Gender, Race, and Power in Colonial Virginia* (Chapel Hill, NC: University of North Carolina Press, 1996), 297; Elizabeth Fox-Genovese, *Household*, 116.

7 Thomas Jefferson to Martha Jefferson Randolph, New York, April 4, 1790, *Papers*, 16:300.

8 Thomas Mann Randolph to Martha Jefferson, Tuckahoe, 12 February 1785, Nicholas P. Trist Papers, accession #3470 (NcU), microfilm Southern Women and Their Families, Parts 4-6, reel 1, transcribed by author. Other correspondence between the two cousins during the 1785–89 period has not been found.

9 Thomas Jefferson to Thomas Mann Randolph, Jr., Paris, 25 November 1785, *Papers*, 9:591-92.

10 Thomas Jefferson to Thomas Mann Randolph, Jr., Paris, 27 August 1786, Ibid., 10:305-09.

11 Thomas Mann Randolph, Jr. to Thomas Jefferson, Edinburgh, 14 April 1787, Ibid., 11:291-93. Father's "impatience" was with Randolph's younger brother, William, who had neglected his studies, preferred social life, and run up substantial debts. Thomas took exception to this discipline and insisted on returning home with his brother. The Randolph family story is that their Varina plantation had been mortgaged to finance the two boy's education at Edinburgh. See below for how he framed his refusal to stay behind to his mother as wanting to avoid the appearance of "partiality."

12 Thomas Jefferson to Thomas Mann Randolph, Sr., Paris, 11 August 1787, Ibid., 12:20-23; to Thomas Mann Randolph, Jr., Paris, 6 July 1787, Ibid., 11:556-557.

13 Thomas Mann Randolph, Jr. to Anne Cary Randolph, Edinburgh, [17?], May 1788, Nicholas P. Trist Papers, accession #3470 (NcU), microfilm Southern Women and Their Families, Parts 4-6, reel 1, transcribed by the author.

14 On 20 December 1788, Jefferson indicated to Dr. James Currie: "I have not heard from young Mr. R. for more than a year which makes me suppose him returned to America" (*Papers*, 14:367).

15 Peter Carr to Thomas Jefferson, New York, 29 May 1789, *Papers*, 15:155-57. Carr was on vacation from William and Mary College reading under James Madison and "attending the debates of the two houses." This section and other information on the Randolph family, generally, are taken from William H. Gaines, Jr., *Thomas Mann Randolph, Jefferson's Son-in-Law* (Kingsport, TN: Louisiana State University Press, 1966), 29-24; hereafter cited as Gaines, *Randolph*; and Jonathan Daniels, *The Randolphs of Virginia: "America's Foremost Family"* (Garden City, NY: Doubleday & Company, Inc., 1972), passim; hereafter cited as Daniels, *Randolphs*.

16 Thomas Mann Randolph to Martha Jefferson, Tuckahoe, 12 February 1785, Nicholas P. Trist Papers, transcribed by author.

17 Thomas Mann Randolph to Anne Cary Randolph, Edinburgh, [17?], May 1788, Nicholas P. Trist Papers, transcribed by author.

18 Martha Jefferson Randolph to Thomas Jefferson, Richmond, 25 April 1790, *Papers*, 16:384-85

19 Thomas Mann Randolph, "Notebook," copy of ms in Thomas Jefferson Foundation, "Long Files/TMR Notebook"; original in Edgehill-Randolph Papers, Special Collections, Alderman Library, University of Virginia, Charlottesville, Virginia, 220. The poem by "D. Doddridge" has not been further identified.

20 Bear and Stanton, *JMB*, 1:747-49.

21 Thomas Jefferson to James Madison, Monticello, 14 February 1790, *Papers*, 16:182-83 refers to "Mr. Randolph whom you saw here." Near his death, Randolph noted

that he had been at Monticello in December 1789, which was just the time of the family's return from France on December 24th. Madison's visit was to determine whether Jefferson would accept appointment as Secretary of State. Thomas Jefferson to Anderson Bryan, Monticello, 6 January 1790, Ibid., 16:83-84 requested a copy of a survey of property "adjoining Edgehill."

[22] Thomas Jefferson to Madame de Corny, New York, 2 April 1790, Ibid., 16:289-90. Jefferson admitted to the unusual courtship but dissembled to his French friend: "[Y]et according to the usage of my country, I scrupulously suppressed my wishes, that my daughter might indulge her own sentiments freely." Perhaps, he doth protest too much.

[23] The details of this complex set of transactions between Wayles, his partners, the Bristol firm of Farell & Jones, the three executors of the Wayles' estate are discussed in *Papers*, 15: 642-77. It should be noted that the Jefferson and the others had chosen to make themselves personally liable for the estate's obligations by taking a distribution of assets before the will had been probated.

[24] Some of the family accounts are described in Thomas Jefferson to Charles Lilburne Lewis, 22 February 1790, *Papers*, 16:191-92; to Randolph Jefferson, Monticello, 28 February 1790, Ibid., 16:194-95; to John Bolling, Richmond, 6 March, 1790, Ibid., 16:207-08; and to Thomas Walker, Monticello, 25 January 1790, Ibid., 16:127-29. Lewis was the husband of Jefferson's sister, Lucy; Randolph was his brother; John Bolling was married to his sister Mary; and Thomas Walker was one executor/"guardian" of Peter Jefferson's estate. The payments in dispute date from 1766.

[25] Thomas Jefferson to James Madison, Paris, 29 August 1789, Ibid., 15:364-69.

[26] Thomas Jefferson to George Washington, Chesterfield [*sic*], 15 December 1789, Ibid., 16:34-35.

[27] Ibid.

[28] George Washington to Thomas Jefferson, New York, 21 January 1790, Ibid., 16:116-18; It was to James Monroe that Jefferson declared in 1782 that all he ever sought from public service was the "affection" of his countrymen (Thomas Jefferson to James Monroe, Monticello, 20 May 1782, Ibid., 6:184 ff).

[29] George Washington to Thomas Jefferson, New York, 13 October 1789, Ibid., 15: 519-20; Thomas Jefferson to George Washington, Monticello, 14 February 1790, Ibid., 16:184.

[30] Thomas Jefferson to James Madison, 14 February 1790, Ibid.,16:182-3. Such agreements were only valid if completed before marriage.

[31] Thomas Jefferson to Thomas Mann Randolph, Sr., Monticello, 4 February 1790, Ibid., 16:154-55; and to Thomas Mann Randolph, Jr., Monticello, 26 February 1795, Ibid., 28: 283.

[32] Thomas Jefferson to Martha Jefferson, Aix en Provence, 28 March 1787, *Papers*, 11:250-53; Toulon, 7 April 1787, Ibid., 277-78; and Languedoc, 21 May 1787, Ibid., 11:369-70.

[33] Respectively, Thomas Jefferson to Anne Willing Bingham, Paris, 7 February 1787, Ibid., 11:122-124; and to Bingham, Paris, 11 May 1788, Ibid., 13:151-52.

[34] Thomas Jefferson to Martha Jefferson Randolph, New York, 17 July 1790, *Papers*, 17:214-16.

[35] Thomas Jefferson to Martha Jefferson Randolph, Philadelphia, 8 May 1791, Ibid., 20:381-82.

[36] The extensive historical literature on the southern "household" seldom provides a succinct statement of how the term is construed. Daniel Blake Smith's pre-eminent work, *Inside the Great House: Planter Family Life in Eighteenth-Century Chesapeake Society* (Ithaca, NY: Cornell University Press, 1980), as the title implies, seemed to distinguish "family" and "house," but concentrates on the former. Contextually, however, his plantation gentry house[hold] of the late eighteenth century is described as having "open" boundaries, providing "economic and emotional support," and accommodating temporarily "kin and occasionally friends" (191). Given the focus on Carole Shammas' work on "household government," power relations (which she confuses with "authority") are the distinguishing features of "household" in *A History of Household Government in America* (Charlottesville, VA: University of Virginia Press, 2002). She delimits "household" to "those dependent on or subject to the authority of the same head" and co-resident (191, and i-iv). Elizabeth Fox-Genovese (*Within the Plantation Household: Black and White women of the Old South* [Chapel Hill, NC: The University of North Carolina Press, 1988]) describes plantation households as "the primary mediating units between the individual and society." Households are characterized by "pooled income and resources," a "division of domestic functions," and at least intermittent "co-residency" (83-93).

This project builds on this earlier research but adds slightly more form and considerable generalizability to the notion of "household." It considers the Jefferson-Randolph household as a site of production, reproduction, and consumption comprised of structures that mediated between the family as a social unit and individuals within it on one hand and society, the public sphere, and the state on the other. The Jeffersons' meaning of "family" is discussed extensively throughout this work, but here its important feature is determining membership on the basis of mutual affection. Friend Eliza House Trist was considered as much a part of their family as Aunt Marks, Jefferson's sister. This opens the boundaries of the familial social unit beyond consanguinity and concomitantly increases the number of potential household structures. For example, Monticello invoked its web of social and business connections to locate land for Mrs. Trist's son, Hore Browse Trist.

The concept of "structure" itself has a long history in anthropology and sociology, e.g., Claude Lévi-Strauss, *Structural Anthropology* (1963); Pierre Bourdieu, *Outline of a Theory of Practice* (1977); and Anthony Giddens, *The Constitution of Society: Outline of the Theory of Structuration* (1984). This project draws on William H. Sewell, Jr., "A Theory of Structure: Duality, Agency, and Transformation," *The American Journal of Sociology*, Vol. 98, No. 1 (July, 1992), who successfully, I believe, avoids the deterministic results of earlier writers. Following Sewell, "structure" as used herein is comprised of two elements—"schemas" and "resources"—which together constitute processes for carrying out social life. Examples of "schemas" include: conventions, rules-of-thumb, habits, manners, principles of action, metaphors, and assumptions about social and cultural phenomena. The notion of "resources" is construed broadly to include both material and non-material sources of power used in social interactions. The Family-of-Letters and Debt are structures in the Jefferson-Randolph household described in detail in this project. Another "schema" mentioned in passing was Jefferson's "assumption" that women did not engage in political activities which he deployed (unsuccessfully) to maintain social relations with his male political enemies. However mentioned in passing, other processes for mediating with the "world" beyond the family were just as vital to its existence: hospitality, travel logistics, technological adaptations on the farm, etc.

[37] Thomas Jefferson to Mary Jefferson, Lake George, New York, May 30, 1791, *Papers*, 20:462-63.

[38] Thomas Jefferson to Martha Jefferson Randolph, Philadelphia, January 15, 1792, Ibid., 23:44-45.

[39] Thomas Jefferson to Thomas Mann Randolph, New York, 7 July 1790, Ibid., 17:26.

[40] Thomas Jefferson to Martha Jefferson Randolph, Philadelphia, 26 April 1790, Ibid., 16:386-87.

[41] Thomas Jefferson to Maria Cosway, Paris, 12 October 1786, Ibid., 10:443-51

[42] Thomas Jefferson to Martha Jefferson Randolph, Philadelphia, December 1, 1790, Ibid., 18:110-11.

[43] Thomas Jefferson to Martha Jefferson Randolph, Philadelphia, December 23, 1790, Ibid., 18:350.

[44] Thomas Jefferson to Martha Jefferson Randolph, Philadelphia, February 2, 1791, Ibid., 19:239.

[45] Thomas Jefferson to Mary Jefferson, Philadelphia, January 5, 1791, Ibid., 18:476-77.

[46] Thomas Jefferson to Maria Jefferson, Philadelphia, 5 January 1791, Ibid., 18:476-77; 13 June 1790, Ibid., 16:491-92; and 25 July 1790, Ibid., 17:271-72.

[47] Respectively, Martha Jefferson Randolph to Thomas Jefferson, Monticello, 25 April 1790, Ibid., 384-85; Thomas Jefferson to Martha Jefferson Randolph, 4 April 1790, Ibid., 300; Mary Jefferson to Thomas Jefferson, 13 February 1791, Ibid., 19:271; and Thomas Jefferson to Thomas Mann Randolph, Jr., Philadelphia, 30 May 1790, Ibid., 16:448-50.

[48] Respectively, Martha Jefferson Randolph to Thomas Jefferson, Richmond, 25 April 1790, Ibid., 16:384-85; Thomas Jefferson to Martha Jefferson Randolph, New York, 27 June 1790, Ibid., 16:577-78; Thomas Mann Randolph to Thomas Jefferson, Richmond, 25 May 1790, Ibid., 16:441-42; Martha Jefferson Randolph to Thomas Jefferson, Monticello, 16 January 1791, Ibid., 18:499-500; Thomas Mann Randolph to Thomas Jefferson, Monticello, 14 March 1791, Ibid., 19:555-56, and 30 April 1791, 20:327-29.

[49] Respectively, Thomas Jefferson to Thomas Mann Randolph, Jr., Philadelphia, 17 July 1791, Ibid., 20:640-41 and 1 January 1792, Ibid., 23:7-8. Responsibility for the post was lodged in the Treasury Department headed by Jeffeson's political adversary, Secretary Alexander Hamilton.

[50] Thomas Jefferson to Martha Jefferson Randolph, Philadelphia, 25 December 1791, Ibid., 22:446. The Randolph's first child was born 23 January 1791.

[51] Thomas Jefferson to Martha Jefferson Randolph, 23 December 1790, Ibid., 18:350.

[52] Respectively, Martha Jefferson Randolph to Thomas Jefferson, Richmond, 25 April 1790, Ibid., 18:385-85; Thomas Jefferson to Maria Jefferson, New York, 11 April 1790, Ibid., 16: 331-32; Thomas Jefferson to Martha Jefferson Randolph, Philadelphia, 27 April 1792, Ibid., 23:466-67; Martha Jefferson Randolph to Thomas Jefferson, Monticello, 7 May 1792, Ibid., 23:486-87; Thomas Jefferson to Martha Jefferson Randolph, Philadelphia, 26 January 1793, Ibid., 25:97-98; and Martha Jefferson Randolph to Thomas Jefferson, Monticello, 16 May 1793, Ibid., 26:53-54.

[53] Thomas Mann Randolph to Thomas Jefferson, Monticello, 2 February 1791, Ibid., 19: 239-40.

Chapter 5: "Much adverse to it"

[1] Thomas Jefferson to Thomas Mann Randolph, New York, 30 May 1790, *Papers*, 16:448-50.

[2] Thomas Jefferson to Thomas Mann Randolph, Philadelphia, 24 February 1791, Ibid., 19:328-31; 6 April 1791, Ibid., 20:160-61; 15 May 1791, Ibid., 20:414-16; and 12 April 1792, Ibid., 23:411 and Thomas Mann Randolph to Thomas Jefferson, Monticello 14 March 1791, Ibid., 19:555-56, and 30 April 1791, Ibid., 20:327-29. Jefferson was referring to the American Philosophical Society to which Randolph was subsequently elected, not for a study of marsupials but his work on the moulboard plow.

[3] Thomas Mann Randolph, Jr., to TJ, Monticello, 30 April 1791, Ibid., 20:327-29 and 4 June 1792, Monticello, Ibid., 24:33-34

[4] Martha Jefferson Randolph to Thomas Jefferson, 25 April 1790, Ibid., 16:384-85.

[5] Thomas Jefferson to Martha Jefferson Randolph, New York, 26 April 1790, Ibid., 16:386-87.

[6] Thomas Jefferson to Anderson Bryan, Monticello, 6 January 1790, Ibid., 16:83-84.

[7] The Marks-Harvie-Jefferson-Randolph families intertwined as follows: James Marks (1745–1816) married Elizabeth Harvie, sister of John Harvie, Jr. (1747–1807); Jefferson's sister Lucy married Hastings Marks, a relative of James; John Harvie's daughter, Gabriella (1772–97) married in late 1790 Thomas Mann Randolph, Sr., who was then age 50, and gave birth to a child they named Thomas Mann Randolph III.

[8] Anderson Bryan to Thomas Jefferson, 10 January 1790, *Papers*, 16:93.

[9] Marriage Settlement for Martha Jefferson, 21 February 1790, *Papers*, 16:189-91.

[10] Thomas Jefferson to Thomas Mann Randolph, Sr., Monticello, 4 February 1790, *Papers*, 16:154-55; and Thomas Mann Randolph, Sr. to Thomas Jefferson, 15 February 1790, Ibid., 27:776-77.

[11] Thomas Jefferson to John Harvie, Jr., Monticello, 11 January 1790, Ibid., 17:97-100; John Harvie, Jr., to Thomas Jefferson, Richmond, 2 February 1790, Ibid.,17:136-37; Thomas Jefferson to John Harvie, Jr., Monticello, 2 November 1790, Ibid., 17:660-63; Thomas Jefferson to John Harvie, Jr., Monticello, 2 November 1790, Ibid., 17:660-63; John Harvie, Jr., to Thomas Jefferson, Richmond, 25 January 1791, Ibid., 19:74-76; Thomas Jefferson to John Harvie, Jr., Philadelphia, 7 April 1791, 20:162-65; "Memorandum on Land Dispute with John Harvie, Jr., [after 12 February 1790], 27:773-74; and Thomas Jefferson to John Harvie, Monticello, 28 December 1809, *Papers, RS*, 2:101-103.

[12] George Gilmer to Thomas Jefferson, Charlottesville, 13 April 1781, Ibid., 5:430-431.

[13] Bryton Merrill, Jr., *Jefferson's Nephews: A Frontier Tragedy* (Lexington, KY: University of Kentucky Press, 1987, 2nd edition), 23. Another truly family "affair" may have been operating in the Governor's unprecedented action of rejecting promotion of Thomas Walker, Jr. During the election of 1800, a newspaper alleged Jefferson had fathered children by his slave, Sally Hemings and had had an affair in 1769 with his friend's wife, Mrs. John Walker (Elizabeth "Betsey" Moore). John and Tom were sons of Dr. Thomas Walker, Sr., who had been one of Jefferson's guardians on the death of Peter Jefferson. President Jefferson never answered the first accusation regarding Hemings, but in 1805 he acknowledged privately: "I plead guilty to one of their charges, that when young and single I offered love to a handsome lady, I acknowledge it's incorrectness" (Dumas Malone, *Jefferson the Virginian* [Boston: Little, Brown and Company, 1948], 153-55).

¹⁴ Thomas Jefferson to John Harvie, Jr., Monticello, 11 January 1790, *Papers,* 16:97-100. Harvie was a Richmond lawyer, builder, and from 1780–91 Register of the Virginia Land Office and well versed in property law. His daughter, Gabriella, married Thomas Mann Randolph, Sr. in November 1790; and his father, John Harvie, had been appointed one of Jefferson's guardians in Peter Jefferson's will.

¹⁵ John Harvie, Jr., to Thomas Jefferson, Richmond, 2 February 1790, *Papers,* 16:136-37.

¹⁶ Thomas Mann Randolph, Sr. to Thomas Jefferson, 30 January 1790, Ibid., 16:135. Received 4 February 1790.

¹⁷ Thomas Mann Randolph, Jr., to Thomas Jefferson, Richmond, 25 May 1790, Ibid., 16:441-41.

¹⁸ Thomas Jefferson to Thomas Mann Randolph, Sr., Monticello, 4 February, 1790, Ibid., 16:154-55. Interestingly, a copy of this letter includes on its reverse a sketch of the tracts in dispute with Harvie (155n). This suggests Jefferson was already considering an Edgehill home, despite being "perfectly contented to leave to [TMR, Sr.] the provision for [his] son" (16:154).

¹⁹ Respectively, Thomas Jefferson to Martha Jefferson, New York, 6 June and 27 June, and 17 July 1790, Ibid., 16:474-45, 577-78, and 17:214-16. Almost four decades separated the ages of the newlyweds and two of Gabriella Harvie's Randolph stepdaughters (Judy and Anne Cary) were only two and four years her junior, respectively.

²⁰ Thomas Jefferson to Nathaniel Burwell, Monticello, 14 March 1818, Ford, *Works,* 12:93-94.

²¹ Thomas Jefferson to Martha Jefferson, Toulon, 7 April 1787, *Papers,* 11:277-78 and to Peter Carr, Paris, 6 August 1788, Ibid., 13: 470-71.

²² Thomas Jefferson to Francis Wayles Eppes, Monticello, 21 May 1816, Betts and Bear, *JFL,* 414-15. For women's contribution to garnering social esteem, see Cynthia A. Kierner, "Hospitality, Sociability, and Gender in the Southern Colonies," *The Journal of Southern History,* 62, no. 3 (1996), 449-80, passim, http://www.jstor.org/ (March 31, 2005).

²³ Thomas Jefferson to Martha Jefferson Randolph, New York, 17 July 1790, *Papers,* 16:214-216.

²⁴ Thomas Jefferson to Elizabeth Wayles Eppes, New York, 25 July 1790, Ibid., 17:265-66.

²⁵ Thomas Jefferson to Thomas Mann Randolph, Jr., New York, 25 July 1790, Ibid., 17:274.

²⁶ Thomas Jefferson to Thomas Mann Randolph, Sr., New York, 25 July 1790, Ibid., 17:274-76.

²⁷ Thomas Jefferson to Nathaniel Anderson, New York, 25 July 1790, Ibid., 17:262-63.

²⁸ Thomas Jefferson to John Harvie, New York, 25 July 1790, Ibid., 17:270-71.

²⁹ Thomas Jefferson, "Opinion on McGillivray's Monopoly of Commerce with Creek Indians, July 29, 1790, *Papers,* 7:288-89. His father, John Harvie, Sr. (1706–67) had been a commissioner with Dr. Thomas Walker, Sr. and Jasper Yates in 1776 to negotiate with Indians at the troubled Fort Pitt (Allen Johnson and Dumas Malone, eds. *Dictionary of American Biography,* [New York: Scribner's, 1931], vol. IV, 375.).

³⁰ John Harvie to Thomas Jefferson, Richmond, 3 August 1790, Ibid., 16:296.

³¹ Thomas Jefferson to Francis Eppes, Monticello, 8 October 1790, Ibid., 17:581-82.

³² Thomas Jefferson to Thomas Mann Randolph, Jr., Monticello, 22 October 1790, Ibid., 17:622.

[33] Ibid., 17:623-24. In fact, the final deed to Randolph, Jr. was for 1152 ½ acres with the residual of the 2400 acres sold to John Harvie, Jr. on 1 January 1792, two months after this letter and two months before the date on the Edgehill deed to the son (Betts and Bear, *JFL*, 55n).

[34] Respectively, Thomas Jefferson to John Harvie, Jr., Monticello, 2 November 1790, and John Harvie, Jr. to Thomas Jefferson, Richmond, 25 January 1791, *Papers*, 17:660-63 and 19:74-76.

[35] Thomas Jefferson to Elizabeth Wayles Eppes, New York, 7 March 1790, Ibid. 16:208-09.

[36] Thomas Jefferson to Mary Jefferson, New York, 11 April 1790, Ibid., 331-32.

[37] Kathleen M. Brown, *Good Wives, Nasty Wenches & Anxious Patriarchs: Gender, Race, and Power in Colonial Virginia* (Chapel Hill, NC: University of North Carolina Press, 1996), 297.

[38] *Life, Letters, and Journals of George Ticknor*, 2 vols., eds. G. S. Hilliard and Anna Eliot Ticknor (Boston: Houghton Mifflin, 1909), 1:36 as cited in James L. and Alan L. Golden, *Thomas Jefferson and the Rhetoric of Virtue* (Lanham, MD: Rowman & Littlefield Publishers, Inc.), 117.

[39] Respectively, Thomas Mann Randolph to Thomas Jefferson, Monticello, 7 July 1791, *Papers*, 20:605-07; Martha Jefferson Randolph to Thomas Jefferson, Monticello, 16 May 1793, Ibid., 26:53-54; and Thomas Jefferson to Thomas Mann Randolph, Thomas Jefferson to Thomas Mann Randolph, Jr., Philadelphia, 30 march 1792, Ibid., 23:355.

[40] Respectively, Thomas Jefferson to Martha Jefferson Randolph, Philadelphia, 13 December 1792, Ibid., 24:740-41; and Thomas Jefferson to Thomas Mann Randolph, Jr., 28 July 1793, Ibid., 26:576-78.

[41] Respectively, Martha Jefferson Randolph to Thomas Jefferson, Monticello, 22 March 1791, Ibid., 19:598-99; and Thomas Jefferson to Martha Jefferson Randolph, Philadelphia, 17 April 1791, Ibid., 20:236-37.

[42] Respectively, Thomas Jefferson to Thomas Mann Randolph, Jr., New York, 28 August 1790, Ibid., 17:473-74; to Martha Jefferson Randolph, New York, 23 December 1790, Ibid., 18:350; and Martha Jefferson Randolph to Thomas Jefferson, 16 January 1791, Ibid., 18:499-500.

[43] Thomas Jefferson to Martha Jefferson Randolph, Philadelphia, 8 May 1791, Ibid., 20:381-82.

[44] Ibid.

[45] Thomas Jefferson to Martha Jefferson Randolph, Philadelphia, 2 February 1791, Ibid., 19:239.

[46] Thomas Jefferson to Martha Jefferson Randolph, Philadelphia, 9 February 1791, Ibid., 19:264.

[47] Martha Jefferson Randolph to Thomas Jefferson, Monticello, March 22, 1791, Ibid., 19:598-99.

[48] Respectively, Martha Jefferson Randolph to Thomas Jefferson, Monticello, 22 March and 23 May 1791, Ibid., 19:598-99 and 20:477.

[49] John Harvie to Thomas Jefferson, Richmond, 25 January 1791, Ibid., 19:74-6.

[50] Thomas Mann Randolph, Jr. to Thomas Jefferson, Monticello, 5 March 1791, Ibid., 19:420.Thomas Jefferson to Thomas Mann Randolph, Jr., Philadelphia, 6 April 1791, Ibid., 20:160-61. Despite Harvie's claim the parcel had "very little Value" for farming, Jefferson assured his son-in-law it was "a valuable tract and a cheap one."

[51] Thomas Mann Randolph, Jr. to Thomas Jefferson, Tuckaho', 22 August 1791, Ibid., 22:60.

[52] Thomas Jefferson to Philip Mazzei, Philadelphia, 7 January 1792, Ibid., 23:29. Seven letters were exchanged among the Jefferson family without a dot or tittle regarding the property until Jefferson received Martha's on March 1st (*Papers*, 23:125-26).

[53] Thomas Jefferson to Martha Jefferson Randolph, Philadelphia, 15 January 1792, Ibid., 23:44.

[54] Thomas Mann Randolph, Jr. to Thomas Jefferson, Monticello, 16 April 1792, Ibid., 23:429.

[55] Martha Jefferson to Thomas Jefferson, Monticello, 27 May 1792, Ibid., 23:546-47. The bride, Mildred Hornsby, was granddaughter of Jefferson's former guardian, Dr. Thomas Walker, as well as first cousin to her new husband, Nicholas Meriwether Lewis (Anna Robinson Watson, *Some Notable Families of America* [New York, n.p.,1898], 92, http://books.google.com/books [July 26, 2009]). The groom's father, Nicholas Lewis, had managed Monticello during Jefferson's absence.

[56] Martha Jefferson to Thomas Jefferson, Monticello, 2 July 1792, Ibid., 23:147-48.

Chapter 6: "Blush for so near a connection"

[1]Cathleen B. Hellier, "The Adolescence of Gentry Girls in Late Eighteenth-Century Virginia," http://research.history.org (October 27, 2008).

[2] Lucinda Lee Orr, *Journal of a Young Lady of Virginia, 1782* (Baltimore, 1871: John Murphy and Company for the Lee Memorial Association of Richmond), http://www.gutenberg.org/ (November 30, 2007). Lucinda was of the Stratford Lees and the two unwelcome beaus were married to her relatives.

[3] Thomas Mann Randolph to Thomas Jefferson, Bizarre, 1 February 1792, *Papers*, 23:95; Martha Jefferson to Thomas Jefferson, Monticello, 20 February 1792, Ibid., 23:125-26.

[4] Thomas Jefferson to Thomas Mann Randolph, Philadelphia, 18 December 1791, Ibid., 22:418-20. Richard Randolph had married Mann's sister, Judith, and assumed informal guardianship of her younger sister, Ann Cary ("Nancy").
A complete Randolph genealogy can barely be described by a family tree, but briefly the actors in this saga included the following: Anne or Nancy (1774–1836) and Judith (1772–1816) of "Tuckahoe" were cousins of Martha as well as sisters of her husband. While traveling home from Norfolk in 1789, Martha likely attended the wedding of Judith to her cousin Richard Randolph (1770–1796) of "Curles," whose widowed mother had married St. George Tucker. Anne at age sixteen left Tuckahoe in 1790 to live with Richard and Judith at "Bizarre" after the "link of love" was broken with her eighteen-year-old step-mother, Gabriella Harvie Randolph. Also, by her own account, she left "to avoid a Marriage hateful to me." Her father was pressing for a marriage to anyone well-situated financially; candidates were cousin Archibald Randolph and much older widowers Henry Lee or Benjamin Harrison (Anne Cary Randolph Morris to St. George Tucker, 2 March 1815, Tucker-Coleman Papers [Vi-W] as cited in Kierner, *Scandal*, 29). This also was the period Randolph Senior was resisting sale of Edgehill to Randolph Junior, in part, because he needed to raise the marriage "portions" for his youngest daughters (Thomas Jefferson to Thomas Mann Randolph, Sr., New York, 25 July 1790, *Papers*, 17:274-76). Richard's brother, John ("Jack") Randolph of Roanoke (1773–1833), would figure prominently in the story some twenty years later in 1814 when he re-opened the infanticide issue with Anne's then husband Gouverneur Morris of New York. She responded with an acerbic and craftily

written circular letter to Virginians that reignited public interest and bewilderment in the "Bizarre scandal" of a First Family of Virginia.

[5] Thomas Jefferson to Martha Jefferson Randolph, Philadelphia, 25 December 1791, *Papers*, 446. The Randolph's wrote just as they left Monticello on 28 November 1791, but this letter was not received by Jefferson until 22 January 1792. Martha's father chastened her that he and Maria had not received a letter covering the seven weeks prior to 28 November.

[6] Maria Jefferson to Thomas Mann Randolph, Philadelphia, 12 December 1791 and 29 January 1792, Papers of Thomas Jefferson (DLC), Series 1, reel 15, documents 11872 and 12168, respectively, transcribed by author. Perhaps Jefferson's earlier experience with Martha's tutors inclined him to try a different approach with Mary Pine's (Mrs. Robert Edge) boarding school near his residence/office. She was taught the feminine ornaments (drawing, dancing, needlework, music, French) and the "usual subjects" (Bear and Stanton, *JMB*, 2:837n 21).

[7] Thomas Jefferson to Thomas Mann Randolph, Philadelphia, 25 October and to Martha Jefferson Randolph, 13 November 1791, *Papers*, 22: 233 and 294, respectively. Eleanor Parke Custis (1779–1852) was the granddaughter of Martha Washington.

[8] Thomas Jefferson to Thomas Mann Randolph, Philadelphia, 1 January 1792, Ibid., 23:7-8.

[9] Thomas Jefferson to Martha Jefferson Randolph, 15 January 1792, Philadelphia, Ibid., 23:44-45.

[10] Theodorick (1771–1792), brother of Richard and John Randolph, died 14 February 1792, just after the Monticello Randolphs left Bizarre, sometime after 1 February.

[11] Thomas Mann Randolph to Thomas Jefferson, Bizarre, 1 February 1792, and Monticello, 17 February 1792, *Papers*, 23:95 and 121-22.

[12] Martha Jefferson Randolph to Thomas Jefferson, Monticello, 20 February 1792, Ibid., 23:125-26.

[13] As discussed below, John Marshall's notes of Martha's testimony in *Commonwealth vs. Randolph* indicate that she was with "Mrs. Richard Randolph [Judith], in the presence of Miss Nancy" (Anne Cary) on "12th September" 1792 on the same day Jeff Randolph was born (Bear and Stanton, *JMB*, 2:878).

[14] Thomas Mann Randolph to Thomas Jefferson, Monticello, 22 October 1792, *Papers*, 24:512-13. Jane and Peter Carr, children of Jefferson's sister Martha and the deceased Dabney Carr, were living at Monticello at this time. (Thomas Jefferson to Thomas Mann Randolph, Philadelphia, 12 October 1792, *Papers*, 24:474n.) Anne had been ill since sometime in late summer or early fall. A recurrence in early October was described as "want of appetite, and excessive thirst…frequent vomitings and a much lower pulse…" Grand Papa recommended to Martha a "good breast of milk…[but] some other than your own" (Thomas Mann Randolph to Thomas Jefferson, Monticello, 7 October 1792, *Papers*, 24:448-49; and Thomas Jefferson to Martha Jefferson, Philadelphia, 26 October 1792, Ibid., 24:534-35).

[15] Material for this section is drawn from the following sources: Cynthia Kierner, *Scandal at Bizarre: Rumor and Reputation in Jefferson's America* (New York: Palgrave Macmillan, 2004); Alan Pell Crawford, *Unwise Passions: A True Story of a Remarkable Woman and the First Great Scandal of Eighteenth-Century America* (New York: Simon & Schuster, 2000); Christopher L. Doyle, "The Randolph Scandal in Early National Virginia: New Voices in the 'Court of Honor', *Journal of Southern History*, 69 (2003), 283-319; *The Papers of John Marshall*, eds. Charles T. Cullen, Herbert A. Johnson, et al. (Chapel Hill, NC: The University of North Carolina Press for The Institute of Early American History and Culture, 1977), 2:161-178; John Randolph to Ann Randolph Morris, 31 October 1814 and Ann Randolph Morris to John Randolph, 16 January

1815 both available from Thomas Jefferson Foundation, Family Letters Project, http://familyletters.dataformat.com. The ambiguous provenance of even Marshall's "Notes of Evidence" is discussed in an editorial note in Cullen and Johnson, *Marshall*, 161-68.

[16] Mrs. Randolph Harrison in John Marshall "Notes on Evidence," *Marshall Papers*, 171-72. Subsequent citations of her testimony are contained on these same pages. "Gum guiacum" (guaiacum) was a tincture used to treat a variety of disorders (gout, ovaritis, rheumatism, colic, etc.), but was considered by some (including Martha Jefferson Randolph) to induce abortion.

[17] Archibald Randolph, a suitor approved by Nancy's father but spurned by her, was among those citing this odiferous evidence and compounded suspicions of Richard's complicity by noting for "about eighteen months past" he thought that "Mr. Randolph & Miss Nancy were too fond of each other" (Archibald Randolph, *Marshall Papers* , 173). An uncle, also, remembered seeing them "kissing and fond of each other" (Carter Page, Ibid., 168).

[18] Richard Randolph, "To the Public, Mar. 29, 1793," *Virginia Gazette & General Advertiser*, April 3, 1793, as cited in Cullen & Johnson, "Editorial Note," *Marshall Papers*, 163. The Tuckahoe Randolphs, especially William, openly blamed Richard for Nancy's "disgrace" and failure to protect a female under his care. Randolph Senior rebuffed Richard's appeal to bring charges of slander against his own son, who compounded the insult by refusing to even answer his cousin's demand for "satisfaction" (Kierner, *Scandal*, 39-40).

[19] Martha Jefferson Randolph to Thomas Jefferson, Bizarre, 18 November 1792, *Papers*, 24:634.

[20] John Marshall, "Notes of Evidence, Mrs. Martha Randolph," *Marshall Papers*, 168-69. If the date is accurate then the Bizarre sisters may have been attending Martha in the birth of Thomas Jefferson Randolph. Mrs. Carter Page, an aunt, would later offer the most damaging testimony against Richard and Nancy.

[21] James Monroe to Thomas Jefferson, Fredericksburgh, 9 May 1793, *Papers*, 25:696-98.

[22] John Wayles Eppes to Thomas Jefferson, Eppington, 1 May 1793, Ibid., 25:632-33.

[23] Ibid.

[24] Martha Jefferson Randolph to Thomas Jefferson, Monticello, 16 May 1793, Ibid., 26:53-54

[25] Thomas Jefferson to Martha Jefferson, Philadelphia, 28 April 1793, Ibid., 25:621-22.

[26] Martha Jefferson Randolph to Thomas Jefferson, Monticello, 16 May 1793, Ibid., 26:53-54.

[27] St. George Tucker, "To the Public, May 5, 1793," *Virginia Gazette & General Advertiser,* May 15, 1793, as cited in Cullen and Johnson, "Editorial Note," *Marshall Papers*, 167.

[28] Thomas Mann Randolph to Thomas Jefferson, Monticello, 8 May 1793, *Papers*, 25:693

[29] Thomas Jefferson to Martha Jefferson Randolph, Philadelphia, 15 January 1792, Ibid., 23:44-45. Thomas Jefferson to Philip Mazzei, Philadelphia, 7 January 1792, Ibid., 23:29: "He [Randolph] has bought Edgehill of his father and will settle on it."

[30] Thomas Mann Randolph to Thomas Jefferson, Monticello, 18 March 1792, Ibid., 23:294-95.

[31] Thomas Jefferson to Thomas Mann Randolph, Philadelphia, 12 October 1792, Ibid., 24:473-74.

[32] Thomas Mann Randolph to Thomas Jefferson, Monticello, 22 October 1792, Ibid., 25:512-13.

[33] Thomas Jefferson to Martha Jefferson Randolph, Philadelphia, 12 May 1793, Ibid., 26:18-20. His first grandson, Thomas Jefferson Randolph, was born at Monticello on 12 September 1792 with a Mrs. Mary (Polly) Sneed attending as midwife. (Bear and Stanton, *JMB* 2: 878 n94.)

[34] Thomas Mann Randolph to Thomas Jefferson, 7 February 1793, *Papers*, 25:156-57. Jefferson's instructions for "scantling" (rafters, joists, etc.) were very detailed. In addition to dimensions, they prescribed the type of trees to be used, how they were to be sawed, and when the logs were to be carried to the saw pit. (TJ/TMR, Philadelphia, 21 January 1793, Ibid., 25:72-3)

[35] Thomas Jefferson to Martha Jefferson Randolph, 9 February 1791, Ibid., 19:264. The occasion was the birth of Anne Cary on 23 January 1791. The father had written: "The Father and Mother are anxious to know when she will have the honor of kissing her Grandpapas hand." She was attended by Mrs. Nicholas Lewis whose presence "made some amends for the want of [Randolph's] Sympathy" from being away from Monticello (Thomas Mann Randolph to Thomas Jefferson, Monticello, 2 February 1791, *Papers*, 19:239-40).

[36] Martha Jefferson Randolph to Thomas Jefferson, Monticello, 26 June 1793, Ibid. 26:380-81.

[37] Thomas Jefferson to James Monroe, Monticello, 20 May 1782, Ibid. 6:184 ff.

[38] Thomas Jefferson to Martha Jefferson, Aix en Provence, 28 March 1787, Ibid., 11:250-53.

[39] Thomas Jefferson to Martha Jefferson Randolph, Philadelphia, 26 January 1793, Ibid., 25:97-98. Republicans in the House of Representatives had introduced resolutions of censure regarding Alexander Hamilton's administration of the Treasury Department. All were soundly defeated by the large Federalist majority. The best evidence suggests Jefferson was in some way a party to the intrigue, perhaps even drafting the measures introduced by Virginia Congressman William Branch Giles. For a discussion of his efforts to counter Hamilton's fiscal policies and material support of the U. S. Bank from late 1792 through March 1793, see "Jefferson's Questions and Observations on the Application of France" and "Jefferson and the Giles Resolutions," *Papers*, 25:172-182 and 280-296, respectively. The canal being constructed on the Rivanna River was to serve Jefferson's "toll" or grist mill, a commercial enterprise. See *Thomas Jefferson's Farm Book*, ed. Edwin Morris Betts (Charlottesville, VA: University Press of Virginia, 1987), 341-44.

[40] Martha Jefferson Randolph to Thomas Jefferson, Monticello, 27 February 1793, *Papers*, 25:297.

[41] Thomas Jefferson to Thomas Mann Randolph, Philadelphia, 3 February 1793, Ibid., 25:137-39.

[42] Thomas Mann Randolph to Thomas Jefferson, Monticello, 20 February 1793, Ibid., 25:245-46.

[43] Thomas Jefferson to Thomas Mann Randolph, Philadelphia, 19 May 1793, Ibid., 26:64-66.

[44] Thomas Jefferson to George Washington, Monticello, 14 May 1794, Ibid., 28:74-75.

[45] Thomas Jefferson to James Madison, Monticello, 15 May 1794, Ibid., 28:75-76.

[46] Thomas Mann Randolph, Jr., to Thomas Jefferson, Monticello, 8 May 1793, Ibid., 25:693.

[47] Thomas Jefferson to Thomas Mann Randolph, Jr., Philadelphia, 19 May 1793, Ibid., 24:64-66. "Notes on Potash and Pearl Ash" (*Papers*, 28:271-72) contains Jefferson's

calculations on the profitability of a potash manufacturing business that in 1795 he was trying to persuade Staunton merchant Archibald Stuart to initiate.

[48] Bear and Stanton, *JMB*, 2:913-20. Jefferson planned to rent all Shadwell acreage across the Rivanna to Maryland farmers whom he considered more capable of growing wheat and grazing cattle as a way of reducing tobacco acreage and the family's dependence on foreign commodity markets. The addition of a grist mill (also to be rented) combined with wheat production had the advantage of supplying flour to both domestic and foreign markets. See Thomas Jefferson to Thomas Mann Randolph, Philadelphia, 18 February 1793, *Papers* 25:230; 3 March 1793, Ibid., 25:313-14; 19 May 1793, 16:64-66; and 8 December 1793, 27:496-97.

[49] Thomas Jefferson to Thomas Mann Randolph, Monticello, 14 July 1794, *Papers*, 28:104. See Gaines, *Randolph*, 39.

[50] Thomas Jefferson to Thomas Mann Randolph, Monticello, 7 August 1794, Ibid., 28:111-12.

[51] Thomas Jefferson to Thomas Mann Randolph, Monticello, 27 October 1794, Ibid., 28:182. This was the "first" Ellen Wayles, who was born 30 August 1794 and died 26 July 1795 in Staunton, Virginia, as her mother and father were traveling for his health to the "Sweet Springs" in what is now Monroe County WV(*Papers* 28:439 n).

[52] Thomas Jefferson to Thomas Mann Randolph, Monticello, 27 October 1794, Ibid., 28:182; 26 December 1794, Ibid., 225-227; and 8 January 1795, Ibid., 242.

[53] Martha Jefferson Randolph to Thomas Jefferson, Varina, 15 January 1795, Ibid., 28:246-47

[54] Thomas Jefferson to Thomas Mann Randolph, Monticello, 5 February 1795, Ibid., 28:260-61.

[55] Bear and Stanton, *JMB*, 2:928 & 930. On 14 May 1795, Jefferson gave "TMRandolph 18.92 D." in cash; and on 25 July he received from Staunton merchant Archibald Stuart "TMRandolph's order...for 120.D."

[56] Thomas Jefferson to Thomas Mann Randolph, Monticello, 26 July 1795, *Papers*, 28:419. The sisters were Mary Bolling (Mrs. John), Martha Carr (Mrs. Dabney), and Anna Scott Marks (Mrs. Hastings).

[57]*Papers*, 28:419n. A letter from Randolph to Jefferson written at Staunton on 23 July 1795 and received 25 July, which may have included information on the child's death, has not been found. This is one of the very rare instances in which Jefferson closed a letter to his family with "God bless..."He recorded in the Memorandum Book on 26 July: "Pd. a man sent by A [Archibald] Stuart from Staunton with the body of our dear little Eleonor 6.D." (Bear and Stanton, *JMB*, 2:930 and n35.)

[58] Thomas Jefferson to Martha Jefferson Randolph, Monticello, 31 July 1795, Ibid., 28:429; and to Thomas Mann Randolph, 11 August 1795, Ibid., 28:434-35.

[59] Most of the letters from Randolph for this period have not been found, nor have many from similar periods of family distress resulting from his behavior.

[60] Thomas Jefferson to James Madison, Monticello, 27 April 1795, *Papers*, 28:338-40. A description of Jefferson's ostensive "silence" in the face of others promoting his candidacy is presented in Malone, *Jefferson and the Ordeal of Liberty* (Boston: Little, Brown and Company, 1962), 273-294. The seeds of raucous partisan politics were planted in the Jay Treaty ratification that Hamilton (nominally "federalist") supported and Madison (nominally "republican") opposed. Nascent parties emerged during the election of 1796 with "federalists" generally arrayed around John Adams (71 electoral votes) and Thomas Pinckney (55); "republicans," around Jefferson (68) and Burr (30). Thus, the top vote-getters created a mixed "party" government of President Adams

and Vice President Jefferson. Though silent, Jefferson contributed mightily to the schismatic debates with a letter to Philip Mazzei on 24 April 1796 that was interpreted as critical of George Washington personally and was published in Italian, French, and American newspapers. He wrote: "In the place of that noble love of liberty and republican government which carried us triumphantly thro' the war, an Anglican, monarchial and aristocratical party has sprung up, whose avowed object is to draw over us the substance as they have already done the forms of the British government....It would give you a fever were I to name to you the apostates who have gone over to these heresies, men who were Samsons in the field and Solomons in the council, but who have had their heads shorn by the harlot England" (*Papers*, 29:73-88).

[61] Thomas Jefferson to Philip Mazzei, Monticello, 30 May 1795, Ibid., 28:368-71.

[62] Thomas Jefferson to Eliza House Trist, Monticello, 23 Sept. 1795, Ibid., 28:478-79. On 21 September 1795, Jefferson wrote to Madison: "Mr. Randolph and my daughter will be back from the springs in the ensuing week. He is almost entirely recovered by the use of the sweet springs" (*Papers*, 28:475-77).

[63] Thomas Jefferson to Wilson Cary Nicholas, Monticello 19 October 1795, Ibid., 28:512.

[64] John Wayles Eppes to Thomas Jefferson, Monticello, 25 September 1796, Ibid., 29:186. Jefferson's responses to this letter and several others between them during this period have not been found.

[65] John Wayles Eppes to Thomas Jefferson, 19 December 1796, Ibid., 29:226

[66] They were married on 13 October 1797 at Monticello. "Marriage Settlement for John Wayles Eppes" and "Marriage Settlement for Mary Jefferson," Ibid., 29:547-50. Her husband's share was 750 acres at "Bermuda Hundred" in Chesterfield County, southeast of Richmond, and a small worthless tract of about 130 acres called "Martin's swamp."

[67] Thomas Jefferson to Thomas Mann Randolph, Monticello, 18 January 1796, Ibid., 28:592-93.

[68] Martha Jefferson Randolph to Thomas Jefferson, 1 January 1796, Ibid., 28:569. Jeff Randolph, just over three years old, remained at Monticello.

[69] Thomas Jefferson to Francis Eppes, Monticello, 4 August 1796, Ibid., 29:166-67.

[70] Documents Relating to the 1796 Campaign for Electors in Virginia, Ibid., 29:193-199. The charges carried sufficient political salience to warrant a rebuttal also in the *Virginia Gazette* on 19 October 1796.

[71] Thomas Jefferson to Martha Jefferson Randolph, Philadelphia, 8 June 1797, Ibid., 29:424-25.

[72] Thomas Jefferson to Martha Jefferson Randolph, 27 March 1797, Ibid., 29:327-28.

[73] Martha Jefferson to Thomas Jefferson, Varina, 31 March 1797, Ibid., 29:334.

[74] Thomas Jefferson to Thomas Mann Randolph, Philadelphia, 30 May 1790, Ibid. 16:448-50. He encouraged his new son-in-law to study law as a "most certain stepping-stone to preferment in the political line"; but, at the same time, he should mix that with "a good degree of attention to the farm."

[75] Thomas Jefferson to Thomas Mann Randolph, Monticello, 23 March 1797, Ibid. 29:322-23; to Thomas Mann Randolph, Monticello, 9 April 1797, Ibid., 29:349-50; and to Martha Jefferson Randolph, Monticello, 9 April 1797, Ibid., 29:349. The circular letter to militia captains was written on 9 April, as well, but has not been found. Obviously aware the election's date, Randolph nonetheless chose to have his children inoculated for small pox in Richmond on the same day. The winners were Wilson Cary Nicholas, whose daughter much later married Thomas Jefferson Randolph, and Francis Walker, the son of Jefferson's guardian, Dr. Thomas Walker.

76 Thomas Jefferson to Angelica Schuyler Church, Philadelphia, 24 May 1797, *Papers*, 29:396-97.

77 Thomas Mann Randolph, Jr., to Thomas Jefferson, Dunginess, 6 November 1797, Ibid., 29:568-69.

78 Gaines, *Randolph*, 41-2.

79 Thomas Jefferson to Mary Jefferson Eppes, Philadelphia, 7 January 1798, *Papers*, 30:14-16.

80 Thomas Jefferson to Thomas Mann Randolph, 20 December 1798, Ibid., 30:604-05.

81 Ibid., and 3 January 1799, Ibid., 30:613-14;

82 Thomas Mann Randolph to Thomas Jefferson, Belmont, 19 January 1799, Ibid., 30:626-67.

83 Thomas Jefferson to Thomas Mann Randolph, 30 January 1799, Ibid., 30:667-69.

84 Thomas Mann Randolph to Thomas Jefferson, Belmont, 13 January 1798, Ibid., 30:26-28. Pantops was across the Rivanna River north of Monticello Mountain and adjacent to Edgehill. It was part of Maria's settlement in her marriage to John Wayles Eppes, the son of Francis and Elizabeth Wayles Eppes, the one-half sister to Martha Wayles Jefferson. The couple had married on 13 October 1797.

85 Martha Jefferson Randolph to Thomas Jefferson, Bellmont, 22 January 1798, Ibid., 30:43-44. Martha routinely used the spelling "Bellmont."

86 Thomas Mann Randolph to Thomas Jefferson, Belmont, 28 Jan 1798, Ibid., 30:62-63.

87 Thomas Mann Randolph to Thomas Jefferson, Belmont, 13 January 1798, Ibid., 30:26-28. Jefferson's apologetic and ambiguous response: "I had directed the managers at both to apply to you for your counsel when at a loss, and have only been prevented by the state of your health from asking a more onerous attention." Then, he directs him on how to supervise each overseer and hired craftsman; to reassign tools among the smiths; to hurry "George...to get the tobacco down"; to write the sawyer about floor planking for the house, &c.

88 Thomas Mann Randolph to Thomas Jefferson, Belmont, 28 January 1798, Ibid., 30:62-63. A postscript to MJR to TJ, 22 January 1798, Ibid.

89 Thomas Mann Randolph to Thomas Jefferson, Belmont, 13 January 1798, Ibid., 30:26-28.

90 Martha Jefferson Randolph to Thomas Jefferson, Bellmont, 22 January 1798, Ibid., 30:43-44.

91 Thomas Jefferson to Martha Jefferson Randolph, Philadelphia, 8 February 1798, Ibid., 30:91-92. On father's "plan," the Randolph family of five would occupy a one-over-one detached "south pavilion," and in the main house a small study and a public space (Parlour) that were the only two rooms with a roof. (Jack McLaughlin, *Jefferson and Monticello: The Biography of a Builder* [New York: Henry Holt and Company, 1988], 265.)

92 Martha Jefferson to Thomas Jefferson, Bellmont, 12 May 1798, *Papers*, 30:346-47.

93 Ibid.

94 Thomas Jefferson to Martha Jefferson Randolph, Philadelphia, 31 May 1798, Ibid., 30:380-81.

95 Martha Jefferson Randolph to Thomas Jefferson, Bellmont, 22 January 1798, Ibid., 30:43-44.

96 Thomas Jefferson to Martha Jefferson Randolph, 8 February 1798, Ibid., 30:91-92.

97 Thomas Jefferson to Maria Jefferson Eppes, Monticello, 8 march 1799, Ibid., 32:75

[98] Maria Jefferson Eppes to Thomas Jefferson, Eppington, 26 June 1799, Ibid., 31:139-40.

[99] Thomas Jefferson to Thomas Mann Randolph, Philadelphia, 4 February 1800, Ibid., 31:359-61

[100] Martha Jefferson Randolph to Thomas Jefferson, Edgehill, 30 January 1800, Ibid., 31:347-48; and Betts & Bear, *JFL,* 183 fn 2.

[101] Thomas Jefferson to Maria Jefferson Eppes, Philadelphia, 17 January 1800, Ibid., 31:314-16.

[102] John Wayles Eppes to Thomas Jefferson, Eppington, 1 January 1800, Ibid., 31:286.

[103] Thomas Jefferson to Martha Jefferson Randolph, Philadelphia, 21 January 1800, Ibid., 31:331.

[104] Martha Jefferson Randolph to Thomas Jefferson, Edgehill, 30 January 1800, Ibid., 31:347.

[105] Thomas Jefferson to Maria Jefferson Eppes, Philadelphia, 12 February 1800, Ibid., 31:267-68.

[106] Maria Jefferson Eppes to Thomas Jefferson, Bermuda Hundred, 28 December 1800, Ibid., 32:364.

[107] Thomas Jefferson to Thomas Mann Randolph, Philadelphia, 24 May 1798, Ibid., 30:365-66.

[108] Thomas Jefferson to Thomas Mann Randolph, Philadelphia, 30 January 1799, Ibid., 30:667-69.

[109] Thomas Jefferson to George Jefferson, Monticello, 18 May 1799, Ibid., 31:111-12.

[110] Thomas Jefferson to Thomas Mann Randolph, Philadelphia, 13 January 1800, Ibid., 31:304-07.

[111] Thomas Jefferson to Littleton Waller Tazewell, Monticello, 30 October 1799, Ibid., 31:229-31. Tazewell (1774–1860) had been a student of Wyeth and went on to serve in the Virginia legislature, Congress, and governor of Virginia.

[112] Thomas Mann Randolph to Thomas Jefferson, Edgehill, 12 April 1800, Ibid., 31:497.

[113] Thomas Jefferson to Thomas Mann Randolph, Philadelphia, 4 March 1800, Ibid., 31:413-15

[114] Thomas Mann Randolph to Thomas Jefferson, Richmond, 1 March 1800, Ibid., 31:403. When portions of Randolph's Varina estate did not sell, the family's commission agent (George Jefferson) interceded to buy the parcels, thus clearing one obligation by incurring another. Jefferson not only diverted his own tobacco proceeds to repay George Jefferson but, also, used receipts due other persons whose affairs he managed (Jefferson to Randolph, Philadelphia, 4 March 1800, and 7 March 1800, *Papers* 31:413-15 and 420-21, respectively).

[115] Martha Jefferson and Thomas Mann Randolph to Thomas Jefferson, 31 January 1801, *Papers*, 32:526-28 and Thomas Jefferson to Martha Jefferson Randolph, Washington, 5 February 1801, Ibid.,32:556-57.

[116] Thomas Jefferson to Maria Jefferson Eppes, Washington, 15 February 1801, Ibid., 32:593.

[117] Maria Jefferson Eppes to Thomas Jefferson, Eppington, 18 April 1801, Ibid., 33:611.

[118] Martha Jefferson Randolph to Thomas Jefferson, Bellmont, 22 January 1798, Ibid., 30:43-44.

Chapter 7: "Dreary and monotonous"

[1] Martha Jefferson Randolph to Thomas Jefferson, Edgehill, 25 July 1801, Betts and Bear, *JFL*, 209. A sense of just how tedious adult women's plantation life could be was aptly chronicled in a daily diary kept for one year by Frances Baylor Hill, *The Diary of Frances Baylor Hill of "Hillsborough" King and Queen County Virginia (1797)*, eds. William K. Bottorff and Roy C. Flannagan, *Early American Literature Newsletter*, 2:3 (Winter, 1967), 4-53. "And [I] now make a conclusion of my journal," Frances wrote on December 31, 1797, "which has been rather more tedious then I suppos'd it would have been when I first began" (53). Indeed, Frances described everyday much like yesterday and tomorrow's plans were strikingly similar: arose late, read, dressed for dinner, visited whomever, etc.

[2] Martha Jefferson Randolph to Thomas Jefferson, Edgehill, 16 April 1802, *Papers*, 222-223.

[3] Thomas Jefferson to Martha Jefferson Randolph, Washington, 19 October 1801, Ibid., 209-10.

[4] Thomas Jefferson to Martha Jefferson Randolph, Philadelphia, 5 February 1801, Ibid., 32:556-57 and to Maria Jefferson Eppes, Washington, 15 February 1801, Ibid., 32:593.

[5] "Public sphere," as used herein, closely approximates Cynthia Kierner's usage in *Beyond the Household: Women's Place in the Early South, 1700–1835* (Ithaca, NY: Cornell University Press, 1998). The author defines "public sphere" as "the site of actual or figurative [symbolic] exchanges on extradomestic ideas or issues and…[embraces] not only formal political participation but also informal civic and sociable life, the world of letters, certain business and market transactions, and religious and benevolent activities" (2). The Jefferson-Randolph letters reveal that "domestic"/"house" and "farm" were considered as constitutive parts of their "plantation household." As noted above, "household" is treated here as an array of mediating structures linking sites (i.e., domestic/house and farm to whatever they considered the "world outside."

[6] Thomas Jefferson to Maria Jefferson Eppes, Monticello, 11 April 1801, Betts and Bear, *JFL*, 201.

[7] Thomas Jefferson to Martha Jefferson Randolph, Washington, 16 July 1801, Ibid., 207-08.

[8]Thomas Jefferson to Martha Jefferson Randolph, Washington, 27 January 1803 and 21 November 1806, Ibid., 242 and 290 (socks and shirts); Thomas Jefferson to Maria Jefferson Eppes, Washington, 24 June 1801, Ibid., 206 and to Martha Jefferson Randolph,16 July 1801, Ibid., 207-08 (coming to Monticello). These examples are just a minor sampling of Jefferson's many, varied, and unremitting instructions on and involvement in domestic matters; farming, finances, and manufacturing were detailed similarly.

[9] Thomas Jefferson to Maria Jefferson Eppes, Washington, 28 May 1801, Ibid., 203.

[10] Thomas Jefferson to Noah Webster, Monticello, 4 December 1790, *Papers*, 18:131-33.

[11] Jurgen Habermas, "The Public Sphere: An Encyclopedia Article [1964]," *New German Critique*, No. 3 (Autumn, 1974), translated by Sara Lennox and Frank Lennox, http://www.jstor.org/ (October 19, 2005), 49-55; various authors in *The William and Mary Quarterly*, Vol. 62, Issue 1, (January, 2005), http://www.historycooperative.org (October 12, 2005); Mary P. Ryan, *Civic Wars: Democracy and Public Life in the American City during the Nineteenth Century* (Berkeley, CA: 1997); David Waldstreicher, *In the Midst*

of Perpetual Fetes: The Making of American Nationalism, 1776–1820 (Chapel Hill, N.C., 1997); Rogan Kersh, *Dreams of a More Perfect Union* (Ithaca, NY: Cornell University Press, 2001); Len Travers, *Celebrating the Fourth: Independence Day and the Rites of Nationalism in the Early Republic* (Amherst, MA: University of Massachusetts Press, 1997); and Simon P. Newman, *Parades and the Politics of the Street: Festive Culture in the Early American Republic* (Philadelphia: University of Pennsylvania Press, 1997).

[12] Jefferson, too, made this distinction between government (state) and society. Stung by newspapers in 1809 for importing merino sheep, cotton seed, and a French plough contrary to his Administration's embargo, he claimed these actions simply continued a long practice of exchanging such items "between societies instituted for the benevolent purpose of communicating to all parts of the world whatever useful is discovered in any one of them." Nations may be at or near war, but "societies are always in peace." He continued: "Like the republic of letters, they form a great fraternity spreading over the whole earth, and their correspondence is never interrupted by any civilized nation" (Thomas Jefferson to John Hollins, Washington, 19 February 1809, *The Portable Jefferson*, ed. Merrill Peterson [New York: Penguin Books, 1975], 515-16).

[13] Thomas Jefferson to Angelica Schuyler Church, Philadelphia, 24 May 1797, *Papers*, 29:396-97. Examples of his keeping Martha abreast of political events include: Thomas Jefferson to Martha Jefferson Randolph, Philadelphia, 26 May 1793, Ibid., 23:122-23; Philadelphia, 5 April 1798, Ibid., 30:248-49; Philadelphia, 31 May 1798, Ibid., 30:381; Philadelphia, 1 December 1793, Ibid., 27:467-78; Philadelphia, 22 December 1793, Ibid., 27:608-09; and Monticello, 27 March 1797, Ibid., 29:327-28.

[14] 15 Thomas Jefferson to Martha Jefferson Randolph, Philadelphia, 26 May 1793, Ibid., 23:122-23.

[15] Thomas Jefferson to Thomas Mann Randolph, Philadelphia, 28 January 1800, Ibid., 31:341-42; Bear and Stanton, *JMB*, 2:964 and 1017n34; and Sowerby #589 and #590.

[16] Martha Jefferson Randolph to Thomas Jefferson, Edgehill, 11 July 1807, Betts and Bear, *JFL*, 310-11. The "affair of the Chesapeake" referred to England's fifty-gun *H. M. S. Leopard* firing on and boarding the U. S. frigate *Chesapeake* on 22 June 1807 in pursuit of alleged British citizens who had deserted the Royal Navy.

[17] Thomas Jefferson to Thomas Mann Randolph, Jr., Philadelphia, 16 March 1792, *Papers*, 23:288.

[18] See "Editorial Note: The Threat of Disunion in the West," *Papers*, 19:442-69; and Malone, *Jefferson and the Rights of Man* (Boston: Little, Brown and Company, 1951), 290 and 435-36.

[19] Thomas Jefferson to Maria Jefferson Eppes, Philadelphia, 17 February 1800, *Papers*, 31:314.

[20] Thomas Jefferson to Martha Jefferson Randolph, Philadelphia, 11 February 1800, Ibid., 31:364-66.

[21] Thomas Mann Randolph to Thomas Jefferson, Edgehill, 18 January 1800, Ibid., 31:323-34 and Martha Jefferson Randolph to Thomas Jefferson, Edgehill, 15 May 1800, Ibid., 31:582-83.

[22] Thomas Jefferson to James Monroe, 12 January 1800, Ibid., 31:300-301.

[23] James Barbour to Thomas Jefferson, Richmond, 20 January 1800, Ibid., 31:325-26. Barbour (1775–1842) began his first term in 1798, became speaker in 1809, governor in 1812, and a United States Senator in 1814 (*Papers*, 31:326n).

[24] Philip Norborne Nicholas to Thomas Jefferson, 2 February 1800, Ibid., 31:356-57. Nicholas sketched two potentially effective *national* issues for the budding organization (viz., to oppose a bill by Charles Pinckney to make English common law a part U.S. law and the Sedition Act) that "would obtain more completely the sympathy of the

people." Also, he strategized that Monroe's position as Governor would "form a center around which our interest can rally."

25 Thomas Jefferson to Philip Narbonne Nicholas, Philadelphia, 7 April 1800, Ibid., 31:485-86.

26 Thomas Jefferson to Maria Jefferson Eppes, Philadelphia, 17 January 1800, Ibid., 31:314-15; to Martha Jefferson Randolph, 21 January, Ibid., 331-32; and to John Wayles Eppes, 22 January, Ibid.,333-34. Maria's husband wrote on February 7th: "...her right breast—It has broke in four or five different places & is still much inflamed. Her fever had left her...it returned" yesterday (John Wayles Eppes to Thomas Jefferson, Eppington, 7 February 1800, Ibid., 31:362).

27 Thomas Jefferson to Thomas Mann Randolph, Philadelphia, 2 February 1800, Ibid., 31:357-59. This particular Varina episode, the household's speculative tobacco marketing decisions, and foreign affairs can be traced in Randolph's letters of 22 February; 1, 11, 31 March; and 4, 12 April 1800 and Jefferson's letters of 3, 7, 9, 11, 31 March and 4 April 1800.

28 Bear and Stanton, JMB, 1017-20; Thomas Jefferson to John Wayles Eppes, Philadelphia, 21 April 1800, Papers,31:531-32; and to Martha Jefferson Randolph, Philadelphia, 22 April 1800, Ibid., 31:535-36.

29 Thomas Jefferson to Judge Spencer Roane, Poplar Forest, 6 September 1819, L&B, Writings, 15:212; The Revolution of 1800: Democracy, Race, & the New Republic, eds. James Horn, Jan Ellen Lewis, and Peter S. Onuf, (Charlottesville, VA: University of Virginia Press, 2002), passim;

30 Thomas Jefferson to Martha Jefferson Randolph, Washington, 16 January 1801, Papers, 32:475-76.

31 Ibid.

32 Thomas Jefferson to Thomas Mann Randolph, Washington, 1 January 1801, Ibid., 32:385. Jefferson in practical politics drew finer, more rhetorically divisive, partisan distinctions (Thomas Jefferson to Levi Lincoln, 11 July and 26 August 1801, L&B, Writings, 10:263-66 and 273-76).

33Joanne Freeman, Affairs of Honor: National Politics in the New Republic (New Haven, CT: Yale University Press, 2001), 250-53. Bayard's letter to the Federalist tax collector in Wilmington (Allen McLane) on the day of the vote reported that Burr intended to remove all officeholders. "I have direct information that Mr. Jefferson will not pursue that plan." He assured McLane. "I have taken good care of you, and think if prudent, you are safe" (Papers, 33:3-4n).

34 Margaret Bayard Smith, The first forty years of Washington society, portrayed by the family letters of Mrs. Samuel Harrison Smith (Margaret Bayard) from the collection of her grandson, J. Henley Smith, http://www.perseus.tufts.edu/ (2 July 2007), 20-21 and 18-19, respectively. Hereafter cited as Smith, Forty.

35 Martha Jefferson Randolph to Thomas Jefferson, 31 January 1801, Papers, 32:526-28. Randolph was the informant of what he termed his wife's "slight indispositions" that she diagnosed as pregnancy related. "[Martha] has not resolution to wean Cornelia [b. 26 July 1799] altho' she is so robust as to have got her mouth set with teeth without our notice. Martha will yield to our persuasions and separate her shortly I am satisfied" (10 January 1801, Papers, 32:440-41).

36 Respectively, Thomas Jefferson to Dolley Madison, 27 May 1801 in The Dolley Madison Digital Edition, http://rotunda.upress.virginia.edu/dmde/ (December 2, 2007) and Thomas Jefferson to Martha Jefferson Randolph, Washington, 28 May 1801,

Betts and Bear, *JFL*, 202-03. The "ladies" may have made 27 May, missed breakfast on 4 June, but the President hoped they would be available to dine that day with "Miss Butters" and the next "with Mrs. Gallatin and Mrs. Mason" (Thomas Jefferson to Dolley Madison, Washington, 4 June 1801, in *The Dolley Madison Digital Edition*, http://rotunda.upress.virginia.edu/dmde/ [December 2, 2007]).

[37] Thomas Jefferson to Maria Jefferson Eppes, Washington, 28 May 1801, *Papers*, 203. He, also, was preparing the rest of the Monticello household for his daughters' visits: "Mr. and Mrs. Madison and Miss Payne are lodging with us till they can get a house," he informed Randolph. "Great desires are expressed here that Patsy and Maria should come on. But that I give no hopes of till Autumn" (Thomas Jefferson to Thomas Mann Randolph, Washington, 14 May 1801, L & B, *Writings*, 10:241-42).

[38] Thomas Jefferson to Maria Jefferson Eppes, Washington, 24 June 1801, Betts and Bear, *JFL*, 206.

[39] Thomas Jefferson to Martha Jefferson Randolph, 8 June 1797, *Papers*, 29:424-25.

[40] Maria Jefferson Eppes to Thomas Jefferson, Bermuda Hundred, 2 February 1801, Ibid., 32:537-38.

[41] Maria Jefferson to Thomas Jefferson, Varina, 27 February 1797, Ibid., 29:308.

[42] Thomas Jefferson to Maria Jefferson, Philadelphia, 11 March 1797, Ibid., 29:314-15.

[43] Martha Jefferson Randolph to Thomas Jefferson, Bellmont, 12 May 1798, Ibid., 30:346-47; Thomas Jefferson to Maria Jefferson Eppes, Philadelphia, 6 June 1798, and 4 July 1800, Ibid., 30:390-91 and 32:39.

[44] Thomas Jefferson to Maria Jefferson Eppes, Washington, 15 February 1801, Ibid., 32:593.

[45] Thomas Mann Randolph to Thomas Jefferson, 14 March 1801, Ibid., 33:290-91

[46] Ruth H. Bloch, "Inside and Outside the Public Sphere," *The William and Mary Quarterly*, 62:1, (January, 2005), 9, http://www.historycooperative.org, (October 12, 2005); Eric Slauter, "Being Alone in the Age of the Social Contract," *William and Mary Quarterly*, 3rd Series 62, no. 1, Forum: Alternative Histories of the Public Sphere (2005) 31-66; and The polyvalence of "private" and "public" as they relate to gendered "spheres" in late eighteenth century England is discussed by Lawrence E. Klein, "Gender and the Public/Private Distinction in the Eighteenth Century: Some Questions about Evidence and Analytic Procedure," *Eighteenth-Century Studies*, 29:1 (1996), 97-109.

[47] Thomas Jefferson to Martha Jefferson Randolph, Philadelphia, 5 February 1801, *Papers*, 32:556-57.

[48] Thomas Jefferson to Martha Jefferson Randolph, Philadelphia, 8 June 1797, Ibid., 29: 424-25.

[49] Thomas Jefferson, *Autobiography*, L & B, *Writings*, 1:73

[50] John Hancock to Thomas Jefferson, Philadelphia, 30 September 1776, *Papers*, 1:523-24.

[51] Richard Henry Lee to Thomas Jefferson, Philadelphia, 27 September 1776, Ibid., 1:522-23.

[52] Thomas Jefferson to John Hancock, Williamsburgh, 11 October 1776, Ibid., 1:524.

[53] Thomas Jefferson to Benjamin Franklin, Virginia, 13 August 1777, Ibid., 2:26-27.

[54] Thomas Jefferson to Edmund Randolph, Monticello, 16 September 1781, Ibid., 6:117-118.

[55] Thomas Jefferson to James Monroe, Monticello, 20 May 1782, Ibid.,6:184 ff. The details of Jefferson's temporary return to service in Virginia's legislature are discussed in Chapter 2.

⁵⁶ Thomas Jefferson to George Washington, Chesterfield [*sic*], 15 December 1789, Ibid., 16:34-35.
⁵⁷ Thomas Jefferson to Martha Jefferson Randolph, Philadelphia, 5 February 1801, Ibid., 32:556-57.
⁵⁸ Ibid.
⁵⁹ Thomas Jefferson to Martha Jefferson Randolph, Washington, 17 July 1804, Betts and Bear, *JFL*, 261-61. Louis André Pichon was Chargé d'Affaires for the French Empire. Thomas Jefferson to Martha Jefferson Randolph, Washington, 16 June 1806, Ibid., 284-85. These were wives of Jefferson's cabinet: Albert Gallatin, Secretary of Treasury, Robert Smith, Secretary of Navy, and Henry Dearborne, Secretary of War. Thomas Jefferson to Martha Jefferson, Washington, 20 October 1806, Ibid., 289.
⁶⁰ Shirley Samuels, "The Family, the State, and the Novel in the Early Republic," *American Quarterly*, 38:3 (1986), 385. Samuels notes that in republican ideology there was "neither an absolute separation nor identification or joining of the state and family, but an unstable relation with permeable and unfixed boundaries."
⁶¹ Thomas Jefferson to Thomas Mann Randolph, Washington, 12 March 1801, *Papers*, 33:259-60. Jefferson believed that David Randolph (1760–1830), as U. S. Marshall in Richmond, had "packed" the jury trying and convicting James Callender under the Sedition Act and compounded his "malconduct" by delaying remittance of Callender's $200 fine following President Jefferson's pardon. Randolph denied complicity. See Malone, *Jefferson the President: First Term, 1801–05* (Boston: Little, Brown and Company, 1970), 207-11. A short description of David and Mary Randolph's decline from planter elite to penury is presented in Jonathan Daniels, *The Randolphs of Virginia* (Garden City, NY: Doubleday & Company, Inc., 1972), 196-202.
⁶² George Jefferson, Jr. (1766–1812) to Thomas Jefferson, Richmond, 4 March 1801, *Papers*, 33:158-60. See John Garland Jefferson to Thomas Jefferson, Amelia, 1 March 1801 Ibid., 33:110-11. This Jefferson (d. 1815) had read law with his cousin's assistance while living in the area of Monticello.
⁶³ Thomas Jefferson to Thomas Mann Randolph, Washington, 8 October and 16 November 1801, Ibid., 35:414-15 and 35:677-68, respectively. The call on the note was immediate, but Jefferson's solution was to give Randolph and Eppes Poplar Forest parcels and hire "10 laboring men" to clear land. After a year, each would have "a fresh farm opened of 300 as. which [they] could either occupy or rent." A generous but financially empty offer.
⁶⁴ Thomas Jefferson to Thomas Mann Randolph, Philadelphia, 18 February 1793, Ibid., 25:230.
⁶⁵ Thomas Jefferson to Thomas Mann Randolph, 29 January 1801, Ibid., 32:516-17 (garden and wine); 18 March 1793, Ibid., 25:403-04 (land lease); Martha Jefferson Randolph to Thomas Jefferson, 10 July 1802 and 12 July 1803, Betts and Bear, *JFL*, 233 and 246-47 (household items); and Thomas Jefferson to Richard Richardson, Philadelphia, 10 February 1800, Ibid., 31:363-64. Richardson began working as a brick mason and plaster at Monticello in 1796 and was overseer of labor at the time of his leaving in 1801 (*JMB*, 945 n66)
⁶⁶ Thomas Jefferson to Stevens Thomson Mason, Monticello, 27 October 1799, *Papers*, 31:222-23. Mason (1760–1803), a nephew of George Mason, served in the Virginia House, Senate, Constitutional ratification convention, and the U.S. Senate from 1794 until his death. He actively and financially supported James T. Callender during his prosecution and conviction under the Sedition Act (Ibid., 31:13n). The

theme of lost farming skills as a consequence of public service is a central feature of "The Jefferson Family Story" described in later chapters.

[67] Thomas Jefferson to Thomas Mann Randolph, Philadelphia, Ibid., 25:230.

[68] Thomas Jefferson to Thomas Mann Randolph, New York, 7 July 1790, Ibid., 17:26.

[69] Thomas Jefferson to Thomas Mann Randolph, Philadelphia, 17 July 1791, Ibid., 20:640-41.

[70] Thomas Jefferson to Thomas Mann Randolph, Philadelphia, 21 December 1792, Ibid., 24:774-75. The devastating effects of this pest are described by Brooke Hunter, "Creative Destruction: The Forgotten Legacy of the Hessian Fly," ed. Cathy Matson, *The Economy of Early America: Historical Perspectives & New Directions* (University Park, PA: The Pennsylvania State University Press, 2006), 236-262.

[71] "Indenture with Craven Peyton for the Lease of Fields at Shadwell," 1 October 1799, *Papers*, 31:197-200. Peyton (1775–1837) was formerly of Loudon County and lived at Milton with his wife, who was Jefferson's niece by his sister Lucy Jefferson Lewis (Mrs. Charles Lilburne).

[72] Thomas Jefferson to Thomas Mann Randolph, Philadelphia, 4 February 1800, Ibid., 31:359-61.

[73] "Agreement with John H. Craven," 11 August 1800, Ibid., 32:108-09. Jefferson typically during this period was converting Virginia pounds to dollars at the rate of 3.33, so returns from Craven's lease were slightly over $1,165 cash plus the added value (if any) of 100 acres of cleared lands over woodlands during the 5-year term of the agreement.

[74] Thomas Jefferson to Thomas Mann Randolph, Washington, 16 November 1801, Thomas Jefferson Foundation file, "Correspondence: Thomas Mann Randolph," transcript of manuscript by Cinder Stanton (DLC). Hereafter, cited as "TJF, Stanton" followed by depository in parentheses.

[75] Thomas Jefferson to Martha Jefferson Randolph, Washington, 27 November 1801, Betts and Bear, *JFL*, 214-15.

[76] Martha Jefferson Randolph to Thomas Jefferson, Edgehill, 19 June 1801, Ibid., 205-05. Martha Jefferson Carr (Mrs. Dabney) and Lucy Jefferson Lewis (Mrs. Charles Lilburn, Jr.) were Jefferson's sisters; Jane Cary Randolph Randolph (Mrs. Thomas Eston) was a sister of Thomas Mann Randolph.

[77] Martha Jefferson Randolph to Thomas Jefferson, [10 November 1801], Ibid., 212-13. Virginia Jefferson Randolph, just 2 ½ months old, also was "in the same state, coughing most violently so as to endanger strangling." Maria's second child, Francis was about three weeks old when he became ill (Mary Jefferson Eppes to Thomas Jefferson, Monticello, 6 November 1801, Betts and Bear, *JFL*, 211).

Chapter 8: "No subject ...so dear and interesting"

[1] Thomas Jefferson to Martha Jefferson Randolph, Washington, 14 May 1804 and Martha Jefferson Randolph to Thomas Jefferson, 31 May 1804, Betts and Bear, *JFL*, 259-60 and 261-62, respectively.

[2] Thomas Mann Randolph to Thomas Jefferson, Monticello, 7 February 1793, *Papers*, 25:156-57, scantling; Thomas Jefferson to Thomas Mann Randolph, Washington, 1 January 1802, TJF, Stanton (DLC), instructions; Thomas Mann Randolph to Thomas Jefferson, 18 July 1801, TJF, Stanton, (DLC), financial; Thomas Jefferson to Thomas Mann Randolph, Washington, 21 February 1802, TJF, Stanton, (DLC), leases; 3 February 1802, TJF, Stanton, (DLC), dignitaries; and Thomas Jefferson to Martha Jefferson, Philadelphia, 5 February 1792, *Papers*, 23:103, reports.

3 Thomas Mann Randolph to Thomas Jefferson, Monticello, 7 July 1791, *Papers*, 20:605-07.

5 Thomas Mann Randolph to Thomas Jefferson, Monticello, 4 June 1792, TJF, Stanton (ViU).

6 Thomas Jefferson to Thomas Mann Randolph, Philadelphia, 4 March 1800, *Papers*, 31:413-15 and Washington, 8 October 1801, TJF, Stanton (DLC). Jefferson could not help in a "pecuniary way," because of the "extraordinary expences of an outfit" in Washington. He proposed, instead, to divide off for Randolph and Eppes two parcels of "6 or 800 or 1000" acres that they could "occupy or rent" to make their "situation...easy." Ironically, this ostensibly generous act would cause a major dispute and estrangement between the two sons-in-law while they were living at the President's House as Congressmen from Virginia. Even Jefferson in this letter acknowledged that it "may require a difference in size...to produce in inferior lands a rent equal to those of superior quality."

6 Thomas Jefferson to Anne Cary, Thomas Jefferson, and Ellen Wayles Randolph, Washington, 2 March 1802, Betts and Bear, *JFL*, 218. In a refrain similar to what he had instructed young Patsy, Grand Papa wrote: "It is a charming thing to be loved by everybody: and the way to obtain it is, never to quarrel or be angry with anybody and to tell a story. Do all the kind things you can to your companions, give them everything rather than to yourself. Pity and help anything you see in distress and learn your books and improve your minds. This will make everybody fond of you, and desirous of doing it to you." Emphasis added.

7 Thomas Mann Randolph to Thomas Jefferson, Edgehill, 6 March 1802, *Papers*, 35:14-16. With the impending return of Louisiana to French jurisdiction in 1801, Randolph had augured just such emigration would result from the transfer: "I fear a speedy effect on our population & and the price of our lands." Climate, fertile soils, French enterprising, convenient shipping, and an abundance of eastern citizens with "no means" would "affect seriously the next generation...: opening an immense new, rich country must [he thought] lower the price, profit & rent of land" in the East (Thomas Mann Randolph to Thomas Jefferson, Edgehill, 23 May 1801, *Papers*, 34:174-75).

8 Thomas Mann Randolph to Thomas Jefferson, 6 February 1802, Ibid., 36:530-32.

9 Martha Jefferson to Thomas Jefferson, 31 January 1801, *Papers*, 32:526-28; 25 July 1801, Betts and Bear, *JFL*, 209, and 18 November 1801, Ibid., 212-13.

10 Martha Jefferson to Thomas Jefferson, Richmond, 25 April 1790, *Papers*, 16:384-85.

11 Thomas Mann Randolph to Thomas Jefferson, Richmond, 30 November 1793, Ibid., 27:464-65.

12 Jefferson to Thomas Mann Randolph, Washington, 12 March 1802, Ibid., 37:64-67

13 Ibid. Jefferson's practice of following numerals with a period is ignored here and throughout. Abraham Baldwin (1754–1807) was a "Connecticut Yankee," graduate of Yale, and U.S. Senator from Augusta, GA, where he moved in 1784, and authored the charter for the University of Georgia. James Jackson (1757–1806) emigrated from England in 1772 to Savannah and served as U.S. Senator and Governor (1798–1801). John Milledge (1757–1818) was a native Georgian who served as Congressman (1795-1802), Governor (1802–06), and Senator (1806–09) of that state (*Biographical Directory of the United States Congress*, http://bioguide.congress.gov/ [July 23, 2007]).

14 Thomas Mann Randolph to Thomas Jefferson, 13 March 1802, *Papers,* 37:71.

15 Thomas Jefferson to Thomas Mann Randolph, 20 March 1802, Ibid., 37:95-97. Given these and other estimated (and optimistic) figures in this letter, Randolph could

expect a gross return of $2,400 (18%) annually on an initial investment of $13,400 in land and slaves; although at about $120 per laborer, it was substantially less than the $300 return that Jefferson had conveyed in his earlier letter.

[16] Thomas Mann Randolph to Thomas Jefferson, Monticello, 4 June 1792, *Papers*, 24:33-34 and Thomas Jefferson to Thomas Mann Randolph, 15 June 1792, Philadelphia, Ibid., 24:83.

[17] Thomas Mann Randolph to Thomas Jefferson, Edgehill, 20 March 1802, Ibid., 37:97-98. Randolph was referring to Napoleon's sending a fleet to St. Domingo to retake the island from Toussaint Louverture. The Administration considered this an unfavorable prelude to Spain's retrocession of Louisiana to France, whom they thought less desirable for the control of New Orleans. The President's dilemma was that he opposed France's re-colonization but in an 1801 conversation with French Chargé d'Affaires, André Pichon, had allegedly stated: "[N]othing would be easier than to furnish your army and fleet with everything, and to reduce Toussaint to starvation." While the "official" line from Madison was reasonably congenial to Napoleon's action, Jefferson in private letters was more bellicose, implying it would result in an Anglo-American alliance (Thomas Jefferson to Pierre Samuel du Pont de Nemours, Washington, 25 April 1802, *Correspondence between Thomas Jefferson and...de Nemours*, ed. Dumas Malone and trans. Linwood Lehman [Boston: Houghton Mifflin Company, The Riverside Press Cambridge, 1930], 46-49. For the intricate diplomatic gambit the President was running in 1801-03, see Dumas Malone, *Jefferson the President: First Term, 1801-1805* (Boston: Little, Brown and Company, 1970), 249-261; quotation from 252 citing "Statement as reported by Pichon to Talleyrand, July 22, 1801, Affaires Étrangères, Correspondance Politique, États-Unis, 55:178.

[18] Thomas Jefferson to Thomas Mann Randolph, Washington, 28 March 1802, Ibid., 37:127-30.

[19] Thomas Jefferson to Maria Jefferson Randolph, Washington, 29 March 1802, Betts and Bear, *JFL*, 220-21.

[20] Thomas Jefferson to Martha Jefferson Randolph, Washington, 3 April 1802, Ibid., 221-22.

[21] Thomas Jefferson to Marbois, Annapolis, 5 December 1783, *Papers*, 6:373-74

[22] Martha Jefferson Randolph to Thomas Jefferson, Edgehill, 16 April 1802, Betts and Bear, *JFL*, 222-23. Emphasis in the original. Anne was 10 ½ years old, Jeff nearly 9, Ellen 6, Cornelia approaching 3, and Virginia just 7 months.

[23] Nathaniel Burwell, Monticello, 14 March 1818, *A Jefferson Profile As Revealed in His letters*, ed., Saul K. Padover (New York: The John Day Company, 1956), 297-98.

[24] Bear and Stanton, *JMB*, 2:1071-72.

[25] Bear and Stanton, *JMB*, 2:1067-68. Jefferson undertook this exercise on 8 March 1802 and later that week made payments for wine totaling $811 and "25 D. charity for meetg. house for blacks" (1068). On June 21, he prepared "A view of the consumption of butcher's meat from Sep. 6. 1801. to June 12,1802." Eleven "servants" were consuming from 15 to 18 pounds a day; the "masters," 20-23 (*JMB*, 1075-76). Originally a businessman in Philadelphia, Barnes moved to Georgetown adjacent to Washington City with the government, where he regularly served as Jefferson's "banker" and commission agent (*JMB*, 2:927 n27).

[26] Thomas Jefferson to Martha Jefferson Randolph, Washington, 3 June 1802, Betts and Bear, *JFL*, 226-28.

[27] Thomas Jefferson to Maria Jefferson Eppes, Washington, 2 July 1802, Ibid., 232.

[28] Thomas Jefferson to Martha Jefferson Randolph, Washington, 18 June 1802, Ibid., 228-29 and Maria Jefferson Eppes to Thomas Jefferson, Eppington, 21 June 1802, Ibid., 229-30. As it turned out, Martha's children at Edgehill "escaped the measles"

rampant on the mountain top, but she expressed "regret" as "the season was so favorable...and mild" (Martha Jefferson Randolph to Thomas Jefferson, Edgehill, 10 July 1802, Ibid., 233).

29 Thomas Jefferson to Martha Jefferson Randolph, Washington, 18 June 1802, Ibid., 228-29.

30 Martha Jefferson Randolph to Thomas Jefferson, Edgehill, 10 July 1802, Ibid., 233.

31 Bear and Stanton, *JMB*, 2:1075-76 and 1083. In another eleven-week period (July-August), the "outfit" cost him over $440 (2:1083). Even if this was untrimmed, bone-in meat, it was an unusual amount; perhaps, some was "walking" out the back door! The Monticello farms were contributing almost nothing to Jefferson's plan for reducing debt. The 1801 Poplar Forest tobacco crop was 18,579 pounds (sold at $5.50 cwt.) as compared to 30,160 in 1799 at $6 and 32,459 in 1800 for which he received $7 cwt. (Ibid., 2:1075, 1026, and 1035). The Hessian fly, transported they believed by British mercenaries during the War, was a perennial pest "laying waste" to the wheat (Thomas Jefferson to Thomas Mann Randolph, Washington, 16 November 1801, TJF, Stanton (DLC). Toll mill construction was faced persistently with obstacles (Thomas Jefferson to James Walker, 1 October 1802, Jefferson Papers (MHi) as cited in *Thomas Jefferson's Farm Book*, ed., Edwin Morris Betts, [Charlottesville, VA: University Press of Virginia, 1987], 353-54).

32 Bear and Stanton, *JMB*, 2:1080, 1085 and 1081, respectively; Thomas Jefferson to Maria Jefferson Eppes, Washington, 7 October 1802, Betts and Bear, *JFL*, 236-37; and to Martha Jefferson Randolph, Washington, 18 October and 7 October, 1802, Ibid., 237and 236, respectively.

33 Thomas Mann Randolph to Thomas Jefferson, Edgehill, 16 October [1802], The Papers of Thomas Jefferson (MHi, reel 13), transcribed by author.

34 Thomas Jefferson to General Thomas Sumpter [*sic*], Washington, 22 October 1802, typescript Thomas Jefferson Foundation, Missouri Historical Society, St. Louis, (MoSHi, reel 1). Nicknamed the "Carolina Gamecock" for his fancy dress and confident style, Thomas Sumter (1734–1832) fought in the French and Indian and Revolutionary Wars and served in the First, Second, and Fifth through Seventh Congresses (*Biographical Directory of the United States Congress*, http://bio guide.congress.gov, [July 15, 2007]). His sister Mary Suddarth, whom Jefferson considered to have "great experience and a sound judgment," was midwife to Maria Eppes for the birth of Francis (Bear and Stanton, *JMB*, 2:1051 n11; and Thomas Jefferson to Maria Jefferson Eppes, Washington, 26 October 1801, Betts and Bear, *JFL*, 210-11).

35 Thomas Jefferson to Thomas Mann Randolph, Washington, 22 October 1801, *Papers*, 38:532-33.

36 Thomas Mann Randolph to Thomas Jefferson, Edgehill, 29 October [1802], The Papers of Thomas Jefferson, Massachusetts Historical Society (MHi, reel 13 out of chronological order near the end), transcribed by author. The other cites to Randolph also from this source. This letter is quoted extensively to convey the intensity of Randolph's emotion and sense of isolation. Martha, also, on 29 October wrote her father: "We received your letter and are preparing with all speed to obey its summons; by next Friday we hope we shall be able to fix a day...Tho as yet it is not entirely certain that we can get off so soon." She requested he buy two wigs for her and Maria (see below).

The author acknowledges the essential assistance of Lisa Francavilla of the Thomas Jefferson Foundation, Jefferson Papers:Retirement Series, Family Letters Project, in locating another transcription (anon.) for corroboration of this difficult-to-find letter.

[37] Gaines, *Randolph*, 41-42.

[38] Thomas Mann Randolph to Thomas Jefferson, Edgehill, 29 October 1802, TJF Stanton (MHi).

[39] Thomas Jefferson to Maria Jefferson Eppes, 12 February 1800, *Papers*, 31:267-68; Maria Jefferson Eppes to Thomas Jefferson, Eppington 26 June 1799, Ibid.,31:139-40; Martha Jefferson Randolph to Thomas Jefferson, Bellmont, 22 January 1798, Ibid., 30:434-44.

[40] Thomas Jefferson to Thomas Mann Randolph, Philadelphia, 3 may 1798, Ibid., 30:325-27; and to Martha Jefferson Randolph, Philadelphia, 8 June 1797, Ibid., 29:424-25.

[41] Thomas Jefferson to Maria Jefferson Eppes, Washington, 15 February 1801, Ibid., 32:593.

[42] Thomas Jefferson to Thomas Mann Randolph, Washington, 2 November 1802, Ibid., 38:623.

[43] Ibid.

[44] Thomas Jefferson to Martha Jefferson Randolph, 2 November 1802, Betts and Bear, *JFL*, 238-39. Anna Scott Marks (1755–1828), also called "Nancy," was Jefferson's sister, twin to Randolph Jefferson and married to Hastings Marks of Louisa County.

[45] Martha Jefferson Randolph to Thomas Jefferson, 9 November 1802, Ibid., 239.

[46] Maria Jefferson Eppes to Thomas Jefferson, 5 November 1802, Ibid., 239.

[47] Bear and Stanton, *JMB*, 2:1085–86 and Martha Jefferson Randolph to Thomas Jefferson, Edgehill, 9 November 1802, Betts and Bear, *JFL*, 239.

[48] Maria Jefferson Eppes to Thomas Jefferson, 5 November 1802, Betts and Bear, *JFL*, 239 and Thomas Jefferson to Martha Jefferson Randolph, 6 June 1802, Ibid., 226-28. Interestingly, Martha's letter four days later made no mention of Randolph's being away from home and there is no evidence of the reason. There were detailed instructions for the trip to Washington City: pack or buy their own "cold victuals; Brown's tavern, about 24 miles south of the Georgetown ferry, was "a poor house but obliging people"; whereas, "Colo. Wren's tavern" was "a very decent house and respectable people."

[49] Thomas Jefferson to Martha Jefferson Randolph, Washington, 2 November 1802, Ibid., 238-39.

[50] Martha Jefferson Randolph to Thomas Jefferson, 9 November 1802, Ibid., 239.

[51] Bear and Stanton, *JMB*, 2:1085.

[52] Martha Jefferson Randolph to Thomas Jefferson, 29 October 1802, Betts and Bear, *JFL*, 238 and Bear and Stanton, *JMB*, 2:1089. Mary Ann Pica was a milliner in Washington, not Philadelphia as Martha supposed (2:1089 n96)

[53] Bear and Stanton, *JMB*, 2:1087-90 and Thomas Jefferson to Martha Jefferson Randolph, Washington, 27 January 1803, Betts and Bear, *JFL*, 242.

[54] Margaret Bayard Smith to Susan Bayard Smith, 26 December 1802, Smith, *Forty*, 34-35.

[55] Maria Jefferson Eppes to Thomas Jefferson, Edgehill, 11 January 1803, Betts and Bear, *JFL*, 240. Randolph and Jefferson's Washington servant, John Shorter, accompanied them on their return.

[56] Thomas Jefferson to Martha Jefferson Randolph, Washington, 27 January 1803, Betts and Bear, *JFL*, 242.

⁵⁷ Bear and Stanton, *JMB*, 2:1094-96 and 1104. Jefferson at this time used a factor of 3.33 to convert Virginia pounds to dollars. Poplar Forest's meat consumption for a year was only slightly less than the amount used at the President's House during Martha and Maria's seven-week visit—2,981 pounds (*JMB*, 2:1086-92). In 1801 to avoid public criticism, Jefferson began buying through tenant Craven Peyton 1,162 acres owned by heirs of Bennett Henderson that adjoined his Tufton farm at the foot of Monticello, along the Rivanna River, and surrounding the town of Milton. He may have embarked on such a course as a way of protecting his plan for developing mills on the River to diversify out of farming and reduce his, now, even larger debt (*JMB*, 2:1047 n94). Even his payments to Craven, however, were later made with money borrowed from commission agent John Barnes (Thomas Jefferson to Thomas Mann Randolph, Washington, 5 July 1803, TJF, Stanton (DLC).

⁵⁸ Thomas Jefferson to Gentlemen of the Senate, and of the House of Representatives, 18 January 1803, manuscript viewed at http://www.ourdocuments.gov (July 26, 2007) and transcribed by author. In this "Confidential" letter, the President was requesting $2,500 for "ten or twelve chosen men" and their officer to explore the Missouri River, "even to the Western Ocean." Obliquely referencing the Administration's diplomatic efforts at the time, he assured Congress: "The nation [France] claiming the territory, regarding this as a literary [scientific] pursuit, which is in the habit of permitting within its dominions, would not be disposed to view it with jealousy, even if the expiring state of its interests there did not render it a matter of indifference."

⁵⁹ Respectively, Thomas Jefferson to Thomas Mann Randolph, Washington, 22 November, 25 November, 15 December, 1802 and 17 January 1803, TJF, Stanton (DLC). (Perhaps sensitive to the recent "silly bird" letter, Jefferson closed each of the first two with a new phrase: "Accept assurances of my affectionate attachment and respect.") John Drayton (1767–1822) was a native South Carolinian who attended the College of New Jersey and served in the State's House and Senate, two gubernatorial terms (1800–02, 1808–09), and as U.S. District Court Judge until his death (http://www.sciway.net, July 26, 2007).

⁶⁰ Thomas Jefferson to Maria Jefferson Eppes, Washington, 18 January and to Martha Jefferson Randolph, 27 January 1803, Betts and Bear, *JFL*, 241 and 242. Eppes ran for the seat being vacated for health reasons by Jefferson's faithful ally, William Branch Giles.

⁶¹ John Wayles Eppes to Thomas Jefferson, 14 April 1803, Edgehill-Randolph Papers (ViU) and Thomas Jefferson to Samuel J. Cabell, 25 April 1803, Jefferson Papers (DLC) as cited in Gaines, *Randolph*, 50. (This description of the public-private conundrum and Randolph's political career, generally, is indebted to Gaines, Ibid. 50-67.) Earlier chapters describe Randolph's youthful political aspirations, his neglect of campaigning for family reasons in 1797 and Jefferson's encouragement in the early years. Cabell (1756–1818) was born in Albemarle County, attended William and Mary, attained the rank of lieutenant colonel during the Revolutionary War, and served in Congress from 1795 to 1803 (http://bioguide.congress.gov, July 15, 2007).

⁶² Thomas Mann Randolph to Thomas Jefferson, Edgehill, 29 April 1803, TJF, Stanton (ViU).

⁶³ Thomas Mann Randolph to Thomas Jefferson, Edgehill, 30 May 1803, TJF, Stanton (ViU). Mary Jefferson Randolph (their seventh) was born 3 November 1803.

⁶⁴ Thomas Mann Randolph to Thomas Jefferson, Edgehill, 22 May 1803, TJF, Stanton, (DLC).

[65]Ibid., and Thomas Mann Randolph to Thomas Jefferson 14 March 1801, *Papers*, 33:290-91. The May 1803 letter seems to end abruptly and was not docketed by Jefferson so may not have been sent. One reason for this may be that it probably concerned the "Walker affair." This is suggested in the first paragraph referencing a 13 April, unfound letter from Jefferson that he had specifically asked be shown to Martha. The content of the letter provoked a heated and indignant outburst from Randolph. "With respect to others no occasion...has occurred since, for me to do anything; and perhaps never may, that subject having ceased I believe to afford discourse to the malignant, as well as the idle and inquisitive. Should it again arise I shall with the warmth my zeal inspires represent to those disposed to agitate it the danger they incur of being charged with baseness or folly for reviving and propagating a story engendered itself by hatred and begetting the misery of individuals who are never heard of in good or in evil. Nothing farther."

Information on the Walker affair was circulating in writing at least in early 1803, which makes it likely the subject of Jefferson's missing 13 April letter he asked Randolph to show Martha. What became labeled the "Walker affair" occurred in 1768, while Elizabeth Walker's husband, John, was accompanying his father and Jefferson's former guardian, Dr. Thomas Walker, to treat with the Indians. Late in 1802, Thomas Callender had published in a Richmond newspaper the stories of Jefferson's indiscretion with neighbor Elizabeth as well as his relationship with Sally Hemings. In March 1803, Jefferson invited John Page to Monticello for the summer and acknowledged that he had "unhappily fallen out" with their mutual friend, John Walker. Malone cites Page's emotional reply: "Curses on the Tongue of Slander! Perdition seize the wretches who would open the scars of wounded Friendship, to gratify private resentment & party spirit," (John Page to Thomas Jefferson, 25 April 1803 as cited Malone, *Jefferson*, 1:451 n12; original in Jefferson Papers [DLC]). Also in April, Malone notes that James Madison wrote Monroe to the effect that "the affair had been happily cleared up" (Malone, 1:218). Jefferson referenced the forthcoming visit by Page and his wife in his letter of 5 May with kudos to his friend implying a controversy was afoot: "We were affectionate friends and inseparable companions in youth, and have always preserved our feelings with mutual fidelity to each other through the stormy times into which we were thrown." But, the affair was not "happily cleared up: and there was something "farther" in 1805, when Walker himself made the allegations public by circulating his correspondence with Jefferson among some Federalists. He sent one letter to South Carolina that specifically referenced discussions he had with Jefferson early in 1803. News of the "affair" (and presumably some letters) reached Connecticut in 1805 at the instigation of David Meade Randolph, Jefferson's distant in-law whom he had turned out of office in 1801 (Malone, 1:219).

One can only imagine the shocking effect such confirmation of theretofore neighborhood gossip had on his daughter. Callender's printed diatribes could be dismissed as the ranting of an embittered and disappointed office seeker; but, Father had probably confirmed the essential facts that "when young and single [he] offered love to a handsome lady." (Thomas Jefferson to Robert Smith, 1 July 1805, as cited in Malone, Ibid., 1:222; original in *Thomas Jefferson Correspondence Printed from the Originals in the Collections of William K. Bixby*, 114-15). Not only did it reflect negatively on the person she most loved but it also soured neighborhood comity her Father had so insistently promoted. The family was quickly learning that the ideal of strictly separated private and public spheres was, in practical politics of the Republic, a wholly deceptive illusion. For a discussion of the Walker affair, see Malone, *Jefferson*, 1: 445-51 and 3:216-23.

66 Thomas Jefferson to Thomas Mann Randolph, Washington, 5 May 1803, TJF, Stanton (DLC).
67 Thomas Mann Randolph to Thomas Jefferson, Edgehill, 30 May 1803, TJF, Stanton (ViU).
68 Thomas Jefferson to Thomas Mann Randolph, 8 June, 1803, TJF, Stanton (DLC).
69 Thomas Jefferson to Thomas Mann Randolph, Washington, 5 July 1803, TJF, Stanton (DLC).
70 Ibid.
71 Respectively, Thomas Jefferson to Anne Willing Bingham, Paris, 11 May 1788, *Papers*,13:151-52; and to Angelica Schuyler Church, Philadelphia, 24 May 1797, Ibid. 29:396-97 For an excellent discussion of women's nascent political influence in Washington City, see Catherine Allgor, *Parlor Politics In Which the Ladies of Washington Help Build a City and a Government* (Charlottesville, VA: University Press of Virginia, 2000).
72Thomas Jefferson to Martha Jefferson Randolph, Philadelphia, 17 May 1798, *Papers*, 30:354-55.
73 Anon., *Aurora* ,13 February 1804 as cited in Dumas Malone, *Jefferson the President: First Term, 1801–05* (Boston: Little, Brown and Company, 1970), 388.
74 This account drawn from Malone, *Jefferson the President*, 376-91.
75 Thomas Jefferson to Martha Jefferson Randolph, Washington, 23 January 1804, Betts & Bear, *JFL*, 254-55.
76 Rosalie Stier Calvert to Mme. H. J. Stier, Riversdale, 29 December 1803 and 2 March 1807, *Mistress of Riversdale: The Plantation Letters of Rosalie Stier Calvert, 1795–1821*, ed. and trans., Margaret Law Callcott (Baltimore: Johns Hopkins University Press, 1991), 70 and 77, respectively. Emphasis in the original. Hereafter, Calvert, *Letters*.
77 Margaret Bayard Smith (Mrs. Samuel Harrison) to Jane Bayard Kirkpatrick (Mrs. Andrew), Washington, 23 January 1804, Smith, *Forty*, 44-46. The youngest brother of Napoleon, Jerome (1784–1860) entered the U.S. in 1803 at the beginning of war between England and France, when the French ship on which he served was forced to New York harbor. His marriage with Elizabeth Patterson (1785–1879) was annulled by his brother in 1807. "Godwin" referred to Mary Wollstonecraft's *Vindication of the Rights of Women* (1792). Rosalie, also, reported on the "display" by Mrs. Bonaparte in a "dress so transparent that you could see the color and shape of her thighs, and even more."
78 Rosalie Stier Calvert to Mme H. J. Stier, Riversdale, 2 March 1804, Calvert, *Letters*, 62.
79 Eleanor Parke Custis Lewis to Elizabeth Bordley Gibson, Woodlawn, 23 March 1806, *George Washington's Beautiful Nelly*, ed., Patricia Brady (Columbia, SC: University of South Carolina Press, 1991), 67.
80 Charlene Boyer Lewis, "Elizabeth Patterson Bonaparte," *Journal of Women's History*, Vol. 18 No. 2 (Summer, 2006), 33-34.
81 Margaret Bayard Smith (Mrs. Samuel Harrison) to Jane Bayard Kirkpatrick (Mrs. Andrew), Washington, 23 January 1804, Smith, *Forty*, 44-46.
82 Martha Jefferson Randolph to Thomas Jefferson, Edgehill, 14 January 1804, Betts and Bear, *JFL*, 251-52.
83 Thomas Jefferson to Maria Jefferson Eppes, Washington, 29 January 1804, Betts and Bear, *JFL*, 255-56.
84 Maria Jefferson Eppes to Thomas Jefferson, Edgehill, 10 February 1804, Ibid., 256-57. Martha, also, reminded Father of his promise. He sat for the physiognotrace by

Charles-Balthazar-Julien Févret de Saint-Mémin sometime in November and ordered forty-eight impressions of the roughly three-inch, round engraving on copper plate. Saint-Mémin emigrated to New York in 1793, moved to Philadelphia in 1798, and traveled to other cities doing portraits. See Noble E. Cunningham, Jr., *The Image of Thomas Jefferson in the Public Eye: Portraits for the People, 1800–1809* (Charlottesville, VA: University Press of Virginia, 1981), 79-84.

[85] Thomas Jefferson to Maria Jefferson Eppes, Washington, 26 February 1804, Betts and Bear, *JFL*, 258.

[86] Thomas Jefferson to Maria Jefferson Eppes, Washington, 3 March 1804, Ibid., 258-59.

[87] Martha Jefferson Randolph to Thomas Jefferson, Edgehill, 31 May 1804, Betts and Bear, *JFL*, 261-62.

Chapter 9: A harbour from cares and storms"

[1] Thomas Jefferson to Martha Jefferson Randolph, Washington, 7 October 1804, Ibid., 262.

[2] Thomas Jefferson to Martha Jefferson Randolph, Washington, 3 December 1804, Ibid., 265.

[3] Thomas Jefferson to Martha Jefferson Randolph, Washington, 7 October, 6 November and 7 January 1804, Betts and Bear, *JFL*, 262-263 and 266, respectively. Martha Jefferson to Thomas Jefferson, 31 May 1804, 30 November and 28 February 1805, Ibid., 260-61, 263 and 268, respectively. The "hysterick" diagnosis encompassed a wide-range of what were considered up to the early twentieth century "nervous diseases" and was almost universally associated with women. Presumed "causes" included exposure to cold, "irritation of the nerves of the stomach," "violent passions...[such] as fear, grief, anger, or great disappointments," and "suppression of the menses." See W. Buchan, *Domestic Medicine* (Prepared for the British Royal Society, 1785 second edition), http://www.americanrevolution.org/medicine (August 29, 2009).

[4] Martha Jefferson to Thomas Jefferson, 28 February 1805, Ibid., 268.

[5] Thomas Mann Randolph to Thomas Jefferson, Edgehill, 27 April and 16 June 1805, TJF, Stanton (ViU).

[6] Martha Jefferson Randolph to Thomas Jefferson, Edgehill, 26 October 1805, Betts and Bear, *JFL*, 280. "Jane" was most likely Mann Randolph's sister, the wife of Thomas Eston Randolph and a neighbor near Monticello.

[7] Respectively, Thomas Jefferson to Dolley Madison, Washington, 1 November 1805, in *The Dolley Madison Digital Edition*, http://rotunda.upress.virginia.edu/dmde (December 2, 2007); and Thomas Jefferson to Martha Jefferson Randolph, Washington, 7 November 1805, Betts and Bear, *JFL*, 280-81.

[8] This and the following from Annals of Congress, House of Representatives, 9th Congress, 1st Session (Washington, D. C.: Gales and Seaton, 1834–35), http://memory.loc.gov/ammem/amlaw/lwac.html (September 18, 2007), 1102-1106. See Gaines, *Randolph*, 60-63. John Randolph used his position as chair during the 9th Congress to mount a strong opposition to various initiatives by the Administration. His comments in this instance were presumably directed toward Pennsylvanian William Findley (ca. 1741–1821), whom he suggested by his language was intoxicated, for charging that salt tax repeal was "part of a system to throw the gauntlet, to destroy the Administration." (Interestingly, Findley had chaired the House Committee on Elections that certified Randolph's narrow, 13-vote margin in the 1803 election.) The

calls for order were in response to David Rogerson Williams of South Carolina (1776–1830) speaking in favor of repeal.

[9] Ibid.

[10] Ibid.

[11] Richmond *Enquirer*, June 17 and 24, July 1 and July 4, as cited in Gaines, *Randolph*, 62 n62, n63, and n67.

[12] Thomas Jefferson to Thomas Mann Randolph, Washington, 12 January 1806, TJF Stanton (MHi, reel 14).

[13] Ibid.

[14] Ibid.

[15] Thomas Jefferson to Thomas Mann Randolph, Washington, 23 June 1806, TJF, Stanton (ViU).

[16] Thomas Jefferson to Martha Jefferson Randolph, Washington, 6 July 1806, Betts and Bear, *JFL*, 285-86. Jefferson used similar language ten years earlier to describe the conflict between his need for public approval and desire for tranquility amid those whom he loved (Thomas Jefferson to Martha Jefferson Randolph, Philadelphia, 8 June 1797, *Papers*, 29:424-25).

[17] Thomas Jefferson to Martha Jefferson Randolph, Washington, 6 July and 20 October 1806, Betts and Bear, *JFL*, 285-86, and 289, respectively,

[18] Thomas Jefferson to Martha Jefferson Randolph, Philadelphia, 8 June 1797, *Papers*, 29:424-25.

[19] Cornelia Jefferson Randolph to Ellen Wayles Randolph Coolidge, New London, 11 December 1826, FLP (ViU), http://familyletters.dataformat.com/ (September 11, 2006). Also, see below regarding Martha's concern for her son's "Randolph character."

[20] Gaines, *Randolph*, 65n80.

[21] Thomas Jefferson to Thomas Mann Randolph, Washington, 18 February 1807, TJF, Stanton (DLC).

[22] Thomas Jefferson to Thomas Mann Randolph, Washington, 19 February 1807, TJF, Stanton (DLC). These charges of disloyalty were not mitigated by Randolph's retreating to a boardinghouse considered "Federalist" (Gaines, *Randolph*, 66).

[23] Thomas Jefferson to Thomas Mann Randolph, Washington, 28 February 1807, TJF, Stanton (DLC).

[24] Thomas Jefferson to Martha Jefferson, Washington, 2, 6, 9, 23 and 27 March 1807, Betts and Bear, *JFL*, 297-299, 304, and 305.

[25] Martha Jefferson Randolph to Thomas Jefferson, Edgehill, March 20, 1807, Ibid., 303.

[26] Ibid.

[27] Martha Jefferson Randolph to Thomas Jefferson, Edgehill, 17 February 1809, Ibid., 381-82.

[28] Martha Jefferson Randolph to Thomas Jefferson, Edgehill, 18 November 1808, Ibid., 359-61 and Thomas Jefferson to Martha Jefferson Randolph, 29 November 1808, Ibid., 366-67. In 1809, John Eppes remarried to nineteen-year old Martha Burke Jones of Halifax, N.C. (Ibid., 285n1). At some point, Eppes developed a relationship and had children with a Hemings descendent, Betsey (1783–1857), daughter of Mary, whom Jefferson in 1792 sold at her request to Thomas Bell, a Charlottesville merchant; however, Jefferson required Betsy's return to Monticello, where she lived until given as part of Maria's marriage settlement with John Eppes in 1797. She was interred with Eppes in the family plot at Millbrook plantation, Buckingham County,

VA, and his wife was buried elsewhere (www.buckinghamhemmings.com [October 20, 2011].)

[29] Martha Jefferson Randolph to Thomas Jefferson, Edgehill, 30 November and 14 January 1804, Betts and Bear, *JFL*, 263-65 and 251-52.

[30] Respectively, Martha Jefferson Randolph to Thomas Jefferson, Edgehill, 2 January 1808, Ibid., 317-18 and Thomas Jefferson to Martha Jefferson Randolph, Washington, 10 January 1809, Ibid., 377-78.

[31] Respectively, Thomas Jefferson to Martha Jefferson, Aix en Provence, 28 March 1787, *Papers*, 11:250-53; New York, 4 April 1790, Ibid., 16:300; Philadelphia, 8 February 1798, Ibid., 30:91-92; and Washington, 23 November 1807, Betts and Bear, *JFL*, 315-16.

[32] Thomas Jefferson to Martha Jefferson Randolph, 5 January and Martha Jefferson Randolph to Thomas Jefferson, 16 January 1808, Betts and Bear, *JFL*, 319-20 and 322-23, respectively.

[33] Thomas Jefferson to Thomas Mann Randolph, Washington, 17 January 1809, TJF, Stanton (MHI, reel 14).

[34] Thomas Jefferson to Thomas Mann Randolph, Washington, 31 January 1809, L & B *Writings*, 18:262-64.

[35] Thomas Jefferson to Thomas Mann Randolph, Washington, 17 January 1809, TJF, Stanton (MHi, reel 14). Jefferson estimated by his own account of the year beginning 4 March 1803 that his rents were $1089; net tobacco revenues, $916; and his government salary, $25,000. Expenses, including the President's house were an estimated $27,721; however, he included over $7,000 in what should be considered capital items, such as purchasing land, building construction costs, and household furnishings. Such commingling of current expenses with investment outlays was typical for Jefferson but distorts and makes it challenging to decipher his financial situation (*JMB*, 2:1098-99). A sense of what this income would buy can be gained by comparison to some common expenses: Stage from Philadelphia to Baltimore, $8, and from thence to Alexandria, $4; one pound of bacon, 7 1/2 cents; a cow, $20; barrel of corn, $2; a year's subscription to Samuel Harrison Smith's *National Intelligencer*, $5; one month wages for house servants in Washington, $200; and a pipe of "Brasil Quality" Madeira, $350 (*JMB*, 2:1018-19, 1023, 1027-08, and 1031, 1040, respectively). Jefferson's 1800 tobacco crop of over 42,000 pounds returned $2974 gross in May 1801, when he paid a month's salary of $200 to household servants. For a summary of 1802–1803 expenses, which was discussed earlier, see Bear and Stanton, *JMB*, 2:1098-99.

[36] The store account with merchant David Higginbotham in Milton was £1920–6–7 (Virginia currency) on 31 August 1807 and slightly over £2011 by 21 June 1810. Using Jefferson's conversion rate of 3.33 Virginia dollars to Virginia pounds, the latter was about $6,697 as compared, say, to his Poplar Forest tobacco from the prior year that brought $2,005 on 14 April. See Bear and Stanton, *JMB*, 2:1258 and 1255, respectively.

[37] Jefferson thought his government salary would provide for his "maintenance" and "profits from [his] estate" would ease the "burthens of debt" (Thomas Jefferson to Thomas Mann Randolph, Washington, 16 November 1801, TJF, Stanton [DLC]). He realized a few months after assuming office that his 1800 "plan" was unworkable. "[S]uch are the extraordinary expences of an outfit here, while the current expences must be going on that I am not only unable to do anything in the pecuniary way [for you] at present, but am so far in anticipation that were any accident to happen to me for some time to come, it would leave my private fortune under serious embarrasment" (Thomas Jefferson to Thomas Mann Randolph, Washington, 8

October 1801, TJF, Stanton [DLC]). To protect the interests of the Randolph and Eppes families, he proposed gifts to each of Bedford County property.

38 Thomas Jefferson to Martha Jefferson Randolph, Washington, 5 January 1808, Betts and Bear, *JFL*, 319-20. The marriage settlement of Bedford property was to "Martha Jefferson and her heirs."

39 Martha Jefferson Randolph to Thomas Jefferson, Edgehill, 16 January 1808, Ibid., 322-23.

40 Thomas Jefferson to Thomas Mann Randolph, Washington, 31 January 1809, L & B, *Writings*, 18:262-64. In early 1809, both Randolph and Jefferson were discussing sale of land to settle debts: Varina by the former and certain "detached" tracts by Jefferson. When Varina's sale fell through, Jefferson offered his land to pay that debt. In proposing to Randolph the sale of land, he proclaimed that nothing can be more profitable, "that is, yield so much happiness, as the payment of debts, which are an unsufferable torment. …" Though Grand Papa euphemistically referred to a "joint family," he effectively behaved as the household's patriarch. The nuanced language he and Martha used regarding their commingled debt clearly suggests they were trying to imagine the solution to Randolph's financial troubles separate from their own and attribute his problems largely to his personal character and imprudent biological family.

41 Thomas Jefferson to Thomas Mann Randolph, Washington, 17 January 1809, TJF, Stanton (MHi, reel 14). His estimates of Poplar Forest sales were consistent with the prior years but, typical for Jefferson, did not net expenses that included building another house. The Bedford detached tract of 474 acres was sold in early 1810 to Samuel J. Harrison for £1,200 (approximately $4,000) or $8.43 per acre, but a portion was subject to conflicting claims. See Bear and Stanton, *JMB*, 2:1254 n66 and "Notes on Ivy Creek Lands," *Papers RS*, 1:670-71.

42 Martha Jefferson Randolph to Thomas Jefferson, Edgehill, 31 May 1804, Betts and Bear, *JFL*, 261-62.

43 Martha Jefferson Randolph to Thomas Jefferson, Edgehill, 15 July 1808, Ibid., 348-49.

44 Martha Jefferson Randolph to Thomas Jefferson, Edgehill, 31 January 1801, *Papers*, 32:526-28; Thomas Jefferson to Martha Jefferson Randolph, Washington, 5 February 1801, Ibid., 32:556-57; and Martha Jefferson Randolph to Thomas Jefferson, Edgehill, 16 April 1802, Betts and Bear, *JFL*, 222-223;

45 Martha Jefferson Randolph to Thomas Jefferson, Edgehill, 30 November 1804, Ibid., 263-65.

46 Thomas Jefferson to Caspar Wistar, Washington, 21 June 1807, Bergh, *Writings* (1907),11:78-85. This passage was not included in *Memoirs, Correspondence, and Miscellanies from the Papers of Thomas Jefferson*, (4:91-95) edited by Thomas Jefferson Randolph, perhaps for obvious reasons; also excluded from this edition of Jefferson documents was a request for information on the costs of boarding, professors' fees, etc.

47 Thomas Jefferson to Thomas Mann Randolph, Washington, 22 November 1808, TJF, Stanton (DLC).

48 Thomas Jefferson to Martha Jefferson Randolph, Washington, 11 July 1808, Betts and Bear, *JFL*, 347-48.

49 Martha Jefferson Randolph to Thomas Jefferson, Edgehill, 18 November 1808, Ibid., 359-61. She was referring to Louis Dubroca, *Le ton de la bonne compagnie, ou régles de la civilité à l'usage des personnes des deux sexes*, (Paris: np, 1802).

[50] Thomas Jefferson to Thomas Jefferson Randolph, Washington, 24 November 1808, *JFL*, 326-65. Jefferson does advise Jeff on "politeness," "never entering into an argument," "good humor," avoiding "bad company," etc.—i.e., manners and genteel behavior, just as his mother wanted. Jefferson was exceptionally strident in describing to Jeff how the political world might be injected into their family affairs. "You will be more exposed than others to have these animals shaking their horns at you, because of the relation in which you stand with me and to hate me as a chief in the antagonist party your presence will be to then what the vomit-grass is to the sick dog, a nostrum for producing an ejaculation."

[51] Martha Jefferson Randolph to Thomas Jefferson, Edgehill, 16 January 1808, Ibid., 322-23.

[52] Thomas Jefferson, *Notes on the State of Virginia*, ed. with and introduction by Frank Shuffelton (New York: Penguin Books, 1999), 153.

[53] Martha Jefferson Randolph to Thomas Jefferson, Edgehill, 16 January 1808, Betts and Bear, *JFL*, 322-23.

[54] Martha Jefferson Randolph to Thomas Jefferson, Edgehill, 26 October 1805, Ibid., 280 and Bear and Stanton, *JMB*, 2:1168. Other than $465 given directly to "Patsy" or "Mrs. Randolph," other expenses for this December-May period noted in the Jefferson's Memorandum Book were not appreciably different from similar periods in prior or subsequent years. For example, meat consumption at the President's House from mid-December to early February a year earlier averaged 325 pounds, compared to 343 pounds during Martha's visit (Ibid., 2:1143-1145 and 1171-73). December to early March was the legislative "campaign season" that always entailed higher expenses as a consequence of the President hosting many dinners with Senators and Congressmen.

[55] Bear and Stanton, Ibid., 2:1179 is one example of these sixty-day notes being renewed that were still outstanding in 1809, when Jefferson left Washington. He initially paid them by a private loan with a six month term from a Virginia resident and later refinanced again with the Richmond Branch of the U.S. Bank (Ibid., 2:1238). These notes likely were what Jefferson was referring to when he informed Randolph that he was to "fall short 8. or 10,000 D." (Washington, 17 January 1809, TJF, Stanton [MHi, R-14]).

[56] Martha Jefferson Randolph to Thomas Jefferson, Edgehill, 26 October 1805, Betts and Bear, *JFL*, 280.

[57] Martha Jefferson Randolph to Thomas Jefferson, Edgehill, 16 January 1808, Ibid., 322-23. In his January 5th letter, Jefferson reassured Martha that their lands held separately from Randolph, "if we preserve them, are sufficient to place all the children in independence" (Ibid., 319-20). The husband's "estate being employed entirely for meeting his own difficulties, would place him at ease."

[58] Martha Jefferson Randolph, to Thomas Jefferson, Edgehill, 2 January 1808, Ibid., 317-18. Gaines notes that Randolph gave a deed of trust for $5,600 to Monroe's son-in-law, George Hay in late 1807 (*Randolph*, 77 and n47.)

[59] Thomas Jefferson to Martha Jefferson Randolph, Washington, 5 January 1808, Betts and Bear, *JFL*, 319-20.

[60] Ibid.

[61] Thomas Jefferson to Nathaniel Burwell, Monticello, 14 March 1818, *A Jefferson Profile As Revealed in His letters*, ed., Saul K. Padover (New York: The John Day Company, 1956), 297-99. This letter on female education with a list of books used in his daughters' education, Jefferson noted, was prepared with the help of Martha and one of the "elèvés." A full description of the referenced reading list was first published in Billy Wayson, " 'Considerably different for her sex':" A Reading Plan for

Martha Jefferson," *The Libraries, Leadership & Legacy of John Adams and Thomas Jefferson,*
eds. Robert C. Baron and Conrad Edick Wright (Golden, CO: Fulcrum Press, 2010),
133-158.
[62] Martha Jefferson Randolph to Thomas Jefferson, 30 January 1808, Betts and Bear,
JFL, 325; Thomas Jefferson to Thomas Mann Randolph, Washington, 6 February
1808, TJF, Stanton (DLC); and to Martha Jefferson Randolph, Betts and Bear, *JFL*,
327. Edmund Bacon was Monticello overseer; Jonathan Shoemaker and son Isaac,
mill tenants. Randolph and Jefferson exchanged unusually few letters in 1808 (eleven).
Randolph was enlisted in two very "little commissions" over the balance of the year.
Soon after Martha's offer, her husband was to retrieve a manuscript copy of a court
decision located somewhere in "one of the 3 or 4 volumes of MS laws"; have it
copied; certify its correctness; and forward immediately (Thomas Jefferson to Thomas
Mann Randolph, Washington, 26 February 1808, TJF, Stanton [MHi, reel 14]). In an
another instance, Randolph was asked to locate somewhere in Jefferson's cabinet and
mail immediately a "bundle of papers" labeled "to be answered and acted on" that
Jefferson's "forgetfulness" left at home (Thomas Jefferson to Thomas Mann
Randolph, Washington, 4 and 11 October 1808, TJF, Stanton [MHi, reel 14] and TJF,
Stanton [DLC], respectively; and Thomas Mann Randolph to Thomas Jefferson, 14
October 1808, TJF, Stanton [ViU]).
[63] Thomas Jefferson to Thomas Mann Randolph, Washington, 28 June 1808, TJF,
Stanton (DLC).
[64] Thomas Jefferson to Martha Jefferson Randolph, Washington, 2 February 1808,
Betts and Bear, *JFL*, 325-27. Richard S. Hackley was a persistent supplicant for public
office. He began as early as 1805 trying to secure a consulship in Bordeaux, France
(Thomas Mann Randolph to Thomas Jefferson, 22 June 1805, TJF, Stanton [ViU]).
Clearly intending his message would be forwarded, Father informed Martha of the
political situation in Spain and suggested Hackley should "cultivate" the sitting
consul's "good will" (Thomas Jefferson to Martha Jefferson Randolph, Washington, 2
February 1808, Ibid., 325-27).
[65] Martha Jefferson Randolph to Dolley Payne Todd Madison, Edge hill, 15 January
1808, in *The Dolley Madison Digital Edition,* http://rotunda.upress.virginia.edu/dmde/
(December 12, 2007). Martha was referring to William Beverley Randolph. Dolley's
action was swift, because on 10 February his mother, Mary, expressed her
"gratitude...for [Mrs. Madison's] very friendly attention in procuring so eligible a
situation" and closed with asking her to "believe me with cordial esteem" (Mary
Randolph to Dolley Madison, 10 February 1808, Richmond, Ibid.). Even ardent
Federalists, it seems, were not adverse to soliciting patronage from Jeffersonian
republicans or pleading their promotions fourteen years later. Ellen Randolph was
"enjoying the gaieties" of Richmond with Mary in the winter of 1822, when her aunt
once again unabashedly asked the long-retired Montpelier planter to intervene on
Beverley's behalf to become head of one department in the newly expanded federal
land office (Mary Randolph to Dolley Madison, [Richmond], 7 March 1822, Ibid.).
These efforts, joined with those to secure an appointment (also successful) for
another son, Burwell Starke Randolph, were considered by Mary as critical to
recovering the social esteem she had lost in their family's bankruptcy. "My situation
here [Washington City] will now be intirely [*sic*] agreeable." She wrote Dolley. "I have
a circle of valuable acquaintances whose manners suit my taste, and I associate with
them on terms of equality." After being "brought low" in Richmond, "the attentions
[she] received...savoured strongly of that patronage which a superior is willing to give

to an inferior who they think not altogether destitute of merit"—traditional genteel condescension (Mary Randolph to Dolley Madison, Washington, 22 September 1820, Ibid.). Her sons' <u>combined</u> salaries of less than $2,000 are an index of just how substantial was respect in Mary's estimation.

[66] Martha Jefferson Randolph to Thomas Jefferson, Edgehill, 17 February 1809, Betts and Bear, *JFL*, 381-82. Beverley, son of William Randolph and Martha's nephew, was traveling through Washington to enter West Point. He had received the appointment on the President's recommendation and the official letter was forwarded through Martha (Thomas Jefferson to Martha Jefferson Randolph, Washington, 18 October 1808, Ibid., 351-52). Martha's involvement as intermediary in other patronage appointments was discussed in several letters from this period, including one of 17 February 1809, Ibid., 381-82, concerning a West Point position for the son of a South Carolina acquaintance, Dr. James Moultrie.

[67] Martha Jefferson Randolph to Thomas Jefferson, Edgehill, 16 January 1808, Ibid., 322-23. The cousin was Tarlton Webb, the grandson of Randolph's aunt Mary (Mrs. Tarlton) Fleming.

[68] Martha Jefferson Randolph to Thomas Jefferson, [received 1 January 1809], Ibid., 375.

[69] Ibid.

[70] Martha Jefferson Randolph to Thomas Jefferson, 24 and 17 February 1809, Ibid. 384 and 381-82;

[71] Thomas Mann Randolph to Thomas Jefferson, 6 January 1809, TJF, Stanton (ViU).

[72] Thomas Jefferson to Thomas Mann Randolph, 17 January 1809, TJF, Stanton (MHi, reel 14). This assignment to Randolph essentially made him responsible for Jefferson's "maintenance" and that of the household. The management of Tufton was also broached with Martha a few weeks later: "Ignorant too, as I am, in the management of a farm, I shall be obliged to ask the aid of Mr. Randolph's skill and attention, especially for that of Tufton, when it comes to me. It will be my main dependence, and to make it adequate, with my other Albemarle resources, to support all expences, will require good management" (to Martha Jefferson Randolph, 27 February 1809, Betts and Bear, *JFL*, 385-86).

[73] Thomas Jefferson to Thomas Mann Randolph, Washington, 31, January 1809, L & B, *Writings*, 18:262-64.

[74] Thomas Jefferson to Jonathan Shoemaker, Monticello, 6 April 1809, *Papers RS*, 1:108-110; Bear and Stanton, *JMB*, 2:1246 n45; and Betts, *Farm Book*, 365-76. The first payment of only $490 was finally made on August 6th and was used immediately to pay on the substantial account with Milton merchant David Higginbotham (*JMB*, 2:1246). Jonathan Shoemaker (1756–1837) had been manager of the Pennsylvania Hospital from 1781–1790 and opened his Rock Creek establishment in 1804, where he remained while son Isaac ran the Shadwell mill (*Papers RS*, 1:109-110n).

[75] Martha Jefferson Randolph to Thomas Jefferson, 2 March 1809, Betts and Bear, *JFL*, 386-88.

[76]Respectively, Martha Jefferson Randolph to Thomas Jefferson, Edgehill, 18 November 1808, Betts and Bear, *JFL*, 359-61; Thomas Jefferson to Anne Cary Randolph Bankhead, Washington, 8 November 1808, Ibid., 357; and Martha Jefferson Randolph to Thomas Jefferson, Edgehill, 24 November 1808, Ibid., 361-62. Virginia (Jenny) had wed Wilson Jefferson Cary on 5 August 1805 but lived primarily in the Monticello household until 1808. Montaigne, whom her father recommended Martha read as a youngster, attributed this quotation to Solon as uttered by King Croesus before being executed by Cyrus: "Men, no matter how Fortune may smile on them, can never be happy until you have seen them pass through the last day of life..."

(Michel De Montaigne, *The Complete Essays*, "19. That we should not be deemed happy till after our death." trans. M. A. Screech (New York: Penguin Books, 1987, 1991), 85.

Chapter 10: "Elate from Monticello"

[1] Margaret Bayard Smith, *The First Forty Years of Washington Society* as cited in *Visitors to Monticello*, ed. Merrill D. Peterson (Charlottesville: University Press of Virginia, 1989), 51.

[2] Thomas Jefferson to Louis H. Girardin, Monticello, 31 October 1809, *Papers RS*, 1:633-34. Jeff studied mathematics and natural philosophy at this school from November 1809 to the following summer. In an ironic twist, he roomed with Mary Randolph (Mrs. David Meade) who had opened a successful Richmond boarding house after her husband's removal as U. S. Marshall and ultimate bankruptcy. Girardin (1771–1825) was a royalist who fled France during the Revolution. He taught at William and Mary, operated the Richmond Academy from 1807–10, and later had similar enterprises in Milton and Stanton (633-34n).

[3] Martha Jefferson Randolph to Ellen Wayles Randolph Coolidge, Washington, April 1st [1831], FLP (ViU), http://familyletters.dataformat.com (May 25, 2007); and to Margaret Bayard Smith, 10 November 1828. A family friend offered to foster thirteen-year-old George during a three year cruise on the "John Adams," thereby giving him a two year advantage for promotion. The young boy began receiving his pay immediately by an order to service whose reporting date set-off six months. Meriwether Lewis Randolph (1810–1837) as an adult moved to Arkansas territory where he died of bilious fever soon thereafter.

[4] Martha Jefferson and Thomas Mann Randolph to Thomas Jefferson, 31 January 1801, *Papers*, 32:526-28; Thomas Jefferson to Martha Jefferson Randolph, Washington, 5 February 1801, Ibid., 32:556-57; and Martha Jefferson to Thomas Jefferson, Bellmont, 22 January 1798, Ibid., 30:43-44.

[5] Martha Jefferson Randolph to Thomas Jefferson, Edgehill, 24 February 1809, Betts and Bear, *JFL*, 384.

[6] Thomas Mann Randolph to Thomas Jefferson, Edgehill, 18 January 1800, *Papers*, 31: 323-24; Thomas Jefferson to Martha Jefferson Randolph, Philadelphia, 8 February 1798, Ibid., 30:90-91; Maria Jefferson Eppes to Martha Jefferson Randolph, Eppington, 4 April 1798, Southern Women and Their Families, Parts 4-6, Nicholas P. Trist Papers (UnC), microfilm reel 1, transcribed by author.

[7] Respectively, Martha Jefferson Randolph to Thomas Jefferson, Monticello, 16 January, 1793, *Papers*, 25:64; Thomas Jefferson to Martha Jefferson Randolph, Monticello, 27 March 1797, Ibid., 29: 327-28); Martha Jefferson Randolph to Thomas Jefferson, Monticello, 12 May 1798, Ibid., 30: 346-47; and Martha Jefferson Randolph to Thomas Jefferson, Edgehill, 19 June 1801, Betts and Bear, *JFL*, 204-05.

[8] Thomas Jefferson to Martha Jefferson Randolph, Washington, 5 January 1808, Betts and Bear, *JFL*, 319-20.

[9] Mary Jefferson Randolph to Ellen W. Randolph Coolidge, Monticello, 30 October 1826, FLP (ViU), http://familyletters.dataformat.com (October 27, 2007).

[10] Cornelia Jefferson Randolph to Ellen W. Randolph Coolidge, Monticello, 6 July 1828, FLP (ViU), http://familyletters.dataformat.com (October 24, 2007); Martha Jefferson Randolph to Ellen W. Randolph Coolidge, Monticello, September 1826, (ViHi, 77-45), transcribed by author; Cornelia Jefferson Randolph to Ellen W.

Randolph Coolidge, New London, 11 December 1826, FLP (ViU), http://familyletters.dataformat.com/ (September 11, 2006); and Ellen W. Randolph Coolidge to Nicholas P. Trist, Boston, 27 September 1826, FLP (ViU), Ibid., (January 22, 2007).

[11] For a detailed description of Jefferson's attentiveness to the historical record, see Robert M. S. McDonald, "Thomas Jefferson and Historical Self-Construction: The Earth Belongs to the Living?," *The Historian*, 61:2, 289-310.

[12] Martha Jefferson Randolph to Thomas Jefferson, Richmond, 25 April 1790, *Papers*, 16:384-85; 22 January 1798, Ibid., 30:434-44; and 31 May 1804, Betts and Bear, *JFL*, 261-62.

[13] Martha Jefferson Randolph to Elizabeth House Trist, Monticello, 12 November 1811, FLP (ViU), http://retirementseries.dateformat.com (September 21, 2009); Bear and Stanton, *JMB*, 1268-69; and Thomas Jefferson to Martha Jefferson Randolph, Poplar Forest, 17 February 1811, Betts & Bear, *JFL*, 398-99. Her son Meriwether Lewis had been born on 1 January 1810, some eighteen months before the miscarriage, and she had just spent three months at Edgehill.

[14] Thomas Jefferson to Thomas Mann Randolph, 17 January and 31 January 1809, TJF, Stanton (MHi, reel 14) and L & B, *Writings*, 18:262-64, respectively.

[15] Thomas Mann Randolph's and Martha Jefferson Randolph's Conveyance of Bedford County Land to Anne Moseley, 19 February 1810, FLP (Vi, Bedford County Deed Book), http://retirementseries.dataformat.com (September 21, 2009).

[16] Thomas Mann Randolph to Thomas Jefferson, Monticello, 5 March 1791, *Papers*, 19:420; 6 March 1802, Edgehill, TJF, Stanton (MHi, reel 13); Monticello 29 April 1803, TJF, Stanton (ViU); Thomas Jefferson to Thomas Mann Randolph, Washington, 13 July 1806, TJF, Stanton (MHi, reel 14); Thomas Jefferson to Martha Jefferson Randolph, Washington, 2 March 1807, Betts and Bear, *JFL*, 297; and, Gaines, *Randolph*, 70. Randolph's son, Jeff, would later marry Jane Hollins Nicholas, the daughter of Wilson Cary Nicholas.

[17] Thomas Mann Randolph to Joseph Carrington Cabell, Edgehill, 23 March 1810, TJF, Stanton (ViU).

[18] Thomas Mann Randolph to Francis Walker Gilmer, 11 June 1809, FLP (DLC, Randolph Family), http://familyletters.dataformat.com (May 26, 2007).

[19] Eliza House Trist to Catharine Wistar Bache, Monticello, 28 December 1819, FLP (PPAmP, Bache), http://familyletters.dataformat.com (May 26, 2007).

[20] Thomas Jefferson to Eliza House Trist, Monticello, 1 February 1814, TJF files transcription.

[21] Thomas Mann Randolph to John Baptiste de Walbach, Monticello, 23 February 1814, http://familyletters.dataformat.com (November 10 2007).

[22] Note on letter of John Baptiste de Walbach to Thomas Mann Randolph, Washington, 13 March 1814, Ibid. John Baptiste de Barth, Baron de Walbach (1766–1857) was a German national that served both in Europe and in 1799 began his American military career. He served under such luminaries as William Macpherson and Charles C. Pinckney in cavalry, artillery, and engineering units. His rank was Adjutant-General in the War of 1812. See Appleton's Cyclopedia of American Biography, eds. James Grant Wilson, John Fiske, and Stanley L. Klos (New York: D. Appleton and Company, 1887–89), http://famousamericans.net/johnbaptiste debarthwalbach/ (November 14, 2007).

[23] Martha Jefferson Randolph to Elizabeth House Trist, Monticello, 31 May 1815, FLP (ViHi, Trist), http://familyletters.dataformat.com (September 10, 2006).

[24] Martha Jefferson Randolph to Elizabeth House Trist, Monticello, 31 May 1815 FLP (ViHi, Trist), http://familyletters.dataformat.com (September 10, 2006).

[25] Martha Jefferson Randolph to Thomas Jefferson, Monticello, 20 November 1816, Betts and Bear *JFL*, 416-17. Nancy experienced trials of her own to preserve Morris' estate for their son, Gouverneur, from legal challenges by his nephews.

[26] Elizabeth Trist to Catherine Wistar Bache, Henry County, 22 August 1814, FLP (PPAmP, Bache), http://retirementseries.dataformat.com (September 24, 2009).

[27] Martha Jefferson Randolph to Thomas Jefferson, Monticello, 20 November 1816, Betts and Bear *JFL*, 416-17. Her son-in-law had forfeited his bond pending trial for assaulting Jeff Randolph with a knife in the courthouse square and may have been jailed had they returned to Albemarle County (Ibid., 430 n1).

[28] Martha Jefferson Randolph to Thomas Jefferson, Monticello, 7 August 1819, Ibid., 429-30.

[29] Eliza House Trist to Nicholas P. Trist, Farmington, 3 February and 9 March 1819, FLP (DLC, Trist), http://retirementseries.dataformat.com (September 4, 2009).

[30] James Madison to Thomas Mann Randolph, Washington, 11 November 1813, FLP (MHi), http://farmilylettersproject.dataformat.com (November 12, 2007) and Gaines, *Randolph*, 92.

[31] Thomas Jefferson to Thomas Eston Randolph, 21 January 1815; Thomas Eston Randolph to Thomas Jefferson, 21 January 1815; and Thomas Jefferson to Thomas Eston Randolph, Monticello,18 June 1816, Edwin Morris Betts, *Thomas Jefferson's Farm Book* (Charlottesville, VA: University Press of Virginia, 1987), 399-400.

[32] Respectively, Gaines, *Randolph*, 77; Conveyance of Bedford County Land to Anne Moseley, http://familyletters.dataformat.com (November 10, 2007) from original in Bedford County Deed Book, 13:487; Gaines, *Randolph*, 104; and Thomas Mann Randolph to Edmund Bacon, 9 May 1819, in Reverend Hamilton Wilcox Pierson, "Jefferson at Monticello: The Private Life of Thomas Jefferson," *Jefferson at Monticello*, ed. James A. Bear, Jr. (Charlottesville: University Press of Virginia, 1967), 92-93. These transactions were documented with a bill of sale and a receipt Bacon provided his interviewer.

[33] *Richmond Enquirer*, December 22, 1821, vol. XVIII, No. 68, http://newsbank.com (November 13, 2007). According to Randolph, the council had routinely acted in his absence, even though he considered his being away warranted by constitution, precedent, and courtesy. There apparently also was a dispute over whether the Governor had "concurred" (i.e., encouraged) six months before to a group of Richmond and Norfolk militia that a July 4th celebration be held, even though the Council (in his absence) had voted to prohibit it as liable to "violent and criminal excitement."

[34] Thomas Jefferson to Wilson Cary Nicholas, Monticello, 26 March 1818 and Wilson Cary Nicholas to Thomas Jefferson, 19 April 1818, The Thomas Jefferson Papers, Series 1 (DLC), http://memory.loc.gov/ (October 16, 2007), transcribed by author; Bear and Stanton, *JMB*, 2:1342 (note to Bank of the U. S.); and 2:1344 (endorsed notes of Nicholas). Jefferson first approached Nicholas, who was President of the Richmond Branch of the U. S. Bank, in the summer of 1817 regarding the prospects of the Bank (which he had much reviled) doing business with "country people." The state-chartered Bank of Virginia had notified him that his $2,000 note with them would not be renewed after sixty days (10 June 1817, Ford, *Works*, 12: http://olldownload.libertyfund.org/ [May 29, 2006]). In an unusual twist of fate for Jefferson, the Bank of Virginia President, Dr. John Brockenbrough had married Gabriella Harvie Randolph, the grieving widow of Mann Randolph's father. This original note, in turn, had been used as partial payment on a long overdue Amsterdam

account that Jefferson claimed had "arisen from mistakes in the complicated matters of account" and from the fact he was not an "accountant." Whether intentional or not, Jefferson agreed to pay $9000, including interest for the intervening thirty years and was propelled even further down the hole by exchanging one favor for another with a near relative. Nicholas' son-in-law and Jefferson's grandson, Jeff Randolph, was asked to co-sign renewal of the $20,000 note, saddling him with legacy debt and mortgaging Monticello. Jefferson assured the bank he would convey land he valued at $20,000 to Jeff as collateral for his signature and retained the unencumbered remained to support his own endorsement (Thomas Jefferson to Joseph Marx, Poplar Forest, 24 August 1819, Ford, *Works*, 10:139-140). The College of William and Mary paid the bank in 1823 with money received from the sale of Nicholas' land on which the College held a lien but, in turn, assigned responsibility for repaying this advance on the Nicholas estate to executor Thomas Jefferson Randolph. The loan was finally retired on Jeff Randolph's death in 1878, after some sixty years of substantially more than "the slightest inconvenience" to remnants of the Monticello household and ninety years after the original debt was incurred with an Amsterdam bank (*JMB*, 2:1392).

This episode was not the only instance demonstrating that Jefferson most certainly was not an "accountant" or sufficiently sensitive to the political ramifications of paying personal accounts with government vouchers and then dutifully recording his debt with the public treasury—essentially using the U. S. Treasury as a banker. "I had no private account with [Grand, the creditor of the U.S. Government]; my account as minister being kept with the treasury directly." (See Thomas Jefferson to Messrs. Ritchie and Gooch, Monticello, 13 May and 10 June 1822, L & B, *Writings*, 15:365-70 & 347-82.) The amount in question in this case was $1,148 incurred in 1789 to pay freight on the return home from Paris; it became a publicized issue as late as 1822 in a Maryland election by a "Native of Virginia" writing in the *Federal Republican*.

Wilson Cary Nicholas (1761–1820) was born in Williamsburg, served in the Revolutionary Army, Virginia General Assembly, and the U. S. Senate and House of Representatives. Jefferson appointed him collector at the port of Norfolk (1804–07). He was Governor of Virginia (1814–17) before assuming the position with the revived U. S. Bank in Richmond. (Biographical Directory of the U. S. Congress, http://bioguide.congress.gov/ [October 19, 2007]). He died penniless in his daughter's home, Tufton, at the foot of Monticello Mountain.

Patrick Gibson was partner with George Jefferson before the latter left to become a consul in Europe.

[35]Ellen Wayles Randolph to Martha Jefferson Randolph, Poplar Forest, 11 August 1819, FLP (ViU), http://familypapers.dataformat.com (April 18, 2007)

[36] Martha Jefferson Randolph to Nicholas P. Trist, Monticello, 4 April 1824, TJF ms copy (NcU, Trist Papers), transcribed by author.

[37] Martha Jefferson Randolph to Ellen W. Randolph Coolidge, Monticello, 1 September 1825, FLP (ViU), http://familyletters.dataformat.com (January 22, 2007); Virginia J. Randolph Trist to Ellen W. Randolph Coolidge, Monticello, 4 December 1825; and Ellen W. Randolph Coolidge to Martha Jefferson Randolph, Boston, 8 February 1826, FLP (ViU), http://familyletters.dataformat.com (January 22, 2007, September 21, 2006, and April 18, 2007, respectively). Jefferson and Jane Hollins Nicholas Randolph were living on Monticello's Tufton farm.

[38] Gaines, *Randolph*, 148

[39] Thomas Jefferson to Nathaniel Burwell, Monticello, 14 March 1818, http://ptjrs2.dataformat.com (April 2, 2009).

[40] Martha Jefferson Randolph to Ann (Nancy) Randolph Morris, Monticello, 8 August 1825, and to Nicholas P. Trist, 4 April 1824, TJF ms copy (NcU, Trist), transcribed by author.
[41] Martha Jefferson Randolph to Ellen W. Randolph Coolidge, Monticello, 1 September 1825, FLP (ViU), http://familyletters.dataformat.com (January 22, 2007).
[42] Martha Jefferson Randolph to Ellen Wayles Randolph Coolidge, Monticello, 13 October 1825, FLP http://retirementseries.dataformat.com (September 4, 2009).
[43] Mary Jefferson Randolph to Ellen W. Randolph Coolidge, Monticello, 23 October 1825, FLP (ViU, Correspondence of Ellen Wayles Randolph Coolidge), http://familypapers.dataformat.com (October 17, 2007).
[44] A sampling of his machinations includes the following. Upon leaving office in 1809, Jefferson moved his loans from Washington to Virginia banks and one large private loan, but these were for short terms of sixty days at which point the creditor could change the terms, as they did with Jefferson. The balance on his account with Milton merchant David Higginbotham increased, and a substantial sum was carried by Leitch in Charlottesville. Holding power of attorney for Kosciusko, Jefferson at the suggestion of his commission agent John Barnes in 1809 "borrowed" $4,900 from his investments and repaid him in 1815 with proceeds from the sale of his library to Congress. See examples for the 1808–1811 period: Bear and Stanton, *JMB*, 2:1238, 1246-48, 1253 n62, 1254 n66, and 1264.
[45] Martha Jefferson Randolph to Ann (Nancy) Randolph Morris, 22 January 1826, FLP (PPAmP, Smith-Houston-Morris-Ogden Family Papers), http://familyletters.dataformat.com (September 9, 2006).
[46] Thomas Jefferson to Thomas Mann Randolph, Monticello, 5 June 1825, *Richmond Enquirer*, Friday September 14, 1827, vol. LXXIV, no. 37 (Ritchie and Gooch), http://newsbank.com/ (November 13, 2007).
[47] Thomas Jefferson to Chastellux, Paris, 2 September 1785, *Papers*, 8:468.
[48] Thomas Jefferson to Thomas Mann Randolph, Washington, 31 January 1809, L & B, *Writings*, 18:262-64; to Martha Jefferson Randolph, Washington, 5 January 1808, Betts and Bear, *JFL*, 319-20.
[49] Thomas Mann Randolph, Edgehill, 29 October 1802, MHi, reel 13 (near end), transcription by author.
[50] Thomas Mann Randolph, "Notebook," 98, copy of manuscript in Thomas Jefferson Foundation file, "TMR Notebook," original in ViU accession 5150.
[51] Martha Jefferson Randolph to Anne (Nancy) Cary Randolph Morris, Monticello, 22 January 1826, FLP (PPAmP, Smith-Houston-Morris-Ogden Family Papers), http://familyletters.dataformat.com (September 9, 2006).
[52] Thomas Jefferson to Martha Jefferson Randolph, Washington 27 February 1809, and Martha Jefferson Randolph to Thomas Jefferson, Edgehill, 2 March 1809, Betts and Bear, *JFL*, 385-388.
[53] Martha Jefferson Randolph and Nicholas P. Trist to Ellen W. Randolph Coolidge, Monticello, 5 April 1826, FLP, http://familyletters.data.format.com (April 22, 2007).
[54] Ibid.
[55] Martha Jefferson Randolph and Nicholas P. Trist to Ellen W. Randolph Coolidge, Monticello, 5 April 1826, FLP (ViU), http://familyletters.dataformat.com (April 22, 2007). If Thomas Mann Randolph was correct, this "bliss" may have been drug induced. He reported to the President of the New York Historical Society that since sometime in 1825 Jefferson had been taking "eighty drops of the strongest laudanum every night for several months" for an "affection of the bladder." Randolph claimed

"several of his family" observed that "his vital powers gave way." See Thomas Mann Randolph to David Hosack, Monticello, 13 August 1826, FLP (NHi), http://familyletters.dataformat.com (November 8, 2007).

[56] Thomas Jefferson to Martha Jefferson, Aix en Provence, 28 March 1787, *Papers*, 11:250-53. It was precisely in this letter that her father is describing for young Patsy the features of plantation society that she is learning vicariously by encountering situations in her convent life. "In the country life of America there are many moments when a woman can have recourse to nothing but her needle for employment. In a dull company and in dull weather for instance. It is ill manners to read; it is ill manners to leave them; no card-playing there among genteel people; that is abandoned to blackguards."

[57] Thomas Jefferson, "Thoughts on Lotteries," February 1826, L & B, *Writings*, 17:448-65.

[58] Thomas Jefferson to Stephen Cathalan, Washington, 29 June 1807, transcript of manuscript located at Thomas Jefferson Foundation (DLC). Cathalan was located at Marseilles where Jefferson regularly bought wine, macaroni, raisins and other supplies. While President, he had a standing, annual order that this letter cancels.

[59] Thomas Jefferson Randolph to Thomas Jefferson, Richmond, February 3, 1826, Betts and Bear *JFL*, 467.

[60] Respectively, Thomas Jefferson to Thomas Ritchie, 28 February and to James Madison, 17 February 1826, Ford, *Works*, 12:220-21 and 12:216-18, http://olldownload.libertyfund.org (May 29, 2006 and October 20, 2005).

[61] Thomas Jefferson to Thomas Jefferson Randolph, Monticello, 8 February 1826, Ibid., 12:215-16.

[62] Thomas Jefferson Papers, Library of Congress, microfilm series 5, reel 59, Commonplace Books, 122-23 as cited in *Thomas Jefferson's Scrapbooks*, edited with an introduction by Jonathan Gross (Hanover, NH: Steerforth Press, 2006), 426-7. Adding to the poem's salience and poignancy is Wilson's observation (*Jefferson's Commonplace Book*, note 151-52) that the last stanza of the complete poem was excised from the manuscript. It read: "My tender Wife—sweet Soother of my Care!/Struck with sad Anguish at the stern Decree,/Fell—ling'ring fell a Victim to Despair,/And left the World to Wretchedness and me." The poem by Thomas Moss appeared in the *Virginia Gazette* (Purdie & Dixon), 28 February 1771 (Ibid.). Jefferson also clipped from a Baltimore newspaper Mary Richardson's poem "The Beggar" whose theme was an impoverished wife of a deceased, intemperate husband.

[63] Thomas Jefferson to Thomas Jefferson Randolph, Monticello, 8 February 1826, Betts and Bear, *JFL*, 469-70.

[64] Ibid.

[65] Thomas Jefferson Randolph to Thomas Jefferson, [Richmond], 31 January and 3 February [1826], Ibid., 466-67.

[66] Thomas Jefferson to Thomas Jefferson Randolph, Monticello, 8 February 1826, Ibid., 469-70.

[67] Nicholas P. Trist to Joseph Coolidge, His bed side, 4 July 1826, FLP (ViU), http://familyletters.dataformat.com (November 8, 2007). The fact this letter was sent to Boston with the knowledge that Coolidge, Ellen, and Cornelia were in transit is an indication of Trist's unsettled state of mind. It reached Boston on 10 July, arrived in Washington on the 15th, and returned to Monticello sometime thereafter.

[68] *Richmond Enquirer* (Ritchie and Gooch), Vol. 23, No. 17, Friday, July 7, 1826, http://infoweb.newsbank.com (October 29 2006).

[69] Martha Jefferson Randolph to Ellen W. Randolph Coolidge, Monticello, September 1826, (ViHi, 77-45), transcribed by author.

[70] Ellen W. Randolph Coolidge to Nicholas P. Trist, Boston, 27 September 1826, FLP (ViU), http://familyletters.dataformat.com (January 22, 2007).
[71] Cornelia Jefferson Randolph to Ellen W. Randolph Coolidge, Monticello, 6 July 1828, Ibid., (October 24, 2007).
[72] Lydia Sigourney to Martha Jefferson Randolph, Hartford CT, August 1826, transcribed by author from copy of ms in TJF/Correspondence/Martha Jefferson Randolph file (DLC, Randolph Family Papers, microfilm reel 59, series 6). Lydia Howard (Huntley) Sigourney (1791–1865) was a prolific writer from Connecticut that authored fifty-three volumes of prose and poetry (http://etext.virginia.edu/eaf/authors/ [September 29, 2009]).

Chapter 11: "Never ashamed of an honorable poverty"

[1] Ellen W. Randolph Coolidge to Martha Jefferson Randolph and Nicholas P. Trist, with Postscript, Joseph Coolidge to Nicholas P. Trist, Boston, 27 September 1826, FLP (ViU), http://familyletters.dataformat.com (October 22, 2007). Coolidge's postscript reveals that this question was posed by "Beach Lawrence," who most likely was William Beach Lawrence (1800–1881) and the book was the first edition of Joseph Blunt's (1792–1860) *The American Annual Register for the years 1825–26 or, the fiftieth year of American Independence* (New York: W. Jackson, 1827). Though known to Jefferson, Lawrence probably did not ultimately write the article, because he departed in 1826 for England to serve as Secretary of the Legation under Albert Gallatin and later Chargé d'Affaires, returning in 1829 (*The New York Times*, "An Eminent Jurist Dead," March 16, 1881, http://query.nytimes.com [October 27, 2007]). That year's issue of the *Register* reported on Lafayette's visit and the deaths of Charles Cotesworth Pinckney, Adams, and Jefferson (240-250). Among the *Register's* items reported from Virginia was the passage of the lottery bill with the caveat that "before the object of this law could be accomplished, this patriot was released from the cares of life" (341).
[2] Thomas Jefferson to Maria Jefferson Eppes, Washington, 15 February 1801, *Papers*, 32:593.
[3] Thomas Jefferson to Thomas Mann Randolph, Washington, 17 January 1809, TJF, Stanton (MHi reel 14); 31 January 1809, L&B, *Writings*, 18:262-64; and to Martha Jefferson Randolph, Washington, 27 February 1809, Betts and Bear, *JFL*, 385-86. "Ignorant too, as I am in the management of a farm," he wrote Martha, "I shall be obliged to ask the aid of Mr. Randolph's skill and attention."
[4] In addition to the many letters directing Mann Randolph cited above, see Thomas Jefferson to Jeremiah Goodman, Monticello, 8 January 1813 and 3 February 1814; Thomas Jefferson Foundation file "Overseers, other than Bacon" (DLC); and Thomas Jefferson to Joel Yancey, Monticello, 18 July 1815, Betts, *Farm Book*, 546-47.
[5] Thomas Jefferson to Joel Yancey, Monticello, 17 January 1819 (MHi), TJF file, Ibid. Jeremiah Goodman was Poplar Forest overseer and Nimrod Darnell served under him for $200 yearly until 1815, when Jefferson dismissed both and hired Yancey. The latter served until 1822 until replaced by Jeff Randolph (Bear and Stanton, *JMB*, 2:1272 n2 and 1317 n16).
[6] Thomas Jefferson to Joel Yancey, Monticello, 18 July 1815, Betts, *Farm Book*, 546047.
[7] For a detailed description of Jefferson's attentiveness to the historical record, see Robert M. S. McDonald, "Thomas Jefferson and Historical Self-Construction: The Earth Belongs to the Living?," *The Historian*, 61:2, 289-310.

[8] Thomas Jefferson to George Loyall, Monticello, 22 February 1826, Ford, *Works*, 12:219-220, http://olldownload.libertyfund.org (May 29, 2006). Loyall (1789–1868) was born in Norfolk and graduated William and Mary College (1808). He served in Virginia's House of Delegates (1818–1827), U. S. House of Representatives, and as Navy agent in Norfolk from 1837–1861 (http://bioguide.congress.gov/ [October 30, 2007]).

[9] Respectively, Thomas Jefferson to James Monroe, Monticello, 8 March 1826, Ford, *Works*, 12:221; and to Thomas Ritchie, Monticello, 28 February 1826, Ibid., 220-21.

[10] Thomas Jefferson to Joel Yancey, Monticello, 22 February and 25 May 1819 [MHi], Thomas Jefferson Foundation file, "Overseers other than Bacon".

[11] Martha Jefferson Randolph and Nicholas P. Trist to Ellen W. Randolph Coolidge, Monticello, 5 April 1826, FLP, http://familyletters.data.format.com (September 10, 2006)

[12] Thomas Jefferson to James Madison, Monticello, 17 February 1826, Ford, *Works*, 12:216-18.

[13] *The Market Revolution in America: Social, Political, and Religious Expressions, 1800–1880,* Melvyn Stokes and Stephen Conway, eds. (Charlottesville, VA: University Press of Virginia, 1996) includes several essays describing the multi-dimensions of the transition to a market economy. Changes in the southern agricultural sector specifically are detailed in Allan Kulikoff, *The Agrarian Origins of American Capitalism* (Charlottesville, VA: University Press of Virginia, 1996, 2nd printing).

[14] Thomas Jefferson to James Madison, Monticello, 17 February 1826, Ford, *Works*, 12:216-218, http://oll.libertyfund.org/ (October 20, 2005). The financial sector and related statutory frameworks are described in Bruce H. Mann, *Republic of Debtors: Bankruptcy in the Age of American Independence* (Cambridge, MA: Harvard University Press, 2002).

[15] Dabney Carr (1773–1837) was born in Louisa County to Jefferson's sister Martha and his close friend Dabney.

[16] Betts, *Farm Book*, 271 and Bear and Stanton, *JMB*, 1406, respectively.

[17] Martha Jefferson Randolph to Ellen W. Randolph Coolidge, Monticello, [September, 1826], Virginia Historical Society, 77-45, transcribed by author.

[18] Mary Jefferson Randolph to Ellen W. Randolph Coolidge, Monticello, 1 October 1826, FLP (ViU), http://familyletters.dataformat.com (October 27, 2007).

[19] Transcript copy in the hand of Trist of Thomas Mann Randolph to Nicholas P. Trist, North Milton, 6 July 1826, FLP (DLC, Papers of Nicholas Philip Trist), http://familyletters.dataformat.com (November 15, 2007).

[20] The boundary was a long-running question dating from the 1780s treaties with Great Britain, to Jefferson's term as Secretary of State, and beyond Randolph's "unsuccessful" (according to the President) survey in 1826–27. Paradoxically, the document John Quincy Adams forwarded to Congress for their 1828 debate on the subject was an extract from Jefferson's report to President Washington of March 18 1792. Congress could not even agree on which committee should receive President Adam's documents! See Report on Negotiations with Spain, 18 March 1792, *Papers*, 23:296-17; Boundary Line Between Georgia and Florida, *American State Papers: Foreign Relations*, 6:836-38; and, Gales & Seaton's Register of Debates in Congress, 20th Congress, 1st Session, January 23, 1828 (1089 ff) both from http://memory.loc.gov/ (October 1, 2007). James Barbour (1775–1842) was born near Gordonsville, Virginia, read law, and served as a Virginia Delegate, Governor, U. S. Senator, John Q. Adam's Secretary of War, and Minister to England. He founded the Orange County Virginia Humane

Society for the advancement of education. (*Biographical Directory of the United States Congress, 1774—Present*, http://bioguide.Congress.gov/ (November 16, 2007).

21 James Barbour to Martha Jefferson Randolph, Washington, 9 November 1826, FLP (DLC, Randolph Family Manuscripts), http://familyletters.dataformat.com (November 16, 2007).

22 Daniels, *Randolphs*, 196-200 and 247-49. First published in 1824, *Housewife* went through six editions over thirty years.

23Martha Jefferson Randolph to Joseph Coolidge, Cary's Brook, 25 January 1829, FLP (ViU), http://familyletters.dataformat.com, (October 23, 2007). Virginia's books were *Letters on female character: addressed to a young lady on the death of her mother* (1828); *Christian parent's assistant, or Tales, for the Moral and religious instruction of youth (1829)*.

24 Martha Jefferson Randolph to Mary Jefferson, 28 December 1826, as cited in Randolph, *Worthy Women*, 57.

25 Martha Jefferson Randolph to Anne (Nancy) Cary Randolph Morris, Boston, 4 December 1826, FLP (PPAmP), http://familypapers.dataformat.com (September 10, 2006).

26 Martha Jefferson Randolph to Anne (Nancy) Cary Randolph Morris, Boston, 22 March 1827, FLP (PPAmP) http://familypapers.dataformat.com (September 10, 2006).

27 Thomas Mann Randolph to Mary Randolph, North Milton, 12 December 1826, FLP (NcU, Southern Historical Collection, Nicholas Philip Trist Papers), http://familyletters.dataformat.com (November 14, 2007).

28 Gaines, *Randolph*, 166-176.

29 Mary Jefferson Randolph to Ellen W. Randolph Coolidge, Monticello, 30 October 1826, FLP (ViU), http://familyletters.dataformat.com (October 27, 2007).

30 Ibid. Thomas Beverley Randolph and Lucy Bolling Randolph were brother and sister. Thomas (1792–?) married Maria Barbara Meyer and Lucy wed William, brother-in-law to Martha Jefferson Randolph. The "Martha" involved in these property transactions has not been identified. Henry ("Harry") Heth was a Richmond businessman whose enterprises included coal mining in which ousted U. S. Marshall David Meade Randolph served as a "technical coal mining advisor" and Beverley Randolph was partner. Heth, also, was among those providing $10,000 bail to Aaron Burr in 1806. See Daniels, *Randolphs*, 197 and 220-21.

31 Martha Jefferson Randolph and Nicholas P. Trist to Ellen W. Randolph Coolidge, Monticello, 5 April 1826, FLP (ViU), http://familyletters.dataformat.com (April 22, 2007). Interestingly, Martha juxtaposed this account of the school with her report on Father's vision of a lottery from the "realms of bliss."

32 The school was advertised in the same *Richmond Enquirer* (Ritchie and Gooch), vol. 23, no. 17, Friday, July 7, 1826, http://infoweb.newsbank.com (October 29, 2006). Francis Eppes, the son of Maria Jefferson and John Eppes, had married Aunt Jane's (1776–1842) daughter, Mary Elizabeth Cleland Randolph. Just as his father, John, had resisted living near Monticello at Pantops, the couple was living at Poplar Forest at this time, though dissatisfied with the house. He "strongly advocated" the move to New London, according to Martha, and in 1826 urged to Nicholas Trist that the Monticello family should move to "Florida, or Kentucky or Tennessee, or Missouri." Eppes relocated near Tallahassee later in the decade, taking the "elder & younger members" of Aunt Jane's family with him and the remainder joined them in October. He bought father-in-law Thomas Eston Randolph "350 acres of very excellent land, some of it first rate sugar land at $1.25 the acre." The family was "well pleased with

their situation," even though living in "log house with the blue sky over their heads." Meanwhile, Aunt Jane was suffering mightily with "an incessant and harassing cough with a discharge of <u>pus</u> and frequent spittings of blood." See Martha Jefferson Randolph to Anne Cary Randolph Morris, Edgehill, 6 September 1829, FLP (PPAmP), http://familyletters.dataformat.com (September 10, 2006).

[33] Cornelia Jefferson Randolph to Ellen W. Randolph Coolidge, Monticello, 11 September 1826, FLP (ViU), http://familyletters.dataformat.com (October 27, 2007).

[34] Cornelia Jefferson Randolph to Ellen W. Randolph Coolidge, New London, 11 December 1826, FLP (ViU), http://familyletters.dataformat.com (September 21, 2006).

[35] Martha Jefferson Randolph to Ann (Nancy) Cary Randolph Morris, Boston, 24 January 1828, and Edgehill, 3 November 1833, FLP (PPAmP), http://retirementseries.dataformat.com (September 2. 2009).

[36] Thomas Mann Randolph, Sr. to Septimia Randolph, 6 August 1827, transcript in Thomas Jefferson Foundation file "People/Thomas Mann Randolph/Correspondence."

[37] Virginia Jefferson Trist to Ellen W. Randolph Coolidge, Tufton, 28 March 1827, FLP (ViU), http://familyletters.dataformat.com (October 27, 2007).

[38] Respectively, "Thoughts on Lotteries; and Thomas Jefferson to Thomas Ritchie, Monticello, 28 February 1826, Ford, *Works*, 12:205-16 and 220 -21, http://olldownload.libertyfund.org/ (May 29, 2006).

[39] Joseph Coolidge to Nicholas P. Trist, Boston, 4 December [1827], http://familyletters.dataformat.com (October 27, 2007).

[40] Mary Jefferson Randolph to Ellen W. Randolph Coolidge, Tufton, 18 March 1827, FLP (ViU), http://familyletters.dataformat.com (October 27 2007).

[41] Cornelia Jefferson Randolph to Ellen W. Randolph Coolidge, Monticello, 18 May 1827, FLP (ViU), http://familyletters.dataformat.com (October 27 2007).

[42] Virginia J. Randolph Trist to Ellen W. Randolph Coolidge, Tufton, 28 March 1827, Ibid., (April 18, 2007).

[43] *Eastern Argus*, Portland, ME, May 18, 1827, *Rochester Telegraph*, Rochester, NY, May 21, 1827, *Newport Mercury*, Newport, RI, May 19, 1827, and *Pittsfield Sun*, Pittsfield, MA, May 31, 1827, http://infoweb.newsbank.com/ (December 14, 2007). Louisiana was the only other State to exercise what in Jefferson's schema would be called "moral sense" to "succor the distress" of his impoverished daughter.

Another form of relief was proposed by Senator George Poindexter (MI), who introduced bills in both the 21st and 22nd Congresses to provide a grant of 50,000 acres in Mississippi from "any unappropriated land of the United States to which Indian title is, or may hereafter be extinguished,..." Though accepting the family's claim that Martha's situation was the result of Jefferson's "services and sacrifices," the Bill offered faint praise by noting he "was unable to make suitable provision for his family (S. 154 and 16, http://memory.loc.gov [January 4, 2008]). On 27 June 1832, the Senate on a roll call voted 15 yeas and 23 nays against even considering a relief bill (*Senate Journal*, Ibid., 370-71).

George Poindexter (1779–1853) was born in Louisa County, Virginia, read law, and practiced from 1800–02 in Milton at the foot of Monticello Mountain. He served in various Territorial offices, the War of 1812, as Governor of Mississippi, and both houses of the U. S. Congress.

[44] *Eastern Argus*, vol. III, issue 272, page 2, 18 May 1827, http://infoweb.newsbank.com/ (December 14, 2007) as forwarded from the Columbia, SC, *Telescope*.

[45] Martha Jefferson Randolph to Ann (Nancy) Cary Randolph Morris, Edgehill, 16 May 1827, FLP (PPAmP), http://familyletters.dataformat.com (September 10, 2006).

46 Jennings L. Wagoner, "'The Knowledge Most Useful to Us:' Thomas Jefferson's Concept of Utility in the Education of Republican Citizens," in *Thomas Jefferson and the Education of a Citizen*, ed. James Gilreath (Washington, D. C.: Library of Congress, 1999), 123-25.
Of her daughters that were of age at the time the household was dissolved in 1827, only Ellen (aged 31) would really "move away" from Monticello while the place remained in the family's hands. Anne, who died in early 1826 from childbirth complications, had left for a short period "down country" to Port Royal but returned to nearby Carlton plantation; Virginia (26) and husband Nicholas Trist, despite not unfavorable prospects in Louisiana, remained in Charlottesville until 1829–30; Cornelia (28) and Mary (24) never left "home," though their residence moved from the mountain top to Tufton farm, Washington, Havana, and finally to Edgehill with brother Jeff.
47 Thomas Jefferson to Thomas Mann Randolph, Monticello, 8 October 1820, transcript TJF, Stanton (MHi, reel 14). Jefferson expressed concern that James (14) was "losing precious time" and offered to assume the "cost and care" of him, Benjamin (12) and Lewis (10), since their father's "necessary absences" made his "close attention...impossible." Nine months later, Randolph expressed his "aversion to have eight of [his] sons brought up to the Bar," nor, was medicine with all its "charlatanism" desirable. Though completely broken financially by this time, he petulantly maintained: "My opinion is unchanged that agriculture is the best employment for young men." Randolph's "anxiety" was that fourteen-year-old James was "living in the midst of idle slaves" that might "give birth to curiosity, and the disposition to pry into the secrets of Nature" (Thomas Mann Randolph to Thomas Jefferson, Richmond, 27 July 1821, transcript TJF, Stanton [ViU]).
48 Virginia Jefferson Randolph to Nicholas P. Trist, Monticello, 5 June 1823, FLP (ViU) http://familyletters.dataformat.com (January 22, 2007).
49 Virginia J. Randolph Trist to Ellen W. Randolph Coolidge, Monticello, 4 December 1825, FLP (ViU), http://familypapers.dataformat.com (September 21, 2006).
50 Mary Jefferson Randolph to Virginia Jefferson Randolph, Monticello, 31 January 1822, Ibid., 163.
51 Virginia Jefferson Randolph to Nicholas P. Trist, Monticello, 16 January 1823, McCrudden, "Childhood," 164, (Trist Papers, DLC). At this time Virginia was reading Moliere and Alain-Rene Lesage's *Gil Blas* in French with "an infinite degree of labor" and the "aid of a dictionary," because, she disparaged, of her "stupidity and want of memory." Ellen was the daughter of the deceased Anne Cary Randolph Bankhead (Mrs. Charles). The "boys" were likely Martha's James Madison (b. 1806), Benjamin Franklin (b. 1808), and Meriwether Lewis (b. 1810) (Bear and Stanton, *JMB*, 2:1392: "Feb. 4. [1823] James, Ben & Lewis enter & begin Mr. Hatch @ 50.D. year each."). Lewis and Ben had begun attending Rev. Frederick Hatch's school in Charlottesville in 1821 (Ibid., 2:1373). Dabney Overton Carr was most likely the grandson of Martha Jefferson Carr and son of Samuel Carr, Jefferson's nephew.
52 Ellen Wayles Randolph to Martha Jefferson Randolph, Poplar Forest, 18 July [1819], FLP (ViU), http://familypapers.dataformat.com (September 21, 2006).
53 Ellen Wayles Randolph to Martha Jefferson Randolph, Poplar Forest, 11 August 1819, FLP (ViU), http://familypapers.dataformat.com (April 18, 2007).
54 Thomas Jefferson to Martha Jefferson, Annapolis, 28 November 1783, *Papers*, 6:359-60.

[55]Ellen Wayles Randolph to Martha Jefferson Randolph, Poplar Forest, 18 July [1819], FLP (ViU), http://familypapers.dataformat.com (September 21, 2006).

[56] Mary Jefferson Randolph to Ellen W. Randolph Coolidge, Monticello, 23 October 1825, FLP (ViU), http://familypapers.dataformat.com (October 17, 2007).

[57] Ellen W. Randolph to Nicholas P. Trist, Monticello, 30 March 1824, FLP (ViU) http://familypapers.dataformat.com (September 21, 2006). As the academy movement was beginning to flourish at about this time in the Northern states, the meaning of "ornamental" was changing and frequently applied to curricula in both female and female schools; typically, it was contrasted with "useful." Opinion was divided on the desirability of such courses (Margaret A. Nash, "'Cultivating the Powers of Human Beings': Gendered Perspectives on Curricula and Pedagogy in Academies of the New Republic," *History of Education Quarterly*, Vol. 41, No. 2 [Summer, 2001], 239-250).

[58] Ellen W. Randolph Coolidge, 15 June 1828, Personal Note, FLP (ViU), http://familypapers.dataformat.com (October 19, 2007). Thomas Mann Randolph died 20 June 1828. Ellen married Joseph Coolidge (1798–1879) on 27 May 1825. They had seven children, six of whom lived to adulthood.

[59] Thomas Mann Randolph, Senior [Junior], to Nicholas P. Trist, Milton, 11 March 1828, FLP (DLC, Trist), http://familyletters.dataformat.com (May 24, 2007).

[60] Cornelia Jefferson Randolph to Ellen W. Randolph Coolidge, Monticello, 6 July 1828, FLP (ViU), http://familypapers.dataformat.com (October 24, 2007).

[61] Martha Jefferson Randolph to Margaret Bayard Smith, 10 November 1828, copy of ms in Thomas Jefferson Foundation file "Notes on Trist Collection," transcribed by author. Trist (1800–1874) served as State Department clerk until 1833, when he became private secretary to Andrew Jackson. Later appointments included Consul in Havana, Chief State Department clerk under Polk, and negotiator of Treaty of Guadalupe Hidalgo ending the Mexican War (1848). He practiced law in Philadelphia and Virginia from 1848 until 1870, when he was appointed postmaster in Alexandria, Virginia by President U. S. Grant (Nicholas Philip Trist, A Register of His Papers in the Library of Congress, prepared by Patrick Kerwin and Lia Apodaca [Washington, D.C.: Manuscript Division, Library of Congress, 2005], http://lcweb2.loc.gov/service/mss [November 24, 2007]).

[62] Martha Jefferson Randolph: Indenture Selling Thomas Jefferson's Land to Martin Dawson, 1 January 1829, FLP, http://familyletters.dataformat.com (May 24, 2007); original in Albemarle County Deed Book, 23:118-19; Virginia Jefferson Trist to Nicholas P. Trist, Edgehill, 5 May 1829 (NcU), "Family Correspondence (1826–1833) Internship," 76; research report compiled by Ann Macon Smith and Ann Lucas, Thomas Jefferson Foundation (1991); Thomas Jefferson Randolph to Nicholas P. Trist, Edgehill, 13 April 1829, FLP (DLC, Trist), http://familyletters.dataformat.com/ (November 20, 2007); Thomas Jefferson Randolph to Nicholas P. Trist, Edgehill, 16 February 1829, FLP (DLC, Trist), Ibid.; Joseph Coolidge to Nicholas P. Trist, Boston, 22 March 1829, Ibid.

[63] Harriet Tucker Randolph Willis to Jane Cary Randolph Randolph, Ballyvoumiere, 19 June 1829, State Archives of Florida, Randolph Family Papers, 1829–1978, Correspondence Transcribed/Dated (with originals), Collection M75, Box 1, http://www.floridamemory.com/ (November 8, 2007). Thomas Eston Randolph was appointed U. S. Marshall in 1831. Harriet and Lucy continued their enterprising proclivities with the first girl's school in Tallahassee (Ibid.).

Francis Eppes, who had married Aunt Jane's daughter (Elizabeth) had been unable in 1826 to convince the Monticello family that a move to the Deep South would be financially advantageous. That same year, his in-laws, Jane and Thomas Eston, left

Albemarle for Bedford County and opened a girls' school (Mary Jefferson Randolph to Ellen W. Randolph Coolidge, Monticello, 12-13 May 1826, FLP [ViU], http://familyletters.dataformat.com, [November 15, 2007]). By spring 1827, Jeff Randolph was disgusted with the faltering lottery scheme and "full of the idea" of our going to Louisiana in a body," but his sister Virginia was sure "Mama [would] never listen to a word on the subject." Robert and Wilson Nicholas of Albemarle also had moved to Louisiana, Virginia reported. "They made this year from their crop of sugar $20,000; as much as, one of the Mr. Barbours [*sic*] said, as he expects to make on his [Virginia] plantation, in twenty years" (Virginia J. Randolph Trist to Ellen W. Randolph Coolidge, Tufton, 28 March 1827, FLP [ViU], http://familyletters. dataforma.com [April 18, 2007]).

64 Martha Jefferson Randolph to Anne (Nancy) Cary Randolph Morris, Edgehill, 6 September 1829, FLP (PPAmP), http://familyletters.dataforma.com, September 10, 2006. "Browse" was Hore Browse Trist (1802–1856), Nicholas's younger brother; after his marriage in 1834, he lived permanently in Louisiana. Burwell Starke Randolph (1800–1854) was the son of Mary ("Molly") and David Meade Randolph.

65 Martha Jefferson Randolph to Thomas Jefferson Randolph, Washington, 7 February 1830, FLP (ViU), http://familyletters.dataformat.com/ (May 25, 2007).

66 Martha Jefferson Randolph to Thomas Jefferson Randolph, Washington, 7 February 1830, FLP (ViU), http://familyletters.dataformat.com/ (May 25, 2007).

67 Cornelia Jefferson Randolph to Virginia J. Randolph Trist, University, 6 August 1831, FLP (ViU), http://familyletters.dataforma.com (April 18, 2007). Martha's "agitation," "soreness of stomach," and "bowel complaint" were being treated with "40 drops of laudanum" and if that dosage was not effective, the doctor had recommended up to "150 or 200." A teaspoon measures about 60 drops, but the strength of laudanum varied.

68 Martha Jefferson Randolph to Thomas Jefferson, Bellmont, 12 May 1798, *Papers*, 30:346-47.

69 Randolph, *Worthy Women*, 67.

70 Martha Jefferson Randolph to Ann (Nancy) Cary Randolph Morris, Washington, 30 June 1833, FLP (PPAmP), http://retirementseries.dataformat.com (September 3, 2009).

71 Martha Jefferson Randolph to Ann (Nancy) Cary Randolph Morris, Boston, 4 December 1835, FLP (PPAmP), http://familyletters.dataformat.com (September 10, 2006),

72 Martha Jefferson Randolph to Ann (Nancy) Cary Randolph Morris, Boston, 5 April 1836, FLP (PPAmP), http://familyletters.dataformat.com (September 10, 2006),

73 Respectively, Martha Jefferson Randolph to Thomas Jefferson, 31 January 1801, *Papers*, 32:526-28 and Thomas Jefferson to Martha Jefferson Randolph, Washington, 5 February 1802, Ibid., 32:556-57.

74 Ellen Wayles Coolidge to Jane Hollins Nicholas Randolph, Geneva, 17 May 1843, FLP (ViU), http://familyletters.dataformat.com (October 23, 2007).

75 Thomas Mann Randolph, Notebook, 98, copy of manuscript Thomas Jefferson Foundation file "TMR Notebook," original in ViU accession 5150.

76 Hamilton W. Pierson, *Jefferson at Monticello: The Private Life of Thomas Jefferson* with an Introduction and edited by James A. Bear (Charlottesville: University Press of Virginia, 1967).

77 Martha Jefferson Randolph to Ellen Wayles Randolph Coolidge, [30 June 1828], FLP (ViU), retirementseries.dataformat.com (September 2, 2009). The second sheet of

this letter has a portion cut away that may be the fragment referenced in the following footnote.

78 Fragment of ALS glued to cover addressed to [Ellen Wayles Coolidge] in Martha Jefferson Randolph's hand; copy of ms from Thomas Jefferson Foundation file "People/Thomas Mann Randolph" located October 24, 2005, transcribed by author; original source noted on ms copy ViU accession #9090, Box 2. Dated "Monticello. July 21.1828." at bottom of ms in another hand.

79 Ellen Wayles Randolph Coolidge to Henry Randall, 27 March 1856, typescript in TJF files of "Ellen Wayles Coolidge Letterbook, 1856–1858," Ellen Wayles Coolidge Correspondence, 1810–1861, Collection 9090, Box 3, Special Collections, University of Virginia, 64.

80 *Jefferson's Literary Commonplace Book*, ed. Douglas Wilson (Princeton, NJ: Princeton University Press, 1989), 224. This quotation in the Edgehill-Randolph Papers (ViU) was likely copied in Martha Jefferson's hand and bears the date 2 October 1833 in another hand. The Bible quotation is from Matthew, Chapter 4:8-9 that reads: "Again, the devil taketh him up into an exceedingly high mountain, and sheweth him all the kingdoms of the world, and the glory of them; And saith unto him, All these things will I give thee, if thou wilt fall down and Worship me" (KJV).

81Randolph, *Worthy Women*, 69-70.

82Sarah N. Randolph, *The Domestic Life of Thomas Jefferson* (New York: Harper and Row, 1871; reprint Charlottesville, VA: University Press of Virginia, 1978), 429.

83 *Jefferson's Literary Commonplace Book*, ed. Douglas Wilson (Princeton, NJ: Princeton University Press, 1989), 224-25. This extract is from a poem written by Anna Laetitia Barbauld (1743–1825) that was inscribed in Martha Jefferson Randolph's hand on the final page of her father's *Commonplace Book*.

Index

Made in the USA
Charleston, SC
25 June 2014